Ethnic and Religious Minorities
in Stalin's Soviet Union

Ethnic and Religious Minorities in Stalin's Soviet Union
New Dimensions of Research

Edited by
Andrej Kotljarchuk & Olle Sundström

Södertörns högskola
(Södertörn University)
Library
SE-141 89 Huddinge

www.sh.se/publications

© Authors

Attribution 4.0 International (CC BY 4.0)
This publication is licensed under a
Creative Commons Attribution 4.0 License.

Cover image: Front page of the Finnish-language newspaper
Polarnoin kollektivisti, 17 December 1937.
Courtesy of Russian National Library.

Graphic form: Per Lindblom & Jonathan Robson

Printed by Elanders, Stockholm 2017

Södertörn Academic Studies 72
ISSN 1650-433X

Northern Studies Monographs 5
ISSN 2000-0405

ISBN 978-91-7601-777-7 (print)

Contents

List of Illustrations 7
Abbreviations 9
Foreword 13

Introduction 15
ANDREJ KOTLJARCHUK & OLLE SUNDSTRÖM

PART 1
National Operations of the NKVD. A General Approach 31

CHAPTER 1
The Great Terror.
New Dimensions of Research 33
HIROAKI KUROMIYA

CHAPTER 2
Ethnification of Stalinism?
Ethnic Cleansings and the NKVD Order № 00447 in a Comparative Perspective 47
ANDREY SAVIN

CHAPTER 3
'He who Is not with Us Is against Us.'
Elimination of the 'Fifth Column' in the Soviet Union, 1937–1938 67
VICTOR DÖNNINGHAUS

PART 2
Ethnic Minorities in the Great Terror. Case studies 87

CHAPTER 4
Propaganda of Hatred and the Great Terror.
A Nordic Approach 89
ANDREJ KOTLJARCHUK

CHAPTER 5
Nation-Building by Terror in Soviet Georgia, 1937–1938 123
MARC JUNGE & DANIEL MÜLLER

CHAPTER 6
A Long Great Ethnic Terror in the Volga Region.
A War before the War 153
EVA TOULOUZE

PART 3
Religious Minorities under Soviet Repression..173

CHAPTER 7
The Ukrainian Evangelicals under Pressure from the NKVD,
1928–1939...175
OKSANA BEZNOSOVA

CHAPTER 8
The Cultural Bases in the North.
Sovietisation and Indigenous Resistance 199
EVA TOULOUZE, LAUR VALLIKIVI & ART LEETE

CHAPTER 9
Repression of Shamans and Shamanism in Khabarovsk Krai.
1920s to the early 1950s 225
TATIANA BULGAKOVA & OLLE SUNDSTRÖM

CHAPTER 10
Where Have the Amur Region's Shamans Gone? 263
YANA IVASHCHENKO

Contributors...279
Södertörn Academic Studies..285
Northern Studies 290

List of Illustrations

1. Map of the nationalities of the Soviet Union. From *Geograficheskiy atlas dlya sredney shkoly*, Moskva: Glavnoe Upravlenie Geodezii i Kartografii pri SNK SSSR (1941).

2. Book cover of *Yaponiya u Manchzhuryi* ['Japan in Manchuria'] written by S. Dashynski [Aleksandr M. Nikonov], the Soviet military intelligence operative. The book was published in 1929 in Minsk by the State Belarusian Publishing House. Photo by Mikola Nikalaieu. Courtesy of the Russian National Library. Aleksandr M. Nikonov was arrested by the NKVD on 5 August 1937 and shot on 26 October 1937 in Moscow.

3. Nikolay Yezhov, People's Commissar for Internal Affairs of the Soviet Union. Portrait from the children's magazine *Chizh*, December 1937.

4. Employment record book from the Volga German Autonomous Soviet Socialist Republic, 1930s. The parallel texts in Russian and German are equally authentic. Private collection of Igor Toporov.

5. Postgraduate diploma of Alexander Held from studies at the Party-Soviet School of the Volga-German Autonomous Soviet Socialist Republic, 1924. Alexander Held was born in 1897 in the Volga-German colony Franzosen; member of the VKP(b) since 1919; Minister of Automobile Transport of the Volga-German Autonomous Soviet Socialist Republic; died in the Ustvymlag in 1944. Private collection of Igor Toporov.

6. Leaders of Sveriges kommunistiska parti kolkhoz ['Swedish Communist Party kolkhoz'] on the cover of the Swedish magazine *Vecko-Journalen*, no. 45, 1932. Photo from Gammalsvenskby, Kherson district. Leftmost: Edvin Blom; in the centre: Karl Ture Grääs; rightmost: journalist Alma Braathen.

7. Front page of the Finnish-language newspaper *Polarnoin kollektivisti*, official organ of the Finnish national district of the Murmansk region. *Polarnoin kollektivisti*, no. 22, 8 March 1937. Courtesy of the Russian National Library.

8. Sergo Goglidze, People's Commissar of Internal Affairs of the Georgian SSR. Museum of the Ministry of Internal Affairs of Georgia.

9. Hard-copy record of meeting no. 44 of the NKVD troika in Georgian SSR from 23 October 1938. Archives of the Ministry of Internal Affairs of Georgia.

10. Kuzebay Gerd (a.k.a. Kuzma Pavlovich Chaynikov, 1896–1937), Udmurt poet accused by the NKVD to be a leader of SOFIN in Udmurtia. Executed by the NKVD in November 1937 in Sandarmoh (Karelia). Courtesy of the Udmurt Institute of History, Language and Literature, Ural branch of the Russian Academy of Science.

11. Members of the Union of the Baptists of the USSR, 1925. In the centre: Aleksey Markovich Bukreev (1884–1929), presbyter of Dnipropetrovsk Baptist Convention. Photo: Aleksey Sinichkin, Archive of the Union of Evangelical Christians-Baptists of Russia.

12. Map over culture bases in the Soviet Union, 1920s–1930s.

13. Photo from Tura culture base, Krasnoyarsk krai, 1920s. Public domain.

14. 'Elect workers to the indigenous council. Don't let the shaman and the kulak in.' Soviet propaganda poster by Georgiy Khoroshevskiy, 1931.

15. Images of *seven*s, kept at the museum in the village Troytskiy, Khabarovsk krai. Photo: Tatiana Bulgakova.

16. A *saola* of the Zaksor clan, supposed to contain the helping spirits of a female shaman, who died in the 1950s. In front of the *saola* are offerings of vodka and candy. Daerga village, Khabarovsk krai, 1994. Photo: Tatiana Bulgakova.

17. 'Attack shamans—a band of charlatans!' Page from *Antireligioznaya azbuka* ['Anti-religious ABC'], Leningrad-Moskva: Utilbyuro Izogiza, 1933.

18. 'Anti-religious skittles.' Children's board game with figures of a "Mongolian shaman," a "German minister," a "Russian priest," the "Jewish god," an Evenk "Tungus hunting god," a Nanai "idol," and the "Christian god." From the Soviet children's magazine *Murzilka* (1932).

Abbreviations

ARAB	*Arbetarrörelsens arkiv och bibliotek* ['The Labour Movement's Archives and Library'], Stockholm, Sweden
Comintern	Communist International
Cheka	*Chrezvychaynaya Komissiya* ['Emergency Committee'], Soviet security service 1917–1922
CP(b)U	*Komunistychna Partyia (bil'shovikiv) Ukrainy* ['The Communist Party of Ukraine']
DADO	*Derzhavnyy Arkhiv Dnipropetrovskoi Oblasti* ['State Archives of Dnipropetrovsk Oblast'], Dnipropetrovsk, Ukraine
DAKhO	*Derzhavnyy Arkhiv Khersonskoi Oblasti* ['State Archives of Kherson Oblast'], Kherson, Ukraine
DAOO	*Derzhavnyy Arkhiv Odeskoi Oblasti* ['State Archives of Odessa Oblast'], Odessa, Ukraine
DAZO	*Derzhavnyy Arkhiv Zaporizhskoi Oblasti* ['State Archives of Zaporizhia Oblast'], Zaporizhia, Ukraine
DPU URSR	*Derzhavne Polytychne Upravlinnia Ukrainskoi Radianskoi Sotsyalistychnoi Respubliki* ['State Political Directorate of the Ukrainian Soviet Socialist Republic']
GDA SBU	*Galuzevyy Derzhavnyi Arkhiv Sluzhby Bezpeki Ukrainy* ['Departmental State Archive of the Security Service of Ukraine']
GAKhK	*Gosudarstvennyy Arkhiv Khabarovkogo Kraya* ['State Archive of Khabarovsk Krai'], Khabarovsk, Russia
GAMO	*Gosudarstvennyy Arkhiv Murmanskoi Oblasti* ['State Archive of Murmansk Oblast'], Murmansk, Russia
GARF	*Gosudarstvennyy Arkhiv Rossiiskoy Federatsii* [State Archive of the Russian Federation'], Moscow, Russia
GPU	*Gosudarstvennoe Politicheskoe Upravlenie* ['State Political Directorate'], Soviet security service 1922–1923

GUGB	*Glavnoe Upravlenie Gosudarestvennoy Bezopasnosti* ['Main Directorate for State Security'], part of the Soviet security service under NKVD 1934–1943
GULAG	*Glavnoe Upravlenie Ispravitel'no-Trudovykh Lagerey i Kolonii* ['Main Directorate of Corrective Labour Camps and Labour Settlements'], Soviet Union
KGB	*Komitet Gosudarstvennoy Bezopasnosti* ['Committee for State Security'], Soviet security service 1954–1991
KVZhD	Kitaysko-Vostochnaya Zheleznaya Doroga ['Chinese Eastern Railway']
LOIKFUN	*Leningradskoe Obshchestvo Issledovateley Kul'tury Finno-Ugorskikh Narodov* ['Leningrad Society of Researchers on the Finno-Ugric Peoples' Culture']
MAE RAN	*Muzey Antropologii i Etnografii Rossiiskoy Akademii Nauk* ['Museum of Anthropology and Ethnography of the Russian Academy of Sciences'], Leningrad/St. Petersburg, Russia
MANAR	*Munitsipal'nyy Arkhiv Nikolaevskogo-na-Amure Rayona* ['Municipal Archive of the Nikolayevsk-on-Amur District'], Nikolayevsk-on-Amur, Russia
MGB	*Ministerstvo Gosudarstvennoy Bezopasnosti* ['Ministry of State Security'], Soviet security service 1946–1953
MVD	*Ministerstvo Vnutrennikh Del* ['Ministry for Internal Affairs'], Soviet Union
NEP	New Economic Policy in the Soviet Union 1921–1928
NKVD	*Narodnyy Komissariat Vnutrennikh Del* ['People's Commissariat for Internal Affairs'], Soviet security service 1934–1946
OGPU	*Ob'edinennoe Gosudarstvennoe Politicheskoe Upravlenie* ['Joint State Political Directorate'], Soviet security service 1923–1934
RA	*Riksarkivet* ['National Archives of Sweden'], Stockholm, Sweden
RGAE	*Rossiiskiy Gosudarstvennyy Arkhiv Ekonomiki* ['Russian State Archives of Economics], Moscow, Russia

ABBREVIATIONS

RGASPI	*Rossiiskiy Gosudarstvennyy Archiv Sotsialno-Politicheskoy Istorii* ['Russian State Archive of Social and Political History'], Moscow, Russia
RSFSR	*Rossiiskaya Sovetskaya Federativnaya Sotsialisticheskaya Respublika* ['Russian Soviet Federative Socialist Republic']
SBU	*Sluzhba Bezpeki Ukrainy* ['Security Service of Ukraine']
SNK	*Sovet Narodnykh Komissarov* ['Council of People's Commissars'], the Soviet central government
SOFIN	*Soyuz Osvobozhdeniya Finskikh Narodov* ['Union for Liberation of Finno-Ugric Peoples'], an underground organization fabricated by the NKVD in 1932–1933
TASS	*Telegrafnoe Agenstvo Sovetskogo Soyuza* ['Telegraph Agency of the Soviet Union']
TsDAGO	*Tsentralnyy Derzhavnyy Arkhiv Gromadskykh Obiednan Ukrainy* ['Central State Archive of the Public Organizations of Ukraine'], Kyiv, Ukraine
TsK VKP (b)	*Tsentralnyy Komitet Vsesoyuznoy Kommunisticheskoy Partii (bolshevikov)* ['Central Committee of the All-Union Communist Party (Bolsheviks)']
UNKVD	*Upravlenie Narodnogo Komissariata Vnutrennikh Del* ['Main Directorate of the People's Commissariat for Internal Affairs'], Soviet security service 1934–1946.
URSR	*Ukrainska Radianska Sotsyalistychna Respublika* ['Ukrainian Soviet Socialist Republic']
VKP(b)	*Vsesoyuznaya Kommunisticheskaya Partiya (bolshevikov)* ['All-Union Communist Party (Bolsheviks)']
VTsIK	*Vserossiyskiy Tsentral'nyy Ispolnitel'nyy Komitet* ['All-Russian Central Executive Committee'], RSFSR
VUTsVK	*Vseukrainskiy Tsentralny Vykonavchy Komitet* ['All-Ukrainian Central Executive Committee'], URSR
ZAGS	*Zapis Aktov Grazhdanskogo Sostoyaniya* ['Soviet Civil Registry Office']

A Short Note on Transliteration, Abbreviations, and Names in this Volume

Personal and geographical names in the book, as well as official Soviet terms, are transliterated from the Cyrillic script in accordance with the simplified version of the US Library of Congress system. Certain exceptions are made for well-known persons. The abbreviations of Soviet institutions are based on the practice of the modern Russian language. Geographical names are given in the form they have in their present-day location, with a few exceptions for Ukraine.

Foreword

This anthology is the result of academic cooperation between Södertörn University and Umeå University within the research projects "Soviet Nordic Minorities and Ethnic Cleansing on the Kola Peninsula" (The Foundation for Baltic and East European Studies) and "Repression of 'Shamans' in the Soviet North" (Swedish Research Council) as well as the multidisciplinary network "The Baltic and Arctic Area under Stalin. Minorities in the Soviet Union" that united scholars from nine countries and was supported by the Swedish Institute. This printed volume and open-access digital anthology has been published thanks to the financial support of the Foundation for Baltic and East European Studies, the Royal Skyttean Society, the Södertörn University Publications Committee, the Swedish Institute, and Umeå University.

Our special thanks go to the members of the network: Dr Arseniy Roginskiy, Dr Aleksandr Daniel, and Boris Belenkin (Memorial, Russia); Prof. Igor Nabok, and Dr Yuliya Kustova (Institute of the Peoples of the North, St. Petersburg, Russia); Levan Avalishvili (Institute for Development and Freedom of Information, Tbilisi, Georgia); Dr Iryna Ramanava (National Academy of Sciences of Belarus); Prof. Bogdan Musial (Cardinal Stefan Wyszyński University, Warsaw, Poland); Erika Aronowitsch (The Living History Forum, Sweden); Dr Irina Takala (Petrozavodsk State University, Russia); Prof. Timo Vihavainen (University of Helsinki, Finland); Dr Nikolay Morozov (Syktyvkar Academy, Russia); and Stella Sevander (Umeå University, Sweden).

We thank Dr Lars Hübinette (Umeå University, Sweden) for careful proofreading of the English language in this anthology. The editors also wish to thank Prof. Norbert Götz (Södertörn University, Sweden), Marianne Yagoubi and Erika Jansson (The Foundation for Baltic and East European Studies, Sweden), Jonathan Robson (Södertörn University Publications Department), Prof. Lars-Erik Edlund (Umeå University and The Royal Skyttean Society, Sweden), Dr Lena Eskilsson (Umeå University, Sweden), Dr Tomislav Dulić and Dr Matthew Kott (Uppsala University, Sweden), Prof. Kristian Gerner, Prof. Barbara Törnquist-Plewa, and Prof. Klas-Göran Karlsson (Lund University, Sweden), Prof. Håkan Rydving (University of Bergen, Norway), Dr Aleksandr Tolstikov (Petrozavodsk University, Russia), Dr Tatiana Shrader (Russian Academy of Sciences), Prof. em. Gerhard Simon

(University of Cologne, Germany), and Prof. Andrea Graziosi (University of Naples, Italy) for their contributions to the realization of the project and this anthology.

Tumba and Umeå, September 2017
Andrej Kotljarchuk & Olle Sundström

Introduction

Andrej Kotljarchuk & Olle Sundström

The Problem of Ethnic and Religious Minorities in Stalin's Soviet Union

Robert Conquest, who popularized the term *the Great Terror* in his classic account of Stalin's purges in 1937–1938, depicts these events as massive repressions first of all of Soviet political, cultural, and military elites (Conquest 1971). But Conquest did not particularly address the role in the turmoil of the 1930s of ethnicity and religious belonging—two categories of central importance in so much of Soviet politics. The Russian "archival revolution"—the newly acquired access to previously unavailable sources from former Soviet archives after 1991—has brought to light new facts on the history of the Great Terror, among other things data on the so-called national operations of the security service (NKVD) against ethnic minorities and details on the repression of religious groups (Samuelson & Sorokin 2007). Even though much information on the repression is still difficult to uncover—as several of the authors in this volume show—the archival revolution has undoubtedly brought new possibilities for research.

The inter-war Soviet Union was unlike many other states in Europe. The differences concern not only the abolition of private property and the establishment of the one-party system, but also a nationality policy based on internationalism (in the sense of 'inter-ethnicity') or the solidarity and unity among different ethnic groups. The Soviet Union was in practice the first major state power in the world that systematically promoted the national consciousness of indigenous peoples and established institutional forms characteristic of a modern nation for them. While small-numbered ethnic groups faced discrimination, the Soviet Union proclaimed in 1923 a policy of self-determination and cultural and linguistic rights for all minorities, which they tried to implement during the 1920s (Martin 2001).

However, in the beginning of the 1930s this policy changed radically, and in 1937 the NKVD initiated top-secret "national operations." The situation in the ethnic and religious communities was rather specific. The Bolsheviks believed that ethnic and religious minorities of rural areas remained behind the progressive development of the population of industrial cities. The cultural and linguistic factors and the isolation of minority communities from the rest of the population thus required additional surveillance of ethnic as well as religious groups by the secret service. At a meeting of the Politburo on 20 July 1937, Stalin initiated the German operation by writing a proposal that "all Germans working in our military and chemical factories, electrical stations and at construction sites in all regions, must be arrested" (Okhotin & Roginskiy 1999: 35). In total, in 1937–1938, 56,787 ethnic Germans were arrested, of whom 41,898 were shot. Only 820 of them were citizens of the German Reich (Okhotin & Roginskiy 1999: 73–74). The next operation was the "Polish" one, in which 139,815 Soviet Poles were arrested and 111,071 of them executed (Petrov & Roginskiy 1997: 37–38). A number of other secret national operations were organized by the central government in accordance with the models of the German and the Polish operations. Among them were the Korean, Chinese, Afghan, Iranian, Greek, and Bulgarian-Macedonian operations as well as the Finnish and Estonian operations. The local NKVD of Smolensk initiated a national Latvian operation. During this operation, which started on 3 December 1937, 17,851 Soviet citizens, mainly of Latvian origin, were arrested and 13,444 were executed (Kott 2007). A number of smaller operations along so-called "national lines" and in accordance with the national operation model were designed and performed by local police against Japanese, Lithuanians, Norwegians, Sami, and Swedes (Kotljarchuk 2014a; Kotljarchuk 2014b; Kotljarchuk 2015). Altogether within the period of fourteen months, August 1937 to October 1938, 335,513 people were arrested in the national operations of the NKVD and 247,157 of them were shot (Werth 2003: 232). The victims of national operations made up 34 per cent of all the murdered victims of the Great Terror.

Historians have put forward many explanations for the mass repression of various ethnic groups committed by Stalin's regime, and two approaches are particularly relevant. Most scholars focus on the security dilemma in the border areas, suggesting the need to secure the ethnic integrity of Soviet space *vis-à-vis* neighbouring capitalistic enemy states. They stress the role of international relations and believe that representatives of "Western" minorities were killed not because of their ethnicity, but rather because of their possible connections to countries hostile to the USSR and fear of disloyalty in case of an invasion (Werth 2003; Mann 2005; Kuromiya 2007). Other scholars argue that the Soviet terror against minorities was actually genocide based on ethnic criteria (Kostiainen 2000; Naimark 2010; Snyder 2010: 92–108).

In contrast to the repression of certain ethnic groups, the repression of religious associations, organisations, and individuals was motivated by basic tenets in the Marxist-Leninist doctrine. As Lenin himself put it, dialectical

INTRODUCTION

Marxism was "unconditionally materialist and resolutely hostile to any religion" (Lenin [1909] 1954: 8; cf. Lenin 1973: 402). While he proclaimed religion to be a private matter of no concern for the state—and indeed freedom of religion and conscience were inscribed in the Soviet constitution—Lenin at the same time made it clear that for the Party it was imperative to fight against "ignorance and obscurantism in the shape of religious beliefs." In fact, he claimed that this was the very reason why the Party was founded (Lenin [1905] 1954: 5–6; cf. Lenin 1965: 85–86). This line of thought was phrased in the official slogan for the second congress of the League of the Militant Atheists (Ru. *Soyuz voynstvuyushchikh bezbozhnikov*)—a Party-run voluntary organization with the mission to propagate atheism in publications, lectures, study groups, and rallies—in June 1929: "The struggle against religion is the struggle for socialism" (see Pospielovsky 1987: 49).

If one, as James Ryan (2012: 2) writes, "accepts that Stalin and his colleagues' professed Leninism was genuinely important for their political practice, then Stalinism should be studied in the light of Leninism." And Stalin was indeed the one who canonized Lenin's writings and proclaimed Marxism-Leninism to be the world-view of the Party, and thus of the Soviet state once the Party took totalitarian control. Lenin's analysis of religion, in an oft-cited passage in his 1905 article "Sotsialism i religiya" ['Socialism and religion'], explains why fighting against religion became integral to the Bolsheviks' revolutionary re-creation of society into a new socialist one among the big city elites, factory workers, peasants, and "savage" hunter-gatherers in the periphery of the Soviet Union:

> Religion is one of the forms of spiritual oppression which everywhere weighs down heavily upon the masses of the people, crushed by their perpetual work for others, by want and solitude. The impotence of the exploited classes in their struggle against the exploiters just as inevitably gives rise to the belief in a better life after death as the impotence of the savage in his struggle with nature gives rise to belief in gods, devils, miracles, and the like. To those who all their lives toil and live in want religion teaches humbleness and patience while here on earth, and to take comfort in the hope of a heavenly reward. But to those who live by the labour of others religion teaches the practicing of charity while on earth, thus offering them a very cheap way of justifying their entire exploiting existence and selling them, at a fair price, tickets to well-being in heaven. Religion is the opium of the people. Religion is a sort of spiritual hooch [Ru. *sivukha*], in which the slaves of capital drown their human image, their demand for a reasonably worthy human life. (Lenin [1905] 1954: 3–4; cf. Lenin 1965: 83)

For Lenin, as for Marx, religion was both an effect of unjust socio-economic relations, as well as of impotence before the forces of nature, and an impediment for overcoming these unjust relations and for increasing humans' command over nature. The opium and alcohol metaphors are therefore quite pertinent for their analysis.

Besides being at the heart of the Marxist-Leninist world-view, the Soviet struggle against religion was also motivated by the Bolshevik intolerance of ideological and organizational competitors of all sorts (and some of them were, of course, outright counter-revolutionary). For both of these reasons, the Russian Orthodox Church became the main target of anti-religious measures in the immediate post-Revolutionary years. As the state church of the tsarist Russian Empire, gathering some 70 per cent of the population, for the revolutionaries this church was synonymous with the monarchy that had just been overthrown (Corley 1996: 13). Thus, emptying the cathedrals of clerics and turning the buildings into museums of atheism and the history of religion was an act in the same vein as throwing out the royal family and transforming the Winter Palace into a state museum (Sundström 2007: 84). In both instances, the killing of the representatives of the monarchy and the church was obviously seen as a justified method by the revolutionaries. James Thrower (1983: 117–118) has noted that Lenin's and the Party's attitude toward religion became more uncompromisingly hostile from 1917 onwards. Lenin's notorious letter of March 1922 to Molotov and the Politburo on how to handle the resistance against the collection of church valuables (for aid to the starving in Ukraine) is an example of that (see e.g. Ryan 2012: 178–181; Troyansky [ed.] 1991: 3–11). In this letter, Lenin elevates violence and terror to a legitimate revolutionary strategy that very well might have set the tone for the subsequent decades of Bolshevik tactics towards real and imagined opponents of socialist reconstruction:

> [...] if it is necessary to resort to harsh methods in order to implement a given political objective, then it is necessary to implement these measures in the most energetic manner and in the shortest period of time, because the popular masses will not tolerate a long application of harsh measures. (Lenin cited and translated in Troyansky [ed.] 1991: 4)

And later in the same letter he specified what "harsh measures" in this case concretely meant: "The more reactionary clergy and reactionary bourgeoisie we are able to execute by firing squad regarding this matter, the better" (Lenin in Troyansky [ed.] 1991: 6).

The combination of the ideological imperative—that religion should be combatted and was predicted to perish in the socialist society—and the ousting of competitors in directing the thoughts and behaviours of Soviet citizens led to recurrent onslaughts on religious representatives and associations in the Soviet Union. However, the religious policy of the Bolshevik regime fluctuated between periods of harsher and more lenient methods of combatting religion. Oksana Beznosova in this volume presents a periodisation of the authorities' treatment of Evangelical associations in Ukraine between 1918 and 1941. There have been many attempts at periodisations of Soviet religious policy in previous research (see e.g. Vorontsov 1973; Pospielovsky 1987; Corley 1996), and P. Walters (1993: 3) comments, while presenting his own, that any such attempt will be disputable. This is due, among other things, to the fact that different religious groups were treated differently during different years and in different areas of the vast Union, and local authorities at times took measures that were not in phase with central policy. For instance, what Beznosova describes as the "Golden Decade" for Ukrainian Evangelists, 1918–1928, was at least in the first years one of the most severe times for the Russian Orthodox Church. But for Protestants and some other minority religions, including shamanism (see Bulgakova & Sundström in this volume), the decade meant relative religious freedom during the NEP, even compared to pre-revolutionary times when Russian Orthodoxy claimed hegemony over the souls in the empire.

Periodisations of various kinds might be instructive in order to connect the fluctuations to the varying conditions for fulfilling the Marxist-Leninist vision of an atheist society, to other projects of Soviet authorities, and to concrete decrees and laws passed by the Party. As some of the studies in this book shows, the default hostility towards religion among Soviet communists became entangled in other campaigns and policies such as the nationality policy, dekulakisation, collectivisation, and the hunt for "counter-revolutionaries," "enemies of the people," and "foreign spies" as well as in the appeal from Stalin for patriotic unity during the Second World War and the cleansing of occupied areas after the war. In the case of the indigenous peoples of the Soviet North, the fight against shamanism was not only a consequence of the general struggle against religion (once shamanism had been classified as a religion), but also of a general civilisation project by Soviet authorities. Shamanism was seen as an integral part of the old indigenous societies that were to be reconstructed under socialism, and it was to be liquiddated together with illiteracy, ignorance, slavery, patriarchalism, the abuse of women, malnutrition, bad hygiene, infant mortality, rampant diseases, etc. (Sundström 2007: 111-164).

This Anthology

The present anthology is the outcome of an international research network created by the editors, Andrej Kotljarchuk and Olle Sundström. Kotljarchuk, as an historian, has previously studied the destiny of ethnic Swedes in Soviet Ukraine, and Sundström, being an historian of religions, has undertaken research specialising in Soviet religious and ethnic policies against the indigenous peoples of the Soviet North. To elucidate unsolved research issues on the consequences of the Great Terror for these and closely related minority groups, we invited a range of specialists to a workshop at Umeå University in Sweden, 26-27 January 2011, under the heading "The Baltic and Arctic Areas under Stalin. Ethnic Minorities in the Great Soviet Terror of 1937-38." At the workshop, 17 papers by scholars from nine different countries (Belarus, Estonia, Georgia, Germany, Poland, Russia, Sweden, Ukraine, and the United States) were presented. As a follow-up to this event, a limited group of the network—Boris Belenkin and Tatiana Bulgakova (Russia), Marc Junge (Germany), Art Leete (Estonia), and Andrej Kotljarchuk and Olle Sundström (Sweden)—met in Umeå for a one-day workshop in June 2012 to plan the present publication. In the discussions at the latter workshop, the scope of the project was somewhat widened to include studies of the situation for various ethnic and religious minorities during the Soviet repression of the 1930s. Finally, the network held a conference, "Soviet Minorities in the Great Terror," in Umeå, 28-31 January 2013, with support from the Foundation for Baltic and East European Studies and the Swedish Institute.

This anthology presents studies of Stalinism in the ethnic and religious borderlands of the Soviet Union. The authors not only cover hitherto less researched geographical areas, but have also tried to address new questions related to the research material. Most of the contributors to this book use a micro-historical approach. With this approach, it is not the entire area of the country with millions of separate individuals, but rather isolated and cohesive ethnic and religious communities that are in focus. This micro-historical method allows the researcher to significantly reduce the scale of observations and thus to concentrate on a particular social group, but only after having processed a massive complex of written and oral sources (Levi 2001). Micro-history does not mean ignoring a macro-historical perspective. What happened on the local level had an all-Union context, and communism, like

Nazism, was a European-wide phenomenon. This means that the history of local minorities in the Soviet Union during Stalin's reign cannot be grasped outside the national and international context. The selection of original papers for this volume is by no means exhaustive for the theme "Ethnic and Religious Minorities in Stalin's Soviet Union." Rather, the chapters are case studies on different minority groups that hopefully can encourage further micro-historical studies on other minorities so that a more complete picture of the causes and effects of the repression during Stalinism can be achieved.

The Soviet Union was one of the most multi-ethnic and multi-confessional states in the world. The first complete census in the Soviet Union (1926) included 188 ethnic categories classified around numerous linguistic groups. According to the census, the Eastern Slavs (Russians, Ukrainians and Belarusians) constituted the majority, or 77.5 per cent, of the total population of 146 million. The next largest ethnic groups in the Soviet Union were the Kazakhs (3,968,289 individuals), the Uzbeks (3,904,622 individuals), the Tatars (3,271,842 individuals), the Jews (2,672,499 individuals), the Georgians (2,199,461 individuals), the Armenians (1,567,568 individuals) and the Mordvins (1,340,415 individuals). Since early modern times, hundreds of thousands of non-Russian Europeans had either moved to Russia or become subjects of the tsar as a result of Russian conquest. The 1926 census reported 1,238,549 Germans, 782,334 Poles, 398,998 Finns (including Karelians), 213,765 Greeks, 154,666 Estonians, 141,703 Latvians and 111,296 Bulgarians (*Vsesoyuznaya perepis'* 1926).

Some thirty indigenous peoples populated the country, from the Sami people (1,720 individuals) on the Kola Peninsula to the Nivkh people (4,076 individuals) in the basin of the Amur River and on Sakhalin. The largest ethnic minority of the Soviet Far East was the Koreans (86,999 individuals). There were also 390,385 foreign citizens residing in the country.[1] Apart from the Roma, practically all ethnic groups in the Soviet Union had their own compact territory and achieved administrative and cultural autonomy after 1922.

The Soviet Union had large communities of adherents of major religions such as Christianity, Islam, Buddhism and Judaism. After the Great Northern War and the partitions of Poland-Lithuania, Christianity was represented in the Russian Empire not only by Orthodoxy, but also by Catholicism and Protestantism of various branches. The North Caucasus, Central Asia and

---

[1] Calculated by Andrej Kotljarchuk from the 1926 All-Union census; http://demoscope.ru; access date 1 October 2017.

Volga regions were the traditional centres for Muslim communities, while Kalmykia, Buryatia and Trans-Baykal were centres of Buddhism, and Ukraine and Belarus of Judaism. So-called shamanism was the religious practice among the various indigenous peoples of northern Russia, Siberia and the Far East.

In the first part of this volume, the contributors discuss the general approach of the national operations of the NKVD. The second part focuses on three case studies of the Great Terror in Soviet ethnic regions. The third part analyses the situation of the religious minorities in the inter-war Soviet Union, both in Ukraine and in the Soviet North.

In the first chapter, "The Great Terror. New dimensions of research," Hiroaki Kuromiya examines the aims of the Great Terror and, in particular, the national operations of the NKVD. He points out that access to the formerly closed Soviet archives in Russia has serious shortcomings and tends to neglect questions of intelligence and counterintelligence. These kinds of sources remain classified. However, the lack or paucity of information should not obscure the understanding of the Great Terror. In the 1930s, Germany, Poland, and Japan were among the most actively engaged countries in undercover activities against the Soviet Union. Their methods were known as "total espionage." Stalin took no chances, turning the tables on these countries by practising "total counter-espionage." Thus, according to Kuromiya, the Great Terror should be seen as the culmination of Stalin's total counter-espionage and the elimination of any possible foreign penetration into the Soviet Union.

In Chapter 2, Andrey Savin turns the attention to the "ethnification" of Stalin's terror. Seen from the perspective of recent studies and newly available archival sources, Savin argues that the NKVD directives and the documents of prosecutors' inspections describe sweeping mass arrests of members of "Western" minorities without any evidence for any crimes. He also shows that the Stalinist leadership and the NKVD perceived certain national minorities as hostile and "counter-revolutionary" as early as the 1920s. In the mid-1930s, this concept was taken as the ideological basis of ethnic cleansing. The specificity of the national operations minimized Party and state control over the actions of the NKVD, which had the main influence on the magnitude of arrests and executions. Savin notes that on the one hand the determinant factor in the fate of the victims of the national operations was the outer signs of their belonging to a "malicious" ethnic group. On the other hand, his local study on the implementation of the German operation in Western Siberia casts doubt on the unambiguity of such an interpretation.

Chapter 3, "'He who is not with us is against us.' Elimination of the 'fifth column' in the Soviet Union, 1937–1938," provides an insight into the political language and nature of the German operation of the NKVD. Victor Dönninghaus shows how Stalin's ideas of the state-and-military confrontation directed the national operations against everyone that in some way was related to the states of the "hostile capitalist encirclement." Thus, he argues that the selection criterion for the national operations was not ethnicity. Rather, potential ties with hostile foreign countries were taken as the primary reason for repression. This marks a difference between these national operations and Stalin's deportations during the Second World War, which touched upon all representatives of purportedly "disloyal" minorities without exception.

In the fourth chapter, entitled "Propaganda of hatred and the Great Terror. A Nordic approach," Andrej Kotljarchuk discusses the propaganda of hatred during the national operations of the NKVD. Drawing on genocide studies, the author examines mechanisms and targets of state-run mass media propaganda on the eve of national operations of the NKVD against Soviet Nordic minorities. Kotljarchuk argues that the media campaign of hatred was orchestrated from Moscow, and often the local newspapers just reprinted materials from the central press. However, in many other cases contents were adapted for local circumstances. The propagandist preparation of the national operations included two main phases. The first phase concerned the conceptualisation of state-run mass violence against certain minorities, and the second was the translation of the propaganda of hatred to broad layers of the population. Through propaganda, the population and local authorities were prepared for subsequent ethnic cleansing. Unlike in urban areas, hiding the knowledge of mass arrests in ethnic borderlands was not possible, and the exact number of arrested people became known to the local community the very next day. Soviet propaganda campaigns during the national operations of the NKVD are an example of what we today call *fake news*—attempts at creating a reality out of nothing.

In Chapter 5, "Nation-building by terror in Soviet Georgia, 1937–1938," Marc Junge and Daniel Müller look at the factors that accelerated the national operations of the NKVD through the prism of persisting inter-ethnic conflicts in the Caucasus. Based on newly obtained access to archival material in Georgia, it is possible to reconstruct "which ethnic groups suffered the most in the Great Terror in absolute and relative terms." The chapter analyses the nature of national operations in Soviet Georgia in terms of ethnic conflicts. Specific Georgian, as opposed to general all-Union, interests seem to be an indispensable basis for understanding the mass operations in Georgia, but admittedly these interests explain only part of the deadly dynamics involved, especially concerning the diaspora nationalities. The authors show how the Georgian leadership used the national operations in order to marginalize and diminish ethnic minorities, especially in Abkhazia.

The ethnic issue is also highlighted in Chapter 6 by Eva Toulouze titled "A long great ethnic terror in the Volga religion. A rehearsal for the Great Terror." Toulouze notes that ethnicity was not at the core of the Marxist understanding of society. But for the Bolsheviks, inheriting a multi-ethnic empire, various ethnicities were a reality that they had to deal with, and Lenin took particular interest in the questions of ethnicity. In the 1920s the Soviet nationality policy was characterised by a striving for *korenizatsiya* ['indigenisation'] in which non-Russian populations were supposed to be actively involved in building a socialist society on their own specific terms. Ethnic cultures were encouraged under the Stalinist slogan that they should be "national [i.e. ethnic] in form, socialist in content." Toulouze's study of the destiny of the intelligentsias of Finno-Ugric descent in the Volga region shows that the encouraging attitudes toward ethnic culture changed by the end of the 1920s in favour of the unity of Soviet culture (modelled after Russian culture). The author concludes that the repression that struck Finno-Ugric (communist) intellectuals during the first half of the 1930s was not primarily motivated by the fact that the Finno-Ugric peoples had sister nations outside the Soviet Union (Finland and Hungary), even though loyalty to purportedly hostile foreign nations was used in the (paranoiac) accusations against individuals and organisations. Rather, what the Stalinist regime really feared was nationality/ethnicity as such, and the purpose of the terror was to control and subjugate local nationalism and ethnic loyalty. Toulouze suggests that the repression of the Finno-Ugric intelligentsia was a foreboding of the Great Terror. In essence it was a rehearsal of the same logic, methods, and tactics that would be used in the purges of 1937–1938 and that had already been tested during the collectivisation and dekulakisation campaigns.

Oksana Beznosova, in Chapter 7 on the fate of Ukrainian Evangelists (Baptists, Evangelical Christians, Pentecostals, Adventists, and Mennonites) between 1928 and 1939, compares the Communist Party to a totalitarian religion with the Marxist-Leninist-Stalinist theory as its doctrine. In that perspective, the NKVD played the role of a "Holy Inquisition" in the fight against "heretics" that potentially could compete with the hegemony of the Party. Beznosova shows that repression of Evangelism in Ukraine, in the form of arrests of pastors and preachers, peaked in 1930, 1932–1933, 1935 and, above all, in 1937–1938. The peaks can be connected to certain Party decrees and resolutions sharpening the anti-religious policy of the state. In Dnipropetrovsk Oblast[2]—the province which in the 1930s was the main centre for Evangelism in the Ukrainian SSR—all legal, registered Evangelical congregations had been disbanded by the time of the Second World War. This happened due to repression in the form of administrative measures, high taxation, and, not least, mass arrests and executions of "cult leaders." Beznosova emphasizes, however, that the full extent of how repressions struck ordinary members of the Evangelical denominations during the Great Terror is still unknown due to the fact that people were not officially arrested on charges of religious belonging.

It is not self-evident what should be defined as "repression" or not. The intentions behind a certain measure taken by authorities might be the opposite of repressive acts, but the outcome, in its entirety or in parts, can still become repressive, at least from some points of view. In the case of the so-called culture bases in the Soviet North, which Eva Toulouze, Laur Vallikivi, and Art Leete treat in Chapter 8, it is one thing what the planners of these bases had in mind, another how the actual bases worked in each individual case, and yet another how the recipients—the northern indigenous minorities—reacted towards them. Culture bases were a form of missionary stations for the new Soviet ideology and administration with the aim of reaching the small-numbered indigenous peoples of the Soviet North. From the start in the late 1920s, these bases were supposed to bring culture, schooling, health-care, and infrastructure to the "backward" peoples inhabiting the vast taigas and tundras of Northern Russia, Siberia, and the Far East. The vision was to emancipate the natives from both external exploitation (traders) and internal inequalities (between men and women, rich and poor, old and young) and make them the "agents of their own fate," as the authors put it. Being among the very few Soviet outposts on the northern frontier in the late 1920s and early 1930s, the culture bases also had the responsibility to administer dekulakisation, class struggle, and the fight against shamans, which led to disfranchisement and exclusion of precisely those persons in the indigenous communities that had the highest internal authority and prestige. To the indigenous peoples, it was obvious that the culture and reforms that the culture bases and their schools tried to implement were based on Russian norms and values, which often collided with

---

[2] Dnipropetrovsk Oblast and the city of Dnipropetrovsk were recently renamed Dnipro Oblast and Dnipro. In this book, we use the Soviet Ukrainian names of the region and the city.

indigenous traditions and world-views. This sometimes led to violent resistance from the indigenous populations, as in the so-called Kazym uprising among a group of Khanty and Nenets, which in turn resulted in repressive retaliation from Soviet authorities.

The uncertainty regarding the extent to which people were arrested because of religious belonging that Beznosova emphasizes is also noted by Tatiana Bulgakova and Olle Sundström concerning the repression of shamans in the Soviet Far East in Chapter 9. Shamanism in many respects flourished among the indigenous peoples of the North in the beginning of the Soviet era, when the Russian Orthodox Church—which before the revolution had combatted shamanism—was forced to withdraw due to the anti-church measures taken by the revolutionaries. Only towards the end of the 1920s was shamanism highlighted as a "religion" or "religious cult"—and hence shamans and shamanism became caught up in the general Soviet struggle against religion. Written sources and archival documents of the time, as well as oral sources from late- and post-Soviet times, present a rather complex situation. Officially, the struggle against shamanism was supposed to be completed through propaganda, enlightenment, education, and a general development plan for these purportedly "backward" and "primitive" peoples. Between 1926 and 1936, putative "shamans," together with "kulaks," were constitutionally excluded from participating in local councils and in decision-making. The official attitudes towards shamans and shamanism at times led to general harassment of shamans, and expropriation and destruction of drums and other ritual objects connected to their activities were common. On the local level, this repression seems to have been carried out by newly "converted" indigenous communists, members of the Komsomol. Because being a shaman or practicing shamanism was not an official accusation in court files, it is impossible to assess how many people were arrested or executed on such grounds in the Far East. But the study of both archival materials and later oral sources indicates that while arrest was a constant and implicit threat to shamans, few were actually brought up on legal charges. The many complaints to authorities that shamans were performing their rituals in the open, both before and after the Second World War, speak for that.

While Bulgakova and Sundström try to trace how Soviet authorities and communist zealots concretely repressed shamanism in light of the overall struggle against religion, Yana Ivashchenko, in Chapter 10, addresses the more direct question of why shamanism in the Soviet Far East had all but disappeared by the 1970s (which she concludes that it had). Was it the communists' education and propaganda campaigns that turned peoples' minds away from the traditional world-view and rituals? Or was it the Soviet modernisation, socio-economic reconstruction, and health-care that made the shamans and their services unnecessary and obsolete? Or was it perhaps arrests and violent purges that reduced the number of shamans—those who knew the traditional world-view system and rituals and would have been capable of transferring the tradition to the next generation—and intimidated others from continuing shamanic practices? Ivashchenko bases her study mainly on her own fieldwork among indigenous peoples in the Lower Amur region. Even though there was a ban on the practice of shamanism, and despite the fact that participants were threatened with arrest for participating in shamanic activities, none of Ivashchenko's informants could recall that anyone was ever arrested or deported due to shamanism. Gradually, shamanism became stigmatized and unpopular among the indigenous peoples during the Soviet era. These attitudes were, of course, intentionally disseminated by the Soviet regime. But Ivashchenko suggests that the main reason why shamanism died off was the internal processes of desacralisation and rationalisation of knowledge among the indigenous peoples themselves—processes that started with the indigenous peoples' contacts with other cultures already in the nineteenth century.

References

Conquest, R. (1971). *The Great Terror. Stalin's Purge of the Thirties*, Harmondsworth: Penguin.

Corley, F. (1996). *Religion in the Soviet Union. An Archival Reader*, London: Macmillan Press LTD.

Kostiainen, A. (2000). "The Finns of Soviet Karelia as a target of Stalin's terror," in *Ethnic and National Issues in Russian and East European History. Selected Papers from the Fifth World Congress of Central and East European Studies, Warsaw, 1995*, ed. J. Morison, Basingstoke: Palgrave Macmillan, pp. 214–229.

Kotljarchuk, A. (2014a). *In the Forge of Stalin. Swedish Colonists of Ukraine in Totalitarian Experiments of the Twentieth Century* (Södertörn Academic Studies 58), Stockholm: Acta Universitatis Stockholmiensis.

Kotljarchuk, A. (2014b). "The Nordic threat. Soviet ethnic cleansing on the Kola Peninsula," in *The Sea of Identities. A Century of Baltic and East European Experiences with Nationality, Class, and Gender* (Södertörn Academic Studies 60), ed. N. Götz, Stockholm: Elanders, pp. 53–83.

Kotljarchuk, A. (2015). "Norwegians in the Stalinist terror. New perspectives for research," *Fortid*, 2, pp. 18–22.

Kott, M. (2007). "Soviet genocide in Latvia. Stalin's Great Terror (1937–38) as antecedent and other aspects of the recent historiography," *Latvijas*

Okupācijas Muzeja Gadagramāta/Yearbook of the Museum of the Occupation of Latvia, 2007, Riga: Latvijas 50 gadu okupācijas muzeja fonds, pp. 42–54.

Kuromiya, H. (2007). *The Voices of the Dead. Stalin's Great Terror in the 1930s*, New Haven: Yale University Press.

Lenin, V. I. (1954). В. И. Ленин, *Социализм и религия / Об отношении рабочей партии к религии* ['Socialism and religion / The attitude of the workers' party to religion'], Moscow: Gospolitizdat.

Lenin, V. I. (1965). *Collected Works* 10. *November 1905–June 1906*, Moscow: Progress Publishers.

Lenin, V. I. (1973). *Collected Works* 15. *1908–1909*, Moscow: Progress Publishers.

Levi, G. (2001). "On microhistory," in *New Perspectives on Historical Writing*, ed. P. Burke, Cambridge: Polity, pp. 97–119.

Mann, M. (2005). *The Dark Side of Democracy. Explaining Ethnic Cleansing*, New York: Cambridge University Press.

Martin, T. (2001). *The Affirmative Action Empire. Nations and Nationalism in the Soviet Union, 1923–1939*, Ithaca: Cornell University Press.

Naimark, N. M. (2010). *Stalin's Genocides*, Princeton: Princeton University Press.

Okhotin, N. & Roginskiy, A. В. (1999). Охотин, Н. & Рогинский, А. Б. "Из истории 'немецкой' операции НКВД 1937–1938 гг." ['From the history of the "German" operation of the NKVD 1937–1938'], *Наказанный народ. Репрессии против российских немцев. Материалы конференции*, Moscow: Zven'ya Press, pp. 35–74.

Petrov, N. V. & Roginskiy, A. В. (1997). Петров, Н. В. & Рогинский А. Б. "Польская операция НКВД 1937–1938 гг." ['The Polish operation of the NKVD 1937–1938'], *Репрессии против поляков и польских граждан*, Moscow: Zven'ya Press, pp. 22–43.

Pospielovsky, D. V. (1987). *A History of Marxist-Leninist Atheism and Soviet Antireligious Policies. Volume 1 of A History of Soviet Atheism in Theory and Practice, and the Believer*, New York: St. Martin's Press.

Ryan, J. (2012). *Lenin's Terror. The Ideological Origins of Early Soviet State Violence*, London: Routledge.

Samuelson, L. & Sorokin A. (2007). "Den ryska 'arkivrevolutionen.' Källvolymer belyser sovjetepokens mörka sidor" ['The Russian "archival revolution." Source volumes enlighten the dark sides of the Soviet era'], *Historisk Tidskrift*, 4, pp. 739–756.

Snyder, T. (2010). *Bloodlands. Europe between Hitler and Stalin*, London: Bodley Head.

Sundström, O. (2007). *Kampen mot "schamanismen." Sovjetisk religionspolitik gentemot inhemska religioner i Sibirien och norra Ryssland* ['The struggle against "shamanism." Soviet religious policy towards the indigenous religions of Siberia and Northern Russia'] (Studies on Inter-Religious Relations 40), Uppsala: Swedish Science Press.

Thrower, J. (1983). *Marxist-Leninist "Scientific Atheism" and the Study of Religion and Atheism in the USSR* (Religion and Reason 25), Berlin: Mouton.

Troyansky, I. (ed.) (1991). *Religion in the Soviet Republics. A Guide to Christianity, Judaism, Islam, Buddhism, and Other Religions*, San Francisco: HarperSanFrancisco.

Vsesoyuznaya perepis' (1926). *Всесоюзная перепись населения 1926 года. Национальный состав населения по республикам СССР* ['The All-Union census of 1926. The national composition of the population in the republics of the USSR']; http://demoscope.ru; access date 1 October 2017.

Vorontsov, I. (1973). Воронцов, И. *Ленинская программа атеистического воспитания в действии (1917–1937 гг.)* ['Lenin's program for atheist education in practice'], Leningrad: Izd. LGU.

Walters, P. (1993). "A survey of Soviet religious policy," in *Religious Policy in the Soviet Union*, ed. S. P. Ramet, Cambridge: Cambridge University Press, pp. 3–30.

Werth, N. (2003). "The mechanism of a mass crime. The Great Terror in the Soviet Union, 1937–1938," in *The Specter of Genocide. Mass Murder in Historical Perspective*, eds. R. Gellately & B. Kiernan, Cambridge: Cambridge University Press, pp. 215–240.

Illustration 1 (next page): Map of the nationalities of the Soviet Union. From *Geograficheskiy atlas dlya sredney shkoly*, Moskva: Glavnoe Upravlenie Geodezii i Kartografii pri SNK SSSR (1941).

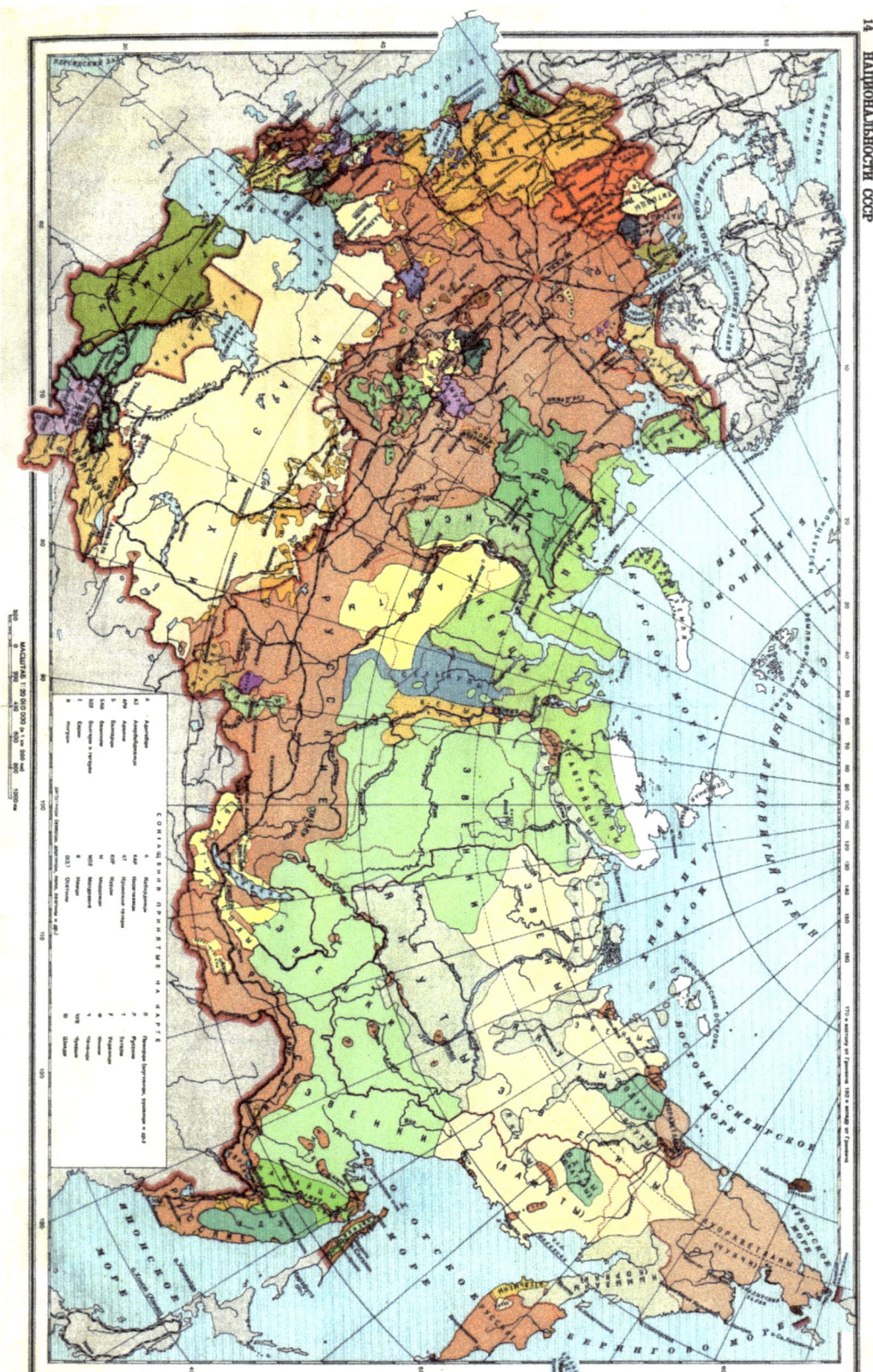

PART 1
National Operations of the NKVD.
A General Approach

CHAPTER 1
The Great Terror.
New Dimensions of Research

Hiroaki Kuromiya

Research on the Great Terror has been making rapid progress, even though access to relevant archives is still far from free. Empirical research is being done all over the world. The Terror touched nearly all groups of people who lived in the Soviet Union, from top Party leaders and military commanders to workers, peasants, the unemployed and invalids, from ethnic Russians, Ukrainians and Belarusians to Poles, Germans, Latvians, Koreans, Japanese, and Buryats, and from people living on the western borderlands to the residents in the Far East. Some results of the current research are presented in the present volume. Here I should like to discuss what new territory needs to be covered to advance research on the Great Terror.

First of all, one has to acknowledge that like many other questions in Soviet history, the Great Terror is enigmatic. This is in part because Iosif Stalin, the Soviet dictator, was careful not to show his hand, but also, more generally, because the most important archives are still largely closed. (One should add, however, that the recent opening-up of the former KGB archives in Ukraine and Georgia has made many historical documents on the Great Terror available to historians.) One knows that there are many, many items in the *osobye papki* ['special files'] of the Communist Party Politburo, Stalin's personal files, and many other archival files that are still classified. These appear to be related largely to intelligence and defense matters. Equally importantly, the secret police archives are still largely closed. The foreign intelligence archives are almost completely inaccessible. One has to assume that many of the most important documents of the Great Terror still remain secret and are likely to remain so in the future.

This means two things. First, we still have only a partial picture of the Great Terror. Second, we need to explore the full range of possibilities based on bits and pieces of information that have become available to us. One would hope that, as Stalin once said, secrets will be revealed in the end: "One cannot hide anything. In the end, everything will be known, everything will become public" (Mgeladze 2001: 116).

The new territory I am discussing here concerns two issues that remain largely hidden in scholarly discussion: 1) international espionage and counter-espionage and 2) political provocation by Soviet authorities. They may not easily be reflected in our discussion of the Great Terror at this or any other conference, but they constitute a larger framework within which any discussion of the Great Terror should take place.

International Espionage and Counter-Espionage

International espionage and counter-espionage were, and are, a fact of international life. The Soviet Union and all major states engaged in them. They belong to the nether world of international life, however. Much vital information never comes to light, and one may never know how and why such and such an event took place. Stalin said in May 1937, just before he launched mass terror operations in the country: "From the point of view of intelligence, we cannot have friends: there are real enemies and there are potential enemies. So we cannot reveal any secrets to anyone" (Petrov & Jansen 2008: 291). Today Moscow still adheres to this position. Consequently, Moscow still tightly guards its intelligence archives. We therefore know little about Soviet intelligence and counter-intelligence operations in Stalin's time. Yet we cannot avoid them in discussing the Great Terror, because they were *the* central factor.

The secretiveness of the Soviet government prompted capitalist countries to intensify their espionage against the openly anti-capitalist communist state. Stalin correctly assumed that all capitalist countries were hostile to the Soviet Union and that they engaged constantly in subversive work. Even before the Great Terror of 1937–1938, Stalin had numerous Soviet citizens and some foreigners arrested and executed as spies. In 1937–1938 the numbers shot up: 265,039 were sentenced to death for foreign espionage (Khaustov *et al.* 2004: 660). A variety of other political crimes were charged against victims of the Great Terror. Yet almost all charges had foreign implications.

What triggered the mass terror operation in the summer of 1937 is a difficult question. Yet several factors seem to be clear. First, Stalin was convinced that war was sure to come, if not in 1937 or 1938, then within a few years (Kuromiya 2011: 247). Stalin's sense of foreign threat was dramatically heightened by several factors. In November 1936 Nazi Germany and Japan concluded the Anti-Comintern Pact (which was in fact an anti-Soviet Union pact). Then, in January 1937, Turkey devised a secret strategic military plan against the Soviet Union, with the expectation of forthcoming war between the Soviet Union and Japan or Germany or both. The plan envisaged the occupation of the southern Caucasus: in the event of war between the Soviet Union and "some great power" and with all or parts of the Soviet forces mobilized out of the Caucasus or "in the event of the fall of Stalin's government," Turkey was to cross the Soviet-Turkish borders and occupy parts of Georgia, Armenia, and Azerbaijan. This plan became known to Moscow via France (Yampol'skiy *et al.* [comp.] 1995: 304). Then in May 1937, pursuant to the Anti-Comintern Pact, Germany and Japan signed "An Additional German-Japanese Agreement on the Exchange of Intelligence Concerning Soviet Russia [USSR]." It detailed plans for anti-Soviet plotting and subversion (*bōryaku*, *Zersetzungsarbeit*) focused on national minority movements (Kuromiya & Mamoulia 2009: 1,427–1,428). Given the long-standing Polish-Japanese cooperation in intelligence against the Soviet Union (Kuromiya & Pepłoński 2009), this constituted, in Stalin's eyes, a German-Polish-Japanese triple intelligence alliance in preparation of war against the Soviet Union. Furthermore, Latvia, Estonia, and Finland secretly assisted the three countries. At that time Japan also sought to establish a "Turkish-Japanese Intelligence Association for the purpose of gathering information concerning Russian activities" (Kuromiya & Mamoulia 2009: 1,428).

Stalin promptly reacted in a manner peculiar to him, namely terror. Undoubtedly it was the threat of war that prompted Stalin. True, in the west, Germany's (and possibly Poland's) threat was almost certainly not imminent, as Stalin correctly understood. However, Japan's threat, in Stalin's own assessment, appeared imminent (Kuromiya 2011: 248). Unfortunately, critics of views that emphasize the threat of war as the cause of the Great Terror ignore the Far East. These critics point out that in 1938, precisely at the time when the threat of war had heightened dramatically in the West, the Great Terror had come to an end (Naimark 2010: 136–137; Baberowski 2012: 31, 218, 516). What they fail to see is that Stalin's terror was a response to the growing threat of war, a pre-cautionary measure in anticipation of war. Stalin meant to place the country on a war footing by securing the home front. It was, in other words, a political preparation for war. *Pace* the critics of the war factor, it was not advanced as a retrospective justification. In June 1938, L. M. Kaganovich, Stalin's right-hand man at the time, stated clearly that had the numerous "enemies of the people" not been destroyed, "perhaps we would have had war already." The terror "delayed war," Kaganovich added (RGASPI, 81, op. 3, d. 231, ll. 73, 79).

Nikolai Bukharin, who was executed in March 1938 after the third Moscow show trial, understood Stalin very well. After several of Lenin's closest colleagues such as Grigoriy Zinov'ev and Lev Kamenev were executed in the wake of the first Moscow trial in the summer of 1936, Bukharin declared:

> I am happy that this entire business [of destroying "our enemies"] has been brought to light before war breaks out and that our [NKVD] organs have been in a position to expose all of this rot before the war so that we can come out of war victorious. Because if all of this had not been revealed before the war but during it, it would have brought about absolutely extraordinary and grievous defeats for the cause of socialism. (Getty & Naumov 1999: 309)

Like Bukharin, Pavel Milyukov, a Russian liberal and fierce opponent of the Soviet government, also came to terms with Stalin's view of war threat. Milyukov's capitulation had begun already after Hitler's ascension to power in 1933 and culminated with the Moscow show trials, which he practically accepted as rational for the survival of "Russia" (Nielsen 1983). At any rate, as Bukharin suggested, the mass terror had to end before war began, and indeed Stalin ended the Great Terror in late 1938. Now Stalin's political terror returned to "routine levels." The Great Terror of 1937–1938, which accounted for 86.6 per cent of all the death sentences passed for political crimes during Stalin's entire reign from 1924 to 1953 (Popov 1992: 28), cannot be reduced simply to one of Stalin's genocides.

Obviously Stalin believed that physical isolation was not enough but that physical liquidation was the ultimate guarantee of security. Otherwise how could one explain the fact that, at the time of the Great Terror, tens of thousands of those political prisoners already incarcerated in the Gulag were executed (Binner *et al.* 2009: 658)? Karl Radek put it well on this matter. A one-time Trotskyite turned Stalin's unofficial spokesman, Radek was known for his loose tongue, and was killed by Stalin after he rendered an invaluable political service to the dictator. He once frankly told an American diplomat why political killing in general was necessary to Stalin:

> Radek said that in his opinion the old tsarist police were unbelievably stupid. They arrested Bolshevik leaders again and again only eventually to release them or allow them to escape. Bukharin agreed. He said, "Yes, our Stalin was arrested several times yet he lived to destroy the police who had failed to destroy him." Radek continued, "But we Bolsheviks are not so stupid. When we arrest enemies of the state we either execute them or we put them away so that no one ever hears of them again." Bukharin again agreed. Neither one of them apparently had any idea that within the next three years Bukharin would be executed and Radek would be sentenced to ten years in prison. (Baer [ed.] 1986: 426).

1 - THE GREAT TERROR - NEW DIMENSIONS OF RESEARCH

No one ever heard of Radek again after he was "put away," because in 1939 he was in fact killed in prison by Stalin's order (Petrov 2005: 314–315). Clearly both Radek and Bukharin understood the logic of Stalin's Great Terror, including the fate of themselves, when it actually came.

How does one explain the fact that the Great Terror hit not merely those who were *ipso facto* already politically suspect (such as former political opponents of Stalin, former members of non-Bolshevik political parties, and ministers of cloth) but also children, beggars, the unemployed, prostitutes, criminals, and others who appeared to have nothing whatsoever to do with foreign countries, let alone foreign intelligence?

Even though foreign factors may not be apparent to historians of today, they were evident to Stalin's contemporaries. It was precisely those people existing on the political and social fringes of Soviet society that Stalin suspected to be the targets of recruitment by foreign espionage. That people far from borders or from any foreign organizations or foreigners could be such targets may be hard to believe, but this was a matter of crass political judgment and not of likelihood. At the very least, it was these people who Stalin suspected could stand up against his power in the event of war. In his mind, not supporting the Soviet government in the event of national emergency was as good as treachery and those not in support of his government were outright traitors and foreign agents. In other words, Stalin meant to eradicate by the terror even the remotest *possibility* of subversion and foreign machinations. In this sense, the mass terror Stalin used was a coldly calculated measure of "total counter-espionage."

Illustration 2 (next page): Book cover of *Yaponiya u Manchzhuryi* ['Japan in Manchuria'] written by S. Dashynski [Aleksandr M. Nikonov], the Soviet military intelligence operative. The book was published in 1929 in Minsk by the State Belarusian Publishing House. Photo by Mikola Nikalaieu. Courtesy of the Russian National Library. Aleksandr M. Nikonov was arrested by the NKVD on 5 August 1937 and shot on 26 October 1937 in Moscow.

The term "total counter-espionage" is one I have appropriated from the term "total espionage," used to describe Japanese intelligence operations before and during the Russo-Japanese War of 1904–1905 (Kuromiya & Pepłoński 2014: 79). Japan used priests, prostitutes, merchants, barbers, photographers, and all kinds of people to spy on the Russian military forces at the time. Officers, of noble origin, for example, were disguised as barbers or merchants in Manchuria, and sent to spy on the Russians. Such practices would have been unimaginable for Russian officers at the time who were overwhelmingly noble and who had adhered to a rigid sense of class. Unknown numbers of "sleeper cells" were also placed in various locations. Japan's intelligence proved far foresighted with devastating results for the Russian Empire. This lesson was not lost on Stalin. Stalin perfected "total espionage" to penetrate many capitalist countries, including Japan, Germany, Poland, Britain, France, and the United States. Japan's "total espionage" came to be emulated by European powers as well and, most importantly for Moscow, by Germany and Poland. Germany's ideas for total espionage were first articulated by Karl Haushofer, a prominent Japanologist and geographer (the father of the Nazi doctrine of *Lebensraum*) who became a teacher of Adolf Hitler and his "deputy" Rudolph Hess. Hess is said to have developed Haushofer's work (Kuromiya & Pepłoński 2014: 80). According to Curt Riess, Germany's total espionage, which "began to function toward the latter part of 1934," reached its top efficiency "by the middle of 1937" (Riess 1941: 86–95), the year of the Great Terror.

Stalin countered foreign "total espionage" with his own "total counter-espionage." Any foreign connection became politically suspect in the Soviet Union. The majority of foreign consulates were closed in the Soviet Union precisely at the time of the Great Terror. Their closure cut off what little contact still existed between foreign officials and ordinary Soviet citizens. Certain ethnic groups became suspect by dint of their ethnicity. Political refugees, former prisoners of war (from the First World War!), foreign refugees, and anyone whose weak political and social standing could be exploited by foreign powers, however remote the possibility, became *ipso facto* politically suspect. Former kulaks, even in the middle of a remote Siberian hinterland, were no exception. After all, even there, foreign connections survived in one form or another, and there were many ethnic Poles, Germans, and others in residence. In Novosibirsk both Germany and Japan maintained a consulate until 1937–1938. In any case, in Stalin's mind, these former kulaks would act as foreign agents by subverting the Soviet government on the home front in the event of war. In practical terms, there was no significant difference in this respect among the "kulak operations," "militia operations," and "national operations" of the Great Terror. All operations pursued the same goal of securing the rear by eliminating any political danger in preparation for war. Even hooligans were politically dangerous, according to this reasoning. As the NKVD chief Genrikh G. Yagoda said in 1935, there was "merely one step" in the transition "from a hooligan to a terrorist," and "hooliganism" was "an element leading to the emergence of diversionary groups" (Khaustov 1997: 334). In Stalin's mind there was no guarantee that there were no foreign "sleeper cells" in remote corners of Siberia. Such was the logic of Stalin's Great Terror. This logic was evident at the time, albeit not always detailed clearly. As a former secret police officer noted, the rank-and-file officers of the NKVD were told that the mass terror operations were to cleanse the home front and eliminate the "fifth columns" in the country. However, who was to be eliminated was solely Moscow's concern (Leybovich [ed.] 2006: 266). The purpose of the terror is not apparent in every document at the time. However, this omission should not obscure the fundamental logic underlining Stalin's Great Terror.

Political Provocation

Stalin meant to eradicate all possible sources of internal opposition and subversion. As he tirelessly contended, such subversion would appear in conjunction with foreign military intervention in the Soviet Union in order to overturn his power. Yet how could he be sure that he was hitting the right targets? Stalin's logic was to kill a hundred people in order to catch the one possible spy among them. Yet even Stalin could not have killed off everyone in order to attain absolute security. Consequently, political provocation was widely deployed in order to detect and entrap suspect people.

Moscow was quite adept at political provocation in the realm of international espionage. The most famous case is the "Trust" operation carried out in the 1920s employing fake "anti-Soviet" organizations allegedly working within the country. Through such operations, Sidney Reilly, the model for James Bond 007 by Ian Fleming and "the World's Greatest Spy" according to some commentators, was lured to the Soviet Union, captured, and then killed in 1925. Such operations were not always successful. They were dealing after all with professional spies of foreign countries.

It was far easier to organize political provocation internally. My research suggests that during the Stalin period the police use of provocateurs was so consistent and widespread that it was likely ubiquitous. Police operational materials are almost completely out of reach for historians, who therefore need to be extraordinarily attentive to the possibility of such hidden operations. One example of a provocation comes from Siberia. In Western Siberia, where resided Poles who fled from the famine in the west of the country, the police engaged in provocation. They had an informer marry a local Polish girl and insinuate himself into the Polish community. Then, pretending to be a representative of the *Dwójka* (Department of Intelligence) of the Polish Army, he filled in questionnaires on all adults of the Polish community, allegedly members of the "Polish Party of People's Heroes." Then he buried the papers in a pre-arranged place agreed upon with the police. The informer staged a flight to Kaluga, as the police uncovered the alleged Polish subversion. The police duly discovered the questionnaires of the members of the "Polish Party of People's Heroes" in the "hiding place" and arrested those adult Poles, including the wife of the informer. In connection with this affair, more than 3,000 people were repressed in 1933–1934 (Kuromiya 2010: 423). This is a good example of mass terror resulting from provocation. Whether these Poles in the middle of Siberia actually presented any risk to security was moot. Based on the assumption that they were risks, the secret police framed "evidence."

Another example, more appropriate for the present volume, comes from the Kola Peninsula. A man named Trofimov (pseudonym), a game warden, lived, with his wife and two children, on a Soviet reservation land in the border area with Finland. The police received reports that he entertained anti-Soviet feelings and began investigation. They dispatched to Trofimov a man named Rylsky in Finnish clothing and with Finnish food and other equipment. Rylsky was fluent in both Russian and Finnish. He approached Trofimov's house on skis from the western direction so as to give the impression that he came from Finland. As soon as Trofimov saw that Rylski came from the west (border regions), he greeted the guest with a remark, "I can see that you are our man." Trofimov invited Rylsky to stay in his house. Over dinner Trofimov spoke of the "contrast between living conditions in the old days and at present," while the guest offered Trofimov Finnish cigarettes, rum, and canned food, which he accepted "with visible pleasure." Trofimov mentioned several of his friends in the neighboring town of Monchegorsk (in Murmansk region), whom Rylsky could trust in his "illegal" journey through Karelia. The younger son of Trofimov guided Rylsky to Monchegorsk. On their way, he disclosed to the police agent that his father had a "well-hidden cache of weapons—detonators, hand grenades, two pistols, rifles, and ammunition" which he hoarded "in expectation that one day he might need them."

Rylsky reported this to the secret police. The police then sent another Finnish-speaking agent who reached the Trofimov house as Rylski had, and informed him that his earlier guest had safely crossed the border and returned to Finland. The new guest gave Trofimov Finnish canned food, rum, and cigarettes as a gift from Rylski in gratitude for his hospitality. They then discussed hunting in the area. In the course of the conversation Trofimov spoke of the cache of weapons to which the guest was invited to use if he ever need them. This was duly reported to the police. The police acted swiftly and arrested Trofimov and his family as well as all the people of Monchegorsk mentioned by Trofimov to Rylsky (Deriabin & Gibney 1959: 300–302).

In interrogating Trofimov, the police informed him that a "Finnish spy had been caught on the border and confessed to Trofimov's complicity in various Finnish espionage missions." The Finnish spy also "confessed" that Trofimov had a hidden cache of firearms. Trofimov never knew the true identity of the two guests. Thus, the "entire case against him had been artificially developed as a result of provocation methods." Without ever knowing the police machination, Trofimov became a "Finnish spy" (Deriabin & Gibney 1959: 302–303).

In most cases, even a perusal of individual case files compiled by the police does not yield hints of these secret operations. Often those individuals used for particularly important operations were subsequently physically eliminated in order to destroy the evidence. As a result, it is extremely difficult to know the methods used by the police to build "criminal cases" against individuals who were repressed. To miss the ubiquitous presence of police provocation means to misunderstand or at the very least not to understand fully the cases one examines.

This is an important lesson for historians, which I emphasized years ago in a discussion with another historian concerning post-war political dissent (Kuromiya 2003: 631–638). It also teaches an important lesson to Russian historians who seek to justify the Great Terror by attacking foreign intelligence services. It is patently absurd to claim, as some Russian historians do, that Finnish intelligence, for example, was indirectly "guilty" of Stalin's Great Terror against ethnic Finns, because it spied relentlessly on the Soviet Union (Laidinen & Verigin 2004: 221). If one follows the same logic, ethnic Russians and Soviet citizens in many countries could have been terrorized on a massive scale in light of the fact that Soviet intelligence penetrated these countries deeply.

Conclusion

Given the fact that the archives of Soviet security organs (the secret police and the military and foreign intelligence) are tightly closed, one needs to be extraordinarily careful in interpreting the voluminous records on the Great Terror that have become available after the collapse of the Soviet Union. Here two issues, foreign intelligence/counter-intelligence and political provocation, are particularly relevant, because, although not necessarily new issues, they are inadequately addressed by today's historians of the Great Terror.

Stalin knew well that numerous foreign countries were engaged widely in intelligence against the Soviet Union, a country hostile to the capitalist world. The extreme secrecy of the Soviet Union only intensified foreign intelligence. Taking advantage of this fact, Stalin turned the tables on the capitalist world by eliminating any possibility of foreign intelligence and subversion in the Soviet Union. Stalin used the Great Terror to secure the rear, even though, by any account, Moscow had very successfully foiled foreign intelligence and subversion. The Great Terror was a means of "total counter-espionage." Stalin meant to subjugate the Soviet population to his will in preparation for war. For this reason he terrorized the Soviet population into accepting that there was no alternative but to submit. All the same, even now, some Russian historians selectively publish documents from intelligence archives in order to denounce some of the foreign countries which they hold accountable for the Great Terror!

As part of "total counter-espionage," Moscow extensively used political provocation to identify and entrap "enemies of the people." True, it cannot possibly have been the case that every Soviet citizen lived happily in the Soviet Union in the 1930s. Undoubtedly, political discontent existed. Yet the political system drove all unofficial political sentiment underground. Stalin used provocation in order to ferret out any suspected dissent. As a result, numerous "enemies" were artificially created. These two aspects of Stalin's terror rarely emerge from the documents that we, today's historians, are allowed to examine. Therefore, there is all the more reason for us to be attentive to the unwritten aspects of the Great Terror.

References

Archives

RGASPI. Российский государственный архив социально-политической истории ['Russian State Archive of Socio-Political History'], Moscow, Russia.

Literature

Baberowski, J. (2012). *Verbrannte Erde. Stalins Herrschaft der Gewalt* ['Scorched earth. Stalin's rule of terror'], Munich: Verlag C.H./Beck.

Baer, G. W. (ed.) (1985). *A Question of Trust. The Origins of U.S.-Soviet Diplomatic Relations. The Memoirs of Loy W. Henderson*, Stanford: Hoover Institution Press.

Binner, R., Bonwetsch, B. & Junge, M. (2009). *Massenmord und Lagerhaft. Die andere Geschichte des Großen Terrors* ['Mass murder and detention. The other history of the Great Terror'], Berlin: Akademie Verlag.

Deriabin, P. & Gibney, F. (1959). *The Secret World*, New York: Doubleday.

Getty, J. A. & Naumov, O. V. (1999). *The Road to Terror. Stalin and the Self-Destruction of the Bolsheviks, 1932–1839*, New Haven-London: Yale University Press.

Khaustov, V. N. (1997). Хаустов, В. Н. "Деятельность органов государственной безопасности НКВД СССР (1934–1941 гг.)" ['The activity of the organs of the state security NKVD USSR (1934–1941)'], diss., Moscow: Akademiya federal'noy sluzhby bezopasnosti.

Khaustov, V. N., Naumov, V. P. & Plotnikova, N. S. (2004). Хаустов, В. Н., Наумов, В. П. & Плотникова, Н. С. *Лубянка. Сталин и главное управление госбезопасности НКВД 1937–1938* ['Lubyanka. Stalin and the Main State Security Directorate of the NKVD 1937–1938'], Moscow: MFD.

Kuromiya, H. (2003). "Political youth opposition in late Stalinism. Evidence and conjecture," *Europe-Asia Studies*, 4, pp. 631–638.

Kuromiya, H. (2010). "Stalin, Poles, and Ukrainians," in *Ofiary imperium. Imperia jako ofiary. 44 spojrzenia* ['Imperial victims. Empires as victims. 44 views'], ed. A. Nowak, Warsaw: IH PAN, pp. 417–428.

Kuromiya, H. (2011). "Stalin's Great Terror and international espionage," *The Journal of Slavic Military Studies*, 2, pp. 238–252.

Kuromiya, H. & Mamoulia, G. (2009). "Anti-Russian and anti-Soviet subversion. The Caucasian-Japanese nexus," *Europe-Asia Studies*, 8, pp. 1,415–1,440.

Kuromiya, H. & Pepłoński, A. (2009). *Między Warszawą a Tokio. Polsko-japońska współpraca wywiadowcza 1904–1944* ['Between Warsaw and Tokyo. Polish-Japanese intelligence cooperation 1904–1944'], Toruń: Adam Marszałek.

Kuromiya, H. & Pepłoński, A. (2014). "Stalin, espionage, and counter-espionage," in *Stalinism and Europe. Imitation and Domination, 1928–1953*, eds. T. Snyder & R. Brandon, Oxford: Oxford University Press.

Laidinen, E. P. & Verigin, S. G. (2004). Лайдинен, Э. П. & Веригин, С. Г. *Финская разведка против Советской России* ['Finnish intelligence against Soviet Russia'], Petrozavodsk: Kompaniya RIF.

Leybovich, O. L. (ed.) (2006). Лейбович, О. Л. *"Включен в операцию." Массовый террор в Прикамье в 1937–38 гг.* ['"Included in the operation." Mass terror in Prikam'e in 1937–38'], Perm: Perm State Technical University.

Mgeladze, A. (2001). Мгеладзе, А. *Сталин каким я его знал* ['Stalin as I knew him'], Tbilisi.

Naimark, N. M. (2010). *Stalin's Genocides*, Princeton: Princeton University Press.

Nielsen, J. P. (1983). Нилсен, Е. П. *Милюков и Сталин. О политической эволюции Милюкова в эмиграции (1918–1943)* ['Milyukov and Stalin. On Milyukov's political evolution in emigration (1918–1943)'], Oslo: University of Oslo.

Petrov, N. (2005). Петров, Н. *Первый председатель КГБ Иван Серов* ['The first chairman of KGB Ivan Serov'], Moscow: Materik.

Petrov, N. & Jansen, M. (2008). Петров, Н. и Янсен, М. *"Сталинский питомец"—Николай Ежов* ['"Stalin's foster-child"—Nikolay Yezhov'], Moscow: ROSSPEN.

Popov, V. P. (1992). Попов, В. П. "Государственный террор в советской России. 1923–1953 гг. Источники и их интерпретация" ['State terror in Soviet Russia. 1923–1953. Sources and their interpretation'], *Отечественные архивы*, 2, pp. 20–31.

Riess, C. (1941). *Total Espionage*, New York: G. P. Putnam's Sons.

Yampol'skiy V. P. *et al.* (comp.) (1995). Ямпольский В. П. и др. (сост.). *Органы государственной безопасности СССР в Великой Отечественной войне. Том. 1. Книга вторая (1 января–21 июня 1941 г.)* ['The Soviet organs of state security in the Great Patriotic War. Vol. 1. Part 1 (1 January–21 June 1941)'], Moscow: Kniga i biznes.

CHAPTER 2
Ethnification of Stalinism? Ethnic Cleansings and the NKVD Order № 00447 in a Comparative Perspective

Andrey Savin

In recent years, the thesis of ethnification of Stalinism has been gaining increasing popularity in historiography, especially in the West. The backers of the thesis believe that at the time of the Revolution, Civil War and NEP, Bolsheviks regarded representatives of "exploiting" classes and groups as their main enemies, whereas in the 1930s, and especially in the 1940s, the national minority and "hostile" ethnic groups became the main victims of the Stalinist regime. Thus, biological, racial aspects allegedly received priority over social ones in the Stalinist policy.

Jörg Baberowski suggested a relevant line of arguments that can be regarded as the quintessence of the general attitude to this question among the proponents of ethnification of Stalinism theory. The famous German historian states that for the Stalinist leadership there were not only social classes, but also an ethnic issue. The more backward a nation was before the Revolution, the more proletarian and advanced it became afterwards, and vice versa. Thus, the "Eastern" nations were considered as the most revolutionary, and the "Western" (Germans, Poles, Jews) the most counter-revolutionary. "Nothing is farther from the truth than the idea that nationality meant nothing to the Bolsheviks," Baberowski says. Bolsheviks perceived any nation as a cultural community, linked by a common destiny, and this was why they believed that members of the counter-revolutionary nation could not change their nation into a more revolutionary one, just as the "formers" (Ru. *byvshiye*, i.e. people who used to belong to the upper class before 1917) could not change their social history and become real proletarians (Baberowski 2003: 195–196).

Another prominent representative of the concept of ethnification of Stalinism is American historian Timothy Snyder, whose book *Bloodlands. Europe between Hitler and Stalin* generated international headlines and was translated into several languages (Snyder 2010). Describing the mass operations of the NKVD in 1937–1938, Snyder focuses on the Polish operation, which he characterizes as "ethnic murder" and emphasizes the apparent "ethnic character" of this large-scale NKVD operation. As Jürgen Zarusky notes in his acute critical review: "The idea of ethnification of Stalin's repressive policy is the main feature of Snyder's book" (Zarusky 2012: 13).

National Operations and the NKVD Order № 00447 in a Comparative Perspective

National operations of the NKVD during the Great Terror, as well as ethnic cleansing and deportation, especially during the Second World War, are regarded as the culminating results and the main evidence of the ideological drift of the Stalinist regime, from a class paradigm to an ethnic one. In this paper I attempt to verify the thesis of the ethnification of Stalinism by studying primarily the German operation as an example of the implementtation of the national operations. I also compare the national operations with the most notorious operation of the Great Terror known as "the kulak operation." It is only through such an empirical approach "from below" that one can confirm or refute a theoretical construct of the ethnification of Stalinism.

In 1937–1938, mass repressive actions were carried out against a number of ethnic minorities, especially Poles, Germans, Latvians, Estonians, Finns, Bulgarians, Macedonians, Greeks, Romanians, Iranians, Afghans, Chinese and Koreans. According to the latest data, 340,000–350,000 people were the victims of these actions, including about 140,000 in the Polish operation and about 55,000 in the German one (Savin 2010: 462–465). It is generally agreed that it was during the "ethnic operations" that the absurdity, blindness and abuse of the Great Terror was clearly revealed: it was not the personal, individual guilt or the past social life of a person, but solely ethnicity that was the determinative factor in the selection of victims of the repressive operation.

In favour of this point of view, there are many relevant arguments, the most important of which may be ranked in the following way:

1. The Stalinist leadership and secret police perceived certain national minorities as hostile and "counter-revolutionary" as early as the 1920s. In the 1930s, this concept was taken as the ideological basis of ethnic cleansing.

Thus, long before Nazism came to power and the problem of a military threat emerged, the top leaders of the secret police of the USSR had already formulated the view of the German Diaspora as being a spy and sabotage base. On 9 July 1924, the Deputy head of the OGPU Genrikh Yagoda and the head of the Soviet counter-intelligence service of the OGPU Artur Artuzov signed the OGPU circular letter № 7/37 "On the German intelligence service and the combat against it," and a year later, on 14 July 1925, Artuzov, in response to Felix Dzerzhinsky's request of 6 July 1925, sent to the chief of the OGPU a set of documents entitled "On the activities of the Germans in the USSR," consisting of a cover letter and five analytical notes. Obviously, the main authors of these documents were counter-intelligence service officers, so this fruit of their collective efforts can be called the "Artuzov notes." The logic of the authors of the circular letter of July 1924, "On the German intelligence service and the combat against it," and the Artuzov notes, "German counter-revolutionary work in the USSR" (July 1925), is as follows: under the guise of an agreement in Rapallo, German intelligence, with the help of nationalist organizations in Germany, began to conduct with impunity espionage and subversive activities in the territory of the USSR. Diplomatic missions, aid agencies and joint ventures played the role of "covers" for the German intelligence:

> the basis of German intelligence in Russia is the millions of Germans by descent [...] who are the main sources in the gathering and receiving of information that Germany focuses on very much.

According to the OGPU, German colonies could be regarded as monarchic cells within the Soviet Union, on which the nationalists in Germany build most of their anti-Soviet policy upon, in order to destroy the USSR from inside. The documents yield a picture of a "natural" base for German espionage in the form of the nationalist and pro-fascist German population of the USSR, which acts as a united front, primarily the Volga Germans, the Ukrainian and Siberian German colonies (Hedeler & Savin 2006).

Interestingly, the Cheka officers did not mention in their note any significant social differentiation among the German population. Artuzov said that German colonies in Russia, by their numbers, social composition ("kulaks") and political aspirations ("fascist-national"), are the largest threat to communism and the USSR as a hostile population on the one hand, and on the other, as groups which tend to strengthen German national interests among the national minorities. He provided data on the social composition of the German colonists in Ukraine and stated that 40–50 per cent of them are "kulaks," i.e. former landowners and rural intelligentsia. The rest are mid-income peasants (Ru. *serednyaky*), and 5–6 per cent are poor peasants (Ru. *bednyaky*), but they are under the absolute influence of the kulaks, too. Thus, the leaders of the counter-intelligence, the OGPU, believed that there had been a number of favourable conditions for espionage by ethnic Germans:

reliable connections with foreign countries and the German diplomatic missions that allowed Russian Germans to provide a systematic correspondence with people abroad and prepare open counter-revolutionary actions. From the point of view of Artuzov, a dense population of Germans in the border areas, large industrial areas and rich agricultural areas would be especially dangerous in the event of war. The general conclusion made by Artuzov was pessimistic:

> There is no doubt that the German nationalists in Russia are doing a great job in all respects and have a much greater influence on the German colonies in the USSR than we have. The latter [our influence] seems to be extremely weak. (See Hedeler & Savin 2006).

The concept of the German "fifth column," devised by the OGPU in the middle of the 1920s, only works for the thesis of the ethnification of Stalinism. The attempt at sovietisation of German villages with the help of national "tools" in the 1920s was a failure, and it only reinforced the Stalinist leadership's perceptions of the counter-revolutionary nature of ethnic Germans. The total resistance by all German village social groups to collectivization in the form of attempts at mass emigration in the 1929–1930s clearly demonstrated the failure of the concept of *korenizatsiya* ['indigenization'] in respect of ethnic Germans (Dönninghaus 2009: 407–435).

When we try to reconstruct the view of one of the protagonists of the Great Terror, People's Commissar for State Security Nikolay Yezhov, that the ethnic Germans were a "fifth column," we are inevitably faced with the scarcity of materials available to researchers. At a meeting of the NKVD top staff on 3 December 1936, Yezhov spoke about a possible reform of the district offices of the Government Security (GUGB). He criticized the work of local offices and offered his solution to the problem. In his opinion, there was a need for GUGB district offices only in three groups of areas—border, industrial and national ones. It was in the "national and major industrial areas" that a "strong GUGB machinery is contemplated, [...] so that we may know that we have their support" (Petrov & Jansen 2006: 279). This focus on places densely populated by Diasporas in anticipation of mass operations is certainly symptomatic. At a meeting of the NKVD leadership on 16 July 1937, the heads of department were informed about the upcoming mass repression, and Yezhov also talked about the forthcoming arrests of Poles and Germans as well as of the so called "Harbinites."¹ This indicates that the national operations were planned simultaneously with the execution of order № 00447 (Teplyakov 2008: 366). On 24 January 1938, in his speech to the People's Commissar for Internal Affairs of the Soviet and Autonomous Republics and heads of the regional departments and divisions of the NKVD, Yezhov was more specific in his summing up of the results of the mass operations in 1937. Discussing a possible reform of the counter-intelligence service of the NKVD, he suggested the creation of a separate German Department, which

> should watch the Embassy, the whole German colony and the entire German population of the Soviet Union, in other words, is a base for German espionage in the Soviet Union, i.e. to control a German line from top to bottom. It should keep records of the Germans, the colonies, the embassies and relevant organizations. This Department must, of course, have a base abroad. That is necessary (Petrov & Jansen 2006: 316–317; *my italics*).

Yezhov also planned to create a Polish department, as well as a number of other "national" departments on the same pattern. Thus, it seems to be quite clear that Yezhov, in the spirit of the Artuzov notes, regarded the German population of the Soviet Union as a spying and subversive base and that he had no doubts about the increasing counter-revolutionary nature of the ethnic Germans.

2. In addition to the concept of the "fifth column," the tradition of repression against a number of "hostile" national groups had already been established by 1937.

As for the ethnic Germans, almost immediately after the mass campaign of repression against the participants of the emigration movement in 1929–1930, the NKVD began to combat the so-called receivers of "Hitler's aid." The economic situation of the German farms in the USSR suffered from a number of years of bad harvests in the early 1930s, which together with the forced requisition of grain had caused famine in the German villages. A campaign titled "Brothers in Need," organized in Germany and aimed at

---

¹ The NKVD operation against "Harbinites" consisted in mass arrests of former personnel of the Chinese Eastern Railway (KVZhD), who had lived in Harbin and re-emigrated to the Soviet Union after 1935, when the KVZhD was sold to Manzhouguo. The operation was not a part of the national operations. However, the NKVD stated that of the about 25,000 registered Harbinites, the absolute majority were former White Russians who, according to the secret police, worked for the Japanese intelligence service.

assisting Germans in the Soviet Union who suffered from famine, caused another anti-German NKVD campaign, the victims of which were the receivers of food parcels and remittances. They were accused of having spread information abroad about the economic plight and famine among Germans in the USSR.

Illustration 3: Nikolay Yezhov, People's Commissar for Internal Affairs of the Soviet Union. Portrait from the children's magazine *Chizh*, December 1937.

A circular of the OGPU of the USSR entitled "On combating reconnaissance and sabotage by the German Fascists against the Soviet Union" was issued in July 1932, directing the local bodies of the OGPU to increase all forms of control of the ethnic Germans. In particular, they were instructed to identify people of German nationality who were in correspondence with relatives in Germany and other countries, and to strengthen the surveillance of German experts working in the defence industry, as well as of soldiers of German nationality doing their military service in the Red Army. The main anti-Soviet activities of the ethnic Germans were believed to be the spreading of open fascist propaganda, in particular by comparing living conditions in Germany with those in the USSR, and disseminating "fascist" literature.[2]

In a telegram of November 1934,[3] the Central Committee of VKP(b) demanded that the local party organizations and the NKVD take punitive measures against "counter-revolutionary and anti-Soviet elements" in the German areas. It marked a new stage of state repression against the ethnic Germans, and made, without a doubt, a significant contribution towards the reinforcement of the concept of the German "fifth column." The direct reason for the telegram was that the starving German population of the USSR was receiving humanitarian aid from abroad.

In January 1935, Yagoda reported to Stalin on the progress of the NKVD in combating the "counter-revolutionary fascist organizations," in response to directives from the Central Committee of the VKP(b). According to Yagoda, the activities of the organizations Brothers in Need and Union of Foreign Germans had been stopped; the activists of the organizations had given over 600,000 marks and 14,500 dollars to ethnic Germans who lived in Ukraine, the North Caucasus region and the autonomous republic of Volga Germans. In total, during the repressive campaign in 1934, about 4,000 of the ethnic Germans were arrested (Khaustov 1999: 77; Khaustov 2008: 223). During 1934–1936, the bodies of GUGB of the NKVD conducted a large-scale operation, Brown Web, whereby all those who had any relationship with the German diplomatic missions were identified and recorded. The state security kept an eye on hundreds of Soviet citizens of German nationality, but the Special Department of the GUGB failed to "expose" the mythical "illegal centre of the German Nazi Party" (Khaustov 2008: 224). Nevertheless, 1935–1936 saw a number of major "spy" cases "revealed" by the NKVD in which the main accused were ethnic Germans. During 1935 the NKVD uncovered 24 German "groups" in the Azov-Black Sea region, the ASSR of Volga Germans, Kuibyshev region and Ukraine (Chentsov 1998: 71). In the fourth quarter of 1935, 218 people were arrested in the ASSR of Volga Germans and brought to trial in a case against five "fascist German organizations" and 17 subgroups (Khaustov 1999: 81). In May 1935, the Secret Political Department of the NKVD sent out a circular entitled "On the German fascist organization in the USSR" which directed the NKVD staff to expose the spying anti-Soviet organizations among the German intelligentsia, and once again it emphasized the role of the German colonies as potential

---

[2] For the text of the circular, see Khaustov 1999: 75–76.
[3] The text of the telegram was first published by Shishkin (1992: 28; 1994: 102–103).

subversive rebel bases. In June 1936, the leadership of the NKVD decided to eliminate all communication between the German diplomatic missions in the USSR and the ethnic Germans. As Vladimir Khaustov noted: "unlike in the previous years, at the end of 1936, the purpose of the investigation of the German missions was to isolate almost completely their staff from Soviet citizens" (Khaustov 2008: 224). In the research literature, there is also information about the directives of the GUGB of the NKVD "On measures to combat the destructive activities of the German Intelligence Service in the national economy," dated 14 October, 1936, and "On the growing activity of the German Intelligence agencies and the special institutions of the fascist party in the Soviet Union" on 2 April 1937. The texts of these directives have never been published, but there is reason to believe that they, too, described the ethnic Germans as potential rebels and as a recruiting spy base of the German intelligence service. Thus, as regards the former circular, Khaustov briefly reports that "some measures were planned to limit the rights of foreigners who were Soviet citizens" (Khaustov 2008: 221).

The tradition of repression against the ethnic Germans had been so well established by 1937 that there was no need to issue a special NKVD order in order to carry out the German operation in 1937–1938. The NKVD order № 00439 of 25 July 1937, which is sometimes mistakenly considered as having been issued with a view to starting the German operation, was not directly related to the subsequent mass German operation, it was only aimed at clearing the Soviet defence plants of German citizens (Okhotin & Roginskiy 1999: 35–74). The reports of the NKVD of the Ukrainian regions, which provided information on all mass operations, including national ones, indicate that the repression in the German operation was conducted "as required by order № 00485" (i.e., the order to carry out repression against Poles), and not by order № 00439 (Junge, Binner, Kokin *et al.* [eds.] 2010).

The NKVD staff was not confounded by the fact that the object of repression was virtually the entire German population of the USSR, in contrast to, for example, the Polish operation, which required an order of the NKVD of the USSR № 00485 and accompanying detailed instructions.

In March 1939, Comrade Stalin wrote to the leader, the officer of the NKVD for the Altai Krai, sergeant of the GB Timofey Baranov, who was expelled from the VKP(b) for "excesses" during the German operation.

> Before the end of my statement, I want to say that I remember your words about the capitalist environment. I and the others only considered it an action to arrest counter-revolutionary elements—that is to remove not only the active enemy activists, but also their base, Germans, Poles, Harbinites and

other scum who are still lurking and ready at any moment to take up arms and oppose the country of socialism. (Savin [ed.] 2009: 675)

3. Plenty of evidence of survivors, the NKVD executives and materials relating to the prosecutor's inspections describe sweeping mass arrests of members of Diasporas despite a lack of incriminating evidence against them.

In 1939, the head of the Intelligence Service Department of the NKVD of the Novosibirsk region, Vladimir Kachurovskiy, wrote to the Secretary of the Novosibirsk Regional Committee of the VKP(b) Gennady Borkov:

> I, like many others, heard that the Deputy People's Commissar for State Security [Mikhail] Frinovskiy directed, before the second operation [spring 1938], that if a sabotage happens anywhere in the region and there is a "lineynik"[4] nearby, i.e. Poles, Latvians etc., then the officer who was responsible for the safety of the object will be criminally charged, along with the saboteur.

A direct consequence of this directive has been a significant expansion of the number of arrested within the national operations. According to Kachurovskiy, "the aim was to completely eliminate these categories of people" (Junge, Bordyugov & Binner [eds.] 2008: 460). Kachurovskiy's statement is a very striking example, but anyone who is interested can easily find a collection of similar statements in published documents containing the testimonies of the NKVD officers who were convicted of "violations of socialist law" during mass repression campaigns (Bednarek *et al.* [eds.] 2010: 1,626–1,861).

It should be noted that the security officers, trying to justify their actions and methods used in operation № 00447 against the "formers," freely admitted that it was against "nationals" they had been "complete blunderers." Thus, on 20 December 1938, in his statement to Stalin, the convicted former senior officer of the NKVD of West Siberia, Pavel Egorov, wrote:

> Around the end of September or the beginning of October 1937, the aim of the operation was only to defeat the counter-revolutionary groups and it did not involve the general public. After September, numerous strict directives were received to intensify the actions. Cipher telegrams ordered the arrest of

---

[4] *Lineynik* was a person involved in and repressed during the so-called *natsional'naya liniya operatsiya* ['national line operation']. In NKVD officers' slang, a "national line operation" meant operations against ethnic minorities.

all refugees, Poles, Latvians, Iranians, and those who worked at the KVZhD. (See Junge, Zhdanova, Rasgon et al. [eds.] 2010: 468–487)

While in Egorov's statement, the initiator of the repression against the "nationals" is not directly named, the testimony of Victor Pazin, former Assistant of the Head of the 11th Department of the NKVD in the Krasnoyarsk Region, indicates that the directives came from the very top: "At the daily NKVD briefing, the secretary of the regional committee Sergey Sobolev directed that all Poles, Latvians, Germans etc. should be arrested." However, Sobolev claimed that he just passed on instructions from Stalin:

> Stop playing internationalists. We must beat all these Poles, Koreans, Latvians, Germans etc., all these corrupt nations should be exterminated [...] all nationals should be caught, put down and exterminated like mad dogs. (See Teplyakov 2008: 366–367)

4. The specificity of the national operations minimized Party and state control over the actions of the NKVD.

The significant differences between the national operations and the operation by order № 00447 was, firstly, the lack of so-called "quotas" and, secondly, the lack of uniformity in the conviction procedure. As has already been proved, the notorious "quotas" of people to be shot or imprisoned in the camp were the result of a cynical bargaining between Moscow leadership and local authorities, and at the same time a kind of way for the central authority to control the scope and direction of the repression under order 00447 (Junge, Bonwetsch & Binner [eds.] 2009). Non-use of the "quotas," which had been approved by Politburo, in the national operations suggests a lack of any quantitative limits in the repressive activities of NKVD bodies against Diasporas.

While the victims of the operation under order № 00447 were sentenced by the specially appointed NKVD troikas, the victims of the "national line" operations were also sentenced by the Special Council of the USSR NKVD, the Military Collegium of the Supreme Court of the USSR, the military tribunals and, after 17 September 1938, by "special troikas." It is believed that most of the "nationals" were convicted by the Commission of the NKVD and the Prosecutor of the USSR using the so-called album procedure. The introduction into the practices of the NKVD of the "album procedure" meant that local bodies of the NKVD, after an investigation had been finished, had to write minutes for each prisoner with a sentencing proposal (execution or 5–

10 years of imprisonment). The minutes, collected in what was called "albums," were signed by a panel of two people—the head of the regional NKVD and the prosecutor (hence the colloquial name of the body, *dvoika*, which did not appear in official correspondence), and the album was then forwarded to Moscow. The final sentence was imposed by the People's Commissar for Internal Affairs and the Prosecutor of the USSR (Yezhov and Andrey Vyshinskiy). Typically, careful consideration of the albums was not made in Moscow, and so the proposals of the local bodies were usually approved mechanically. On return of the album to the local bodies of the NKVD, sentences were executed. As a result, the lax control at higher levels, or rather the total absence of control, gave the local NKVD bodies carte blanche and allowed them to carry out repressive actions against "nationals" at their own discretion.

Taken together, the above arguments would seem to suggest that the determinant factor when it comes to the fate of the victims of the national operations was the objective criterion of their belonging to a "malicious" national minority, but not their social past or recurrent anti-Soviet behaveour, past or present. However, the study of the German operation in Western Siberia, conducted mainly through archival investigation of the cases of repressed ethnic Germans, casts doubt on the unambiguity of such an interpretation.

In many ways, the key to understanding the specificity of the national operations is comparing them with the operation under the NKVD of the USSR order № 00447 of 30 July 1937 against "formers" and other "counter-revolutionary elements." This comparison is justified: for historians of the Great Terror it is obvious that national operations in general and the German operation in particular were secondary to the kulak operation in scale, methods and length. Kulak operations were also a kind of motor and model for the national operations.

Not long ago, the essence of kulak operations was graphically illustrated by a famous image by American historian and "revisionist" John Archibald Getty: a crazy person climbed a tower with weapons and opened fire on the crowd. Owing to recent research, especially the international project "Stalinism in the Soviet provinces. Mass operation under order № 00447," conducted by a group of Russian and Ukrainian historians under the direction of Bernd Bonwetsch, Marc Junge and Rolf Binner, this picture of "excessive" terror has undergone a significant correction that cannot be ignored (Junge 2011: 77–98). However, if we accept the fact that 1937 was a year of focus and control by Moscow of the "social" cleansing, which mostly affected those groups that were the traditional targets of persecution and repression by the Bolsheviks, it is still very tempting to describe 1938 as a year of ethnic cleansing. In this case, the state, like Getty's crazy shooter, opened fire on the national Diasporas, not caring who it killed.

We will not get an accurate, complex and differentiated picture of the national operations unless we understand that their specificity, first of all, was determined by the geographical and economic characteristics of the regions of the USSR, as well as the presence or, respectively, the absence of different ethnic groups, "special contingents," on the territory. We must always remember to distinguish between punitive actions carried out by the NKVD in places densely populated by national minorities (national village councils, districts, autonomous regions and republics) on the one hand, and on the other in places sparsely populated by such minorities. Besides, national operations must always be considered in terms of the following oppositions: 1) city—collective farm village, 2) border regions—internal regions of the country, 3) areas of the defence industry—other areas, 4) places with a mixed population with a predominance of the titular nation (Russian)—places predominantly populated by ethnic minorities.

Identification of people with foreign names, identification of the "nationals" through profiles of institutions and plants, was actually carried out in the capital, in industrial and border regions, in large industrial and "secret" industries, in the Party and the Soviet government and in military units. Where more than one of these factors was present, the punitive effects inevitably multiplied. Obviously, it must be admitted that the indiscriminate mass repression of victims based on the objective criteria of their belonging to the "counter-revolutionary" nationalities was actually performed by the NKVD in order to try to create a "homogeneous, modern landscape" (Baberowski 2003).[5] Under these conditions, an order like the following, given by Stalin to Yezhov on 20 July 1937, could be issued: "All Germans in our military, paramilitary and chemical plants, power plants and construction sites, in all areas, must be arrested" (Okhotin & Roginskiy 1999: 35). Also at great risk were the communist-political refugees, defectors, former prisoners of war from Germany and Austria-Hungary, members of the socialist parties, former foreign citizens working in the Soviet Union in the defence industry or transport services, former employees of foreign companies or pre-revolutionary Soviet concessions, "nationals" who were members of the Soviet military, administrative or economic elite. They were repressed almost

---

[5] A. Weiner (2001) considers the things in the same way.

without exception. These punitive practices fit in well with the theory of ethnification of internal enemies.

As for the places densely populated by diasporas, especially in the national regions and republics, where the arrest of all ethnic "special contingents" was physically impossible and absurd, every national operation was primarily a social cleansing in the same way as the operation by order № 00447. To put it figuratively, any of the national orders can be compared to a magnifying glass, tailored to strengthen and sharpen the focus of the NKVD's attention on a specific national group. Undoubtedly, additional risks arose due to the increased repressive attention to that national minority which Stalin's leadership regarded as counter-revolutionary. In fact, whenever a new national order was issued, there was the same pattern as that seen in connection with the formation of the new territorial-administrative units during the Great Terror—this automatically led to more repression in the newly created regions and provinces.

Our study of the German operation in Western Siberia, especially in the Altai and Omsk regions, shows that there was a purposeful pre-selection of victims in areas densely populated by ethnic Germans, performed by the same NKVD staff who simultaneously participated in the kulak operation. The choice of victims was made in close collaboration with the secret police and activists in the villages, who together selected candidates for arrest on the grounds of their links to kulaks, past criminal records, poor work performance in the collective farms, participation in anti-Soviet actions, membership of a religious community/sect etc. There are no serious reasons to doubt that during the German operation the NKVD officers acted that way, through an extremely simplified procedure of arrest and investigation, even compared to the "usual" practice during the operation by order №00447, which gave the NKVD staff a great deal of scope to abuse their power.

Obviously, in the ethnic minority areas, most of the victims of the "national line" operations belonged to those "risk groups" that were constantly being watched by the Soviet secret police, and the criteria of a person's social past was a determinant factor in the choice of victims. However, accidental or arbitrary arrests are of course also likely to have occurred. Thus, the victims of the German operation in Western Siberia belonged to the following risk groups: the clergy, priests and preachers, receivers of "Hitler's aid," dispossessed peasants and previously convicted persons, visitors to the German embassy and consulates and people who had relatives abroad. But the main risk group among the ethnic Germans in Siberia were the members of the mass emigration movement in 1929–1930.

The importance of the latter factor for the German operation in Western Siberia is clearly demonstrated by significant differences in the results in the Altai and the Omsk Region. The number of Germans living in those regions in 1937 was the same—30,000 people in each. But while in the Altai Region, according to our estimates, about 2,000 ethnic Germans were arrested in November 1937–November 1938, only about 600 people[6] were arrested in the Omsk Region in the same period. It is difficult to attribute such a dramatic difference in the number of victims in the German operation to extreme bloodthirst among the Altai Cheka-men or their harbouring a special hatred of the Germans.

But the dilemma can be easily resolved if we take the assumption that targeted capture and extermination of the former emigrants was the main motive of terror against the Germans in Siberia in 1937–1938. As we know, it was the Altai Mennonites who were the main participants in the mass emigration movement: 5,761 people emigrated from the Soviet Union in 1929, about 4,400 of whom left the German settlements in Western Siberia, including about 3,800 people from the territory of the future Altai Region, while only about 250 people emigrated from the Omsk Region (Brandes & Savin 2001: 287, 296–297). Thus, the mass participation of the Altai Germans in the emigration movement had become a fatal circumstance for the emigrants that gave security officers in 1937–1938 every right to arrest and convict the "emigrants" as anti-Soviet "contingents." As already mentioned above, one of the active organizers and executors of the German operation in the Altai Region, Baranov, a sergeant of the security service, wrote to Stalin: "The emigration abroad of the Germans, as has been proved, was the result of [their] hatred of the Soviet government." When being interrogated on 24 of January 1940, Baranov also said:

> Investigations and orders for arrest were based on the fact that a person who was subject to arrest was of a different nationality, had participated in the emigration movement in 1929, and in 1933 had received "Hitler's aid" [...]. The fact that those who were subject to arrest had received "Hitler's aid" was not known prior to the investigation. Remittances and parcels from Germany came through the German consulate in Novosibirsk; besides, it was revealed

---

[6] Yezhov's telegram of 3 of November 1937 demanded intensified operations against anti-Soviet elements, Germans, Poles and "Harbinites." This telegram can be regarded as having the same force as a special order to carry out the German operation in the USSR. Thus, November 1937 was the beginning of the German operation in Siberia, which, from that moment, was conducted simultaneously with the kulak operation. This view is also supported by the mass arrests of the Germans in the Altai Region in early November 1937.

and confirmed during the investigation that this aid was indeed Hitler's [...]. At the time, I thought that this was right and necessary in terms of clearing the area of persons of German nationality who were regarded as "special contingents." Now, in August 1939, while in custody, I am fully convinced that this was absolutely not justified, and that by these unwarranted mass arrests, [we] deeply perverted revolutionary legality. (Savin [ed.] 2006: 466–467)

The testimonies of the convicted officers of the Altai Region NKVD contain interesting information about targeted selection that was applied not before, but after, the arrests. Thus, on 20–23 June, 1938, the head of the Third (counterintelligence) Department of the NKVD for the Altai Region, lieutenant of the security service Ivan Lazarev, arrived in the Novo-Kievskiy (Kulundinskiy) district of the Altai Region, which was densely populated by ethnic Germans. One night before his arrival, the district NKVD officers prepared lists of all the people arrested—about 150 ethnic Germans—with a description of their actual counter-revolutionary activities containing information about their social status, participation in the emigration in 1929 and whether they had received "Hitler's aid" during the famine of 1933–1934. There were about 60 people who were "emigrants" and "receivers." Lazarev looked through the lists and ordered that the cases against these 60 people should be pursued, and that 90 people should be released from prison, "emphasizing that the releases be made gradually, not all at once [...] and this was done." This order was not well received by the district NKVD officers, as they had to start all over again with the cases that they had already completed. Lazarev also released from prison about a half of the Germans in Slavgorod, where about 150 Germans had been arrested by the Novo-Kievskiy District Department of the NKVD. Only members of the emigration movement and the receivers of "Hitler's aid" remained in custody (Savin [ed.] 2009: 690–691).

However, while we maintain the view that the rationality of the actions of the NKVD in the German operation was significantly greater than it is still considered to be, we also believe that the degree of rationality varied a great deal depending on specific conditions, even in the areas densely populated by national minorities. One of the circumstances which could seriously affect it, was the brief amount of time the NKVD bodies had. Thus, the persons involved in the infamous "Slavgorod case," which was concocted by the Third Department (counter-intelligence) of the NKVD for the Altai Region involving the arrest of 298 Germans on 19 and 21 December, were all without exception sentenced to death by the NKVD troika in the Altai region after only a few days, on 29 December, 1937. It is evident that both the scale and pace of the case, and the unprecedented harsh sentences were due to expectations of a speedy completion of the mass operations in the USSR. According to directive № 50194 of 11 December 1937 from the People's Commissar for Internal Affairs N. Yezhov, the deadline for national operations was postponed to 1 January 1938, and submission of reports on the operations to 15 January 1938.

However, the testimonies of the Altai Region NKVD officers, made in 1939–1940, shows that in the "Slavgorod case" the members of the NKVD special team did not conduct random arrests, but that these were based on lists drawn up by the head of the German District Department of the NKVD, Karl Koester. If we take into account that in 1925–1930 Koester worked as a commissioner and a senior commissioner of the Secret Department and then as the Deputy Head of the Slavgorod District Department of the Representative Office of the OGPU for Siberia, that he was an active participant in the struggle against the German emigration movement, and that he since 1935 had been the deputy head and then the head of the German district Department of the NKVD and thus was a well-informed expert on the German "special contingent," we can assume that in these proscription lists there were people who had demonstrated their disloyalty to the regime or displayed recurrent deviant behaviour.

Conclusion

Each of the "national line" operations represented a complex and ambivalent phenomenon. We must distinguish between the indiscriminate victimization solely on the basis of nationality or "foreign" names, and the repression against various "formers," believers, opposition-minded people and real opponents and critics of the Stalinist regime. While the former took place mainly in the big cities and the administrative and industrial centres (which were also places sparsely populated by the "nationals"), the latter occurred in those areas that were densely populated by diasporas, where purposeful terror prevailed over random repression.

The choice of "unreliable nations" as an internal enemy and the "fifth column," as well as the shift in the national policy of the Stalinist regime of the 1930s from internationalism to Russification and "National Bolshevism," is generally consistent with the theory of the ethnification of Stalinism. Nevertheless, an analysis of the actual conduct of one of the most national mass operations of the NKVD—the German operation—suggests that in

1937–1938 the impact of class dogmas and the inertia of social cleansing that had existed since 1917 were too great to be substituted by indiscriminate repression by nationality. As a result, the determinant factors in the choice of the majority of the victims of the national operations were, as a rule, the objective criteria of a "hostile" social past/origin and the subjective criteria of recurrent "anti-Soviet" behaviour. It took an event such as the Second World War to make possible the ethnic mass deportations of entire nations. But, as Zarusky rightly concludes:

> Of course, a number of ethnic minorities in the Soviet Union were victims of Stalinist xenophobia and suspicions of espionage or collective collaboration, which led to a selective or indiscriminate mass repression. However, this was by far nothing like the National Socialist classification and treatment of nations and ethnic groups seen by the Nazis as inferior races. (Zarusky 2012: 13)

Increased hostile attention to ethnic minorities, ethnic cleansing and forced migration, motivated by ethno-political considerations, have become some of the negative distinctive traits of the history of the twenty-first century, not only that of the Soviet Union, but also that of the world as a whole. In Europe alone, 80 million people were affected by forced ethnic migrations. National xenophobia on such a scale gives historians supposedly universal patterns of interpretation of what happened, and makes it tempting to seek "simple" and "obvious" solutions. In the case of the Great Terror, such a solution is to describe 1937 as the year of social cleansing and 1938 as the year of ethnic cleansing. But this speculative logic construct does not find clear support in the archival sources. At best, we can talk about a trend of ethnification of Stalinism punitive policies which was extremely inconsistent, unstable, protracted and undergoing repeated returns to traditional social, class and political reasons for repression.

References

Baberowski, J. (2003). *Der rote Terror. Die Geschichte des Stalinismus*, München: Deutsche Verlags-Anstalt.

Bednarek, E., Kokin, S., Shapoval, Yu. et al. (eds.) (2010). Беднарек, Е., Кокин, С., Шаповал, Ю. и др. (ред.). *Польша та Україна у тридцятих – сорокових роках XX століття. Невідомі документи з архівів спеціальних служб. Том 8. Великий терор. Польска операція 1937–1938* ['Poland and Ukraine in the 1930s–1940s. Secret documents from archives of secret intelligence services. Vol. 8. The Great Terror. Polish operation 1937–1938'], Warsaw & Kyiv.

Brandes, D. & Savin, A. (2001). *Die Sibiriendeutschen im Sowjetstaat 1919-1938* (Veröffentlichungen zur Kultur und Geschichte der Deutschen im östlichen Europa 19), Essen: Klartext Verlag.

Chentsov, V. V. (1998). Ченцов, В. В. *Трагические судьбы. Политические репрессии против немецкого населения Украины в 1920-1930-е годы* ['Tragic fates. Political repressions against Ukraine's German population in the 1920s-1930s'], Moscow: Gotika.

Dönninghaus, V. (2009). *Minderheiten in Bedrängnis. Sowjetische Politik gegenüber Deutschen, Polen und andere Diaspora-Nationalitäten 1917-1938*, München: R. Oldenbourg Verlag.

Hedeler, W. & Savin, A. I. (2006). "Die Deutschen in der UdSSR—eine „fünfte Kolonne?" Die sowjetisch-deutschen Beziehungen Mitte der 1920er Jahre aus der Sicht der OGPU," *Internationale Wissenschaftliche Korrespondenz zur Geschichte der deutschen Arbeiterbewegung*, 2, pp. 305-324.

Junge, M. (2011). "Massenverfolgungen und dogmatischer Import," *Totalitarismus und Demokratie. Zeitschrift für Internationale Diktatur- und Freiheitsforschung*, 1, pp. 77-98.

Junge, M., Binner, R., Kokin, S. A., et al. (eds.) (2010). Юнге, М., Биннер, Р., Кокин, С. А. и др. (ред.). *«Через трупы врага на благо народа». «Кулацкая операция» в Украинской ССР 1937-1941 гг.* ['"Over corpses of enemies to the good of the people." The "kulak operation" in Ukrainian SSR in 1937-1941'], Moscow: ROSSPEN & Germanskiy Istoricheskiy Institut v Moskve.

Junge, M., Bonwetsch, B. & Binner, R. (eds.) (2009). Юнге, М., Бонвеч, Б. и Биннер, Р. (ред.). *Сталинизм в советской провинции 1937-1938. Массовая операция на основе приказа № 00447* ['Stalinism in the Soviet provinces 1937-1938. The mass operation based on order № 00447'], Moscow: ROSSPEN & Germanskiy Istoricheskiy Institut v Moskve.

Junge, M., Bordyugov, G. & Binner, R. (eds.) (2008). Юнге, М., Бордюгов, Г. и Биннер, Р. *Вертикаль большого террора. История операции по приказу № 00447.* ['The vertical of the Great Terror. The history of the operation based on order № 00447'], Moscow: Novyy Khronograf.

Junge, M., Zhdanova, G. D., Rasgon, V. N. et al. (eds.) (2010). Юнге, М., Жданова, Г. Д., Разгон, В. Н. и др. (ред.). *Массовые репрессии в Алтайском крае. 1937-1938 гг. Приказ № 00447.* ['The mass repressions in Altai krai. 1937-1938. Order № 00447'], Moscow: ROSSPEN & Germanskiy Istoricheskiy Institut v Moskve.

Khaustov, V. (1999). Хаустов, В. "Репрессии против советских немцев до начала массовой операции 1937 г." ['Repressions against Soviet Germans before the mass operation of 1937'], in *Наказанный народ. Репрессии против российских немцев. Материалы конференции*, Moscow: Zven'ya Press, pp. 75-83.

Khaustov, V. (2008). Хаустов, В. "Иностранцы и советские граждане иностранного происхождения—потенциальные «агенты буржуазных разведок»" ['Foreigners and Soviet citizens of foreign origins—potential "spies of bourgeois intelligence'"], in *Исторические чтения на Лубянке. 1997–2007*, Moscow, pp. 219–227.

Okhotin, N. & Roginskiy, A. V. (1999). Охотин, Н. и Рогинский, А. В. "Из истории «немецкой операции» НКВД 1937–1938 гг." ['From the history of the "German operation" of the NKVD 1937–1938'], in *Наказанный народ. Репрессии против российских немцев. Материалы конференции*, Moscow: Zven'ya Press, pp. 35–74.

Petrov, N. & Jansen, M. (2006). Петров, Н. и Янсен, М. *«Сталинский питомец»—Николай Ежов* ['Stalin's first lieutenant—Nikolay Yezhov'], Moscow: ROSSPEN.

Savin, A. I. (ed.) (2006). Савин А. И. *Этноконфессия в советском государстве. Меннониты Сибири в 1920–1980-е годы. Аннотированный перечень архивных документов и материалов. Избранные документы* ['Ethno-confession in the Soviet state. Mennonites in Siberia in 1920–1980s. An Annotated list of documents and materials. Selected documents'], Novosibirsk: Posoch.

Savin, A. I. (ed.) (2009). Савин А. И. *Этноконфессия в советском государстве. Меннониты Сибири в 1920–1930-е годы. Эмиграция и репрессии. Документы и материалы.* ['Ethno-confession in the Soviet State. Mennonites in Siberia in 1920s–1930s. Emigration and repression. Documents and materials'], Novosibirsk: Posoch.

Savin, A. I. (2010). "Nationale Operationen des NKVD der UdSSR 1937/1938," in *Lexikon der Vertreibungen. Deportation, Zwangsaussiedlung und ethnische Säuberung im Europa des 20. Jahrhunderts*, hrsg. von D. Brandes, H. Sundhaussen, S. Troebst, Wien-Köln-Weimar: Böhlau Verlag, pp. 462–465.

Shishkin, V. (1992). Шишкин, В. "Советские немцы. У истоков трагедии" ['Soviet Germans. Origins of a tragedy'], *Наука в Сибири*, 28–30, pp. 8–11.

Shishkin, V. (1994). Шишкин, В. "Советские немцы. У истоков трагедии" ['Soviet Germans. Origins of a tragedy'], in *Возвращение памяти. Историко-публицистический альманах*, Novosibirsk, pp. 100–124.

Snyder, T. (2010). *Bloodlands. Europe between Hitler and Stalin*, New York: Basic Books.

Teplyakov, A. G. (2008). Тепляков, А. Г. *Машина террора. ОГПУ-НКВД Сибири в 1929–1941 гг.* ['Terror machine. OGPU-NKVD in Siberia in 1929–1941'], Moscow: Novyy Khronograf.

Weiner, A. (2001). *Making Sense of War. The Second World War and the Fate of the Bolshevik Revolution*, Princeton: Princeton University Press.

Zarusky, J. (2012). "Timothy Snyders *Bloodlands*. Kritische Anmerkungen zur Konstruktion einer Geschichtslandschaft," *Vierteljahreshefte für Zeitgeschichte*, 60:1, pp. 1–31.

CHAPTER 3

'He who Is not with Us Is against Us.' Elimination of the 'Fifth Column' in the Soviet Union, 1937–1938

Victor Dönninghaus

> 1937 was necessary. […] enemies of various tendencies were still around, and in the face of the growing threat of fascist aggression they might unite. Thanks to 1937 we had no fifth column during the war.
>
> Vyacheslav Molotov (cited in Chuyev 1991: 390–391)

According to Stalin's closest associate, the mass repressions were no more than an ordinary "preventive purge" of the Soviet society, without any specific limits or exact criteria. Its principal aim was to prevent enemies from escaping. The amount of innocent victims was of minor importance. "To my mind, Stalin's policy was absolutely correct: better one less innocent head than hesitations during and after the war," Molotov concluded (Chuyev 1991: 416). It is no wonder that the repressions against national minorities of the West took a special place in the process of elimination of a potential fifth column in 1937–1938. They were most closely connected with Stalin's feeling of an impending war, his spy mania and idea of a "hostile capitalist encirclement." It was not accidental that the main victims of the NKVD "national operations" of 1937–1938 were the ethnic minorities comprising nations of certain Western "bourgeois-fascist" states: Poles, Germans, Finns, Estonians, Latvians etc. (Petrov & Roginskiy 1997: 32).

The personal qualities of the "leader of the peoples" became an important factor to predetermine the mass terror of the end of 1930s. Having been convinced of the potential capability of the "capitalist encirclement" to use Western national minorities as a Trojan horse, Stalin no longer trusted their loyalty to the regime, notwithstanding the decades of advancing the slogan of internationalism and the purge of the first half of the 1930s. His doubts were further strengthened by reports from the NKVD leadership, which consistently described "activization" of Western intelligence services on the USSR territory and their preparation of "springboards" for a future invasion. Thus, in January–February 1937 alone, Stalin read top-secret special reports by Nikolai Yezhov, head of the NKVD, such as: "On the Polish Military

Organization" (16 January 1937), "On the Latvian 'counter-revolutionary' organization" (21 January 1937) and "On sabotage activities by foreign intelligence services in the West Siberian Region" (15 February 1937) (*Lubyanka* 2004: 41–44, 52–54, 92–94).

Within this context of spy mania one should not be surprised by Stalin's ideas about the part played by "bourgeois countries," which he shared with participants of the February–March 1937 Plenum of the Central Committee of the VKP(b). According to him, hostile capitalist states "surround the Soviet Union, waiting for an opportunity to attack and defeat it or, at any rate, to undermine its might and weaken it." And above all, if they establish spy networks within each other, "bourgeois states are sure to send to the Soviet Union twice or thrice as many saboteurs, spies, wreckers and murderers" (*Lubyanka* 2004: 97–98; Hedeler & Savin 2006: 305–324). Following Stalin's logic, representatives of Western national minorities were ideally suited for the part of the fifth column, since it was much easier for intelligence agencies of corresponding capitalist states to work in "their own" language and cultural environment. It was precisely these ideas of military and state opposition held by Stalin that led to the national operations of 1937–1938 against everybody directly or indirectly related to the states of "hostile encirclement." According to opinions expressed lately in the literature, up to July 1937 nothing predicted such a scope of repressions. For example, the French historian Gabor Rittersporn points out that judging by many measures taken by law enforcement authorities in 1936 and early 1937, their chiefs never expected such an abrupt turn to a tougher punitive policy in the USSR (Rittersporn 1993: 99–115). On the contrary, the Russian historians Nikita Okhotin and Arseniy Roginskiy see in Stalin's actions a certain "mobilization plan" for pre-war Soviet society, singling out its three main items: 1) "thinning" of the Party-state apparatus, i.e. the "new elite;" 2) general "purging" of the country from "former enemies," i.e. the "old elite" and criminals; and 3) elimination of the "spy-and-saboteur base" in the countries of "capitalist encirclement." Whereas the first two items referred to all and sundry categories of the USSR population, the last one mostly concerned foreigners and representatives of "hostile" nationalities (Okhotin & Roginskiy 1999: 37).

The motives and "planned character" of the NKVD mass operations are still widely discussed in the literature; we cannot go into details now (Junge, Bonwetsch & Binner [eds.] 2009; Zhdanova, Razgon, Junge & Binner [eds.] 2010). But one thing is beyond any doubt—Stalin did not act at random, he knew exactly what he wanted to attain. This supposition was shared by Nikolai Bukharin who wrote about it from prison:

> There is a big and bold political idea of a general purge: a) due to pre-war times, b) due to the transition to democracy. This purge involves: a) those who are guilty, b) those who are under suspicion and c) those who are potential suspects [...]. (Bukharin [1937] 1993: 23)

Nevertheless, analyzing the course of mass repressions of 1937–1938, it is difficult to call it a well thought-out "plan" consistently realized by the Kremlin. It is more likely that, as we speak about the "nature of the Great Terror," including "national operations," we must mean certain "collective efforts"—by the Centre and immediate executors down the line (Hildermeier 2001: 29–32; Khlevnyuk 1996: 187–215).

On 2 July, 1937 the VKP(b) Central Committee Politburo adopted a resolution "On anti-Soviet elements," by which Party organs were charged with "registering all kulaks and criminals who have returned home, in order that the most hostile among them be forthwith administratively arrested and shot" (*Lubyanka* 2004: 234–235). In a week, the Politburo approved the composition of regional and republican extrajudicial "troikas" (commissions of three persons) and "quotas" of former kulaks and criminals who were to be shot or exiled without trial (*Lubyanka* 2004: 239–240). On 31 July 1937 the Politburo confirmed Order № 00447 on the so-called kulak operation "for repressing former kulaks, criminals and other anti-Soviet elements." Meanwhile the Kremlin was preparing special national operations, the first one being a "German operation."

Formally, the German operation started with a short note by Stalin that was added to a protocol of the Politburo meeting on 20 July 1937. The note ran: "All Germans working in our military, semi-military and chemical factories, in electric stations and at building sites, in all regions, are all to be arrested" (Okhotin & Roginskiy 1999: 35). Stalin also wrote the text of the Politburo resolution himself:

> To suggest that Comrade Yezhov give an immediate order to the NKVD organs to arrest all Germans employed in defence plants [...]. To report (daily) to the Central Committee on the course of arrests and number of arrested. (*Lubyanka* 2004: 250–251)

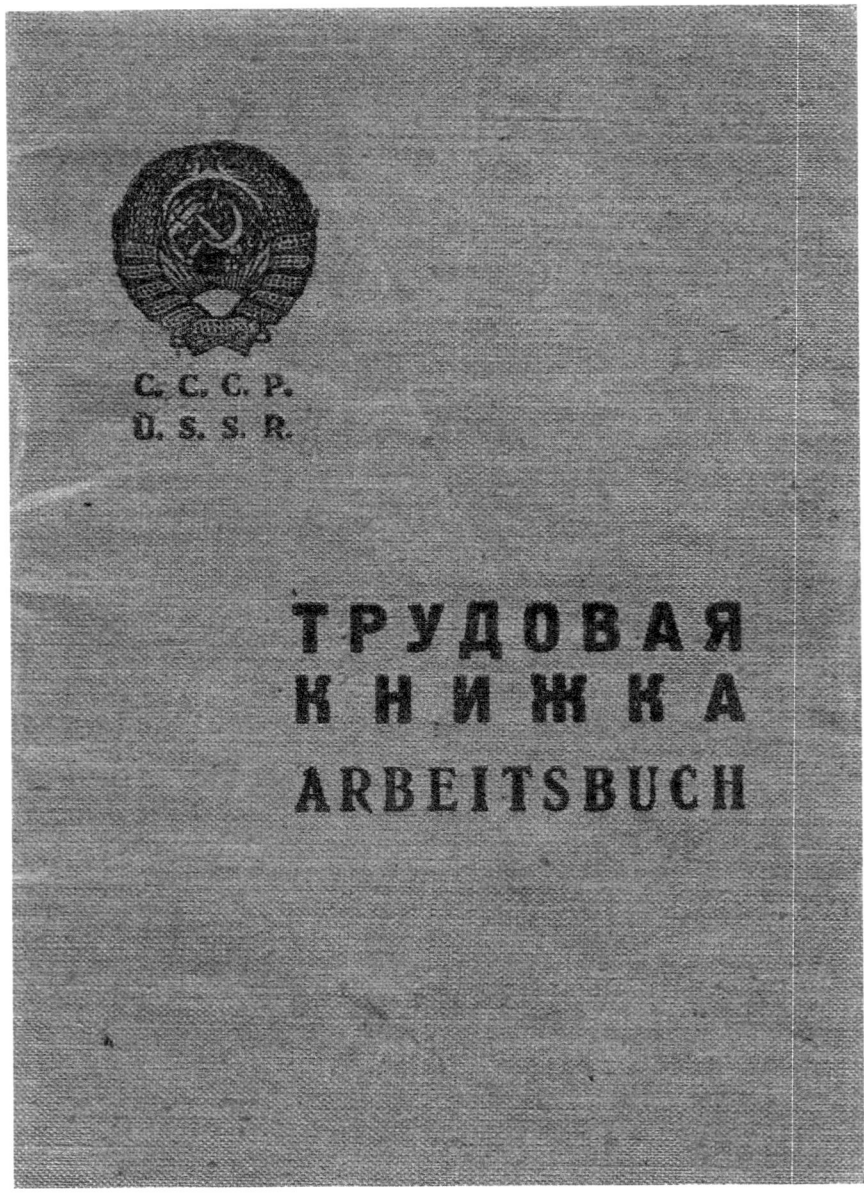

Illustration 4: Employment record book from the Volga German Autonomous Soviet Socialist Republic, 1930s. The parallel texts in Russian and German are equally authentic. Private collection of Igor Toporov.

On 25 July, 1937 Yezhov signed and conveyed by telegraph to all local NKVD organs operational Order № 00439, which demanded that all German citizens—including political émigrés—employed (or having been employed) in the defense industry and on the railroads, should be arrested within five days. Citizens of the USSR were not forgotten in the order either: "German spies, saboteurs and terrorists, newly exposed in the course of investigation [...] from among Soviet citizens [...] are to be immediately arrested, irrespective of their place of employment" (*Lubyanka* 2004: 270–272).

Stalin personally monitored the course of the operation "on German citizens." As soon as on 6 August 1937 Yezhov reported to him the first "successes:" "Altogether in the USSR 340 German citizens arrested [...] 19 spy- and-saboteur residencies exposed" (Okhotin & Roginskiy 1999: 38). By 26 August the number of arrested persons had reached 472, and thereby the operation by Order № 00439 had practically "exhausted itself." According to historians N. Okhotin and A. Roginskiy, the total number of German citizens arrested in the USSR throughout the Great Terror amounted to about 820 people.

On 9 August 1937 the Politburo confirmed a draft of the principal national order by NKVD—the "Polish" Order № 00485, aimed at liquidation of Polish diversionist and espionage groups and structures of the Polish Military Organization (POV) (*Lubyanka* 2004: 299, 301–303). Making national operations a separate trend as well as an opportunity to repress "nationals" within the general framework of Order № 00447 indicates that Stalin followed a certain logic in carrying out the Great Terror. Distinguishing potential "participants of the fifth column" proves the special importance of these operations for the Kremlin. Most probably, Stalin's special interest in the Polish operation could be explained by the fact that after the German-Polish agreement of January 1934 he was sure there existed a certain secret protocol on military co-operation, envisaging their joint actions against the USSR. There are a few other reasons which explain the Kremlin's attention to the Polish operation: 1) it was Poland that posed the biggest threat to peace on the Western border of the USSR; 2) the large number of Polish deserters— i.e. "potential spies and saboteurs;" 3) the multiplicity of Polish diaspora in the country, from which it was concluded that the Polish intelligence service must have a much "broader" base than that of the other foreign intelligences; 4) the "predominance" of Poles in industry, transport, defense and law enforcement agencies (the Army, NKVD), in Party and Soviet authorities (RGASPI f. 17, op. 2, d. 316, 2–10).

In accordance with Order № 00485, six main categories of "the large-scale sabotage and insurgent rank and file of the POV were subject to arrest, untouched up to now, as well as the basic human contingents of the Polish intelligence service in the USSR" (*Butovskiy poligon* 1997: 353–354): a) the most active, not yet identified members of the POV; b) prisoners of war from the Polish army who are in the USSR; c) defectors from Poland, irrespective of time of their desertion to the USSR (Petrov & Roginskiy 1997: 24–25);[1] d) political émigrés and those admitted through prisoners' exchange; e) former members of the Polish Socialist Party (PPS) and other Polish political parties; f) the most active part of local anti-Soviet and nationalist elements in Polish districts. Together with the "Polish" order, the regional NKVD chiefs received a special "secret" letter, also signed by Yezhov: "On the fascist-insurgent, espionage, sabotage, defeatist and terrorist activity of the Polish intelligence service in the USSR." It is noteworthy to mention that both the order and the letter were approved by Stalin (*Lubyanka* 2004: 303–321).

It was necessary to issue these two documents simultaneously, because Order № 00485 referred not only to "Polish spies and saboteurs" but to practically all Poles on the territory of the USSR (Petrov & Roginskiy 1997: 23). Estimating the scale of the "Polish operation," Nikita Khrushchev noted: "When there developed a real 'witch hunt,' [...] all the Poles in the USSR came under suspicion" (Khrushchev 1994: 65). An even more exact evaluation of the range of Order № 00485 was given by A. O. Postel, the Moscow Region UNKVD executive:

> When we, the heads of department, had heard out Yezhov's order to arrest absolutely all Poles, Polish political émigrés, former prisoners of war, members of the Polish Communist Party, etc., this caused not only surprise but also various lobby talks, which stopped when they told us that this order was approved by Stalin and the Politburo, so we should smash the Poles to the utmost. (Petrov & Roginskiy 1997: 23)

Most probably, expecting such a reaction to the "Polish" order, the NKVD authority had to append to it a sort of interpretation.

---

[1] In January 1938, addressing a meeting of GUGB ['Main Directorate for State Security'] NKVD leaders, Nikolay Yezhov estimated that the number of "Polish defectors" exceeded 100,000 men.

As a result, Order № 00485 provided the NKVD with "a model" for decrees in all subsequent national operations of 1937–1938: German,[2] Romanian, Latvian, Finnish, etc. It is noteworthy that this "Polish" order gave birth to something basically new in the NKVD practice of conviction—the so-called album procedure—whereby, at the end of an investigation, NKVD officials prepared special certificates for each arrested person, providing their sentencing recommendations. These certificates, compiled in a special list (i.e. an "album"), were signed by a so-called *dvoika* ['twosome']—the regional NKVD chief and the local prosecutor—after which they were sent to Moscow for a final decision by the People's Commissar for Internal Affairs Yezhov and the Chief Prosecutor of the USSR Vyshinsky. Initially, the Polish operation was planned to be completed within three months. But this term was constantly being prolonged (as well as the terms of other special national operations): at first to 10 December, then to 1 January 1938, 15 April and finally to 1 August 1938 (*Lubyanka* 2004: 538).

In mid-September 1937, Yezhov, in his special report to Stalin on the course of the Polish operation, informed of the arrest of 23,216 people, most of them in Ukraine (7,651 men) (*Lubyanka* 2004: 352). On reading it, Stalin wrote in the margin: "Very good! Dig up and purge this Polish espionage mud in the future as well. Destroy it in the interest of the USSR" (*Lubyanka* 2004: 359). Such notes reflect Stalin's almost professional interest in the NKVD's activities and his scrupulous attention to all the details of investigation and intelligence work of its officers. All in all, as a result of the Polish operation, cases involving 143,810 people were examined, of whom 139,835 were convicted, including 111,091 sentenced to be shot (79.44%) (Petrov & Roginskiy 1997: 33; Danilov [ed.] 2006: 157).

As for the German operation, expansion of the repressed "categories" by Soviet citizens and introduction of the "album procedure" for conviction did not begin until the autumn of 1937. Such a "delay" can be explained by the fact that before the outset of the Great Terror, the Germans had already been exposed to much more severe and large-scale repressions than the Poles. This was partially due to low representation of Soviet Germans in Party and state organs, in industry, transport and the Army, which permitted the Centre to act without haste (RGASPI f. 17, op. 7, d. 316, l. 2–10). It may be supposed that the "Polish operation" precipitated a transfer from the "program" of

---

[2] There never existed a special NKVD order to launch an operation against Germans. Order № 00439 was not directly related to the subsequent mass "German operation." As reports of the NKVD directorates usually indicated, the repressions of the German operation were carried out "likewise as in Order № 00485."

arresting "German citizens" to mass repression against Soviet citizens of German nationality. Specific directives of Order № 00485, especially the practice of carrying it out down the line, determined the principal forms and scope of repression against all "suspicious" national groups. One may agree with the opinion of the historians N. Okhotin and A. Roginskiy that the application of the "Polish" order to other "not too loyal" national contingents often took place spontaneously. In such cases there was only one thing to do for the Centre—to authorize what had already been established down the line. This is, apparently, what happened when the German operation gradually developed from a local operation (regarding "German citizens") into a mass one ("citizens of the USSR").

On 3 November 1937, in his telegram to heads of the republican NKVD divisions and the NKVD directorates, Yezhov noted:

> Operations carried out now [against] anti-Soviet elements, Germans, Poles, Harbinites and wives of traitors of the Motherland [in] a number of regions, are advancing extremely slowly [...] Operations against Germans are conducted inactively in the Gorky and Rostov regions [...]. (*Lubyanka* 2004: 649)[3]

No special order or explanations were issued concerning mass repression against Germans with Soviet citizenship, but it was not particularly necessary to specify the task. The matter is that as far back as 2 April 1937 the GUGB NKVD had sent to the provinces a directive letter "On rising activity of German intelligence agencies and of the Nazi Party's special institutions in the USSR territory," with an extensive "Reference on German Nazis' activities in the USSR." What is more, there were enough supporters of sterner repression against the German population among the Party leadership in Soviet republics. For example, delegates of the January 1937 VKP(b) of Ukraine Central Committee Plenum discussed proposals of mass eviction of Germans from industrial regions of the republic. S. Sarkisov, CP(b)U Central Committee Politburo candidate member, who defended this idea, made a clear announcement:

---

[3] A. I. Savin supposes that this telegram by Yezhov may be a substitute for a special order to carry out a German operation.

> Germans, who are entangled with fascists, have spread their nets over big power stations [...]. I think we should be more active in the deportation of many Germans from Donbass. We don't need them [...]. (Evtukh & Chirko 1994: 62)

The question of expulsion of all the Germans from Ukraine, as representatives of the national group "contaminated with fascist ideology," was also raised at the 13th Congress of VKP(b) in Ukraine held in May–June 1937 (Chentsov 1998: 102).

It should be noted that the first arrests "by the German line" (as by the other "lines') were made on the basis of available NKVD registration data on "counter-revolutionary activities" (which included participating in the émigré movement and receiving the so-called "Hitler's aid"), filing cards on political refugees and former prisoners of war, lists of visitors to German consulates, etc. As these "registration data," "cards" and "lists" ran out, they began to arrest people "without any indication of their belonging to a counter-revolutionary organization," because of "their German nationality or just on mere suspicion of being of German nationality" (Belkovets 1996: 454–455; Vilenskiy [ed.] 1992: 118–120).

Among NKVD officials, "the German line" was considered one of the most "promising," as regards the number of repressed people (Savin [ed.] 2009: 45–55). Germans were accused of espionage, diversions, sabotage, preparation of terrorist acts, creation of insurgent organizations, etc. Every day, NKVD investigation officers "cooked up" cases, compiling them into all kinds of "organizations," "detachments," "groups," "residencies" or "networks," headed, as a rule, by citizens of Germany—either " technicians" or émigrés (Chentsov 1998: 125–126). In 1939, when asked about a mechanism of fabricating "national cases," investigation officers of the Ukrainian NKVD said:

> There was a directive by Uspenskiy [from January 1938, People's Commissar of the Interior of the Ukrainian SSR] to knock out the base from under the Polish and German intelligence services, [...] we should arrest Poles and Germans irrespective of whether there were enough materials for arrest. On these grounds, in our drawing up of certificates for the arrest of Poles and Germans, their ethnicity played the dominant role. (Chentsov 1998: 132)

According to data of the NKVD 1st Special Department, as of 1 July 1938, 65,339 people had been arrested "by the German line," while the total number of Germans arrested from 1 October 1936 to 1 July 1938 amounted to 75,331 people, including 18,469 arrested during the operation by Order № 00447 (Danilov [ed.] 2006: 157, 163; Savin 2010: 462–465). These figures, on the whole, do not contradict the data of N. Okhotin and A. Roginskiy, who state that between 69,000 and 73,000 Germans were convicted (Okhotin & Roginskiy 1999: 71), of whom about 53,000–56,000 (76%) were sentenced to execution (Okhotin & Roginskiy 1999: 71; Krieger 2002: 474–475).[4]

The stepping up of national mass repression involved more and more "unreliable" nationalities. Events preceding the Latvian operation fully reveal the mechanism of a "collective creative effort" (by the Centre and provinces) during the Great Terror. In November 1937, in his report to Yezhov on the progress of "operations" in the Smolensk Region, the head of the UNKVD (regional administration) A. Nasedkin mentioned the so-called Latvian National Centre—he extorted this information during interrogations of arrested Latvians. He described this centre as a wide network of Latvians working in the Latvian section of the Comintern, the "Prometejs" society and other Latvian unions and organizations. To Yezhov's question how many people should be arrested, proceeding from the available operative information,[5] Nasedkin replied 500. According to him, Yezhov was absolutely dissatisfied with this figure and announced: "Nonsense! I'll settle this with the VKP(b) Central Committee. Arrest not less than 1,500 people." Two days later Yezhov informed Nasedkin that the Latvian operation had caused no objection at the top level and offered him to start (before any official order was issued) arresting Latvians who worked in the NKVD of the Belarusian SSR, the Latvian Club, the Latvian National Theatre, as well as the most active members of Latvian cultural organizations and the section of Latvian Riflemen (*Lubyanka* 2004: 662). As a result, on 30 November 1937 a ciphered telegram № 49990, signed by Yezhov, was sent down the line. In this telegram the UNKVD authorities were recommended to pay special attention to "purging" Latvians from defence plants, transport, zones of special regime, and special sectors in different institutions engaged in defence, mobilization and cipher-work (*Lubyanka* 2004: 662; Okhotin & Roginskiy 2000: 5).

It should be stressed that the "Latvian operation" in the USSR resulted in extermination of a considerable number of active participants of Russia's revolutionary underground activities and of its Civil War, major Party, Soviet and military personalities. This was substantiated by a covert predication that Latvians—even celebrated revolutionaries—were apt to espionage for the sake of "their own" bourgeois state. According to A. Radzivilovskiy, one of

---

[4] Altogether, of the 55,000 people convicted as a result of the German operation, about 38,000 were Germans.

[5] According to A. Nasedkin, altogether about 5,000 Latvians were officially registered, including children.

the heads of the USSR NKVD, while explaining to him the procedure of arresting communists who represented Western national minorities, Yezhov said the following:

> Don't stand upon ceremony with these people, their cases will be examined through an "album procedure." It should be proved that Latvians, Poles, Germans and others, members of the VKP(b), are spies and saboteurs [...]. (Vilenskiy [ed.] 1992: 119)

According to the NKVD 1st Special Department, as of 1 July 1938 altogether 23,539 people were arrested "by the Latvian line;" 21,392 of these were Latvians, of whom only 987 were arrested in the course of operation by Order № 00447 (Danilov [ed.] 2006: 157, 163). It is significant that by March 1938, as a result of repression and purges within Party organizations, the number of communists representing Western national minorities (with the exception of Greeks) had dropped below the level of 1927.

Table 1: Total number of VKP(b) members and candidate-members representing the main groups of Western national minorities (1927 and 1938).

Nationality	1927	March 1938
Poles	11,158	10,066
Latvians	12,198	7,215
Germans	5,226	4,562
Estonians	3,682	3,001
Greeks	1,521	2,165
Lithuanians	2,577	1,800
Finns	1,810	1,402

* Source: RGASPI f. 17, op. 7, d. 316, l. 12

Analysis of the national operations gives reasons for a conclusion that they were exceptionally centralized. At the same time, this does not mean that such national operations, like the process of the Great Terror, did not contain a certain amount of local initiative. The facts remain: in some cases the Centre could do nothing but authorize an "additional" act of repression against "nationals," initiated down the line by some zealous heads of the NKVD. This is, for example, what happened in the Romanian operation which began spontaneously in Ukraine in August 1937, as well as in the purge of Finns—launched on their own initiative by the NKVD authorities of the Leningrad Region and Karelia in September–October 1937. There were neither special resolutions of the VKP(b) Central Committee Politburo, nor orders by the USSR NKVD to justify operations against these national contingents. They could at any time simply be "included" in general directives for the prolongation and activization of national operations or in instructions for accounts etc. (Takala 1998: 189).

Mass dismissals of representatives of Western national minorities—including VKP(b) members—from defence plants in the spring of 1938 are a striking example of interlacing of ethnic and "institutional" factors. As follows from a memorandum by the VKP(b) Central Committee Department of Principal Party Organs, of the 37,000 communists who represented "nationalities that are not part of the USSR" (as of 5 March 1938),[6] the majority (about 80%) belonged to 17 regional and republican Party organizations "most important from both, economic and strategic points of view."[7] Nearly half of these people (46.4%) worked in industry, transport, communications and construction. Many communist "nationals" held leading positions in "strategic" People's Commissariats and their directorates.

> As can be seen from these data [the above-mentioned memorandum emphasized] Party members and candidate-members of nationalities that are not part of the USSR, fill leading posts, from heads of industrial works to directors of central institutions and organizations. These are not isolated cases of Germans, Poles, Latvians being placed in charge of very important branches of industry. (RGASPI f. 17, op. 7, d. 316, l. 3–4)

On 23 March 1938 the VKP(b) Central Committee Politburo issued an official order "to purge" all spheres of the defence industry of representatives of Western national minorities. It did not matter at all for the Kremlin what the dismissed person's fault was and whether he had infringed a law—the main thing was that he belonged to an "unreliable" nationality. A Politburo decision of 23 March 1938 stated:

---

[6] The overwhelming majority (around 90%) were representatives of Western national minorities.
[7] For example, the Leningrad Region numbered 7,703 Party members of nationalities that were not part of the USSR; the Ukrainian SSR, 7,602; the Moscow region, 4,572; the Belarusian SSR, 1,242, etc.

3 - 'HE WHO IS NOT WITH US IS AGAINST US.'

> To consider it abnormal that a large number of Germans, Poles, Latvians and Estonians are employed at plants, chief directorates and the central machinery of the People's Commissariat of Defence Industry. To assign Comrades Yezhov and Malenkov, jointly with Comrade M. Kaganovich, the task of purging the defence industry of persons of the mentioned nationalities. (*Lubyanka* 2004: 502)

An analogous approach can clearly be seen in the process of discharges from the army and the NKVD in the summer of 1938. A directive by People's Commissar of Defense K. E. Voroshilov (№ 200 sh, from 24 June 1938) stated that all servicemen "of nationalities that are not part of the USSR" were subject to discharge. According to official data, altogether 35,020 officers were discharged from the Red Army in 1937–1938. Of this number 4,138 (11.8%) (*Voenno-istoricheskiy arkhiv* 1998: 47–49; *Izvestiya TsK KPSS* 1990: 188)[8] were "foreigners" who did not inspire "political confidence," including 717 Latvians, 1,099 Poles, 620 Germans, 312 Estonians, 109 Finns, 128 Greeks, etc.

Contrary to the Kremlin's initial plans, the operation by Order № 00447 was not completed in four months. On 31 January 1938 the VKP(b) Central Committee Politburo supported the NKVD's proposal "concerning the confirmation of additional numbers of former kulaks, criminals and active anti-Soviet elements subject to repression" (*Lubyanka* 2004: 467–468). Ethnicity was a factor that added to the general escalation of repression in the USSR. On the same day, the Politburo members adopted another decision on further purges among representatives of "unreliable nationalities," according to which the national operations were to be extended to 15 April 1938. What is more, the NKVD was ordered "to smash up the Bulgarian and Macedonian personnel" (*Lubyanka* 2004: 468–469). On 1 February, 1938 Yezhov telegraphed to all the NKVD directorates his Directive № 233, which officially prolonged the terms of "national operations" under way and opened up a number of "new lines" (Finnish, Estonian, Romanian, Chinese, Bulgarian and Macedonian). Here, an order was once again issued "to subject to arrest all Germans suspected of espionage, subversive and other anti-Soviet activities who have Soviet citizenship, in accordance with categories enumerated in my Order № 00485" (Okhotin & Roginskiy 1999: 52). Thus, Yezhov again sanctioned, post factum, the German operation, that had long ago been realized down the line.

---

[8] According to a report by E. A. Shchadenko, of 4,138 people, discharged by Voroshilov's directive № 200 sh, 1,919 (46.4%) were later reinstated in the Army.

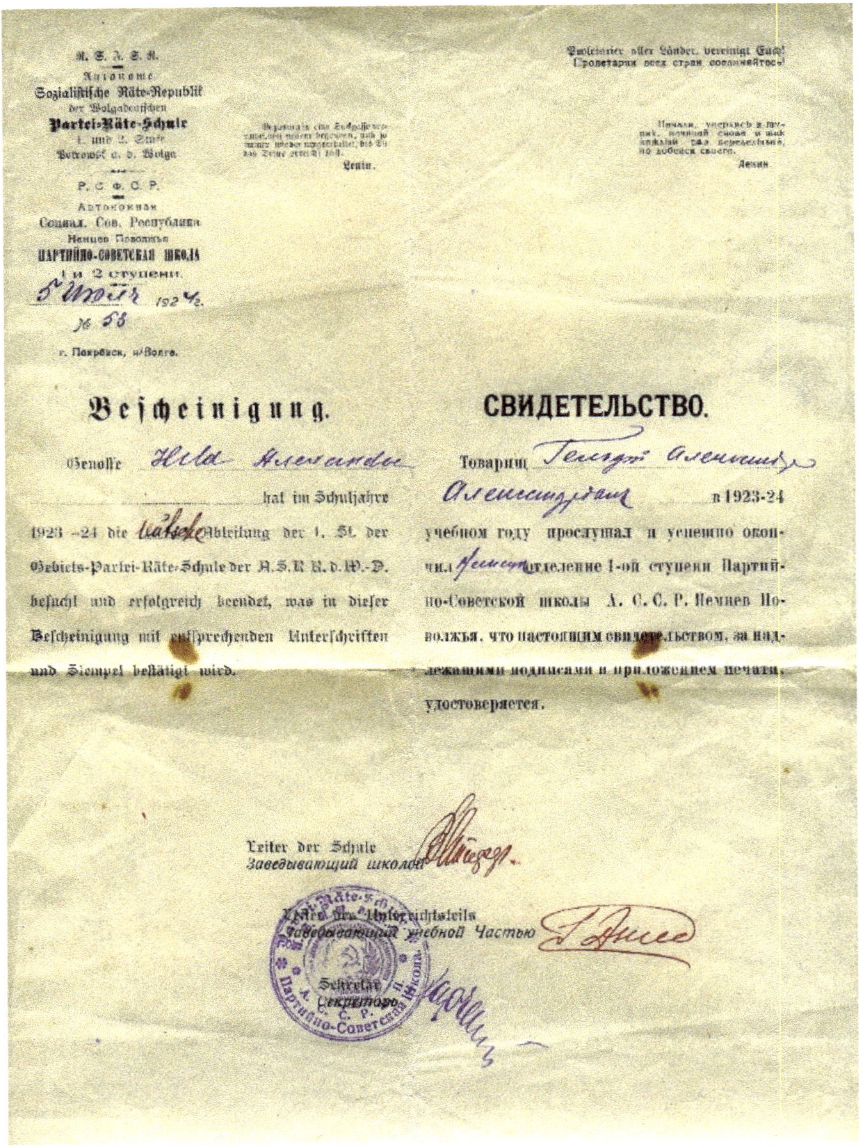

A. S. R. R.
Autonome
Sozialistische Räte-Republik
der Wolgadeutschen
Partei-Räte-Schule
1. und 2. Stufe
Petrowsk a. d. Wolga

Р. С. Ф. С. Р.
Автономная
Социал. Сов. Республика
Немцев Поволжья
ПАРТИЙНО-СОВЕТСКАЯ ШКОЛА
1 и 2 ступени.

5 июля 1924 г.
№ 58
г. Покровск, н/Волге.

Proletarier aller Länder, vereinigt Euch!
Пролетарии всех стран, соединяйтесь!

Lenin.

Ленин

Bescheinigung.

Genosse Held Alexander hat im Schuljahre 1923–24 die ... Abteilung der 1. St. der Gebiets-Partei-Räte-Schule der A.S.R.R. d. W.-D. besucht und erfolgreich beendet, was in dieser Bescheinigung mit entsprechenden Unterschriften und Stempel bestätigt wird.

СВИДЕТЕЛЬСТВО.

Товарищ ... в 1923-24 учебном году прослушал и успешно окончил ... отделение 1-ой ступени Партийно-Советской школы А. С. С. Р. Немцев Поволжья, что настоящим свидетельством, за надлежащими подписями и приложением печати, удостоверяется.

Leiter der Schule
Заведывающий школой

Leiter des Unterrichtsteils
Заведывающий учебной частью

Sekretär
Секретарь

Illustration 5: Postgraduate diploma of Alexander Held from studies at the Party-Soviet School of the Volga-German Autonomous Soviet Socialist Republic, 1924. Alexander Held was born in 1897 in the Volga-German colony Franzosen; member of the VKP(b) since 1919; Minister of Automobile Transport of the Volga-German Autonomous Soviet Socialist Republic; died in the Ustvymlag in 1944. Private collection of Igor Toporov.

The NKVD directive, for the first time providing a whole list of "national operations," sharply intensified the repression against "nationals" throughout the country. Meanwhile, the operation by Order № 00447 was gradually subsiding. From the spring of 1938, the operations "by nationality lines" became the main sphere of mass repression in the USSR. The order "to smash up nationals" was understood literally down the line. For example, Latvians and Poles were arrested in Rostov according to lists of names compiled through data from an address bureau (Kislitsyn 1992: 62). According to M. I. Semyonov, chairman of a special troika for Moscow and the Moscow Region, "in the course of mass operations [...] on withdrawal of Poles, Latvians, Germans and representatives of other nationalities, arrests were made without any incriminating evidence" (Vilenskiy [ed] 1992: 118). To ensure a monthly "limit on spies, i.e. nationals" (Vilenskiy [ed] 1992: 119–120),[9] A. O. Postel, the Moscow Region UNKVD executive noted that

> they arrested and shot whole families, which comprised absolutely illiterate women, youths, even pregnant women, and subjected everybody, like spies, to shooting, without any evidence, just because they were nationals ... (Prudnikova 2007: 113; Golovkova 2010)

When they did not have enough arrested people of a certain nationality for reporting, NKVD investigators, as they confessed, did a very simple thing: "Made a Jew a German, or a Moscow-born person Warsaw-born" (Vilenskiy [ed] 1992: 118–119).

On 28 May, 1938 came a new NKVD Order № 1160 announcing another extension of the term of national operations to 1 August 1938. The work on "arresting persons of Polish, German, Latvian, Estonian, Finnish, Bulgarian, Macedonian, Greek, Romanian [...] nationalities" was so intensive that the Centre could not operatively "digest" all the incoming "albums." In the summer of 1938 albums of more than 100,000 people had accumulated in Moscow. As a consequence of such a delay, the prisons were overcrowded, with a corresponding increase of expenditure for maintenance of practically doomed prisoners. On 15 September 1938 the Politburo decided to abolish the "album procedure" and to establish in each region "special troikas"—commissions of three persons—tasked with carrying out sentences against

---

[9] Officially, there existed no limits for national operations approved by the Centre like those set for the operation by Order № 00447. This could only be a local initiative with figures set by heads of local NKVD directorates. Thus, according to testimony by NKVD investigators of the Moscow Region, from 1938 they were monthly given "limits" for arresting certain groups of "nationals."

"national contingents," whose decisions needed no confirmation from Moscow and were carried out immediately (*Lubyanka* 2004: 549–550). Proceeding from this decision, Yezhov initiated the corresponding NKVD Order № 00606 of 17 September, 1938 whereby all unprocessed albums were to be returned from Moscow to the places where they had been produced. The results of such a "rationalization" were not long in coming. In less than two months, the special troikas examined the cases of nearly 108,000 people from all the national operations—of them 72,254 (68.79%) were sentenced to be shot.[10] The largest number of convictions by special troikas was against Poles (21,258 people), and the second largest against Germans (17,150) (Okhotin & Roginskiy 1999: 62, 70).

The Great Terror ended exactly as it had begun, by an order from Moscow. Thus, the activity of the special troikas was ended by a Politburo resolution of 15 November, 1938 (*Lubyanka* 2004: 606), and two days later the Politburo decided to terminate all mass operations, including the "national" ones (*Lubyanka* 2004: 607–611). Before long, there followed NKVD Order № 00762 of 26 November 1938, signed by a new People's Commissar for Internal Affairs, L. P. Beria, which cancelled all operative orders and directives of 1937–1938 (*Lubyanka* 2004: 612–615).

Conclusion

Altogether, in 15 months, from August 1937 to November 1938, over 1.6 million people were arrested, about 700,000 of whom were shot. The number of convicted persons in the course of the national operations amounted to 335,513,[11] of whom 247,157 (73.66%) were sentenced to be shot (Petrov & Roginskiy 1997: 32–33; Kostyrchenko 2003: 132).[12] The data are far from exhaustive, but even these figures show adequately the scale of repression against national groups of the "hostile capitalist encirclement." So, it was Stalin's ideas of the state-and-military confrontation that directed the national operations of 1937–1938 against everybody who was in one way or another related to the states of "hostile capitalist encirclement." In the context of spy mania and active preparation for the impending war, representatives of Western national minorities became the first target for the Centre, as

---

[10] Of 108,000 cases, examined by special troikas, only 137 people were released. The cases of 2,711 prisoners were returned for further inquiry or submitted to judicial authorities.
[11] As already mentioned, this number includes not only members of minority groups, but also representatives of the majority, the so-called "titular nationalities."
[12] Greeks (81%) and Finns (80%) had the highest death rate among those arrested.

potential "enemies of the regime, spies and saboteurs." The "nature of the Great Terror," including national operations, was shaped by the "collective effort" of the Centre and executors down the line.

Although the national operations were carried out by the NKVD organs "by the lines" of practically all countries of "hostile capitalist encirclement," it was not so much nationality that was the main criterion for repression, but rather birth, having lived abroad or any other kind of ties with these foreign countries. It was this very "selectivity" that cardinally distinguished the national operations of 1937–1938 from the deportations in 1941–1944, which, without exception, involved all representatives of "disloyal" nationalities.

In the national operations of 1937–1938, for the first time in Soviet history, mass repression was not based on class, social or political background, but on so-called "foreign contacts." Thus, the national status outweighed the social one, practically refuting the slogan of proletarian internationalism and class solidarity advanced by the Bolsheviks.

References

Archives

RGASPI. Российский Государственный Архив Социально-Политической Истории ['Russian state archive of social and political history'], Moscow, Russia.

Literature

Belkovets, L. (1996). Белковец, Л. П. "«Большой террор» в немецких селах Западно-Сибирского края" ['"The Great Terror" in German villages of the West Siberian region'], in *Российские немцы. Проблемы истории, языка и современного положения*, Moscow, pp. 452–457.

Bukharin, N. [1937] (1993). Бухарин, Н. "«Прости меня, Коба». Неизвестное письмо Н. Бухарина (10 декабря 1937 г.)" ['"Forgive me Koba." N. *Bukharin's unknown letter to Stalin*, 10 December *1937*'], Источник, 10, pp. 23–24.

Butovskiy poligon (1997). *Бутовский полигон 1937–1938 гг. Книга памяти жертв политических репрессий* ['The Butovskiy polygon 1937–1938. Book of memory of the victims of political repression'], Moscow.

Chentsov, V. (1998). Ченцов, В. В. *Трагические судьбы. Политические репрессии против немецкого населения Украины в 1920–1930-е годы* ['Tragic fates. Political repression against the German population of the Ukraine in the 1920s and 1930s'], Moscow.

Chuyev, F. (1991). Чуев, Ф. *Сто сорок бесед с Молотовым. Из дневника Ф. Чуева* ['One hundred and forty talks with Molotov. From F. Chuyev's diary'], Moscow.

Danilov, V. P. (ed.) (2006). Данилов, В. П. (ред.). *Трагедия советской деревни. Коллективизация и раскулачивание. Документы и материалы. 5:2 (1937–1939)* ['Tragedy of the Soviet village. Collectivization and dispossession. Documents and materials. 5:2 (1937–1939)'], Moscow.

Evtukh, V. & Chirko, B. (1994). Евтух, В. и Чирко, Б. *Німці в Україні (1920-і–1990-і роки)* ['Germans in the Ukraine (1920–1990s)'], Kyiv.

Golovkova, L. (2010). Головкова, Л. *Спецобъект «Бутовский полигон» (история, документы, воспоминания)* ['Special object "Butovo Polygon" (history, documents, reminiscences']; http://www.martyr.ru/content/view/6/15/; access date 12 September 2010.

Hedeler, W. & Savin, A. I. (2006). "Die Deutschen in der UdSSR—eine "fünfte Kolonne?" Die sowjetisch-deutschen Beziehungen Mitte der 1920er Jahre aus der Sicht der OGPU," *Internationale Wissenschaftliche Korrespondenz zur Geschichte der deutschen Arbeiterbewegung*, 2–3, pp. 305–324.

Hildermeier, M. (2001). Хильдермайер, М. "Сталинизм и террор" ['Stalinism and terror'], in *Коммунизм, террор, человек. Дискуссионные статьи на тему «Черная книга коммунизма»*, сост. С. Кройсбергер и др., Kyiv, pp. 19–32.

Izvestiya TsK KPSS (1990). "Из постановлений Политбюро ЦК ВКП(б). О работе за 1939 г. Из отчета начальника Управления по начальствующему составу РККА Наркомата Обороны СССР Е. А. Щаденко, 5.05.1940 г." ['From the decisions of the Central Committee of the VKP(b). On the work from 1939'], in *Известия ЦК КПСС*, 1, pp. 186–192.

Junge, M., Bonwetsch, B. & Binner, R. (eds.) (2009). Юнге, М., Бонвеч, Б. и Биннер, Р. (ред.). *Сталинизм в советской провинции. 1937–1938. Массовая операция на основе приказа № 00447* ['Stalinism in the Soviet provinces. 1937–1938. The mass operation according to Order № 00447'], Moscow.

Khlevnyuk, O. V. (1996). Хлевнюк, О. В. *Политбюро. Механизмы политической власти в 30-е годы* ['The Politburo. Mechanisms of political power in the 1930s'], Moscow.

Khrushchev, N. S. (1994). Хрущев, Н. С. *Мемуары Никиты Сергеевича Хрущева* ['Memoirs of Nikita Sergeyevich Khrushchev'], *Вопросы истории*, 4, pp. 63–79.

Kislitsyn, S. A. (1992). Кислицын, С. А. *Сказавшие «нет». Эпизоды из истории политической борьбы в советском обществе в конце 20-х–первой половине 30-х гг.* ['The ones who said "no." Episodes from the history of political struggle in Soviet society in the late 1920s to the first half of the 1930s'], Rostov-na-Donu.

Kostyrchenko, G. V. (2003). Костырченко, Г. В. *Тайная политика Сталина. Власть и антисемитизм* ['Stalin's secret policy. Power and anti-semitism'], Moscow.

Krieger, V. (2002). Кригер, В. "Некоторые аспекты демографического развития немецкого населения 1930-х–1950-х годов" [Some aspects of demographic development of the German population in the 1930s–1950s], in *Germans of Russia. Socio-Economic and Spiritual Development. 1871–1941*, Moscow, pp. 470–494.

Lubyanka (2004). *Лубянка. Сталин и Главное управление госбезопасности НКВД. Архив Сталина. Документы высших органов партийной и государственной власти. 1937–1938 гг.* ['Lubyanka. Stalin and the Main Directorate for State Security NKVD. Stalin's archive. Documents of higher organs of Party and state power. 1937–1938'], Moscow.

Okhotin, N. & Roginskiy, A. V. (1999). Охотин, Н. и Рогинский, А. Б. "Из истории «немецкой» операции НКВД 1937–1938 гг." ['From the history of the "German operation" of the NKVD 1937–1938'], *Наказанный народ. Репрессии против российских немцев. Материалы конференции*, Moscow, pp. 35–74.

Okhotin, N. & Roginsky, A. V. (2000). Охотин, Н. & Рогинский А. Б. "«Латышская операция» 1937–1938 годов. Архивные комментарии" ['"The Latvian operation" in 1937–1938 . Archival comments'], *Архивные комментарии*, 4, pp. 5.

Petrov, N. & Roginsky, A. V. (1997). Петров Н. В. & Рогинский А. Б. "«Польская операция» НКВД 1937–1938 гг." ['The "Polish operation" of the NKVD in 1937–1938'], in *Репрессии против польских граждан*, сост. А. Гурьянов. Вып. 1, Moscow, pp. 22–43.

Prudnikova, E. A. (2007). Прудникова, Е. А. *Хрущев. Творцы террора* ['Khrushchev. Creators of terror'], Moscow.

Rittersporn, G. (1993). "The omnipresent conspiracy. On Soviet imagery of politics and social relations in the 30s," in *Stalinist Terror. New Perspectives*, eds. J. A. Getty & R. T. Manning, New York, pp. 99–115.

Savin, A. I. (ed.) (2009). Савин, А. И. *Этноконфессия в советском государстве. Меннониты Сибири в 1920–1930-е годы. Эмиграция и репрессии. Документы и материалы* ['Ethno-confession in the Soviet State. Mennonites in Siberia in 1920s–1930s. Emigration and repression. Documents and materials'], Novosibirsk: Posoch.

Savin, A. I. (2010). "Nationale Operationen des NKVD der UdSSR 1937/1938," in *Lexikon der Vertreibungen. Deportation, Zwangsaussiedlung und ethnische Säuberung im Europa des 20. Jahrhunderts*, hrsg. von D. Brandes, H. Sundhaussen, S. Troebst, Wien-Köln-Weimar, pp. 462–465.

Takala, I. (1998). Такала, И. "Национальные операции ОГПУ/НКВД в Карелии" ['National operations of the OGPU/NKVD in Karelia'], in *В семье единой. Национальная политика партии большевиков и ее осуществление на Северо-Западе России в 1920–1950-е годы*, Petrozavodsk, pp. 161–206.

Vilenskiy, S. S. (ed.) (1992). Виленский, С. С. (ред.). *Сопротивление в ГУЛАГе. Воспоминания, письма, документы* ['Resistance in GULAG. Reminiscences, letters, documents'], Moscow.

Voenno-istoricheskiy arkhiv (1998). "Статистика антиармейского террора" ['Statistics of anti-army terror'], *Военно-исторический архив*, 3, pp. 39–51.

Zhdanova, G. D., Razgon, V. N., Junge M. & Binner R. (eds.) (2010). Жданова, Г. Д., Разгон, В. Н., Юнге, М. и Биннер, Р. (ред.). *Массовые репрессии в Алтайском крае 1937–1938. Приказ № 00447* ['Mass repressions in Altai krai 1937–1938. Order № 00447'], Moscow.

PART 2
Ethnic Minorities in the Great Terror. Case studies

CHAPTER 4
Propaganda of Hatred and the Great Terror. A Nordic Approach

Andrej Kotljarchuk

Genocide Studies have shown that the Holocaust was prepared through a propaganda campaign of anti-Semitism that was filtered to society through the mass media (Glass 1997: 129–45; Herf 2006: 17–49; Jones 2011: 487–498). Less is known about the role of propaganda in the so-called national operations of the NKVD in 1937–1938. The Stalin dictatorship was one of the first modern propaganda political regimes (Kenez 1985; Brandenberger 2011). The Soviet state monopolized the press, cinema and theather and almost totally controlled the public space. One can believe that, because unlike the Moscow trials the national operations were secret, the use of propaganda was minimal. This is not correct. Unprecedented mass arrests of members of the ethnic communities required massive propaganda. The aim of this paper is to analyse the ideas, technologies, aims and target groups of the propaganda campaign during the national operations of the NKVD. The study is focused on the local press in the Swedish and Finnish minority areas.

The early Soviet Union was unlike many other states in Europe, not just because of the abolition of private property and the dictatorship of the Communist Party, but also because of its nationalities policy based on internationalism. The Soviet Union was practically the first great power in the world that systematically promoted the national consciousness of ethnic minorities and established for them institutional forms characteristic of a modern nation. In 1923, the Bolsheviks proclaimed a policy of self-determination and cultural and linguistic rights for all minorities, referred to as Lenin's nationalities policy (Martin 2001). This policy changed dramatically when, in 1937, the NKVD began its national operations aimed at executing members of various ethnic minorities. In the first operation, personally initiated by Stalin, Germans were the target, while the second and largest was directed against Poles. Numerous national operations organized by the NKVD in August 1937–November 1938 targeted people of Finnish, Greek, Latvian, Romanian, Bulgarian, Iranian and Afghani descent (Okhotin & Roginsky 1999: 35–74; Kott 2007: 42–54). According to official data, a total of 335,513 people were arrested in the course of the national operations, and 247,157 of those arrested were shot (Werth 2003: 232).

In Karelia alone, the Finnish operations resulted in the arrest of 4,700 individuals of Nordic origin, including 27 former members of Finland's parliament (Takala 1998: 199; List 2016). The Great Terror practically destroyed the Executive Committee of the Communist International (Chase 2001). Among the victims of the Great Terror were the prominent figures of the Nordic communist movement, top politicians and military commanders.[1] Altogether, 694 Finns, 23 Norwegians, and 6 Swedes were arrested in the Murmansk region in 1937–1938, approximately half of the adult population belonging to these nationalities (Mikolyuk 2003: 62–63). A total of 27 Finns were arrested in Uura, the administrative centre of the Finnish national rayon, accused of being members of a fictitious Finnish underground espionage counter-revolutionary organization (Kotljarchuk 2017).[2] Similarly, 22 Swedes were arrested in Gammalsvenskby and accused of being members of a fictitious Swedish underground espionage counter-revolutionary organization (Kotljarchuk 2014a: 132–191). The arrested people

---

[1] Among them were: Allan Wallenius (1890–1942), a Swede from Finland. One of the most prominent leftist intellectuals and Director of the Communist International Library in Moscow. Arrested by the NKVD on 16 February 1938 and sentenced to 5 years in prison. Died in the NKVD prison in Kuybyshev (for more information about him, see Mustelin 1984); Victoria Vilhelmsson (1899–1937), member of the VKP(b), editor-in-chief at the publishing house Foreign Workers in the USSR. Arrested on 27 July 1937 and executed on 15 November 1937; Edvard Gylling (1881–1938), a Swede from Finland, Finnish and Soviet politician, member of the Social Democratic Party of Finland, Associate Professor of statistics at Helsinki University, member of Finland's parliament, head of the Central Bank of Finland (1918), a resident of the Soviet Union since 1920, head of the Karelian autonomy. In 1935–1937 Research Fellow at the Institute of International Economics in Moscow. Executed on 14 June 1938 (see Baron 2007); Valter Bergström (1899–1938), born in Helsinki in a Swedish family. Member of VKP(b) and general-in-chief of the Soviet Marine Air Forces. Executed on 27 July, 1938; Eyolf Mattsson-Ignaeus (1897–1965), a Swede from Åland. Member of VKP(b), commander of *Karjalan jääkäriprikaati* ['Karelian infantry brigade']. Head of Department at Moscow Military Academy. On 1 January 1937 he was convicted to death, but was instead sentenced to 10 years in prison (see Kivalo & Mittler 2000); Peter Åkerman (1888–1938), born in Sweden, member of the Communist Party of Sweden. Head of Archangelsk paper pulp factory. Arrested on 14 December 1937 and executed on 19 February 1938; Erik Tamberg (1893–?), born in Oslo, member of the Communist Party of Norway. Senior Researcher at the state company Karelles. Arrested by the NKVD on 11 October 1937 and sentenced to 10 years imprisonment in the Gulag; Arist Serk (1895–?), born in Finland to a Norwegian family, member of the Communist Party of Finland, senior economist at Kola State Geological-Exploration Company. Arrested by the NKVD on 2 March 1938 and sentenced to 10 years imprisonment in the Gulag.

[2] Rayon (also spelled raion in English) is a type of administrative unite in the Soviet Union such as a part of an oblast.

simply disappeared. In reality, most of them were murdered and their corpses buried in secret places. The executions were decided not by a court, but by a so-called troika—a three-person body made up of the local NKVD chief, the local prosecutor and the local secretary of the Communist Party.

The organisation of Nordic national operations is complicated. Finns were subject to a special Finnish operation (Kostiainen 2000; Golubev & Takala 2014: 121–156; Kotljarchuk 2014b; Kotljarchuk 2017) while small-numbered communities of Soviet Swedes and Norwegians were not the target of national operations. However, the mass-violence against them was designed in the same way as the national operations (Kotljarchuk 2014a; Kotljarchuk 2015). The Sami is an indigenous minority of Russia and yet they were one of the principal targets for the national operations of the Murmansk NKVD (Kotljarchuk 2012). This chapter presents a comparative study of the propaganda hatred campaign in the course of the national operations of the NKVD in the Nordic minority areas. The author discusses the ideas, the aims and the target groups of the state-run propaganda, and the role of the mass media in the preparation, progress and support of mass violence.

Method, Theoretical Frameworks and Aims of the Study

Kristina Lundgren, Birgitta Ney and Torsten Thurén developed a method that was adopted for this study consisting of a set of analytical tools for the investigation of newspapers. First, one must look more carefully at the newspaper in which the article is published: its language, circulation, area of distribution and political complexion. Second, the scholar should note how the article was published, that is, where in the newspaper the editorial board placed the article, the length of the text, primary or reprint publication etc. Third, the researcher should look at images and photographs and their relation to the content, and whether they are an interplay with other items in the newspaper in question. The next step is to study what the article is about, what facts, terms and quotations have been used, and whether it refers to past events. Then one should look at how the article is structured. The publication might be also linguistically analyzed with a focus on the tone of the text, interpretation and the selection of keynote words, the so-called wording. In addition, it is important to study how events have been dramatized and how the dramatic sequence in the text is presented: who is guilty and who are heroes and observers (Lundgren, Ney & Thurén 1999).

Leo Kuper points out that mass violence is not triggered by already existing conditions within a society. Rather, they occur when powerful groups—e.g., politicians and media opinion-makers—decide to define and isolate a specific group of people (Kuper 1982: 40–56). Jacques Sémelin (2007) sees ethnic discrimination as part of a dynamic state structure with, at its core, the matrix of a social imaginaire that, responding to social fears, proposes the need to identify, exclude and, possibly, eliminate an internal enemy. Sémelin's method helps to identify the mechanisms by which mass media propaganda can become a legitimate tool for political action.

The scholars have put forward different points regarding the performance of propaganda in Stalin's Soviet Union from the succesful indoctrination of the population (Kotkin 1997; Bonell 1997) to popular resistance (Davies 1997) and systematic failure (Brandenberger 2011). Some scholars argue for a highly centralized implementation of the national operations, the design and progress of which were planned in detail in Moscow. Other scholars have suggested that the exceptional scale of the mass arrests during the national operations might be explained by the role of local authorities, who turned a well-planned scheme of repressions into "a flight into chaos" (Werth 2003: 216–217).

How was the propaganda hatred campaign organized on the eve, during the progress and in the final stage of the national operations? What ideas, aims and target groups did the propaganda campaign have? Was the campaign orchestrated from Moscow or very much dependent on the initiative of local authorities? What about the results of the state-run propaganda campaigns in 1937–1938? A comparative study of the press in the remote areas of the Soviet Union can bring some light on this issue.

Historians have put forward many explanations for the mass repression of various ethnic groups committed by Stalin's regime. Two approaches are particularly relevant. Most scholars focus on the security dilemma in the border areas, suggesting a need to secure the ethnic integrity of Soviet space against neighbouring capitalistic enemy states. They stress the role of international relations and believe that representatives of the so-called "Western minorities" were killed or deported not because of their ethnicity, but rather because of their connection to countries hostile to the Soviet Union and fear that they might be disloyal to the Bolshevik regime (Werth 2003; Mann 2005: 318–328; Dönninghaus 2011). Other scholars argue that the Soviet terror against minorities was similar to a genocide, based on ethnic criteria (Kostiainen 2000; Norman 2010, Snyder 2010: 92–108). The results of this study may contribute to the discussion about the systematic nature of Stalin's terror and the role of mass propaganda.

Historical Background

Two remote areas in the northern and southern borderlands of the Soviet Union were chosen for this study: the Finnish national rayon (Ru. *Finskiy natsional'nyy rayon*) on the Kola Peninsula and the Swedish national rural council (Ukr. *Shveds'ka natsyonal'na sil'ska rada*) in the Ukrainian steppes. The 1928 regional census counted 2,111 Finns in Murmansk region, making up approximately 7.7 per cent of the region's entire population of 27,229. Like elsewhere in the North Calotte, fishermen and hunters of sea animals coexisted there with reindeer herders and farmers, creating a mix of Scandinavian and Finno-Ugric cultures (Elenius *et al.* 2015: 219–220). The Finnish national rayon was established in 1930. Its administrative centre was Murmansk and later Ura-Guba (Uura in Finnish). Fishermen from Finland and Sweden-Norway founded Ura-Guba in 1864. A Finnish school was opened in the village in 1868 and the Finnish Lutheran church in the village was founded the same year. With a population of 450 people, Uura was the largest settlement of the Finnish national rayon. About 58 per cent (1,297) of the population of the rayon at that time was Finnish. Together with Sami, Norwegians and Swedes, they made up the majority, 72 per cent, of the entire population (*Murmanskiy okrug* 1929: 10–12). The Finnish national rayon was abolished in 1939 and is today a part of Kola District of the Murmansk region, Russia.

Staroshveds'ke (*Gammalsvenskby* in Swedish) was founded in 1782 in the Kherson region, by a group of 965 Swedish fishermen from the island of Dagö. Here, the Swedish islanders were to build a prosperous fishing industry centre. Before the 1917 Revolution, Gammalsvenskby was a small town with a population of about 1,200 people, the administrative centre of the Swedish district and the largest Swedish settlement east of Finland (Malitska 2014: 61–85). By 1926, Swedes made up 4 per cent of the rural population of Beryslav Rayon. A part of the Swedes' Kherson district was inhabited by ethnic Ukrainians, Germans, Russians and Jews (Kotljarchuk 2014a: 46–49). In 1929, the entire Swedish population of Kherson region emigrated to their original homeland. In Sweden, the emigrants were denied a separate settlement and were dispersed throughout the country to undergo "instructtion in the Swedish norms of activities of economic nature and of everyday kind" (Wedin 2007). The colonists who disagreed with this policy (around 300 individuals) returned to the Soviet Union, accompanied by a dozen families of Swedish communists. In 1931, under the auspices of the Communist International, the Swedish Communist Party's kolkhoz was established in

Gammalsvenskby (Kotljarchuk 2014c: 111–149). Today, Gammalsvenskby is called Zmiivka and is located in the Beryslav Rayon, Kherson Oblast, Ukraine.

Soviet Press as the Major Transmitter of State-Run Propaganda

As Peter Kenez point out the Bolsheviks were pathbreakers since they introduced a new approach to politics and a new concept of propaganda (Kenez 1985). The Communist Party attached great weight to the development of local mass media. In 1923, Stalin announced the building of a national-wide network of local press:

> The role of a newspaper, however, is not limited solely to the dissemination of ideas, to political education, and to the enlistment of political allies. A newspaper is not only a collective propagandist and a collective agitator, it is also a collective organizer [...] This network of agents will form the skeleton of precisely the kind of organization we need—one that is sufficiently large to embrace the whole country (Stalin [1923] 1953: 289).

In 1937, more than 8,500 titles of newspapers were published in the Soviet Union, 2,500 of which were in the minority languages. The overall circulation of newspapers was 36.2 million copies and they were available to most of the literate population (Ovsepyan 1999: 127). As a rule, the editor-in-chief was a member of the Party nomenclature and took part in the meetings of Soviet and Party leadership.

The central media are represented in this study by three newspapers: *Pravda*, *Izvestiya* and *Pionerskaya Pravda*. *Pravda* ['Truth'] was a leading Party newspaper—an organ of the Central and Moscow Committee of VKP(b). It was established in 1912 and was issued daily in Russian in the 1930s. By 1937, *Pravda*'s circulation was more than two million copies, distributed throughout the country. *Izvestiya* ['News'] was a leading nationwide official newspaper, published in Russian. It was established in 1917 as the organ of the Supreme Soviet Council and Soviet Central Government. In the early 1930s, its circulation was 1.1 million copies. *Pionerskaya Pravda* ['Pioneer Truth'] was a nationwide newspaper for Soviet youth and the organ of the Central and Moscow Committee of Komsomol and had a circulation of 450,000[3] copies in the early 1930s.

---

[3] The circulation of Soviet newspapers is based on an open report published in 1931, see *Vsya Moskva*. In the mid-1930s the circulation of Soviet newspapers was classified.

The press was a principal mediator between the government and the rural population in the ethnic borderland. In the 1930s, radio was not yet widespread in Kherson and Murmansk regions. With the growth of literacy among the adult population, more and more people were able to read newspapers. Official newspapers were financed both through subscriptions and governmental funding. Such newspapers were subject to a mandatory subscription for officials, Party and Komsomol members. In rural areas, the mandatory subscription to newspapers was incumbent on local *izba-chital'-nya* ['reading rooms']. Being subsidized by the state, the state newspapers were cheap, and they could thus be afforded also by farmers and fishermen. As early as 1925, the newly established reading room in Gammalsvenskby started subscribing to newspapers. The residents of Gammalsvenskby subscribed individually to more than 100 copies of newspapers (Kotljarchuk 2014a: 60). Newspapers were also available through the so-called *doska pechati*—public noticeboards usually located outside local offices.

Three local newspapers were chosen for the present study. *Naddniprians'ka Pravda* ['On-the-Dnepr truth'] is a Ukrainian-language daily established in 1928 as an official organ of Kherson district where the Swedish national rural council was situated. By 1937, the circulation of *Naddniprians'ka Pravda* was 11,000 copies. *Polarnoin kollektivisti/Polyarnyy kollektivist* ['Polar collective worker'] was an organ of the Finnish national rayon. This newspaper was established as a bilingual four-page Finnish-Russian newspaper, which often had parallel texts in these two languages. The newspaper was issued every five days and had a circulation of about 500–600 copies. From January 1938 until July 1940 the newspaper was issued only in Russian. After the deportation of the entire Finnish population from Murmansk region, the publication of the newspaper was stopped on 3 July 1940.

Polyarnaya Pravda ['Polar truth'] was an organ of the Murmansk regional government and VKP(b). This daily was established in 1920 and published in Russian. In 1937 the newspaper had a circulation of 12,000 copies. Starting in 1933, *Polyarnaya Pravda* also had an irregularly appearing page in the Sami language (Osipov, E. U. 1933; Osipov, O. O. 1933). The Russian language in the Murmansk press had a lot of Scandinavian loanwords that was not used by the central media, for example: *buksy* ['pair of trousers,' *bukser* in Norwegian], *rokon* ['overcoat,' *rocken* in Swedish], *bot* ['boat,' *båt* in Scandinavian languages], *snurrevad* ['seine net, drag net,' *snurrevad* in Norwegian and Swedish].

Illustration 6: Leaders of Sveriges kommunistiska parti kolkhoz ['Swedish Communist Party kolkhoz'] on the cover of the Swedish magazine *Vecko-Journalen,* no. 45, 1932. Photo from Gammalsvenskby, Kherson district. Leftmost: Edvin Blom; in the centre: Karl Ture Grääs; rightmost: journalist Alma Braathen.

Eläköön maaliskuun 8:s päivä — Kansainvälinen kommunistinen naistenpäivä!

KAIKKIEN MAIDEN PROLETAARIT, YHTYKÄÄ!   ПРОЛЕТАРИИ ВСЕХ СТРАН, СОЕДИНЯЙТЕСЬ!

Maaliskuun 8 pnä v. 1937.
8 марта 1937 г.
№ 22 (368)

Polarnoin kollektivisti
Полярный коллективист

NKP(b):n POLARNOIN RK:n JA RAJONIN TpK:n ÄÄNENKANNATTAJA.
ОРГАН ПОЛЯРНОГО РК ВКП(б) И РАЙИСПОЛКОМА

Kansainvälisenä kommunistisena naistenpäivänä

Inään, maaliskuun 8 päivä Sovettimaassamme ja koko ilmassa vietetään Kansainvälista kommunistista naistenpäivää. Sovettiliitossa me tämän juhlanä vuonna otamme vastuuden Konstitutsion lialla, Konstitutsion, johon kirjoitettu kansojemme oikeudet, jotka on valloitettu näissä taisteluissa ja työssä suuressa Konstitutsio-cokutissa, jonka on luonut kansan johtaja ja ystävä, nero Josef Vissarionovitsh Stalin, astuu myöskin naistemme vat saavutukset, heidän ensä ja iloinen elämä... aisten suurista oikeuksista uu Konstitutsion pykälä johon on kirjoitettu:

Naiselle annetaan SSTL:ssa at oikeudet kuin miehelle adelliseen, yhteiskunnalliseen ja yhteiskunnallis-poisen elämän kaikilla aloilla, aisten näiden oikeuksien utlamismahdollisuuden turvat yhtenäisen oikeuden iminen niin naiselle kuin hellekin työhön, työpalk-, lepoon, yhteiskunnalli-y vakuutukseen ja sivistyk-, valtion turvaama äidin ja intereisen suojelus, lo antaminen naiselle rasden aikana, säilyttäen työön, synnytyslaitosten, lastemien ja— tarhojen laaja :osto".

akainen nainen maassamme ypeä näistä oikeuksista, silän voi täydellisesti nauttia ä.

eidän maassamme ei ole än tuotannon tai työn alaa, n ei osallistuisi nainen. inen-insinööri, nainen-lennainen- professori, tieteellityön tekijä, tuotantolain johtaja," — ja paljon on , jolla työskentelee nainen naassamme, osoittaen työn nkytteitä.

tinka paljon onkaan kasvamaassamme sankaritareja! Stahanovilaisten Dusja ja Maria Vinogradovain, traktoristien Pasha Angelingan ja Pasha Kovardakin ja monien muiden maamme mainittavien ihmisten nimet tuntee koko maa. Sana nainen— se kaikuu ylpeästi Sovettien maassa!

Kokonaan toisenlaisissa olosuhteissa viettävät naiset Kansainvälistä kommunistista naistenpäivää kapitalistisissa maissa. Kurjuus, työttömyys, nälkä,— kaikki nämä ovat langenneet naisen osalle rajojemme takana.

„Sivistyneessä" Japanissa aina tähän päivään asti säilyy sananlasku: „Jos japanilainen kutojatar katsotaan ihmiseksi, silloin puhelinpylväskin voi kukkia." Ja tuo järjetön sananlasku osaltaan selvittääkin sitä kauheaa asemaa, jossa japanilainen kutojatar on.

Japanissa edelleenkin on voimassa naisten osto ja myynti. Yksistään vuonna 1933 myytiin yli 30.000 16—23 ikävuodista tyttöä.

Tällainen on naisen asema kapitalistisissa maissa.

Vihalla ja kiihtymyksellä on täyttyneet naisten sydämet ristijä-vihollisiaan kohtaan. Laajenee ja kasvaa kansainvälistama fasismia ja sotaa, nälkää ja kurjuutta vastaan. Sankarillisesi Espanjan naiset kulkevat tämän taistelun eturiveissä. Verellään he puolustavat vapautustaan.

Sovettiliiton Konstitutsio kuin majakka valaisee maailman työtätekeville tietä. Se on ohjelmana heidän taisteluissaan vapautensa ja onnensa puolesta.

Maaliskuun 8 päivänä — naisten kansainvälisenä solidaarisuuden päivänä — me loivotamme rajantakaisille sisarillemme pikaista vapautumista kapitalistien orjuudesta ja 'sorrosta.

Eläköön Kansainvälinen kommunistinen naistenpäivä!

Eläköön työtätekevät naiset koko maailmassa!

OLEMME VALMIINA

ätsin kylän naiset osallisaktiivisesti yhteiskunnallityöhön.

nsainvälisen kommunistinaistenpäivän edellä he pat kylään Punaisen ristin kylän, jonka jäseninä on 4 henkilöä.

jestettyän Punaisen ristin ikan, naiset tekevät ahkeilyötä sanitäärimininin

opiskelemaan. He ovat järjestäneet sanitääripiirin, jota ohjaa lääkäripunktin lääkäri tov. Grigorjev. Säännöllisesti joka sunnuntai naiset ja yleensä piirin jäsenet kokoontuvat opiskelemaan. Voimme sanoa, että naiset ovat ymmärtäneet opiskella sanitääritaitoa.

M. ILLE.

Työskennelleen kesällä heinätöissä, hän sai kaikista korkeimman työnkorvauksen. Nyt hän on verkonkorjaus- ja kuto-

HÄNESTÄ VOI OTTAA ESIMERKKIÄ

Kukapa ei tuntisi Paro Anderssenia Läätsin kylässä. Hän on iäkkään puoleinen nainen, jonka kasvoille on raskas työ alkoinaan painanut leimansa.

Paro Anderssen työskentelee kylän klubilla siivoojana. Mutta hänen työnsä ei sisälly ainoastaan tähän. Kollektivisti eivät näe häntä ainoastaan klubilla, Paro osallistuu kolhoosin kaikissa aputöissä. mistöissä. Ollen aina elämäniloinen ja innokas, hän innostaa esimerkillään myöskin toista kolhosnikkanaisia.

Anderssenin taio on kylässä kaikkein pienin talo. Mutta se on samalla kaikkein kulttuurisin asunto.

Parolla on pieni lapsi, mutta se ei estä häntä ottamasta osaa yhteiskunnalliseen työhön. Paro onkin MOPRin jäsen, Punaisen ristin jatsheikan jäsen ja kaikkien kolhoosin ja kylän kokouksien aktiivinen osanottaja.

Paro oli lukutaidoton. Nyt hän lukee ja kirjoittaa vapaasti.

— Minä olen ,vanha, — puhelee hän. — Lukemaan ja kirjoittamaan olen oppinut vasta vanhoilla päivilläni. Ennen minulla ei ollut oikeutta sivistykseen. Opiskelisin enemmänkin, mutta näkö on jo mennyt huonoksi. Mutta nuorison, jonka nuoruuden päivät kuluvat näin ihanaan aikana, on opiskeltava enemmän.

Tov. Anderssen on mainio kollektivistinainen. Hänestä voi ottaa kaikki meidän kylän toiset naiset esimerkkiä.

ILLE.

Illustration 7: Front age of the Finnish-language newspaper *Polarnoin kollektivisti*, official organ of the Finnish national district of the Murmansk region. *Polarnoin kollektivisti*, no. 22, 8 March 1937. Courtesy of the Russian National Library.

1937. New Ideas and New Enemies

The start of the national operations was conceptualized in two main steps. The first concerned the ideological orchestration of the massive ethnic cleansing and the second was the translation of the new ideas to the population. So what kind of ideas did the Soviet leadership formulate in 1937?

At the end of March 1937, *Pravda* and the Central Party Publishing House printed a speech that Stalin gave at the Plenum of the Central Committee of the Communist Party on 3 March 1937 titled "On the errors of Party work and further steps to eliminate the Trotskyite and other hypocrites" (Stalin 1937). The local newspapers reprinted Stalin's speech (Toveri 1937). In the speech, Stalin formulated the idea of a new wave of repressions and selected the target groups. Prior to 1937, the Soviet terror was directed against various social groups (i.e. kulaks, tsarist military officers and priests), but now Stalin warned about the cleansing of the entire state apparatus and Soviet organizations with a special focus on foreign agents. According to the dictator "the sabotage and subversive spy work of agents of foreign states have beset the Soviet state and our organisations from top to bottom" (Stalin 1937). In 1937, the media dictionary of Soviet newspeak was enriched by a number of Stalin's neologisms (Pöppel 2007). Stalin's formula of *kapitalisticheskoe okruzhenie* ['capitalist encirclement'] resulted in a dramatic turn in both foreign and domestic politics. For the first time, Stalin did not make any exceptions and the Nordic countries entered the list of primary Soviet enemies. The idea of international solidarity with the global working class was abandoned in favour of isolation and distrust of all foreigners. Stalin paid special attention to Scandinavia. Discussing a base for a spy network in the Soviet Union, the leader used Norway as an example and referred to Nordic communists as potential spies:

> Take, for example, a group of the shuffler Scheflo in Norway, who gave shelter to the chief spy Trotsky and helped him play mean tricks on the Soviet Union. Doesn't it look like a reserve team. Who can deny that this counter-revolutionary group will henceforth continue to provide its services to Trotskyite spies and saboteurs? (Stalin 1937)[4]

Stalin's concept of *vykorchevyvanie* ['uprooting'] that was mentioned several times in his March speech is of interest. The technical meaning of *uprooting* is to remove the stumps and roots of trees and shrubs when clearing an area

---

[4] Olav Scheflo (1883–1943) was the founder of the Communist Party of Norway. He supported Leon Trotsky during Trotsky's stay in Norway in 1935–1936.

in preparation for road construction works. The political meaning of the term signified a course towards the complete extermination of arrested people. In his address to the deputies of the Supreme Soviet of the Soviet Union, Stalin repeated this idea, which was enthusiastically supported by the political elite:

> We are now rich and therefore we have become an object of attention for avaricious countries and fascist states. What counter-weapon do we have? To uproot their agents, to uproot them—this is our counter-weapon. Tumultuous applause, Hurrah! Long live Comrade Stalin! (Khaustov, Naumov & Plotnikova [eds.] 2004: 499)

The title of Stalin's speech contains the word "elimination" that is reminiscent of the concept of "elimination of the kulaks as a class," which in the early 1930s was the ground for deportations of well-to-do farmers. Stalin's March speech also contains a new definition of the enemies of the Soviet regime that differed from previous conceptions of the class enemy: *internal and external enemies, enemies of the Soviet Union* and finally, *enemies of the people*. The creative efforts of Stalin were here focused on finding a better ideological alternative to the concept of *class enemy*. Of all of Stalin's alternative terms, the concept of *vragi naroda* ['enemies of the people'] was the most widely spread by Soviet propaganda during the Great Terror. This unclear term was included already in the wording of the 1936 Constitution (article 131). Unlike the concept of *class enemy*, a broader term like *enemies of the people* enabled the arrest of any individual, regardless of class origin and Party and Komsomol membership. The March speech also launched the start of a spy mania campaign:

> To take the necessary measures to ensure that our comrades, party and non-party Bolsheviks, know the goals and objectives of the practice and techniques of subversive work, of sabotage and of espionage by foreign agents. (Stalin 1937)

Fulfilling the directive of Stalin, the Soviet intelligence prepared propagandist material on mass espionage for journalists (Lubyanka 2004: 134–135). Dozens of booklets and thousands of articles were published in 1937–1938 describing destructive espionage activities by foreign agents against the Soviet Union. The booklets addressed different groups in society: Party and Soviet officials, NKVD officers, kolkhoz leaders and children (*O metodakh i priemakh* 1937; Zakovskiy 1937a; *Shpionam i izmennikam* 1937; *Shpionazh i razvedka* 1937; *Shpiguny i diversanti* 1937; Zil'ver 1938). In 1937, the Central

Party Publishing House in Moscow published in 300,000 copies the anthology *On the Methods and Techniques of Foreign Intelligence Agencies and their Trotskyite-Bukharin Agents*. The book consists of 15 chapters written by leading experts: the NKVD, military intelligence officers, journalists and lawyers. Comparing the content of this publication with that of the Kherson and Murmansk newspapers, we can conclude that at least seven chapters from the anthology were reprinted in the local Murmansk and Kherson press (Kolesnik 1937; Sokolov 1937; Rubin & Serebrov 1937a; Rubin & Serebrov 1937b; Rubin & Serebrov 1937c; Kandidov 1938; Uranov 1937a; Uranov 1937b; Zakovskiy 1937c; Zakovskiy 1937d; Zakovskij 1937a; Zakovskij 1937b).

Stalin's idea about a massive espionage activity suggested a wide network of domestic agents. Moscow journalists Nikolay Rubin and Yakov Serebrov were the first to profusely apply Stalin's ideas for propaganda tasks. In the summer of 1937 the Central Party Publishing House printed a book entitled *On the Sabotage Activity of Fascist Intelligence Services and the Task of Fighting it* (Rubin & Serebrov 1937a). On 29 and 30 July, *Pravda* published an abridged version of the book and a few days later, Kherson and Murmansk newspapers reprinted *Pravda*'s article (Rubin & Serebrov 1937b; Rubin & Serebrov 1937c). Rubin and Serebrov presented new categories of people's enemies: the double dealers—communists of foreign origin and Soviet citizens who have relatives abroad.

The propaganda campaign aimed to reach all social groups, including children. In 1938, the Central Committee of VLKSM printed 50,000 copies of a book titled *Prick up your Ears* written by Lev Zil'ver (1938). The aim of the book was to educate Soviet children about the massive espionage activity in the Soviet Union and to inform them of how they could help the NKVD to catch underground agents. The author presented thirteen short novels about agents of capitalistic states unmasked by children. Under the heading "Adults and children alike can help the NKVD" *Pionerskaya Pravda* published a series of articles dedicated to the 20th anniversary of the NKVD, calling on children to actively cooperate with the secret police (Varmuzh 1937). Young assistants of security officers in pre-border kolkhozes were looking for and pointing out foreign intelligence agents' hideouts (Vanya i Anya 1937). Another publication told a story of the second-grade schoolboy Leva who eavesdropped on all the neighbours in the communal apartment and gave valuable information to the NKVD, thus exposing spies and wreckers (Tazin 1937). As Oleg Khlevnyuk points out, hundreds of similar stories were produced which convinced both old and young that the country really was full of spies (Khlevnyuk 1992: 170).

Nordic Nations and Soviet Propaganda

According to the 1926 Soviet census, there were 150,838 Finns (including Izhorians), 2,495 Swedes and 245 Norwegians in the country.[5] In Soviet imaginaire, Finland was a principal enemy of the socialist state. Nevertheless, Soviet propaganda described the people of Finland as being divided into two opposing groups: working class people and the so-called *Belofinny* ['White Finns'], a reactionist part of society hostile to socialism and separatist-minded towards Russia. In 1937, this image has changed dramatically and all emigrants from Finland, as well as Russian Finns, began to be considered by the media as potential enemies. In its instructions to the NKVD, the Politwburo emphasised that not only Finnish citizens but also Russian Finns were to be targeted in the mass operations against Finns.[6] In the fall of 1937 the press reported about how hundreds of Finnish agents had been uncovered in Russia. On 14 September 1937, the special correspondent of *Pravda* in Karelia, Boris Zolotov, informed the readers that the regional authorities in Karelia were totally infiltrated by Finnish agents and that it was "only due to the NKVD that the Finnish espionage network was successfully exposed" (Zolotov 1937b). Four days before, *Pravda* had published a headline article about the subversive activity of Finland's agents at the Kondopoga paper mill (Zolotov 1937a).

Neighbouring Sweden and Norway (until 1905 Sweden-Norway) were not on the list of the primary enemies of the Soviet Union. Sweden and Norway were neutral and did not have a common borderline with the Soviet Union. For the Kremlin leadership, it was significant that, unlike their Finnish counterpart, the communist parties in Sweden and in Norway were legal political parties. The Soviet Union had stable diplomatic, economic, and political relations with Sweden and Norway, and the Kremlin described the relationship with these countries as correct (Ken, Rupasov & Samuelson

---

[5] Calculated from the 1926 All-Soviet census; http://demoscope.ru; access date 1 October 2016.
[6] "О продлении до 15 апреля 1938 года операций по разгрому шпионско-диверсионных контингентов из поляков, латышей, немцев, эстонцев, финн, греков, иранцев, харбинцев, китайцев и румын, как иностранных граждан, так и советских подданных, согласно существующих приказов НКВД СССР," 31.01.1938. Russian State Archive of Social-Political History (RGASPI), fond 17, opis 166, delo 585, l. 27.

2005: 33–34; Chubar'yan & Riste [eds.] 1997: no. 191). However, the spiral of the Great Terror changed this positive image and from 1937, numerous articles were published depicting Norway and Sweden as main bases of espionage against the Soviet Union (Kotljarchuk 2014c: 12–13). Leonid Zakovskiy, the NKVD-chief for the Leningrad Oblast and Murmansk district, published a book on the methods of foreign intelligence services in which he presented the Scandinavian countries as a base for foreign espionage against the Soviet Union (Zakovskiy 1937a: 3).[7] *Journal de Moscou*—the organ of the Soviet Foreign Office printed an article about Sweden in which it was argued that Stockholm had become the main base of the German Gestapo (Hôtes inopportuns 1937). The local press elaborated on such ideas. *Polyarnaya Pravda*, in a special article about Norway, informed their readers that the country had become "awash with spies—agents of German fascism" (Norvegiya 1937).

Izvestiya published an article written by Professor Yevgeny Tarle with the remarkable title "Lessons on History." This renowned Soviet historian contributed to the injection of anti-Swedish sentiments. Released in 1937 from the Gulag, he was subsequently treated kindly by Stalin and published a number of patriotic anti-Western works. Tarle compared the 1938 Munich Agreement to a coalition of states hostile to Russia, created by Sweden in the early eighteenth century (Tarle 1938). *Pionerskaya Pravda* published an article titled "Exposing the conspiracy" about the arrest of a spy at the door to a Norwegian consulate (Razoblachennye zagovory 1937). Soviet propaganda became a matter of great concern for the Swedish embassy in Moscow which realised that the Kremlin was deliberately building a negative image of Sweden.[8] Joseph Davies, the U.S. ambassador to Moscow in 1936–1938 noted that the notion of an "active internal espionage," which had not been used by Soviet propaganda prior to 1937, suddenly appeared on the eve of the Great Terror. The American diplomat described these techniques as having been directly borrowed from Nazi Germany (Davies 1941: 273).

---

[7] Leonid Zakovskiy (aka Henriks Stubis, 1894–1938) was a Latvian Bolshevik, organizer of the Great Terror in the Murmansk region and Deputy Commissar of the NKVD of the Soviet Union. He was arrested on 29 August 1938 and has never been rehabilitated.

[8] "Med artikel över Sverige." Eric Gyllenstierna to Rickard Sandler, 14 October 1937. RA (National Archives of Sweden), Utrikesdepartementet, HP 514, vol. 61.

Spies in the Tundra and in the Steppes

The local media elaborated on Stalin's ideas about total espionage. In 1937, Kherson and Murmansk newspapers reported constantly on a sharp intensification of espionage activities in the entire world and in the deep Soviet hinterland (Buty pil'nymi 1937; Shpionskaya organizatsiya 1937; Derzkaya vykhodka 1937; Zorko okhranyat' 1937; Poymali shpiona 1937; Kolhospniki zatrimali shpiguna 1937; Ribalki dopomogli zatrimati shpiguna 1937; Abuzov 1937a; Shakhnovich 1937; Kandidov 1938).

On 11 July 1937, the chief of the secret political department of the NKVD for the Leningrad Oblast and Murmansk district, Petr Korkin, published an article in *Leningradskaya Pravda* with the remarkable title "On the subversive activities of foreign intelligence services in the rural area." Korkin claimed that in recent time the remote kolkhozes had become an active field for foreign espionage activity:

> Naive people believe that we have to deal with the capitalist encirclement [Stalin's term] only on the borders of the Soviet Union, at frontier points or, finally, in large industrial centers and big cities. Meanwhile the capitalist encirclement, as shown by numerous facts, sends its spies to the most remote areas, small settlements, villages and kolkhozes of our country. (*Leningradskiy martirolog* 1995: ill. 11)

In order to enhance the effect of the breaking news, many such publications were illustrated with propagandist posters. In the article "Crisis of foreign bourgeoisie intelligence services," *Polarnoin kollektivisti* reprinted a poster from the central newspaper *Komsomolskaya Pravda* made by Vasiliy Fomichev. The poster "K nogtiu" ['Crush under a nail'] shows a hand of the NKVD policeman that crushes a foreign spy under his nail (Krizis inostrannykh 1937). On 2 August 1937 *Polyarnaya Pravda* reprinted on its front page the poster "Ezhovye rukavitsy" ['Yezhov's work gloves'] from *Izvestiya*, designed by Boris Efimov. The poster, which became an iconic image of the Great Terror, has a double sense in Russian: on the one hand it shows the NKVD-chief Nikolay Yezhov in gauntlet gloves, and on the other *ezhovye rukavitsy* means 'hedgehog gloves' in Russian.

The publications emphasized that the NKVD was facing not just the activities of individual spies, but also extensive espionage networks covering numerous regions. *Polyarnaya Pravda*, referring to Stalin's March speech, stressed that "according to Stalin and Marxist thinking the capitalist states now have to send twice or thrice as many enemies, spies, moonbeams and murderers to Soviet hinterland as before" (Petrov 1937). Instilment of suspicion was combined with detective stories with a touch of pseudoscientific terminology. *Polyarnaya Pravda* told its readers that in Khabarovsk, Japanese agents hold the phone cord to Japan in order to report the results of espionage activity (Derzkaya vykhodka 1937). At the end of July 1937, both *Polyarnaya Pravda* and *Naddniprians'ka Pravda* reprinted an article from *Izvestiya*, "Parcels of diversionists," written by the well-known journalist Abram Lyass. The first story was about a plant selection breeder who received a parcel from Japan containing a Japanese terry cherry seedling which had been wilfully infected with pest, resulting in the ruining of the whole orchard. The next plot was about an American who "sent to our country cotton seeds, infected with pink worm" (Lyass 1937a; Lyass 1937b). The journalists invented simple stories so that everyone residing in the countryside could easily put himself in the shoes of the characters described. In August 1937, Murmansk and Kherson newspapers reprinted one more article from *Izvestiya*, this time about some kolkhoz farmers who had caught a spy (Poymali shpiona 1937; Kolhospniki zatrimali shpiguna 1937). The non-specific character of such stories (non-named persons, non-concrete geographical places and foreign countries) and the fact that they were based on information that was impossible to verify, made it possible to manipulate public opinion. Additionally, in this way the local press warned people that the next target of mass arrests could be their home area.

In 1937, the local press developed a new propagandist genre. The idea was to reprint in a series of articles booklets about foreign espionage activity written by the country's leading experts. Thus, in a series of fourteen articles, *Polyarnaya Pravda* reprinted in June 1937 the book *Intelligence and Counter-intelligence* from *Pravda*. A Soviet edition of the book *Spy and Counter-Spy*, written by the American journalist Richard Wilmer Rowan (Rowan 1928), was published in 1937 by the Central Social-Economic Publishing House in Moscow in 350,000 copies (Rowan 1937). In July 1937 *Naddniprians'ka Pravda* translated into Ukrainian and edited the brochure "Some methods of subversive activity of Trotskyite and fascist spies" written by Andrey Vyshinsky, the Prosecutor General of the Soviet Union (Sokolov 1937). Before that, Vyshinsky's pamphlet was published by the Central Party Publishing House in no less than 500,000 copies (Vyshinsky 1937).

The local press adopted the plots of the central publications. The Kherson newspapers focused on German spies (Germans were the largest minority group in the region) and the Murmansk press tells stories about the activity of the Finnish intelligence service. In September 1937, *Naddniprians'ka*

Pravda translated into Ukrainian and published the booklet *Gestapo* written by Nikolay Abuzov (Abuzov 1937a). The publication was a reprint of *Pravda*'s edition of the book (Abuzov 1937b). The booklet was published in 1937 in Moscow in four editions. The first was printed by the Central Party Publishing House in 300,000 copies (Abuzov 1937c); the second in 400,000 copies by the same publishing house (Abuzov 1937d), the third by the Central Socio-Economic Publishing House in 200,000 copies (Abuzov 1937e) and finally the fourth in 100,000 copies in German by the Publishing House of the Association of the Foreign Workers (Abuzov 1937f). Thus, the total circulation of Abusov's pamphlet exceeded 2 million copies. The reprints of such publications by local press had two principal purposes, to convince the local population that extensive espionage activities were going on throughout the country and to instruct provincial NKVD policemen how to design cases against internal agents (Kotljarchuk 2014a: 143).

In 1937, the Central Party Publishing House printed 300,000 copies of an anthology on foreign espionage in the Soviet Union. Two chapters were written by Leonid Zakovskiy (*O metodakh i priemakh* 1937). Zakovskiy's pamphlet was also published in 300,000 copies in a separate edition (Zakovskiy 1937a). In 1937, Zakovskiy presented his booklet at the Leningrad Party Conference, which was attended by the leadership of Murmansk region (Zakovskiy 1937b). *Polyarnaya Pravda* reprinted Zakovskiy's pamphlet in July–September 1937. In the first chapter with the remarkable title "Spies, saboteurs and wreckers must be totally destroyed," Zakovskiy quoted Stalin's March speech and argued three main points: First, the Finnish Intelligence service, together with the German General Staff, had started to build an extensive underground network in the Murmansk area as early as during the First World War. Second, Finnish agents had been recruited both among those members of the Communist Party of Finland who had been exiled to the Soviet Union, and from the Finnish secretariat of the Communist International. Finally, Zakovskiy highlighted that in recent times "a foreign consulate" had started to recruit agents among local people in the remote areas of the Murmansk and Leningrad regions. The ethnicity of ordinary agents was not mentioned, but certain geographical names created the desired effect. Zakovskiy told a story about a spy who came to Murmansk from Ozerko—the Finnish village on the Rybachiy Peninsula. The next story was about the wreckers in Kandalaksha (Kantalahti in Finnish), a town on the White See with a Finnish minority (Zakovskiy 1937c). *Polarnoin kollektivisti* translated Zakovskiy's pamphlet into Finnish and published it during August–November 1937 in a series of articles (Zakovskij 1937a;

Zakovskij 1937b). Thus, in the midst of the Great Terror, the NKVD sent a clear signal to potential victims, officials and bystanders about the nature of the ongoing mass arrests.

It was the media that built a propaganda bridge between foreign and domestic agents. The press presented officials in minority areas as agents of foreign intelligence services. But what were spies doing in kolkhozes? Zakovskiy gave an answer to this question: their task was to disorganise the kolkhoz system *ab intra*. Local journalists developed the NKVD-chief's conception. *Polyarnaya Pravda* explained the reasons for the on-going arrests of officials in Finnish national rayons as follows:

> The enemies of the people, hangdog bourgeois nationalists, occupied the leading positions in the rayon and, following the orders of their fascist masters, started to disorganise the kolkhoz system and to destroy the Navy. (Antonov 1937)

In 1937, *Polarnoin kollektivisti* had a special column on the activity of "bourgeois nationalists" and nationalistic public moods in the Finnish rayon. The articles were published both in Finnish and in Russian (Eräs 1937a; Eräs 1937b; Eräs 1937c; Huonon Kasvatustyön 1937; Vykorchevat' ostatki vrediteley 1937; O mestnom natsionalisme 1937; Gore-rukovoditel' 1937; Natsionalnye nastroeniya 1937; Bystree likvidirovat' ostatki 1937; Razgromit' burzhuaznykh natsionalistov 1937). These publications illustrate a dramatic turn in the Soviet policy, described by Stephen Kotkin as "a strategic shift from the task of building of socialism to that of defending socialism" (Kotkin 1997: 357).

The newspapers reported on numerous meetings at which the population enthusiastically supported the mass arrests. For example, *Polyarnaya Pravda* reported about the meeting of the fishermen of the Finnish kolkhoz Tarmo in Ura-Guba at which they "fully supported" the execution of German spies in Moscow. The local Finns promised "to follow the instructions of Comrade Stalin on the capitalist encirclement and from child to old man jealously guard the borderland and unmask the subversive activity of the enemies" (Zorko okhranyat' 1937). At a meeting in Toros, Kola-Norwegians accepted the resolution "On the uprooting of the rest of the wreckers" (Vykorchevat' ostatki vreditelei 1937). In fact, such supposedly spontaneous meetings were organized by the authorities and attendance was compulsory. It was necessary for the Soviet totalitarian regime to obtain the formal support of the ordinary people. Agitation meetings was a propaganda tool that made the majority of society approve the verdict of the NKVD. In the course of such meetings, the participants seemed to have a sense of involvement in what was going on, a feeling of mutual responsibility was created and strangers came to evoke a general fear of repression.

1938. The Abolishment of Native Schools and Propaganda Campaign

Terry Martin drew attention to the connection between the Great Terror and the elimination of the system of native schools and the expansion of the Russian language in education (Martin 2001: 422–423). According to the Soviet plan of *korenizatsiya* ['indigenization'], the nationalities policy, the ethnic borderlands should prioritize native schools in order to promote the ideas of socialism and to nurture a local Party and Komsomol elite. The authorities implied that schooling in their mother tongue would make it easier to involve the young generations of the rural ethnic minorities in the process of socialist construction. Ensuring minority rights meant the creation or development of native pedagogical cadres, schools, textbooks and native-language media. Solving these problems demanded great human and material resources, but the Bolsheviks relied on the reciprocal loyalty of the minorities to the new regime.

Karl Marx' idea of world revolution played an important role in Lenin's nationalities policy. In this regard, Karelia, the Finnish national rayon on the Kola Peninsula and the Swedish village in Ukraine were seen as the "Piedmont of Red Scandinavia" (Martin 2001: 51–52). The Swedish colonists were encouraged to learn modern Swedish, the language of the communist party of Sweden, rather than the archaic native dialect. The Party leadership of the Murmansk district counted on the development of the Finnish literary language and the Kola Sami had been given textbooks in the Latin script, not Cyrillic as before 1917. This policy changed when in the midst of the national operations the regime initiated a radical elimination of native schools. On 24 January 1938 the Central Committee of VKP(b) adopted a resolution "On the reorganization of native schools" in which it was stated that:

> The special inspection found that enemies of people acting in regional Commissariats for Education forced through the creation of separate native schools; German, Finnish, Polish, Latvian, Estonian, Ingrian, Vepsian and others, turning them into centres of bourgeois nationalist and anti–Soviet influence on schoolchildren. (Gatagova [ed.] 2009: 342–343)

The Politburo formed a special commission on this issue represented by Andrey Zhdanov, Andrey Andreev, Nikolay Bulganin and Petr Tyurkin. Native schools were to be reorganized into ordinary schools of the conventional type. The reorganization was to be started immediately and completed in a very short time, by 1 September 1938. Altogether 237 Finnish schools were closed in Russia, as well as one Swedish school in Ukraine. The Finnish Pedagogical College in Leningrad that educated teachers for Finnish schools in Russia closed. The authorities also dissolved the Sami Faculty at the Murmansk Pedagogical College.

The radical elimination of native schools needed a new propagandist vocabulary. The establishment of native schools used to be described as an impressive achievement within the framework of Lenin's nationalities policy. In 1938, however, the central media began to present Lenin's heritage as a subversive activity by bourgeois nationalists. On the first day of the academic year, *Izvestiya* published the headline "New school year" in which the government explained the reasons for the radical school reform:

> Enemies of the people established native schools in which they sabotaged the teaching of the Russian language. Their aim was to separate the fraternal ethnic minorities of the Soviet Union from the Great Russian nation. Now it is time for the Soviet teaching staff to eradicate the results of this sabotage work. (Novyy uchebnyy god 1938)

In the different regions, the local authorities focused on a specific minority. In the Murmansk region it was the Finns. In Ukraine the authorities paid particular attention to Polish, German and Swedish schools. In April 1938, the Politburo of the Communist Party of Ukraine published a regional resolution on the elimination of native schools. The aggressive wording left no room for discussion:

> The special inspection found that the people's enemies—Trotskyites, Bukharinites and bourgeois nationalists, who had operated in the Ukrainian Commissariat for Education, forced through the creation of separate national German, Polish, and Czech, Swedish, Greek and other schools, turning them into centres of bourgeois nationalist and anti-Soviet influence on schoolchildren [...] Based on the decision of the Central Committee of VKP(B), the Politburo of the Communist Party of Ukraine considers the existence of special national schools inexpedient and harmful. (*Nimtsi v Ukrainy* 1994: 100)

4 - PROPAGANDA OF HATRED AND THE GREAT TERROR

In his speech at the XIV Congress of the Ukrainian Communists in June 1938, the leader of the republic, Nikita Khrushchev stressed that:

> The agents of the western intelligence services, as well as the Ukrainian nationalists, imposed in Ukraine so-called national schools. In most of the cases, under the guise of national Polish, German, Swedish and other schools, the enemies created a nest for carrying-out counter revolutionary work. (Efimenko 2001: 47)

Murmansk journalists argued in similar way. Nikolay Ivanov, the deputy editor-in-chief of *Polarnoin kollektivisti* explained that:

> It was the people's enemies—nationalists Peterson, Lahdenperä and Salo—who implemented the Finnization of our rayon, claiming that everything must be in Finnish, despite the fact that only 20 per cent of the population of the Murmansk are Finns. They fought hard against the Russian language, tried to preserve the isolation of the Finnish population and despised everything Russian, that is, the Soviet [sic!]. Their politics achieved some success and we now have Finns living in the Soviet Union who do not know the Russian language and do not want to study it. Our young people who graduate from the seven-year [Finnish] school do not speak Russian at all. As a result, these people's enemies have built on the Kola Peninsula a Chinese wall between the Finnish and Russian nations. (Ivanov 1938)

The NKVD had already arrested the Finnish officials mentioned by Ivanov.[9] The local opinion-makers continued to brainwash the readers into believing that the elimination of Finnish schools and the Russification were for the good of the Finnish population:

> The Finnish language does not allow our Finns to grow culturally together with all the Soviet people and take part in the development of the socialist culture. On the contrary, it paves the way for the development of a bourgeois

---

[9] Karl Peterson (1890–1938) was born in Helsinki in a Swedish family. He was deputy head of the State Fishing Company Murmanryba. Arrested by the NKVD on 7 September 1937 and shot 18 January 1938 in Leningrad. Ejnar Lahdenperä (1898–1937), head of the Finnish national rayon, was born in Ura-Guba in a family of Finnish colonists. In 1932 he graduated from Lenin Party School in Leningrad. In September 1937 he was accused by the secretary of Murmansk Committee of VKP(b) Ermil Babachenko of being "a leader of the underground Finnish nationalist counter-revolutionary organization." Removed from his position, he committed suicide in September 1937. Johannes Salo (1900–1938), head of the Finnish kolkhoz Herätys and a member of the VKP (b), was born in Terioki. He was arrested by the Murmansk NKVD on 5 August, 1937 and shot on 8 January 1938 in Leningrad.

culture in the spirit of nationalism. Ignorance of the Russian language puts Finns below Russians. Finnish literature in the Soviet Union is extremely poor, and lack of a knowledge of the Russian language results in a loss of all perspectives. Universities work in Russian. Therefore, the resolution [On the reorganization of native schools] of the Party and the government is timely and politically correct. The Russian language is the language of Lenin and Stalin, the language of Revolution that opens a wide road for our youth. (Ivanov 1938)

In Ukraine the Russification of native schools was explained in similar way:

The enemies made it so that the teaching in many schools of Ukraine is in German, Polish and other languages, but not in Russian. Now; however, everybody has to learn Russian in order to fight under the banner of Lenin and Stalin for the complete victory of Communism.[10]

Thus, for the first time in history, the Russian language was proclaimed to be the only true Soviet language. Simultaneously with the closing of the national schools, Russian became a compulsory subject throughout the Soviet Union. Stalin initiated this measure personally (Efimenko 2001: 43). The dictator explained the need for non-Russian youth to study Russian by stating that Red Army soldiers had to be able to understand perfectly orders given in Russian (Gatagova [ed.] 2009: 298–299). On 17 January 1938, the Finnish edition of *Polarnoin kollektivisti* was discontinued and the Finnish title disappeared from the front page flag. The explanation was Kafkaesque:

The Finnish-language edition of our newspaper does not meet the demands of the local Finnish population [sic!]. In addition to the absence of control over publications in the Finnish language, the quality of the articles was very low. Therefore the newspaper was totally useless. (Ivanov 1938)

In fact, the Finnish-language press in the Soviet Union was totally eliminated by the authorities in the aftermath of the Great Terror. In 1937, the Leningrad authorities closed down the Finnish-language newspapers *Vapaus*, *Nuori Kaarti* and *Kipinä* (Smirnova 2006: 37–46), calling them "nests of spies and bourgeois nationalists." The leading Finnish newspaper of Karelia, *Punainen Karjala*, was also abolished in 1937. *Polarnoin kollektivisti* was actually the

---

[10] "Språkfrågan i Sovjetunionen och dess politiska bakgrund," Nils Lindh till Hans Excellens Herr Ministern för Utrikes Ärenden Rickard Sandler, den 12 juli 1938. Kungl. Utrikesdepartementet. Avdelning HP 514. Grupp 1. Mål: Er. Politisk allmänt Ryssland. Volym LXII 1938. RA, Riksarkivet ['National Archives of Sweden'].

last Finnish-language newspaper in the interwar Soviet Union. Alongside the abolishment of the newspaper, the NKVD also eliminated its editorial board.[11]

In February 1938 *Polyarnyy kollektivist* published an address of the Murmansk authorities, entitled "To all Finnish workers in the Polar rayon" in which the great benefits of the school reform was once again explained again to the Finns (Ko vsem trudyashchimsya finnam 1938). In reality, the changeover to teaching in a non-mother tongue was accompanied by a stigmatization of native cultures and psychological stress for non-Slavic schoolchildren (Kotljarchuk 2014a: 188–190). In order to obtain formal support for the russification campaign, the authorities organized a meeting in Ura-Guba where the Finns had approved with a solid vote the abolishment of native schools (Miting v Ura-Guba 1938).

The radical shift of Soviet school policy did not go unnoticed in Scandinavia. In July 1938, the Swedish press attaché in Moscow Nils Lindh sent Minister of Foreign Affairs Rickard Sandler the note "The language issue in the Soviet Union and its political background." In particular, the diplomat wrote that the decision to introduce Russian in native schools was, beyond a shadow of a doubt, made in Moscow. He put emphasis on the fact that the radical school reform was connected with a strengthening of Moscow's control over the national autonomies, in which "the issue of the school language is used as a political weapon."[12]

Conclusion

Media propaganda played a significant role in the conceptualization and support of the national operations of the NKVD, as well as in the elimination of native schools. Through propaganda, the minority population and local

---

[11] The editor-in-chief Vilhelm Kivelä (born in 1900 in Belokamenka, Murmansk region) was arrested by the NKVD on 13 September 1937 and sentenced to 10 years in prison. Editor Rickard Hiarkinen (born in 1914 in Vichana, Murmansk region) was arrested by the NKVD on 9 August 1937 and executed on 20 December 1937 in Leningrad. Typographer Rickard Birget (born in 1916 in Ara-Guba, Murmansk rgion) was arrested by the NKVD on 9 August, 1937 and executed on 20 December 1937 in Leningrad. Journalist Verner Ranta (born in 1912 in Rosliakovo, Murmansk region) was arrested by the NKVD 23 February 1938 and sentenced to 10 years in prison. He died in the Gulag.

[12] "Språkfrågan i Sovjetunionen och dess politiska bakgrund," Nils Lindh till Hans Excellens Herr Ministern för Utrikes Ärenden Rickard Sandler, den 12 juli 1938. Kungl. Utrikesdepartementet. Avdelning HP 514. Grupp 1. Mål: Er. Politisk allmänt Ryssland. Volym LXII 1938. RA, Riksarkivet ['National Archives of Sweden'].

authorities were prepared for the subsequent mass violence. On the one hand, the national operations were secret; their dates, progress, concrete results, names of arrested people were not reported. On the other, it was not possible to hide mass arrests in a rural ethnic borderland, and the exact number of arrested people became known the next day. Therefore it was necessary for the state to explain what was going on in order to calm bystanders and to inform local village administrations. Many articles placed special emphasis on information about meetings at which ordinary people had unanimously supported the destruction of foreign agents. In the course of such meetings, the participants seemed to feel a sense of involvement in what was going on, a feeling of mutual responsibility was created and strangers came to evoke a general fear of repression. The state-run propaganda support for the national operations was primarily aimed at:

- creating a negative image of the risk group;
- creating an atmosphere of uncertainty, fear and suspicion in the native borderland;
- redistributing universal fear to a certain ethnic group;
- neutralizing bystanders to make them behave mechanically, co-operate passively with the government and exhibit non-resistance to mass violence;
- introducing specific explanations for the reasons of mass arrests;
- informing local village authorities about subsequent mass arrests;
- appraising denunciations and collaboration with the secret police;
- serving as a source of information helping local NKVD officers to develop the design of the national operations.

The study confirms the thesis that the propaganda hatred campaign in the local press was orchestrated from Moscow and was systematic in nature. It started simultaneously in the Kherson and Murmansk regions on the eve of the national operations and finished in December 1938 after the end of the NKVD mass operations. A cross-analysis of media publications shows that the topic of foreign and domestic agents and espionage activity became a central issue for the local press precisely during the Great Terror. The official pamphlets and publications of the central media were principal frameworks for the local media. The newspapers reprinted *en masse* publications of the central media. Sometimes, the plot of some publications was adapted to local circumstances. However, the ideology of internationalism was never completely rejected and in 1937 the press did not accuse entire minorities of treason. The ethnic cleansing of Finnish and Swedish rural communities proceeded without any protests on the part of the victims and their families. The bystanders, local secret informants and village officials, actively collaborated with the NKVD (Kotljarchuk 2014a: 132–191). The elimination of native schools also ensured that there were no protests from the local population. This means that the propaganda support for the state-run mass violence reached its goal. The Soviet propaganda campaign during the national operations of the NKVD is an early example of what we call today *fake news*—creating a reality out of nothing.

References

Archives

RA. Riksarkivet ['National Archives of Sweden'], Stockholm, Sweden.

RGASPI. Российский Государственный Архив Социально-Политической Истории ['Russian state archive of social and political history'], Moscow, Russia.

Literature

Abuzov, N. (1937a). Абузов, Н. "Підступні методи підривної діяльністі агентури Гестапо в СРСР" ['Underground methods of the subversives activity of Gestapo agents in the USSR'], *Naddniprians'ka Pravda* 24 September.

Abuzov, N. (1937b). Абузов, Н. "Гестапо" ['Gestapo'], *Pravda* 16 and 17 September.

Abuzov, N. (1937c). Абузов, Н. *Гестапо* ['Gestapo'], Moscow: Partizdat.

Abuzov, N. (1937d). Абузов, Н. *Гестапо* ['Gestapo'], Moscow: Partizdat.

Abuzov, N. (1937e). Абузов, Н. *Гестапо* ['Gestapo'], Moscow: Sotsekgiz.

Abuzov, N. (1937f). *Die Gestapo*, Moscow: Verlagsgenossenschaft Ausländischer Arbeiter in der Sowjetunion.

Antonov, P. P. (1937). Антонов, П. П. "Ура-Губа" ['Ura-Guba'], *Polyarnaya Pravda* 2 October.

Baron, N. (2007). *Soviet Karelia. Politics, Planning and Terror in Stalin's Russia, 1920–1939*, London: Routledge.

Bonnell, V. E. (1997). *Iconography of Power. Soviet Political Posters under Lenin and Stalin*, Berkeley: University of California Press.

Brandenberger, D. (2011). *Propaganda State in Crisis. Soviet Ideology, Indoctrination, and Terror under Stalin, 1927–1941*, New Haven: Yale University Press.

Buty pil'nymi (1937). "Бути пильними скрізь і завжди" ['Be vigilant always and everywhere'], *Naddniprians'ka Pravda* 21 September.

Bystree likvidirovat' ostatki (1937). "Быстрее ликвидировать остатки вредительской работы" ['Eliminate the remains of subversive work more quickly'], *Polarnoin kollektivisti* 17 October.

Chase, W. J. (2001). *Enemies within the Gates? The Comintern and the Stalinist Repression, 1934–1939*, New Haven: Yale University Press.

Chubar'yan, A. & Riste, O. (eds.) (1997). Чубарьян, А. и Ристе, О. *Советско-норвежские отношения 1917–1955* ['Soviet-Norwegian relations'], Moscow: Russian Academy of Sciences.

Davies, J. E. (1941). *Mission to Moscow. A Record Of Confidential Dispatches to the State Department, Official and Personal Correspondence, Current Diary and Journal Entries, Including Notes and Comment up to October, 1941*, New York.

Derzkaya vykhodka (1937). "Дерзкая выходка японских шпионов" ['Daring action of Japanese spies'], *Polyarnaya Pravda* 22 May.

Dönninghaus, V. (2011). *В тени Большого брата. Западные меньшинства в СССР 1917–1938 гг.* ['In the shadow of Big brother. Western minorities in the USSR 1917–1938'], Moscow: Rosspen.

Efimenko, G. G. (2001). Єфіменко Г. Г. *Національно-культурна політика ВКП(б) щодо Радянської України (1932–1938)* ['Nationalities and cultural politics of VKP(b) in Soviet Ukraine 1932–1938'], Kiev: Ukrainian Institute of History.

Elenius, L., Tjelmeland, H., Lähteenmäki, M. & Golubev A. (2015). *The Barents Region. A Transnational History of Subarctic Northern Europe*, Oslo: Pax.

Eräs, (1937a) Эряс, "Mitä tekee Tujunen?" ['Who is Tujunen?'], *Polarnoin kollektivisti* 17 May.

Eräs, (1937b) Эряс, "Кто такой Туюнен?" ['Who is Tujunen?'], *Polarnoin kollektivisti* 17 May.

Eräs, (1937c) Эряс, "Отказалась разговаривать" ['Refused to talk'], *Polarnoin kollektivisti* 4 September.

Gatagova, L. S. (ed.) (2009). Гатагова Л. С. (сост.). *ЦК ВКП(б) и национальный вопрос. Книга 2* ['Central Committee of VKP(b) and the nationalities issue. Book 2'], Moscow: Rosspen.

Glass, J. M. (1997) "Against the indifference hypothesis. The Holocaust and the enthusiasts for murder," *Political Psychology*, 18:1, pp. 129–145.

Golubev, A. & Takala, I. (2014). *The Search for a Socialist El Dorado. Finnish Immigration to Soviet Karelia from the United States and Canada in the 1930s*, East Lansing: Michigan State University Press.

Gore-rukovoditel' (1937). "Горе-руководитель" ['Fail manager'], *Polyarnyy kollektivist* 28 July.

Herf, J. (2006). *The Jewish Enemy. Nazi Propaganda during World War II and the Holocaust*, Cambridge, Mass: Harvard University Press.

Hôtes inopportuns (1937). "Hôtes inopportuns et indésirables conseillers (lettre de Stockholm)," *Journal de Moscou* 12 October.

Huonon Kasvatustyön (1937). "Huonon Kasvatustyön tulokset paikallisesta Natsionalismista ja kulttuuri-joukkotyön puuttumisesta Oserkossa" ['About local nationalism and the absence of mass cultural work in Ozerko'], *Polarnoin kollektivisti* 17 May.

Ivanov, N. (1938) Иванов Н. "За изучение русского языка" ['For the study of the Russian language'], *Polyarnyy kollektivist* 1 February.

Jones, A. (2011). *Genocide. A Comprehensive Introduction*, London: Routledge.

Kandidov, B. (1938). Кандидов, Б. "Шпионы в рясах" ['Spies in cassocks'], *Polyarnyy kollektivist* 18 October.

Ken, O. N., Rupasov, A. I. & Samuelson, L. (2005). Кен, О. Н., Рупасов, А. И. и Самуэльсон, Л. *Швеция в политике Москвы 1930–1950-е годы* ['Sweden in Moscow politics of the 1930s–1950s'], Moscow: Rosspen.

Kenez, P. (1985). *The Birth of the Propaganda State. Soviet Methods of Mass Mobilization, 1917–1929*, Cambridge & New York: Cambridge University Press.

Khaustov, V. N., Naumov, V. P. & Plotnikova, N. S. (eds) (2004). Хаустов, В. Н., Наумов, В. П. и Плотникова, Н. С. (сост.). *Лубянка. Сталин и Главное управление госбезопасности НКВД 1937–1938* ['Lubyanka. Stalin and the Main Directorate for State Security of the NKVD in 1937–38'], Moscow: MFD.

Khlevnyuk, O. V. (1992). Хлевнюк, О. В. *1937-й. Сталин, НКВД и советское общество* ['1937. Stalin, the NKVD and Soviet society'], Moscow: Respublika.

Kivalo, E. & Mittler, R. (2000). *Ahvenanmaalaisen Eyolf Mattson-Ignaeuksen elämänura teekkarista puna-armeijan prikaatikenraaliksi*, ['The Ålander Eyolf Mattson-Ignaeus' life cycle. From manufacturing technician to Red Army Brigadier General'], Helsinki: Omakustanne.

Ko vsem trudyashchimsya finnam (1938). "Ко всем трудящимся финнам Полярного района" ['To all Finn workers in the Polar region'], *Polyarnyy kollektivist* 5 February.

Kolesnik, V. (1937). Колесник, В. "Шпигунський Інтернаціонал," ['Espionage International'], *Naddniprians'ka Pravda* 27 September.

Kolhospniki zatrimali shpiguna (1937). "Колгоспники затримали шпигуна," ['Kolkhoz farmers caught a spy'], *Naddniprians'ka Pravda* 16 August.

Kotkin, S. (1997). *Magnetic Mountain. Stalinism as a Civilization*, Berkeley & Los Angeles: University of California Press.

Kotljarchuk, A. (2012). "Kola Sami in the Stalinist terror. A quantitative analysis," in *Journal of Northern Studies*, 6:2, pp. 59–82.

Kotljarchuk, A. (2014a). *In the Forge of Stalin. Swedish Colonists of Ukraine in Totalitarian Experiments of the Twentieth Century* (Södertörn Academic Studies 58), Stockholm: Acta Universitatis Stockholmiensis.

Kotljarchuk, A. (2014b). "The Nordic threat. Soviet ethnic cleansing on the Kola Peninsula," in *The Sea of Identities. A Century of Baltic and East European*

Experiences with Nationality, Class, and Gender, ed. N. Götz, Stockholm: Elanders, pp. 53–83.

Kotljarchuk, A. (2014c) "Little Red Sweden in Ukraine. The 1930s Comintern project in Gammalsvenskby," in *The Lost Swedish Tribe. Reapproaching the History of Gammalsvenskby in Ukraine*, eds. P. Wawrzeniuk & J. Malitska, Huddinge: Södertörn University, pp. 111–149.

Kotljarchuk, A. (2015). "Norwegians in the Stalinist terror. New perspectives for research," *Fortid*, 2, pp. 18–22.

Kotljarchuk, A. (2016). "Ethnic cleansings and 'Russification'," in *Encyclopedia of the Barents Region* 1, eds. M.-O. Olsson et al., Oslo: Pax, pp. 189–191.

Kotljarchuk, A. (2017). "Nordic fishermen in the Soviet Union. Ethnic purges and the cleansing of cultural landscape," in *The Barents and the Baltic Sea Region. Contacts, Influences and Social Change* (Studia Historica Septentrionalia 77), eds. K. Alenius & M. Enbuske, Rovaniemi: Pohjois-Suomen historiallinen yhdistys, pp. 39–56.

Kostiainen, A. (2000). "The Finns of Soviet Karelia as a target of Stalin's terror," in *Ethnic and National Issues in Russian and East European History*, ed. J. Morison, New York: St. Martin's Press, pp. 214–229.

Kott, M. (2007). "Soviet genocide in Latvia. Stalin's Great Terror (1937–38) as antecedent and other aspects of the recent historiography," in *Latvijas Okupācijas Muzeja Gadagrāmata*, 2007, Riga, pp. 42–54.

Krizis inostrannykh (1937). "Кризис иностранных буржуазных разведок" ['Crisis of the foreign bourgeois intelligence services'], *Polyarnyy kollektivist* 15 June.

Kuper, L. (1982). *Genocide. Its Political Use in the Twentieth Century*, New Haven: Yale University Press.

Leningradskiy martirolog (1995). Ленинградский мартиролог 1937–1938, St. Petersburg: Russian National Library.

List (2016). List of the former members of Finland's parliament repressed by the NKVD in Karelia in 1937–1938. Official Internet Portal of the Republic of Karelia; http://www.gov.karelia.ru/gov/Power/Office/FSB/rep.html; access date 21 May 2016.

Lubyanka (2004). Лубянка. Сталин и Главное управление госбезопасности НКВД. Архив Сталина. Документы высших органов партийной и государственной власти. 1937–1938 гг. ['Lubyanka. Stalin and the Main Directorate for State Security NKVD. Stalin's archive. Documents of higher organs of Party and state power. 1937–1938'], Moscow.

Lundgren, K., Ney, B. & Thurén, T. (1999). *Nyheter. Att läsa tidningstext* ['News. To read a newspaper text'], Stockholm: Ordfront.

Lyass, A. (1937a). Лясс, А. "Посылки диверсантов" ['Parcels of diversionists'], *Polyarnaya Pravda* 24 July.

Lyass, A. (1937b). Лясс, А. "Посилки диверсантів" ['Parcels of diversionists'], *Naddniprians'ka Pravda* 26 July.

Malitska, J. (2014). "People in between. Baltic islanders as colonists on the steppe," in *The Lost Swedish Tribe. Reapproaching the History of Gammalsvenskby in Ukraine*, eds. P. Wawrzeniuk & J. Malitska, Huddinge: Södertörn University, pp. 61-85.

Mann, M. (2005). *The Dark Side of Democracy. Explaining Ethnic Cleansing*, New York: Cambridge University Press.

Martin, T. (2001). *The Affirmative Action Empire. Nations and Nationalism in the Soviet Union, 1923-1939*, Ithaca: Cornell University Press.

Mikolyuk, O. V. (2003). Микалюк, О. В. *Политические репресии на Мурмане в 30-ые годы 20 века. Диссертация на соискание степени кандидата исторических наук* ['Political repressions on Murman in the 1930s. PhD dissertation'], Murmansk: Murmansk Pedagogical University.

Miting v Ura-Guba (1938). "Митинг в Ура-Губа" ['Meeting in Ura-Guba'], *Polyarnyy kollektivist* 3 February.

Murmanskiy okrug (1929). *Мурманский округ. Статистико-экономическое описание* ['Murmansk District. Statistical and economical description'], Murmansk: Murmansk District Committee Publishing.

Mustelin, O. (1984). "Allan Wallenius. Biblioteksman, publicist och revolutionär" ['Allan Wallenius. Librarian, publicist and revolutionary'], *Svenska litteratursällskapet i Finland*, 59, pp. 269-389.

Natsionalisticheskie nastroeniya (1937). " Националистические настроения в Западной Лице" ['Nationalistic moods in Zapadnaya Litsa], *Polarnoin kollektivisti* 16 September.

Nimtsi v Ukrainy (1994). *Німці в Україні 20-30-ти рр. XX ст. Збірник документів* ['Germans in Ukraine in the 1920s-1930s. Collection of documents'], Kyiv: Ukrainian Institute of History.

Norman, M. N. (2010). *Stalin's Genocides*, Princeton: Princeton University Press.

Norvegiya (1937). "Норвегия" ['Norway'], *Polyarnaya Pravda* 17 October.

Novyy uchebnyy god (1938). "Новый учебный год" ['New school year'], *Izvestiya* 1 September.

O mestnom natsionalisme (1937) "О местном национализме и отсутствии массовой работы" ['About local nationalism and the absence of mass work'], *Polyarnyy kollektivist* 17 May.

O metodakh i priemakh (1937). *О методах и приемах иностранных разведывательных органов и их троцкистско-бухаринской агентуры* ['On the methods and techniques of foreign intelligence services and their Trotskyite-Bukharin agents'], Moscow: Partizdat.

Okhotin, N. & Roginskiy, A. V. (1999). Охотин, Н. и Рогинский, А. Б. "Из истории 'немецкой' операции НКВД 1937-1938 гг." ['From the history of the "German operation" of the NKVD 1937-1938'], *Наказанный народ. Репрессии против российских немцев. Материалы конференции*, Moscow: Zven'ya Press, pp. 35-74.

Osipov E. U. (1933). "Saam di 16 Oktavr egk" ['Sami celebrate 16th anniversary of the October Revolution'], *Polyarnaya Pravda* 12 November.

Osipov, O. O. (1933). "Səntəv saam opnəja" ['Educating Sami teachers'], *Polyarnaya Pravda* 12 November.

Ovsepyan, R. P. (1999). Овсепян Р. П. *История новейшей отечественной журналистики* ['A history of the modern journalism of the fatherland'], Moscow: Moscow State University Publishing.

Petrov, I. (1937). Петров И. "Ещё раз о коварных приемах иностранной разведки" ['Once again about the deceitful methods of foreign intelligence'], *Polyarnaya Pravda* 27 July.

Pöppel, L. (2007). *The Rhetoric of Pravda Editorials. A Diachronic Study of a Political Genre*, Stockholm: Stockholm University Press.

Poymali shpiona (1937). "Поймали шпиона" ['A spy was caught'], *Polyarnaya Pravda* 8 August.

Razgromit' burzhuaznykh natsionalistov (1937). "Разгромить буржуазных националистов до конца" ['To destroy the bourgeois nationalists completely'], *Polyarnaya Pravda* 16 October.

Razoblachennye zagovory (1937). "Разоблаченные заговоры" ['Exposing the conspiracy'], *Pionerskaya Pravda* 20 December.

Ribalki dopomogli zatrimati shpiguna (1937). "Рибалки допомогли затримати шпигуна" ['Fishermen helped to caught a spy'], *Naddniprians'ka Pravda* 20 September.

Rowan, R. W. (1928). *Spy and Counter-Spy. The Development of Modern Espionage*, New York: Viking Press.

Rowan, R. W. (1937). Роуан, Р. В. *Разведка и контрразведка* ['Intelligence and counter-intelligence'], Moscow: Sotsegiz.

Rubin, N. & Serebrov, Y. (1937a). Рубин Н. и Серебров Я. "О подрывной деятельности фашистских разведок в СССР и задачах борьбы с нею" ['About the sabotage activity of fascist intelligence services and the tasks of fighting it'], Moscow: Partizdat.

Rubin, N. & Serebrov, Y. (1937b). Рубин Н. & Серебров Я. "Про підривну діяльність фашистських розвідок в СРСР і завдання боротьби з нею" ['About the sabotage activity of fascist intelligence services and the tasks of fighting it'], *Naddniprians'ka Pravda* 6 and 8 August.

Rubin, N. & Serebrov, Y. (1937c). Рубин Н. & Серебров Я. "О подрывной деятельности фашистских разведок в СССР и задачах борьбы с нею" ['About the sabotage activity of fascist intelligence services and the tasks of fighting it'], *Polyarnaya Pravda* 2, 3, and 4 August.

Sémelin, J. (2007). *Purify and Destroy. The Political Ideas of Massacre and Genocide*, New York: Columbia University Press.

Shakhnovich, M. (1937). Шахнович М. "Шпигуни і диверсанти в рясах" ['Spies and saboteurs in cassocks'], *Naddniprians'ka Pravda* 30 September.

Shpiguny i diversanti (1937). *Шпигуни і діверсанти за роботою* ['Spies and saboteurs at work'], Kyiv.

Shpionam i izmennikam (1937). Шпионам и изменникам Родины нет и не будет пощады. В помощь библиотекарям ['No forgiveness to the spies and the traitors. To the help of librarians'], Leningrad: Leningrad State Press.

Shpionazh i razvedka (1937). Шпионаж и разведка капиталистических государств. В помощь пропагандисту и беседчик ['Espionage and intelligence of the capitalistic states. For propagandist and moderator'], Leningrad: Leningrad State Press.

Shpionskaya organizatsiya (1937). "Шпионская организация испанских фашистов в США" ['Spy organization of the Spanish fascists in the USA'], *Polyarnaya Pravda* 14 May.

Smirnova, T. V. (2006). "Кадры финской советской печати Петрограда-Ленинграда" ['Cadres of Soviet Finnish press in Petrograd-Leningrad'], in *Санкт-Петербург и Страны Северной Европы*, ред. В. Н. Барышников & П. А. Кротов, St. Petersburg: RKhGI, pp. 37–46.

Snyder, T. (2010). *Bloodlands. Europe between Hitler and Stalin*, London: Bodley Head.

Sokolov, K. (1937). Соколов К. "Деякі методи шкідницько-диверсійної роботи троцькістсько-фашистських розвідників" ['Some methods of subversive-sabotage activity of Trotskyite-Fascist intelligence services'], *Naddniprians'ka Pravda* 16 July.

Stalin, I. V. [1923] (1953). "The Press as a collective organiser," in Stalin, J. V. *Works. Volume 5, 1921–1923*, Moscow: Foreign Languages Publishing House, pp. 286–290.

Stalin, I. V. (1937). Сталин, И. В. *О недостатках партийной работы и мерах ликвидации троцкистских и иных двурушников* ['On the errors of party work and further steps to eliminate the Trotskyite and other hypocrites'], Moscow: Partizdat.

Takala, I. R. (1998). Такала, И. Р. "Национальные операции ОГПУ/НКВД в Карелии" ['National operations of the OGPU/NKVD in Karelia'], in *В семье единой. Национальная политика партии большевиков и ее осуществление на Северо-Западе России в 1920–1950-е годы*, Petrozavodsk, pp. 161–206.

Tarle, E. (1938). Тарле, Е. В. "Уроки истории" ['Lessons of history'], *Izvestiya* 5 November.

Tazin, S. (1937). Тазин, С. "Незнакомец со свертком" ['Stranger with a parcel'], *Pionerskaya Pravda* 20 December.

Toveri, I. V. (1937). "Stalinin puhe" ['Stalin's speech'], *Polarnoin kollektivisti* 6 April.

Uranov, S. (1937a). Уранов, С. "О некоторых коварных приемах вербовочной работы иностранных разведок" ['About some insidious methods of recruiting work by foreign intelligence services'], *Polyarnaya Pravda* 4, 5 and 17 July.

Uranov, S. (1937b). "Eräistä ulkomaiden vakoiluelinten kavalista värväystyön menetelmistä" ['About some insidious methods of recruiting work by foreign intelligence services'], *Polarnoin kollektivisti* 15, 22, 24, 30 June and 4 July.

Vanya i Anya (1937). "Ваня и Аня Кузнецовы—частые гости на пограничной заставе" ['Vanya and Anya Kuznetsova—frequent guests at the frontier outpost'], *Pionerskaya Pravda* 20 December.

Varmuzh, V. (1937). Вармуж, В. "Юные помощники славных чекистов" ['Young helpers of glorious NKVD officers'], *Pionerskaya Pravda* 20 December.

Vsya Moskva (1931). Вся Москва. Адресная и справочная книга, Moscow: Izd. Mosoblispolkoma.

Vykorchevat' ostatki vrediteley (1937). "Выкорчевать остатки вредителей" ['To uproot the remains of saboteurs'], *Polyarnyy kollektivist* 18 June.

Vyshinsky, A. (1937). Вышинский, А. *Некоторые методы вредительско-диверсионной работы троцкистско-фашистских разведчиков* ['Some methods of the subversive activity of Trotskyite and fascist spies'], Moscow: Partizdat.

Wedin, A. (2007). "Gammalsvenskbybornas emigration till Sverige 1929. En studie i svenskhet och etniskt ursprung" ['Emigration of the inhabitants of Gammalsvenskby to Sweden in 1929. A study in Swedishness and ethnic origin'], unpublished BA-thesis in history supervised by Andrej Kotljarchuk, Södertörn University, Sweden.

Werth, N. (2003). "The mechanism of a mass crime. The Great Terror in the Soviet Union, 1937-38," in *The Specter of Genocide. Mass Murder in Historical Perspective*, eds. R. Gellately & B. Kiernan, Cambridge: Cambridge University Press, pp. 215–239.

Zakovskij, L. (1937a). "Vielä ulkomaiden vakoiluelinten metodeista ja menetelmistä" ['Once again about the methods and techniques of the foreign intelligence services'], *Polarnoin kollektivisti* 21 and 24 July, 2 August.

Zakovskij, L. (1937b). "Hävitämme spionit, diversantit ja tuholaiset loppuun asti" ['Spies, saboteurs and wreckers must be totally destroyed'], *Polarnoin kollektivisti* 24, 28 and 30 September, 6, 17, 22 and 27 October, 1 and 17 November.

Zakovskiy, L. M. (1937a). Заковский Л. *О некоторых методах и приемах иностранных разведывательных органов и их троцкистско-бухаринской агентуры* ['About some methods and techniques of foreign intelligence services and their Trotskyite-Bukharin agents'], Moscow: Partizdat.

Zakovskiy, L. M. (1937b) Заковский Л. *О некоторых методах и приемах иностранных разведывательных органов и их троцкистско-бухаринской агентуры, доклад на Ленинградской областной партконференции* ['About some methods and techniques of foreign intelligence services and their Trotskyite-Bukharin agents, report on the Leningrad regional party conference'], Kursk: Kurskoe oblastnoe izdatel'stvo.

Zakovskiy, L. M. (1937c). Заковский Л. "Еще о методах и приемах иностранных разведывательных органов" ['Once again about the methods and the techniques of the foreign intelligence services'], *Polyarnaya Pravda* 2, 3 and 4 July.

Zakovskiy, L. M. (1937d). Заковский Л. "Шпионов, диверсантов и вредителей уничтожить до конца" ['Spies, saboteurs and wreckers must be totally destroyed'], *Polyarnaya Pravda* 15, 16, 17, 20, 21, 22, 23, 24, 26 and 27 September.

Zil'ver, L. (1938). Зильвер, Л. *Быть начеку!* ['Be on the alert!'], Moscow: VLKSM Press.

Zolotov, V. (1937a). Золотов, Б. "На Кондопожском бумажном комбинате" ['On Kondopoga paper mill'], *Pravda* 10 September.

Zolotov, V. (1937b). Золотов, Б. "Кто орудует в Пряжинском районе Карелии?" ['Who operated in Priazhynskiy rayon of Karelia?'], *Pravda* 14 September.

Zorko okhranyat' (1937). "Зорко охранять границы отечества" ['Guard the borders of the fatherland'], *Polyarnaya Pravda* 18 June.

CHAPTER 5

Nation-Building by Terror in Soviet Georgia, 1937–1938

Marc Junge & Daniel Müller

A nation is a historically constituted, stable community of people, formed on the basis of a common language, territory, economic life, and psychological make-up manifested in a common culture.

Iosif Stalin, Marxism and the National Question (1913)

In this contribution the question will be posed whether the Great Terror of 1937–1938 in the Soviet Union had, in addition to political and social, also ethnic and racist or possibly even genocidal, components. Therefore we will take a look at Soviet Georgia, a markedly multi-ethnic society. For the Georgian Soviet Socialist Republic it is possible to reconstruct which ethnic groups suffered the most in the Great Terror in absolute and relative terms. In the light of the persisting significant interethnic conflicts in this Caucasian region, the results are not without brisance. Thus on the territory of Abkhazia, de facto separated since 1993, but regarded as a part of Georgia by the international community with the exception of Russia, repression was especially pronounced, and even more so in the case of the ethnic Abkhaz. On the other hand the Ossetians (the other flashpoint in Georgia being South Ossetia, with heavy fighting in 1991 and 2008) suffered considerably less. Taking into account that the distrust between the nationalities has longer-standing causes, dating back at least to Menshevik rule in Georgia in 1918–1921—those years saw fighting in Abkhazia as well as in the Ossetian region of Georgia, which took on an ethnic character as Georgian troops, regarded as occupation forces, fought Abkhaz and Ossetian forces willy-nilly allying with Russian troops from the North Caucasus, whether "White" or "Red"—, at least for Abkhazia it seems plausible that the decision makers inside the Georgian SSR poured oil on the fire exactly in 1937–1938 during the Great Terror through their now *systematic* persecutions (Dzidzariya [ed.] 1957; Sagariya & Achugba [eds.] 1992).

The project represented in the chapter undertakes a methodological innovation in that it attempts to relate statistical data on the persecution of nationalities in Georgia in the mass operations of the Great Terror to the general nationality policies in the republic. Generally speaking we have a dichotomy between those arguments that seem to individualize the terror (both based on the persecutors' personalities and those of the persecuted), and those that generalize it from an all-Union, indeed globalized, overarching view which insists that foreign-policy concerns ("growing threat of war") are the absolutely dominant, if not sole, movens for the persecution of groups, leading to the categorization of those with foreign roots or links as "enemy nations" (to become "punished peoples") where ethnicity became an almost, or indeed, "objective" marker singling out collectivities for all-encompassing persecution.

Many scholars have plausibly linked the targeted persecution of some nationalities, beginning in the mid-1930s (Poles, Germans, Finns, then Koreans and others) and culminating in the national operations of the Great Terror, to Soviet foreign policy and a growing identification of these ethnic groups with hostile foreign states, especially as the threat of a huge war grew. This concept of "enemy nations," put forward by scholars such as Terry Martin, Jörg Baberowski, Hiroaki Kuromiya and Paul Gregory, looks plausible enough, and of course it is not intended to deny its relevance. On the other hand, it only goes so far in explaining the treatment of various groups (Baberowski 2003; Baberowski 2012: 345, 352; Baberowski & Doering-Manteuffel 2006: 17, 79; Baberowski & Doering-Manteuffel 2009: 216; Dönninghaus 2009: 594; Gregory 2009: 265; Hirsch 2005; Kuromiya 2005: 90–91; Martin 2001; Naimark 2010: 120).

Often, for example, the mass deportations of "diaspora" groups from the borders to the hinterland, both before and during the war, seem a logical conclusion to and culmination of this policy. But then again, even this undeniable aspect of ethnic cleansing only explains part of the activities and leaves many questions unanswered, especially the partial deportations of groups like Greeks, Kurds and others (despite heavy "contamination" and mobility in their cases), and even the post-war deportations, again partial, of various groups from Georgia fit into this picture.

The approach sketched here in a rather declamatory fashion and elaborated in another publication[1] denies neither individual factors, nor the—

---

[1] In the present publication, due to the required brevity, methodological and procedural aspects have been put to the fore and the concrete application, in limited detail, restricted to some few nationalities. An extended version with ample statistics and the treatment of a broader array of nationalities was printed in Junge & Müller (2013). This extended version was co-authored by Wolfgang Feurstein (concerning the Laz) and Ivan Dzhukha (concerning the Greeks), whose gracious input has obviously informed our present shorter interpretation as well. Both the present paper and its extended version originated in the context of a project on the mass persecutions in Georgia in the Great Terror, funded

indeed undeniable—aspect of the war threat and a resulting particular suspicion of anything smacking of foreign links and potential fifth-columnists. But it is here attempted to look closer at another angle which seems clearly relevant. The "enemy nation" school, for all its merits, concentrates on the so-called national operations, and links those with the ethnicity-based deportations; it also concentrates on exactly those groups where the theory fits best: Germans, Poles, Finns and the like. This seems an approach dangerously close to the "self-fulfilling prophecy" fallacy. By extending the view in three directions, it is here attempted to broaden the outlook.

First, the focus—as far as was possible depending on the data—is on the persecution of *all* nationalities. This of course includes the "enemy nations," but also the "imperial" Russians, the titular nationalities of Union Republics (Ukrainians, Georgians, and Armenians etc.), the lesser-titular nationalities of autonomous republics (like the Abkhazians) or even lower-ranked units, and finally other, non-titular groups. Second, and directly linked to that, the source base is no longer restricted to the *national* operations, but is extended to *all* mass operations in the Great Terror, including the *kulatskaya troyka* (Order No 00447) and the dvoika.[2] Only the *militseyskaya troyka* could not be included for lack of data. In addition, as a complementary and corrective element, the "Stalin lists" (*Stalinskie spiski*) were also included as a typical instrument of elite (as opposed to mass) repression.[3] Third, the focus of the study is on Georgia.

This is linked to an attempt to devise an ethno-cultural, political, geographical, economic and social profile of the groups in question from the data restricted here to the *kulatskaya operatsiya* ['Kulak operation'], with additional background information from other sources (census data etc.). This overview of all groups, without a separation of "inner-Soviet" and "foreign"

---

by the VW Foundation and directed by Bernd Bonwetsch. The authors express their thanks to the Ministry of the Interior of the Republic of Georgia, especially Omar Tushurashvili, for their all-encompassing support.

[2] *Kulatskaya troyka* and *natsional'naya troyka*: An extrajudicial committee of three, formed in the capital and in all large administrative units of the USSR, presided over by the respective head of the secret service, the NKVD. Members were the corresponding prosecutors and Party secretaries. A dvoika was an extrajudicial commission of two, which was composed of the federal, regional or local state prosecutor and the current head of the NKVD.

[3] *Militseyskaya troyka* ['police troika']: The chairman was usually the local, regional or federal head of the NKVD or his representative, the other members being the corresponding state prosecutor and the leader of the administration of the civil police (Ru. *militsiya*), as well as the leader of the responsible departments of the police.

or "diaspora" nationalities—a separation which, it might be added, is not always coherent and stringent—is a necessity for this approach. In a sense, an approach focused exclusively on the "foreign" groups leads to results tinged with a sense of "self-fulfilling prophecy." The authors think that by including other groups, and studying differences both between groups in one "category" (e. g., "foreign" ones) and between groups in various categories, it is possible to get both a more accurate appreciation of the *level* of persecution as such, of various groups in the Great Terror, and plausible new evidence for a significant differentiation in *motives* regarding the persecutions of various groups.

The aim, then, would be to move beyond the focus on "ethnic cleansing" of (imperial) "enemy nations," which we deem too narrow and one-dimensional, and on linked matters of foreign policy ("growing threat of war") and to direct the view towards the potentially very varied and distinct interests of the Moscow centre on the one hand and the actors on the Georgian periphery of the empire on the other. In a sense, this also leads to a tentative reversal of perspectives. It is intended to complement the Moscow-centric view with a view which switches sides and puts the periphery in the centre. So the Moscow perspective is augmented by the Tbilisi perspective; and the key interest of the outermost borders (here, with Turkey) is supplemented by an interest in the core issues of Georgian nation-building. To make ourselves clear: Repression along ethnic lines is a strong and obvious fact; but a) one that does not explain everything, especially a sharp differentiation in degree; and b) the ethnic lines in question were several, and criss-crossing one another: they were partly those of the centre, and partly those of the power elites in the periphery.

The connection here taken into view between persecution and the cohabitation of ethnic groups in Georgia does not pertain solely to the titular nationality of the country (the Georgians) or to the lesser titular nationalities (the Ossetians, the Abkhaz, and the Adzhars, whose status was ambivalent to begin with), i.e. those that had "their own" autonomous Soviet socialist republic or area (Ru. *oblast'*), but also other groups linked more or less closely to the core of the Georgian nation: the Laz, Mingrelians, Svans and Batsbii with their ambivalent position and special identity within the Georgian sphere. Besides these, the Southwest of Georgia was home to Kurds and Turks, compactly settled both in parts of Adzharia (annexed by Russia from the Ottoman Empire in 1878) and in Meskhetia, the former Pashalyk of Ahiska (annexed by Russia in 1829); immediately to the eastward and bordering on Armenia, there were compact settlements of Armenians; and again to the east of these, in the southeast of the country bordering Azerbaijan, there were areas settled by Azerbaijanis (called Tatars [Ru. *tatary*] earlier, they were called Turks (Ru. *tyurki*) earlier in the Soviet era, and Azerbaijanis (Ru. *azerbaidzhantsy*) only from 1936 onwards). In the Northeast, on the border with Chechnya, there were Kists, a Muslim subgroup of the Chechen-Ingush; and slightly to the east, on the border with Dagestan, Avars and small Tsezic ("Dido") peoples distantly related to them. Colonies of Greeks, Germans, Jews, Aramaean speakers from Persia, generally called "Assyrians" (Ru. *assiriytsy*) or "Aysors" (Ru. *aysory*) residing in individual villages or groups of villages also existed, as well as colonies of Russians and Ukrainians, many of them sectarians like Molokans (Ru. *molokane*) or Dukhobors (Ru. *dukhobory*). It seems remarkable that a significant part of the recent newcomers (mainly refugees) from the Ottoman and Persian Empires—mainly affected were Greeks, Armenians, Turks, Laz, Aramaeans and Azerbaijanis—were not granted Soviet citizenship, but kept their status of foreigners (Ru. *inostrantsy*). Most of the Azerbaijanis from Persia were generally called "Iranians" (Ru. *irantsy*) in Soviet sources, referring to their country of origin rather than their ethnicity (ethnic Persians were much less numerous).[4] So let us analyze the data regarding our first example, the Abkhazians in comparison with the Ossetians of Georgia.[5]

The Abkhazians and the Ossetians

At slightly under 1 per cent, the degree of repression of the Abkhazians was significantly more than a third higher than that of the Georgians (0.63 per cent) (ratio 1:0,6). Also with regard to the degree of punishment—meaning the rate of executions to the total of repressed persons—the rate of repression is very high: In both respects the percentage of the Abkhazians is twice as high as that of the Georgians.

Remarkably, the degree of repression for the Abkhazians is diametrically opposed to that of the Ossetians, although one might assume they ought to

---

[4] Throughout, we refer to Tsentral'noe statisticheskoe upravlenie, Otdel perepisi (ed.) (1929). This also serves as a corrective for the 1937 data when these are clearly inapplicable (e.g. in the case of the Germans in Georgia), cf. Polyakov, Vodarskiy, Zhiromskaya & Kiselev (eds.) (1991).

[5] Eka Kuchalashvili and Georgiy Lominashvili have compiled the tables on the persecutions in the context of the mass operations according to both ethnicity and social profile. The statistics regarding the "Stalin lists" originate with the Georgian Institute for Free Access to Information, where special thanks are due to Georgiy Kldashvili.

be similar, as both had autonomous entities on the territory of the Georgian SSR. (In our terminology, this means they were both minor titular nationalities of Georgia.) In the Ossetian case, both rates were indeed less than *half* that of the Georgians—i.e., only a quarter of the rate for the Abkhazians (see Table 1).

Table 1: Abkhazians and Ossetians, kulak troika, degree of repression

Nationality	Population 3,376,946	Repressed persons 1937–38		Population/ Repressed persons % 1937–38	
		total	executed	total	executed
Titular nationality					
Georgians, Adzharians	2,080,179	13,177	6,127	0.63	0.30
Lesser titular nationalities					
Abkhazians	55,409	548	308	0.99	0.55
Ossetians	143,604	384	207	0.27	0.14

Admittedly, Abkhazia, being on the Black Sea coast, was repeatedly the object of foreign invasion, as recently as 1918 by the Ottomans, 1919 by the Germans and 1920 by the British. Still, it is difficult to see how these maritime threats on the Black Sea coast alone can motivate such a massive discrepancy. What, then, might be alternative reasons for this unequal treatment?

The working hypothesis would be that besides the *ethnic* attribution, differences in the social background and political status of a given ethnic group played a decisive role in determining the persecutions. Put differently: Nationalities of lower status (like the Ossetians) were persecuted to a much lesser degree than those with a higher one (like the Abkhazians). This thesis refers to social status both past (in the sense of social origins [Ru. *sotsial'noe proiskhozhdenie*]) and present (in the sense of the social position [Ru. *sotsial'noe polozhenie*] at the time of arrest). To ascertain this thesis, we have the data for the kulak operation: Regarding origins we have such classifications as "kulak," "officer" (meaning: of the tsarist or White army), member of the police organs (Ru. *karatel'nye organy*), or descent from the nobility (Ru. *dvoryanskogo proiskhozhdeniya*).

Regarding the social situation we have such information as "worker," white-collar employee, farmer; and in addition data on the educational level attained (from higher education down to illiterates). Let us take a look at these social origins.

The Social Origins of Abkhazians versus Ossetians

Among the Abkhazians, the percentage which had had a higher social standing under tsarism is significantly higher than in the case of the Ossetians; this *social origins* aspect thus fits in with the thesis mentioned above, that higher social status of nationalities was linked to higher degrees of repression. Regarding *current* social status, however, the thesis seems not to hold, as the Ossetians' social status was higher than that of the Abkhazians being repressed (see Table 2).

Now our explanations: First, the main thrust of the kulak operation should be recalled: Throughout the Soviet Union, the stress of the kulak operation was on the cleansing of disloyal rural populations. Among the repressed Ossetians however, only 20 per cent were farmers; in contrast, a remarkable 80 per cent of them were white-collar employees. Among the Abkhazians, in a direct reversal, the rural population was persecuted above average, whereas white-collar persons were relatively speaking underrepresented at some 50 per cent only.

To clear up the exceptional degree of repression of Abkhazian farmers, theories of nation-building might be referred to. The high degree of repression of "farmers" can be seen as an indicator of a process of nation-building having progressed much further among the Abkhazians than among the Ossetians. According to the three-stage model developed by Miroslav Hroch for the creation of national identity, the Abkhazians were already at stage three, meaning the process had already reached the broader Abkhazian population, largely farmers. These processes of identity formation had been catalysed by the social, economic and educational upheavals in the Republic of Abkhazia. Indeed, in the year 1937 itself a massive settlement of the climatically privileged and largely underpopulated autonomous republic had begun. That very year, the Georgian state began the mass colonization of Mingrelians and Western Georgians in Abkhazia. Southern Ossetia, by contrast, which is very mountainous and had only poor soil, was already overpopulated and in addition its infrastructure was much less developed. No

Table 2: Abkhazians, kulak troika, social origins

568 Abkhazians were purged in 1937–1938		total	executed	camp	VKP (b)
Social origins	Farmers	239	124	115	55
	Kulaks	36	25	11	3
	Princes	32	29	3	1
	Nobles	45	20	25	1
	Muslim leaders (hodzhas, beks)	-	-	-	-
	Merchants	1	1	-	-
	'Citizens' (*meshchane*)	2	2	-	-
	(Former) Officers	6	4	2	1
	(Former) Police	10	9	1	5
	total	371	214	157	66
VKP (b) party members		62	42	20	-
Social situation	(Blue-collar) Workers	6	5	1	-
	White-collar workers (*sluzhashchie*)	146	83	63	68
	Farmers	122	55	67	10
	total	274	143	131	78
Education	High education	22	18	4	14
	Medium education	34	23	11	11
	Low education	228	130	98	44
	Illiterate	55	32	23	1
	total	339	203	136	70

comparable colonization policies were pursued there in the 1930s. Flanked by linguistic and colonization policies the persecutions during the mass operations were used in a very differentiated form regarding both minor titular nationalities in order to hollow out their autonomy and transform it into a largely symbolic one, with an unspoken goal to move towards a titular homogenization of the territory of the Georgian SSR. The kulak operation would seem to have been particularly suited to such purposes, as the competence for this repressive operation had especially been transferred from the Moscow centre to the periphery. Looking at the persecution of Abkhazian elites, this was decidedly less important during the Great Terror, i.e. beginning in the summer of 1937. As far as the Abkhazians were concerned, *this had already happened in 1936 and early 1937*, as shown by the "Stalin lists" and other evidence; there were few of that description left to be persecuted. The Ossetian elites, however, were not of the same calibre as the Abkhazians. Their turn therefore only came during the kulak operation. Now, both Party members and white-collar employees were purged (see table 3).

Table 3: Abkhazians and Ossetians, "Stalin lists," degree of repression

Nationality	Population 3,376,946	Repressed persons 1937–38		Population/ Repressed persons % 1937–38	
		total	executed	total	executed
Titular nationality					
Georgians, Adzharians	2,080,179	1,666	1,470	0.08	0.07
Lesser titular nationalities					
Abkhazians	55,409	76	70	0.14	0.13
Ossetians	143,604	56	51	0.04	0.03

In this sense, comparing Abkhazians and Ossetians, not only the "social past" and the "social present" play a role, but also geographic and economic designs and finally the time frame, where we can see a kind of phase model where the Ossetians were "behind" the Abkhazians in time schedule. So let us come to our second example, the Turks of Georgia.

The Turks

Numbering some 82,500 the Turkish population was among the largest minorities in Georgia, living compactly in the border areas with Turkey (see Tables 4 and 5).

Counting all mass operations together—meaning the kulak troika, the dvoika, the national troika and as well as the police troika—, the percentage of Turks purged reaches 0.6 per cent; 44 per cent of the repressed were executed (see Table 6).

Table 4: Turks, kulak troika, degree of repression

Nationality	Population 3,376,946	Repressed persons 1937–38		Population/ Repressed persons % 1937–38	
		total	executed	total	executed
Titular nationality					
Georgians, Adzharians	2,080,179	13,177	6,127	0.63	0.30
Diaspora nationalities					
Greeks	87,385	157	72	0.18	0.08
Turks	82,500	323	201	0.39	0.24

Table 5: Turks, dvoika, degree of repression

Nationality	Population 3,376,946	Repressed persons 1937–38		Population/ Repressed persons % 1937–38	
		total	executed	total	executed
Titular nationality					
Georgians, Adzharians	2,080,179	0	0	0	0
Diaspora nationalities					
Greeks	87,385	156	72	0.18	0.08
Turks	82,500	0	0	0	0

The mass of the persecuted Turks were, unsurprisingly in the view of the Turks' low status, farmers. But Party members and/or white-collar workers, were very disproportionately sentenced to death. So the Turks had very few beginnings of an elite, but in the mass operations this tiny elite was hit particularly hard. Of 187 white-collar workers sentenced, two thirds were sentenced to death, whereas for farmers this applied only to 30 per cent. In addition, the remaining traditional elite was also decimated in an extreme way: 32 mullahs got caught up in the repression machinery; in fact, 25 of them (78 per cent), i.e. nearly four fifths, were sentenced to death.

Table 6: Turks, all mass operations (kulak troika, dvoika, national troika, police troika), degree of repression

Nationality	Population 3,376,946	Repressed persons 1937–38		Population/ Repressed persons % 1937–38	
		total	executed	total	executed
Titular nationality					
Georgians, Adzharians	2,080,179	13,986	6,169	0.67	0.30
Diaspora nationalities					
Greeks	87,385	798	168	0.91	0.19
Turks	82,500	520	231	0.63	0.68

Table 7: Turks, "Stalin lists," degree of repression

Nationality	Population 3,376,946	Repressed persons 1937–38		Population/ Repressed persons % 1937–38	
		total	executed	total	executed
Titular nationality					
Georgians, Adzharians	2,080,179	1,666	1,470	0.08	0.07
Diaspora nationalities					
Greeks	87,385	32	27	0.04	0.03
Turks	90,000	4	4	0.004	0.004

The repression of the Turks did not yet mean resettlement but rather, first and foremost, the securing of the border and the weakening of the possibilities for religious articulation of an ethnic group. During the Great Terror, securing the border without deportation or resettlement meant to discipline the masses of a low-status nationality by decapitating their elites and to sanction, in significant breadth, even the most minor perceived infractions against total loyalty. As a potential source of maintenance of a separate cultural identity, the mullahs were also weeded out at the same time. This was indeed limited to this form of border security and cultural exclusion only. In

1944 the spatial exclusion through deportation followed, though now under the direction of Moscow. Our working hypothesis would be that in the shadow of Moscow-imposed policies of "securing the border," the Georgian central power in Tbilisi was also able to pursue its own agenda and further its own interests (see Table 7).

Ill. 8. Sergo Goglidze, People's Commissar of Internal Affairs of the Georgian SSR. Museum of the Ministry of Internal Affairs of Georgia.

The Germans

Including the Germans in Georgia in the category of persecuted nationalities with foreign ethnic roots is once again somewhat unusual to a certain extent because with Germany, even more so than with Japan, we are dealing with the most important "enemy nation" of the Soviet Union.[6] War threat and the formation of a fifth column within the country in case of war are obvious factors and formed a familiar pattern since before the First World War. Counting up all convictions by the kulak troika (329 persons total, death sentence 188 persons), dvoika (119/13), national troika (57/24) and police troika (8/0) (total: 518/228), we come to a huge degree of repression of 2.1

---

[6] The repressions of the Poles and "Iranians" can not be included here since the data material is insufficient (Poles) or it appears unclear ("Iranians").

per cent in relation to the absolute number; with the death sentence, to a high degree of repression of 44 per cent, and 0.94 per cent executions in relation to the total number of Germans then living in Georgia. Germans, however, were also convicted via the Stalin lists. Just as with the mass operations, here the degree of repression was also very high in comparison to nearly all other nationalities. It came to 0.34 per cent. Solely the degree of repression of the Jews at 0.31 per cent comes close to that of the Germans (see Tables 8, 9 and 10).

Table 8: Jews and Germans, national troika, degree of repression

Nationality	Population 3,376,946	Repressed persons 1937–38		Population/ Repressed persons % 1937–38	
		total	executed	total	executed
Titular nationality					
Georgians, Adzharians	2,080,179	24	4	0.0020	0.00019
Jews and diaspora nationalities					
Jews	29,721	5	2	0.17	0.007
Germans	24,140	57	24	0.24	0.1

Table 9: Jews and Germans, all mass operations (kulak troika, dvoika, national troika, police troika), degree of repression

Nationality	Population 3,376,946	Repressed persons 1937–38		Population/ Repressed persons % 1937–38	
		total	executed	total	executed
Titular nationality					
Georgians, Adzharians	2,080,179	13,986	6,169	0.67	0.30
Jews and diaspora nationalities					
Jews	29,721	264	124	0.90	0.43
Germans	24,135	514	225	2.1	0.94

Table 10: Jews and Germans, "Stalin lists," degree of repression

Nationality	Population 3,376,946	Repressed persons 1937–38		Population / Repressed persons % 1937–38	
		total	executed	total	executed
Titular nationality					
Georgians, Adzharians	2,080,179	1,666	1,470	0.08	0.07
Jews and diaspora nationalities					
Jews	29,721	93	82	0.31	0.30
Germans	24,140	82	70	0.34	0.30

If we now consider the results in a synopsis, then the expressly bloody dynamic of the repression of the Germans comes to the fore, in both quantitative and qualitative terms, directly through the interplay of foreign and internal policy interests, of local and central interests and motives. For the Germans their relatively high social status, the suspect social origin, their noticeably high average level of education, paired with a high degree of participation in the local power structures when viewed from a local perspective, turned into their doom. The Germans presented serious competition for the titular nationality; they were well educated, present in the state and Party apparatus and in industry, as well as in small businesses. The opportunity to apply the brakes on the Germans became significantly less complicated for the repression bodies through their stigmatisation as an "enemy nationality" or potential danger. In this respect, the Moscow "central command" provided ideological and practical help with the central propaganda machine and special orders. Because of this interplay of internal and foreign factors, the traditionally positive image of the Germans could be pushed to the background as the elimination of the political and social competition of this ethnic group gained dominance, even at the local level in Georgia.

Illustration 9 (next page): Hard-copy record of meeting no. 44 of the NKVD troika in Georgian SSR from 23 October 1938. Archives of the Ministry of Internal Affairs of Georgia.

ПРОТОКОЛ № 74

Заседания тройки при Комиссариате Внутренних Дел Грузинской ССР
от „23" X 1938 г.

Председатель тройки НКВД Груз. ССР _____
Члены _____ Прокурор по спецделам _____
Секретарь _____

Слушали:	Постановили:
Следственно-арестанское дело № 3804 Люксембургского РО-НКВД ГССР	ГАРТЕР Готлиб Христианович 1885 года рождения.-
По обвинению ГАРТЕРА Готлиба Христиановича, 1885 г. рожд, ур. м Люксембурги, того же р-на ГССР, немец, сов гр-н, быв кулак лишенец спекулянт ошибочно восстановленный в праве голоса, ныне колхозник, женат, грамотный, б/п, не судившийся, член общества - церковь божия.-	Расстрелять Имущество принадлежащее лично ему конфисковать.
Обвиняется в том, что состоя членом нелегальной контрреволюционной фашистской организации немцев ставившей задачу свержение сов власти путем вооруженного восстания каковую был вовлечен одним из руководителей той же организации высланным Готман Яковом так же находясь в хороших отношениях с упомянутым Готманом Гартер систематически разделял к-р взгляды и вел активную борьбу против мероприятии существующего строя в СССР.- В предъявленном обвинении себя виновным признал полностью.	
Арестован 25/УП-38 года Содержится в Люксембургском РО НКВД ГССР	
ДОКЛАДЧИК:- НАЧ РО (Григолия)	Председатель: Члены: Секретарь:-

Сов. Секретно

Combination Theory versus Ethnification

In Georgia, for the period of the Great Terror, one can distinguish between groups on the one hand who seemed to be "includable" into the Georgian nation, and those on the other to whom that did not apply. Here one can apply the criteria enumerated by Stalin as early as 1913 in his publication "Marxism and the National Question" (Stalin [1913] 1953), in which common language, culture, history and territory play a decisive role. Inclusion and exclusion appear as two sides of the same coin, building the Georgian nation—unified within, clearly delimited from the outside.

All special identities within the Kartvelian groups thus had to be levelled. The Kartvelian languages other than Georgian—Mingrelian, Svan, Laz, as well as the non-Kartvelian East Caucasian languages of Christians (Bats, Udi)—had to be purged, administratively, from linguistic research (which clearly proved to observers near and far that these were not "dialects of Georgian," but languages in their own right mutually unintelligible with Georgian), from schools and media, and indeed from daily use as well. Islam was combatted as the mainstay of the separate identity of Adzhars, Laz and Meskhians, with the prior aim of inclusion. Those who seemed no longer within reach for inclusion—like most of the Laz and those Adzhars and Meskhians more strongly affected by Turkification—were alternatively threatened with exclusion. Ossetians and Abkhaz (with no separate "high culture" in reach, and wholly or largely non-Muslim), too, were targeted for inclusion, but threatened with exclusion and persecution in case of "inclusion failure" at the same time.

Policy towards the diaspora nationalities of no major importance to Georgian nationalism was also directed towards reduction, but not in the sense of inclusion within the Georgian nation. Thus neither Armenians nor Azerbaijanis were targeted for active linguistic assimilation, despite the fact that for example most of the Armenians in the capital Tbilisi (a third of all Armenians in Georgia) were already native speakers of Georgian anyway. In their rural areas of settlements, the South(-West) in the case of the Armenians and the Southeast in the case of the Azerbaijanis, they kept their own (Armenian- and Azerbaijani-language) schools. The other groups, however, were considered of no importance according to these new proceedings and were either delivered over to Russian as the imperial language (i.e. their schools transferred to Russian), or, dependent on geographical proximity, to Georgian, Armenian, or Azerbaijani schools.

The Georgian repression bureaucracy closely followed the predefined path. Already in the simple classification and enumeration of the persecution victims by nationality, the general intent to level the ethnic and cultural diversity of the republic further and to finish off the "national circus" of the preceding years once and for all immediately reveals itself. Some ethnicities simply were not mentioned any longer in the extra-judicial and judicial documents. This way, the Mingrelians and Svans had already disappeared, but now the Adzhars, still in existence in the census of 1937, and theoretically the titular nationality of an ASSR, were also abolished.[7] With the exception of the Laz, all subgroups with South Caucasian (Kartvelian) languages had thus disappeared by mid-1937.[8]

Through this administrative inclusion of whole ethnicities (at least 300,000 in the case of the Mingrelians, some 100,000 in the case of the Adzhars, significant numbers in a republic with just three million inhabitants!), local initiative was well on its way to fulfil the fourth and last Stalinist criterion of what constitutes a nation: commonality of culture (Ru. *Obshchnost' kul'tury*). This was flanked by measures aimed at eradicating minority languages like Mingrelian, Svan, Laz and Batsbi, that propped up group identities that were lacking Stalin's criteria of for example "specific spiritual complexion," "psychological make-up," "peculiarities of national culture," "national character" (Stalin [1913] 1953: 307).

Other groups deemed more or less "includable" received, instead of their Latin-based alphabets developed as recently as 1928–1930, a Georgian alphabet (not a Cyrillic one). This was the case for the Abkhaz, although their close relatives, the Abazinians in the North Caucasus, switched from Latin to

---

[7] The hollowed-out shell of the ASSR remained, as the territory's "autonomy" was guaranteed in the peace treaties with Turkey (Kars and Moscow 1921) and thus had international implications.

[8] It ought to be stressed that even the all-Union census of 1926, in presenting an anomaly in the Georgian case, seems to show the singular strength of Georgian nationalist aspirations. This was an extremely detailed census, accounting for even minor differences. All groups were listed separately, even if separated "only" by religion. Thus (Muslim) Tatars were number 48 in the census list of nationalities (here *narodnosti*, not *natsional'nosti*) and Christian Tatar Misharians (Ru. *mishari*) 49; Buddhist Kalmyks 54 and Muslim Sart-Kalmyks 57; Muslim Kurds 154 and Yezidis (also Kurdish-speaking) 155; etc.. There was only one exception: the Georgians (number 105) alone had only "subgroups:" 105a Adzharians, 105b Mingrelians, 105c Laz, 105d Svans (in Russian *105a/b/v/g*). This totally illogical exception, extended also to the languages, where absurdly "Kartvelian languages" were shown as one with subgroups of Mingrelian, Laz, Svan and "Georgian proper" (Ru. *sobstvenno gruzinskiy*), shows that the basis for the local inclusionary/assimilatory policies was strong within the apparatus at least by then.

Cyrillic at the same time; and even for the Ossetians, although the North Caucasian majority (in and around the North Ossetian ASSR) of this Soviet nationality also switched to Cyrillic. Here the desire for territorial homogenization obviously trumped rational concerns, resulting in two scripts for one (territorially adjacent) Soviet nationality![9] With the introduction of the Georgian script, the Georgian language was also massively strengthened in Abkhaz and Ossetian schools at the expense of the native languages. Indeed, according to Stalin, "a national community is inconceivable without a common language (Stalin [1913] 1953: 304)." Obviously it was not a problem that the administrative language, as shown in the archival documents of the persecution, remained Russian in 1937–1938. Indeed Stalin had explicitly remarked that

> the integrity of Russia and Austria is not affected by the fact that there are a number of different languages within their borders. We are referring, of course, to the spoken languages of the people and not to the official governmental languages. (Stalin [1913] 1953: 304)

The persecution statistics ordered by nationalities mirror not only the administrative aspects of local policies, but also their bloody side, especially regarding those ethnicities straddling the new boundaries of Georgianness, those intended for inclusion but not seen as fully compliant with it, standing in the way of full-scale homogenization. Numbers and information about nationalities other than "Georgians" listed separately in the persecution documents show that the centre in Tbilisi also pursued homogenization through violence, by disempowering and subjecting minorities to the benefit of the titular nationality, through the use of organized violence.

The best example for such procedures are the Abkhaz, who numerically experienced a particularly harsh repression.[10] As early as 1936 their elite had been massively weakened, then in the mass persecutions came the turn of the

---

[9] Again the Georgian case of these two lesser-titular languages switching to the titular languages as opposed to the imperial Russian (Cyrillic) script was *unique*. No other minority switched in this way, e.g. all minorities in Armenia switched to the Cyrillic alphabet, none to the Armenian, not even the Yezidis which had seen a Kurdish book printed in Armenian script in 1921, a tradition that was *not* renewed.

[10] The Abkhaz were not a typical diaspora nation in that in their case, the original homeland was on what became Soviet territory, and the foreign groups, scattered through the former Ottoman Empire but particularly in Turkey and Syria, were the results of emigration (mainly in 1864, 1866–1867, and 1877–1878, called "exile" [Ru. *makhadzhirstvo*] from *muhacir*, 'refugee'); cf. Dzidzariya 1982.

broad masses: many farm workers, but also white-collar workers (Ru. *Sluzha-shchie*) and lowly and middle-ranking Party functionaries. Major priority seems to have been given to a rollback of separate nation-building processes far advanced among the Abkhaz in the wake of the 1918–1921 fighting, the struggle to maintain a separate SSR status (1921–1931)[11] with the aid of good connections to Moscow and to the North Caucasus. These good contacts with Moscow had to be snapped, and the settlement plans of the republic, aimed at denying Tbilisi's hegemony, thwarted. The Abkhaz wanted to counterbalance the influx of Western Georgians, Svans, and Mingrelians by settling there also Greeks, Laz, and others to prevent a full-scale demographic swamping of the Abkhaz by the Georgians and Georgians-to-be. The persecution statistics regarding the Abkhaz is thus a prime example for the repressive implementation of the second and third Stalinist criteria for a nation, those of a "common territory" and of an "internal economic bond." "A common economic life, economic cohesion", i.e. the cultural, political and physical penetration of Abkhaz territory was thus pursued through the massive colonization of Abkhazia with Georgians and Mingrelians (simultaneously with the switching of the Abkhaz media and schools to Georgian language or at least script), including the allocation of economic and technological resources to the settlers, available to the bureaucracy locally because of collectivization (Stalin [1913] 1953: 305, 306).

That this policy of persecution of minorities not necessarily implies an ethnification of perceptions by the Tbilisi-directed persecution bureaucracy, but is rather to be understood as a "punishment" meted out because of a perceived lack of loyalty and a diagnosis of a lack in will to adapt and integrate into the Georgian nation as the policy aims required, is shown through the persecution policies regarding the Laz. The Laz were indeed the most problematic of the "Kartvelian groups" and thus turn up again, and stay distinct, in the persecution documents at a time when all others had been subsumed

---

[11] From Sovietization in 1921 until 1931 Abkhazia was an SSR, a Soviet Socialist Republic (not just "Autonomous") in its own right. In 1925, there was a minor demotion as Abkhazia received the unique status of DSSR, literally 'Treaty SSR' (Ru. *Dogovornaya SSR*), meaning it was an SSR with a special treaty relation with Georgia. Only in 1931 did it indeed become an ASSR. Obviously, Abkhazia was not on a par with Georgia, Armenia and Azerbaijan in 1921–1931, as it was not a direct member of the Transcaucasian SFSR, but *de facto* entered in it through Georgia. Still the more elevated status was not just symbolic, but also included enhanced opportunities to appeal to Moscow and conduct policy independently. Georgian and Georgian-influenced historiography often, for understandable reasons, falsifies the whole SSR and DSSR history of Abkhazia (clearly shown in all contemporary sources) and calls it an ASSR from 1921 onwards.

under Georgians. The Mingrelians and Svans had distinct languages, but they were Christians and their church language was Georgian. The Adzhars were Muslim, and their "high culture" was Ottoman Turkish, but their everyday language was Georgian. The Laz, by contrast, were distinct in both. They spoke a distinct language (rather close to Mingrelian actually) like Mingrelians and Svans *and* they were Muslims whose "high culture" was Turkish like the Adzhars'. Besides, unlike the others, they had a strong diaspora, with a huge majority of the Laz population (about 300,000) residing in Turkey, and most Laz in Georgia actually being refugees from Turkey. Also remarkable is the severity of the punishment, i.e. the high ratio of death sentences, handed out to Laz victims. A generalized reason for this "special"—especially murderous—treatment of the Laz can be found in the lacking of "commonality of culture," as pointed out above. As in the dual matrix of religion and language they were farthest removed of all the Kartvelian groups from the Georgian core.

Another angle arguably affecting the Laz is that they were reasonably seen as in league with the major "problem group" and the major centre of national resistance within Georgia, with the Abkhaz. Laz territory ("Lazistan") only made up one (large) village within Georgia (Sarp, Georgian Sarpi, in Adzharia, through which the Soviet-Turkish border ran). Other Laz were scattered, but a significant concentration, mainly refugees, was in the "Little Lazistan" enclave in Abkhazia. The Abkhaz elites had actively tried to promote this group, among others, to counterbalance Georgian encroachments. Thus, in a pretty direct challenge to Tbilisi, the Abkhaz had enabled the publication of a Laz newspaper and Laz schoolbooks in Sukhum (in 1929), and had also provided land for the foundation of a Laz collective farm. The Laz, through the prolific activist Iskander Tsitashi, also intervened directly in Moscow, through letters to Georgi Dimitrov, Stalin, and others, thus providing a constant embarrassment for the Tbilisi authorities criticizing their national policies and employing Stalinist rhetoric. In these letters Tsitashi exposed how the Tbilisi authorities used their economic powers to distribute machinery, land and other resources gained in collectivization in order to thwart the cultural, political and economic promotion of Laz aspirations by the Abkhaz party. Thus, already the seemingly "nationality-neutral" collectivization drive could be used to provide the titular nationality with economic weapons to fight unwanted national developments. Far from establishing a "Soviet piedmont" for the Laz to put pressure on Turkey and create a magnet for the Laz masses there, the Tbilisi authorities actually encouraged Laz emigration (return movements) to Turkey in order to get rid of them.[12]

Another group caught up in the struggle between Tbilisi and Sukhum were the Greeks. Admittedly the Greeks, too, had foreign connections. They were immigrants, often recently arrived refugees, from the Ottoman Empire and Turkey. "Coastal invasion" paranoia, harking back to the Crimean War but also recent sea-borne interventions across the Black Sea in 1877–1878, 1914–1915 and 1918–1921, may have played a part. But their—numerically very pronounced—persecution in 1937–1938 can equally be read in the context of their concentration in Abkhazia, the major bone of contention. These Greeks were often Turkish-speaking and thus, despite their orthodox religion, not easily included into the Georgian nation, but threatened (like the Laz) to bolster the Abkhaz' defensive shield against a Georgian majority. The Greeks outside Abkhazia seem to have been much less affected by the persecutions. The explanations are here clearly not mutually exclusive, but a focus solely on the threat supposedly posed by these Greeks to the maritime borders of the Soviet Union seems one-sided; inner-Georgian dynamics are at least equally plausible.

This interdependence between persecution and geography, between social, political and economic space can also be seen at work by looking at an example of sub-average persecution, namely, the Ossetians. Both repression coefficients for them are low; their territory, landlocked from an all-Union perspective, but also unproductive, overpopulated and generally very unattractive high in the mountains from a Georgian resource-focused perspective, was not desirable and largely devoid of importance. Isolated from other trouble spots, the Ossetians could be dealt with by focusing on their not very numerous elites (white-collar workers, Party members) and thus pre-emptively decapitating any attempts at nation-building outside the Georgian frame. The lowly social status of the Ossetian subsistence farmers, ready to become fully integrated into the Georgian sphere aided by the accelerated cultural Georginization, was thus cemented.

---

[12] И. Т. Циташи генеральному секретарю Исполкома Коминтерна Г. М. Димитрову о положении Лазов в Грузии ['I. T. Tsitashi to the General Secretary of the Comintern Ispolkom, G. M. Dimitrov, on the situation of the Laz in Georgia']. Не позже 25 июля 1937 г., *Archives of Interior Affairs of Georgia*. First Department. Fond 14, Inventory 102, Document 98, Sheet 3–12.; И. Т. Циташи секретарю ВКП (б) И. В. Сталину о положении Лазов в Грузии. ['I. T. Tsitashi to the secretary of the VKP (b), I. V. Stalin, on the situation of the Laz in Georgia']. Ранее 11 февраля 1935 г., in Chitași 2012: 130–140.

One of the nationalities in Georgia where territorial questions are hardly of any importance at all, but where social and political status predominates, are the Jews. The Jews were nearly all urban dwellers, with heavy concentration in the largest cities, but also a strong presence in mid-size and small towns. In the largest cities, there were both "Georgian Jews" (Ru. *evrey gruzinskie*), speaking Georgian, and *Ashkenazim*, Eastern European Jews (speaking Russian and occasionally still Yiddish as well). In the smaller towns, there were few *Ashkenazim*. Non-proletarian social origins and high status (good education, Party membership) can explain the harsh repression of this group; anti-Semitism may have furthered it.

The persecution of Eastern Slavs (Russians, Ukrainians) on the other hand shows no peculiarities. The paralysis of lesser-titular nationalities (Abkhaz, Ossetians) and other "interior" ethnic groups of Georgia enabling the streamlining of the titular nationality's cultural, social, territorial and economic hegemony can be extended to the persecution of diaspora nationalities. They could not be included within the Georgian nation of the Stalinist type, as shown by administrative aspects (like the lack of an attempt to systematically extend Georgian schooling to them, compared to what was done in the "includable" cases), but their power had to be crippled and their resources destroyed.

In the largest Georgian cities, especially in Tbilisi—a largely Armenian city throughout the nineteenth century, and still with an Armenian plurality in the 1920s! —the high-status urban Armenians (traditionally dominating commerce here) were deprived of their economic might and thus dominance. The Yezidis, forming a tightly knit, closed-off community segregated through religious and cultural boundaries from all neighbours, hierarchically shaped by clan allegiance and all but monopolizing certain professions like inner-city transport (porters, including water carriers, garbage collection) in Tbilisi and to a lesser degree Batumi, often semi-legal or on the fringe of organized crime, were massively persecuted, although, with their total break with the Ottoman Empire/Turkey where the Yezidis had been subject to genocide, they could hardly be counted as an "enemy nation."

Other low-status groups like the Azerbaijanis, Turks and Muslim Kurds— much like the Ossetians—saw their small elites heavily decimated further and thus their low-ranking status confirmed. The German colonist community, once an important cultural, economic and political factor with good contacts with Moscow, had its back finally broken, by persecuting them aggressively, much like the Jews, both in numbers and in degree (executions), and singling out their "disloyal" elites for execution or disappearance in camps.

Georgian Regional Government versus the Kremlin

The Georgian regional government (Party and state apparatus) at Tbilisi was thereby not at all working in secret against the policy of the Moscow centre. The preferential treatment of titular nationalities accompanied by a marginalization of lesser-titular ones (i.e., titular for ASSRs or AOs and even lesser entities only) and other groups was a rather typical Union-wide procedure in this phase of Stalinism (Reisner 2010: 164; Slezkine 1994: 448; Simonsen 1999: 1,070 f.; Martin 2001), picking up steam at the beginning of the 1930s, when national rayons where massively abolished across the USSR, often with the aid of statistical manipulation, ironically often achieved through extensions which drove the percentage of the titular groups below 50 per cent. In Ukraine, where this procedure of massively decimating Polish and German rayons is well-documented, it culminated in the Ukrainian Politburo's decision of 16 February 1938 on the "Transformation of the national rayon and village Soviets in normal rayons." The final nail in the coffin of these entities then came with the corresponding (7 April 1939) decree of the same body, "On the liquidation and transformation of national entities" (Čirko 2007: 272–276). In the Ukraine, school policies accompanying these abolitions very much favoured Russian over Ukrainian, however, showing the relative strength of Georgian versus Russian compared to Ukrainian versus Russian (Borisenok 2006: 229–232). Generally, there was a certain flexibility. If the "includibility" pointed in the Georgian or Ukrainian direction, then that was the language chosen; if it did not, then the imperial Russian language was chosen.

The most important aspect of this policy seems to have been that from 1937 and finally 1938 Moscow no longer acted as arbiter in these inner-SSR disputes. Formerly, even lowly entities and unaffiliated personalities like Iskander Tsitashi had directly appealed to Moscow to seek redress for grievances, finding allies in Moscow and generally a leadership trying to carefully play off one interest against the other. That was no longer the case. The titular nationalities and the SSR leadership now gained hierarchical control. A balancing of interests was replaced by one of fairly total control by the titular nationality power structures; letters from Tsitashi and other gadflies were no longer processed in Moscow but, on the contrary, were delivered back to the "competent" authorities in Tbilisi, setting up Tsitashi as fair game to be persecuted (and executed) by Tbilisi. No longer could the Abkhaz (or Baku) meddle in Laz affairs; no longer could Kurdish school books from Yerevan be used in Tbilisi or Nakhichevan Kurdish schools; the whole system became streamlined. Tbilisi decided for Georgia, Baku for Azerbaijan, Yerevan for Armenia, without interference from Moscow as long as the latter's general directives were meticulously fulfilled.

That extended to history and other sciences. From 1937–1938 onwards, ethnographic expeditions even from Moscow or Leningrad depended on the good-will of the SSR authorities, whereas cross-visits (say kurdological scholars from Armenia visiting the Kurds of Azerbaijan) became for all practical purposes impossible. The very history was fully territorialized; Armenia lost the right to publish books pertaining to the present-day territory of Georgia, even to the Armenians there, at least without the direct and prior approval of the Georgian authorities. The full interpretative authority was decided on a territorial basis (cf. Shnirelman 1996; Shnirelman 2001; Shnirel'man 2010). Cohabitation of cultures within the SSR was no longer wanted. Parallel with the delegation of large swathes of Soviet nationality policy to the Union republics, the regionalization of persecuting power reached new heights in the Great Terror. Only through this development, which began with collectivization but was finalized only now, could nation-building of the Stalinist stamp become the fiery nucleus of mass persecutions in Georgia. For Georgia, then, and the time beginning with the Great Terror, one can postulate the formula: "Socialist in form, national in content." Nation-building based on an inherently multinational idea must be regarded as having failed.

Specific Georgian, as opposed to general all-Union, interests seem an indispensable basis for understanding the mass persecutions in Georgia, but they admittedly do explain only part of the deadly dynamics, especially concerning the diaspora nationalities. Thus regarding more typical "foreign groups," much more than in the case of the Abkhaz and the Laz (coastal strip, diaspora in Turkey), where it also does apply, the interaction between regional interests and the central Moscow perspective has to be taken into account. Only by combining them can the significant, indeed statistically, striking discrepancy in the degree of persecution be explained.

Thus the broad persecution of the Turks, despite their lowly social and political status, and their economically less attractive, overpopulated area of settlement in Meskhetia and the Adzharian hinterland, must be seen on the background of the Union-wide strengthening of borders accelerated in 1929–1931. For the Tbilisi authorities this was, however, an opportunity legitimizing the sharp persecution of the Turks living close to the Turkish border, at the same time incidentally putting pressure on Georgian-speaking

Meskhians to accept inclusion or become part of the out-group. The disproportionate persecution of the Turks, from a Georgian point of view, may thus be said to be an opportunity of combining business with pleasure, fulfilling Moscow's directives and pursuing Georgian nation-building interests at the same time. Aspects of ethnic cleansing to pre-empt Turkish claims when making demands for Turkish territory, as happened in 1945, may also be anticipated here (Kuniholm 1980; Dimitrov 1991: 203; Chuev 1991). That despite all this even the Turks were seen as a largely regional job is made plausible by the fact that only few of them were persecuted through the dvoika and the national troika with their stronger association with foreign policy (as compared to the kulak troika).

Where the pretence of "securing the border" was non-existent or weaker as in the case of the Greeks, this did by no means imply a guarantee of less persecution. On the contrary, inner-Georgian interests could more than offset this. Thus the Georgian repression bureaucracy intensely used the "National Orders" in order to marginalize and diminish this diaspora nationality, important because of its strong presence in Abkhazia. Despite this, for various reasons, the coefficients for the Greeks and especially for executions do not reach the heights of those for the Germans. After all, the Greeks were low-status and their persecution was not based on real "dangers," but more on interior policy, getting and keeping a firm grip on Abkhazia.

With the Germans and presumably also the Poles and "Iranians" we see the full amalgamation of central Moscow and local Tbilisi interests at play. The Germans, of course, are *the* enemy nation *par excellence*. The Germans in the Soviet Union were linked to and associated with the exterior enemy in a unique fashion. Poles and Finns seemed less dangerous, Japanese and British lacked significant representation, the Germans had both: Their state was seen as extremely dangerous, especially so in 1938, and they were heavily represented in the Soviet Union. But through their formerly high social status (wealth, education, Party connections) they offered numerous open flanks for attack, but also made welcome targets in another sense, as they had much wealth to be confiscated. As an almost extra-territorial group they thus stood in the way of Georgian nation-building. This combination arguably led to the extremely high and disproportionately deadly coefficients of repression for this group.

Conclusion

The category "ethnification of perception," heightened to "ethnicity as an objective criterion" seem a far less useful tool to fathom the strong repression of the diaspora nationalities. This is a Moscow-centred perspective neglecting regional/local aspects. A general xenophobia also seems unsatisfactory as an explanation.

That does not mean that ethnicity played no role in Georgia; it obviously did. But it did so in a combination of feared, potential or real political, social and territorial competition inside Georgia; of the Moscow policy of drastically lowering the threshold for what was perceived (and to be draconically punished) as an inacceptable violation of loyalty, collectively and individually; and foreign policy considerations making certain groups and border regions even more likely to be hit hard. There is no either/or here, no dichotomy, but a strongly cumulative and combinatory approach. Therefore it seems somewhat difficult to draw a line of continuity between the persecutions in the Great Terror and the collective—total or partial—deportations of nationalities, although undeniably the total deportation of the Germans from Georgia to Kazakhstan in 1941 objectively constituted the culmination of this group's persecution.[13] The same is true for the deportation of the Turks and Kurds from Adzharistan and Meskhetia in 1944. The very procedure of the deportations differed fundamentally from the repressions used in the mass operations. The deportations were handled administratively, without any participation of courts, not even special courts. The respective groups were deported as contingents or partial contingents, and, in distinction from the mass operations, none of these deportations were directed against individual persons (Polyan 2005: 5–6). The most important difference, however, is that the deportations were ordered and organized from above, from Moscow (Party, government, secret police, in the war through the State Defence Committee), making use of the organizational know-how of central commissions and the central NKVD, brought in force with special trains. Here, a centrally driven policy of resettlement was pursued, ethnic cleansing in combination with securing borders and indiscriminately getting rid of potential fifth-columnists (Polyan 2005: 8–9). Local interests and influences played no or at most a very subservient role; the leeway of local authorities was minimal

---

[13] Only those Germans married to Georgians outside ethnic German villages were immune against the official rationale for the deportation (feared or actual collaboration with the German invaders); they were allowed to stay.

at most. The Great Terror meant systematic persecution carried out on centrally delegated powers by the peripheral power-holders on their own authority and with more loose oversight from Moscow. The deportations, on the other hand, were a (partial) massive central intervention. In that sense, the deportations are by no means a logical consequence of local nationality policies in the Great Terror, nor were they already foreshadowed in the Great Terror (although experience from both the Great Terror and the war-time deportations may have informed procedures followed in the after-war deportations, in 1949–1952). The deportations must be seen in the context of centrally-driven Moscow population policies and of course of the Second World War; that war was at the same time the deeper reason and the immediate occasion. That the deportations created huge empty spaces, some of them rather desirable, to be settled with Georgians and others (Armenians, Azerbaijanis), was arguably only a side-effect, albeit presumably not an unwelcome one.

In contradistinction to the deportations, the Great Terror was no physical exclusion of nationalities from Georgian space, but a systematic and violent disciplining, subjecting and marginalization of nationalities along the lines of a checking of clues and markers (including ethnicity) for individual loyalty or lack thereof. It must also be mentioned that, as elsewhere, already the collectivization drive had burst the seams of normal cohabitation of people and indeed nationalities in Georgia. The Great Terror completed this estrangement, thereby also laying the foundations for the desperate struggle of the Abkhaz and Ossetians to get out from under central Georgian control at any cost, and for the lasting and still dominant "essentialist ethnic-cultural definition of the Georgian nation" (Reisner 2010: 163).

References

Archives
Archives of the Interior Affairs of Georgia

Literature
Baberowski, J. (2003). *Der Rote Terror. Die Geschichte des Stalinismus* ['Red terror. The history of Stalinism'], Munich: Beck.

Baberowski, J. (2012). *Verbrannte Erde. Stalins Herrschaft der Gewalt* ['Scorched earth. Stalin's rule of violence'], Munich: Beck.

Baberowski, J. & Doering-Manteuffel, A. (2006). *Ordnung durch Terror. Gewaltexzesse und Vernichtung im nationalsozialistischen und im stalinistischen Imperium* ['Order through terror. Excesses of violence and destructtion in the National Socialist and Stalinist empires'], Berlin: Dietz.

Baberowski, J. & Doering-Manteuffel, A. (2009). "The quest for order and the pursuit of terror. National Socialist Germany and the Stalinist Soviet Union as multi-ethnic empires," in *Beyond Totalitarianism. Stalinism and Nazism Compared*, eds. M. Geyer & S. Fitzpatrick, Cambridge: Cambridge University Press, pp. 180–230.

Borisenok, E. (2006). Борисенок, Е. *Феномен советской украинизации 1920-1930-е годы* ['The phenomenon of Soviet Ukrainization in the 1920s–1930s'], Moscow: Evropa.

Chitaşi, I. (2012). *Çquni Çhara. Albonişi Supara. Ve Chitaşi'nin diğer yazilari* ['We write. Alphabet book. And other writings by Tsitashi'], Istanbul: Laz Kültür Derneği.

Chuev, F. I. (1991). Чуев, Ф. И. *Сто сорок бесед с Молотовым. Из дневника Ф. Чуева* ['140 interviews with Molotov. From the diary of F. Chuev'], Moscow: Terra.

Čirko, B. V. (2007). "Die Liquidierung des Systems der nationalen Rayons der Ukraine in den Jahren 1934–1939" ['The liquidation of the system of national rayons in the Ukraine in the years 1934–1939'], in *Deutsche in Rußland und der Sowjetunion 1914–1941* ['Germans in Russia and the Soviet Union 1914–1941'], eds. A. Eisfeld, V. Herdt & B. Meissner, Berlin: Lit Verlag, pp. 272–276.

Dimitrov, G. (1991). *Dnevnik. 9 mart 1933–6 fevruari 1949* ['Diary. 9 March 1933–6 February 1949'], Sofiya: Universitetsko izdatelstvo "Sv. Kliment Ochridski."

Dönninghaus, V. (2009). *Minderheiten in Bedrängnis. Sowjetische Politik gegenüber Deutschen, Polen und anderen Diaspora-Nationalitäten 1917–1938* ['Minorities in distress. Germans, Poles and other diaspora nationalities 1917–1938'], Munich: Oldenburg.

Dzidzariya, G. A. (ed.) (1957). Дзидзария, Г. А. (сост.). *Борьба за советскую власть в Абхазии. Сборник документов и материалов 1917–1921* ['The fight for Soviet power in Abkhazia. Collection of documents and materials 1917–1921'], Sukhumi: Alashara.

Dzidzariya, G. A. (1982). Дзидзария, Г. А. *Махаджирство и проблемы истории Абхазии в XIX столетия* ['Exile and problems of the history of Abkhazia in the nineteenth century'], Sukhumi: Alashara.

Gregory, P. R. (2009). *Terror by Quota. State Security from Lenin to Stalin. An Archival Study*, New Haven & London: Yale University Press.

Hirsch, F. (2005). *Empire of Nations. Ethnographic Knowledge and the Making of the Soviet Union*, Ithaca: Cornell University Press.

Junge, M. & Müller, D. (2013). Юнге, М. и Мюллер, Д. "Образование грузинской нации с помощью террора" ['The formation of the Georgian nation with the aid of terror'], in *Большевистский порядок в Грузии*. Том 1. *Большой террор в маленькой кавказской республике* ['The Bolshevik order in Georgia. Vol. 1. The Great Terror in a small Caucasian republic'], сост. М. Юнге, О. Тушурашвили и Б. Бонвеч, Moscow: ROSSPEN.

Kuniholm, B. R. (1980). *The Origins of the Cold War in the Near East. Great Power Conflict and Diplomacy in Iran, Turkey, and Greece*, Princeton, N. J.: University of Princeton Press.

Kuromiya, H. (2005). "Accounting for the Great Terror," *Jahrbücher für Geschichte Osteuropas*, 53, pp. 86–101.

Martin, T. (2001). *The Affirmative Action Empire. Nations and Nationalism in the Soviet Union, 1923–1939*, Ithaca: Cornell University Press.

Naimark, N. (2010). *Stalin's Genocides*, Princeton: Princeton University Press.

Polyakov, Yu. A., Vodarskiy, Ya. E., Zhiromskaya, V. B. & Kiselev, I. N. (eds.) (1991). Поляков, Ю., Водарский, Я. Е., Жиромская, В. Б. и Киселев, И. Н. (сост.). *Всесоюзная перепись населения 1937 г. Краткие итоги* ['The all-Union census of 1937. Short results'], Moscow: Institut istorii SSSR Akademii nauk SSSR.

Polyan, P. (2005). Полян, П. "Депортация и этничность" ['Deportation and ethnicity'], in *Сталинские депортации 1928–1953* ['The Stalin deportations, 1928–1953'], сост. Н. Л. Поболь и П. Полян, Moscow: Materik.

Reisner, O. (2010). "Between state and nation. The debate about 'ethnicity' in Georgian citizens' ID cards," in *Exploring the Caucasus in the 21st Century. Essays on Culture, History and Politics in a Dynamic Context*, eds. F. Companjen, L. Marácz & L. Versteegh, Amsterdam: University of Chicago Press, pp. 157–179.

Sagariya, B. E.-I. & Achugba, T. A. (eds.) (1992). Сагария, Б. Е.-И. и Ачугба, Т. А. (сост.). *Абхазия. Документы свидетельствуют 1937–1953. Сборник материалов* ['Abkhazia. The documents bear witness, 1937–1953. A collection of materials'], Sukhumi: Alashara.

Shnirelman, V. A. (1996). *Who Gets the Past? Competition for Ancestors among non-Russian Intellectuals in Russia*, Washington, D. C.: Johns Hopkins University Press.

Shnirelman, V. A. (2001). *The Value of the Past. Myths, Identity and Politics in Transcaucasia*, Osaka: National Museum of Ethnology.

Shnirelman, V. A. (2010). Шнирельман, В. А. *Многоликая Клио. Бой за историю на постсоветском пространстве* ['Many-faced Klio. The fight for history in post-Soviet space'], Braunschweig: Georg Eckert Institut.

Simonsen, S. G. (1999). "Inheriting the Soviet policy toolbox. Russia's dilemma over ascriptive nationality," *Europe-Asia Studies*, 51, pp. 1,069–1,087.

Slezkine, Y. (1994). "The USSR as a communal apartment, or how a socialist state promoted ethnic particularism," *Soviet Review*, 53, pp. 414–452.

Stalin, I. V. [1913] (1953). "Marxism and the national question," in Stalin, I. V., *Works* 2, 1907–1913, pp. 300–381.

Tsentral'noe statisticheskoe upravlenie. Otdel perepisi (ed.) (1929). Центральное статистическое управление. Отдел переписи (Сост). *Всесоюзная перепись населения 1926 года. Том XIV. Закавказская Социалистическая Федеративная Советскя Республика. Отдел I. Народность, родной язык, возраст, грамотность* ['The all-Union census of 1926. Vol. XIV. The Transcaucasian Socialist Federative Soviet Republic. Section I. Nationality, native language, age, literacy'], Moscow: TsSU Soyuza SSR.

CHAPTER 6
A Long Great Ethnic Terror in the Volga Region. A War before the War

Eva Toulouze

In order to understand the Great Terror in a wider perspective, and to situate ethnical groups within its logic, it is useful to concentrate on its "predecessors," i.e. systematic attacks against ethnicity in previous years, and to widen its geography to regions far away from the Union's borders. From this point of view, the Volga region is in itself an interesting as well as a fruitful field for historical analysis. Moreover, since its integration into the Russian space,[1] it has been a complicated region to rule, where regular protests against Moscow took place.[2]

The Volga region is a mosaic of nationalities. But, unlike Caucasus, ethnic groups are strong and numerous there, although they represent two sets of linguistic, historical and religious traditions. The first is the Turkic family, historically an important player in Russia's history. The ethnical groups whose origins are connected with the Mongol occupation of Russia and the political power following its collapse are very close to one another: while Tatars were at the core of the last Mongol state before its incorporation into Muscovite Russia, and Bashkirs were nomadic tribes difficult to control, they both spoke very close, mutually understandable languages and had a Muslim tradition. Tatars had a ruling tradition, which they had maintained after the Russian occupation. It relied very much on the system set by the Kazan Khanate and its civil servants; Kazan was a local metropolis, with a complex social structure and political life. The ethnical groups of the second set were, in comparison, more complicated and politically much weaker, several of them, mostly peasants in Russian-dominated regions, without any ruling experience, speaking different and mutually incomprehensible languages belonging to the Finno-Ugric language group, and living in more or less compact areas, more or less Christianised on the substrate of animistic world-

---

[1] With the conquest of Kazan in 1552, the lands that previously formed the Kazan Khanate were absorbed by Russia.

[2] The Cheremis wars (1560–1580), Ivan Bolotnikov's (1605–1607), Stepan Razin's (1670–1671), Emelian Pugachev's revolts (1773–1774). These last movements threatened directly the imperial power.

views. They were the Mordvins,[3] the Maris,[4] the Udmurts,[5] and the Komi.[6] There has never been any unity or connection between these communities. None of them has ever ruled a state but they have always been subordinated to other ethnic groups. Historically there were no cities in their territories, and the political organisation was very weak.[7] They have thus never represented any challenging political danger for the central power: even when they participated in the different historical revolts, they were never the initiators. It is thus interesting to follow their fate in Russian Stalinist repressions.

The Soviet State and Ethnicity in the Volga Area in the 1920–1930s

One of the peculiar and unexpected ideological standpoints on which the Soviet state was actually built was the structural power of ethnicity (Slezkine 1994). The stress on ethnicity was not part of the Marxist dogma; ethnicity was viewed by strict Marxists as part of the so-called superstructure that was not at the core of the understanding of society. But strict Marxists did not

---

[3] The Mordvins were (and are) divided into Erzya and Moksha Mordvins, whose languages are not immediately mutually understandable. They were to a large extent Russified and dispersed over a wide area.

[4] The Mari, formerly called the Cheremis, were also divided into two groups speaking different dialects (fixed since the 1920s into two literary languages). The majority of Meadow Maris and a small active minority of Hill Maris lived in a fairly compact area, and while evangelised mostly between 1740 and 1767, they actively retained an animistic world-view and practices (revitalised nowadays) well into the 1930s. Small groups of Maris migrated eastwards to avoid heavy taxes and brutal Christianisation and they still dwell mostly in Bashkortostan.

[5] The Udmurts, formerly called Votyaks, live in a compact area. For centuries, the southern groups of Udmurts were incorporated into the Kazan Khanate while the northern part was encompassed in the Russian Vyatka State. This has left traces on their respective cultures. Starting in the seventeenth century, Russians established metal and later weapon industries on their territory, while in the last few decades oil has been found.

[6] Formerly called Zyrians and Permiak. The two Komi groups are separated by forest areas. The Permiak group fell under the rule of the Stroganov family after the Russian conquest. In the north, the Zyrian group occupied a huge taiga area. They were evangelised in the fourteenth century and were thus better integrated than the others into the Russian world (cf. Toulouze 2010a; Toulouze 2010b).

[7] Actually, I have left aside another Volga ethnic group, the Chuvash, which presents hybrid features. While these descendants of the Volga Bulgars speak a Turkic language (but quite different from Tatar and not mutually understandable), the rest of their history is akin to that of the Finno-Ugric groups. As I have not studied this group, I will not dwell on its history.

have a multicultural empire to manage as the Bolsheviks had after 1917: "Nations might not be helpful and they might not last, but they were here and they were real" (Slezkine 1994: 415). The Bolsheviks had to build support for their rule in complicated conditions and sought the support of the weakest ethnic groups, which had not been previously involved in political life.[8]

The weight of ethnicity in the building of the Soviet State must not be underestimated. Several authors have emphasised that the Soviet Union was a triumph for the principle of ethnicity. This understanding led to the establishing of a territorial network of ethnic groups, which were "given" so-called autonomy at different levels. Among them, the Volga peoples became nations. They were allowed to develop their culture within the Soviet framework, and all of them (except the Mordvins) were allocated a territory[9] in which to develop their own cultural and political goals. A material contribution towards the achievement of this framework was the activity of the autochthonous peoples' young and numerally small intelligentsia, whose aims were more cultural than political. They were given carte blanche to develop their people's culture in return for their loyalty, which was freely and gratefully given. At this stage, indeed, what the Bolshevik offered corresponded to the aims of the local intelligentsia. The latter came from a total absence of recognition and were provided the means to build a cultural life, to develop schools in their own languages, to express themselves and to gain for their communities a dignity they had never had before.

Still, both in Udmurtia and in the Mari region (the two areas I will focus on here), the intellectuals that enthusiastically worked with the Bolsheviks were usually members of the Communist Party, as the Party was smart enough to integrate them at posts of responsibility.[10] Some joined the Party later. Others never did, but this did not lessen their enthusiasm. In this remarkable period, which started as soon as the Civil War was over (or even before), the promotion of the natives was one of the Party's concerns, which is well expressed with the

---

[8] Just after the Revolution, some of the most ethnically aware of Russia's nationalities, the Western groups, either formed their own states (the Finns, the Balts, the Poles), or remained within the borders of the Soviet State, but with difficult relations (the Ukrainians). The Tatars were, as I mentioned, highly politicised, and they were uncomfortable allies for the Bolshevik.

[9] Mari and Udmurt Autonomous Oblast were created in November 1920, the Komi A.O. in August 1921.

[10] Thus, for instance, Kuzebay Gerd, the main Udmurt poet, was called to be the editor-in-chief of the Party's daily newspaper. He asserts: "The February Revolution writers immediately changed their orientation and passed unanimously to the camp of the new literature" (Gerd 1929: 21).

policy of indigenisation (Ru. *korenizatsiya*), the aim of which was to develop proficiency in the vernacular languages by the non-natives, alias mainly Russians, and to ensure the recruiting of native managers and executives, because "nationals" were weakly represented in leading positions (*Kulturnoe* 1970: 149; Sidtikova 1990: 38). Moreover, in some conflicts that emerged in the 1920s, Moscow regularly supported the local national leaders against the Russian-minded Party or state officials.[11] The Party still followed Lenin's approach, which was definitely hostile to Russian nationalism (Slezkine 1994: 414) and sympathised with the cultural development, in accordance with the earlier Russian Orthodox missionary tradetions.[12]

Following these regions' political developments in the 1920s, one can clearly see that two tendencies co-existed in the Party's leadership: the dominant one was quite encouraging and supportive of the Volga intellectuals' involvement in promoting their culture within the socialist system; the other, less dominant in the 1920s, was strongly Russian-minded and hostile to the promotion of nationalities, in line with their understanding that such policies would divert the Party from its main goal, the building of a proletarian nationless society. In the Party's discourse, throughout two decades, these two tendencies appeared in opposition against two extremes that were considered threats to the Party's righteous policy. One was the "great-power chauvinism,"[13] the other, the "local nationalism."[14] While at the beginning, the first was considered as the main peril (Pesikina 1956: 96), the second became perceived as the most subtle and dangerous enemy of the Soviet power in the 1930s (Lallukka 1990: 65).

This Russian-friendly tendency, which was then called "great power chauvinism," was not represented by the Kremlin at the beginning of the 1920s, but was still very much present, especially in Udmurtia (with the strong proletarian Izhevsk factory Party organisation). The newspapers

---

[11] It is very clear in the case of the Udmurt executive committee chairman Trofim Borisov, an ethnic Udmurt, physician and Party member (for his biography, see Pavlov 1991). He was expelled from the Party by an Izhevsk factory Russian lobby and accused of rape. While he was actually expelled from the Udmurt Communist Party, he was rehabilitated immediately afterwards by the centre and appointed Party Leader in Kalmykia (Kulikov 1997: 42; Kuznetsov 1994: 27).

[12] As emphasised by Isabelle Kreindler, Lenin, whose father was supervisor of a missionary school in the Volga region, might have been inspired by this school's implementation of the teaching of vernacular languages, provided that the contents were Christian (Kreindler 1977).

[13] In Russian: *velikoderzhavnyy shovinizm*.

[14] In Russian: *mestnyy natsionalizm*.

reported many protests within the Party against indigenisation, and numerous refusals to learn Udmurt; moreover, as soon as in 1926, the leader of the Udmurt intelligentsia, who was also the leader of the newly created Udmurt Writers' Union, was compelled to resign because of a row with the local Party leadership. These were marginal but clear signs that the officially declared place given to ethnicity, and especially non-Russian ethnicity, was not willingly accepted by many communists.

During the second half of the 1920s, this Russian-minded wing of the Party became the leading one. The rhetoric of the two dangers did not disappear immediately, but it was used in order to show the enemy's cunningness: local nationalists were said to be secretly speaking deceitfully against Great-Russian chauvinism (Dimanshteyn 1937: 7).

On the general level, collectivisation in 1928 was a brutal aggression against those ethnic groups that were mainly rural (such as the Volga Finno-Ugrians), with the elimination of the rural society's more active members, who were repressed as "kulaks;" but while repression *de facto* endangered their vital strength, it did not directly target ethnic groups as such. Still, the impact was huge and may be compared to terror. In Udmurtia, for example, while according to the statistics, the wealthy peasants represented 2.3 per cent of the rural population, more than 30 per cent were eliminated, accused of being "kulaks" (Nikitina 1998: 164). Another area in which repressions started with collectivisation was the spiritual domain. Until the end of the 1920s, Udmurt folk religion was tolerated, partly because the Russian Orthodox Church had fought against it. With collectivisation everything changed. Among other things, animistic rituals were prohibited as they were seen as something that wasted state commodities (e.g. through animal sacrifices). This aspect of collectivisation can, undoubtedly, be likened to ethnic repression (Nikitina 1998: 130–131).

Explicit attacks against ethnicity were to be noticed in the last years of the 1920s and the very beginning of the 1930s, before they transformed into a calculated enterprise to eliminate national intelligentsias. I shall now follow, after these first contextualising sections, the forms of this war against the Volga nationalities with the example of the Finno-Ugrians. But first I will add a last contextualising comment about the notion of "Finno-Ugric." It is clearly a linguistic notion: the languages spoken by these peoples are of the same remote origin and connect them to the westernmost languages of the group—Estonian, Finnish, and Hungarian. Language, for these three state-building communities, is the main identity factor. Since the first decades of the nineteenth century, Finnish and Hungarian scholars have been looking for cognate languages in Eastern Russia and Siberia. The Volga peoples, who spoke Finno-Ugric languages, while living far from Russia's borders, were intellectually and emotionally connected with these countries, whose political sympathies were not with the USSR. While the intellectuals of these minorities in Russia were sincerely devoted to the Bolshevik cause, they were trying to develop meaningful links and relations with Hungary and Finland, not because of their present politics, but because of their history and patrimony. Some examples: the Komi writer and linguist Vasiliy Lytkin (who wrote under the Komi name Illya Vas') received a scholarship in 1926–1927 to study in Helsinki and Budapest (Turkin 1995: 210–212; Turkin 1997: 22–25); Kuzebay Gerd,[15] who, besides being a writer, was also a student in Moscow, was able to get in touch with the Finnish scholar Yrjö Wichmann, who had visited Udmurtia at the beginning of the twentieth century to collect oral poetry. Gerd was keen on returning the treasures of oral culture Finnish scholars had gathered from his people. Wishing to confer with his Finnish colleague, he published an article in Finland through the Finnish embassy (Haltsonen 1964: 359; Kuznetsov 1994: 36, 82–89). Moreover, Finland was in some sense a model for Udmurt intellectuals: the discovery of a collection of Finnish poems translated into Russian showed Gerd the path he had to follow in order to develop Udmurt modern culture (Shklyaev 1982: 141). In his motives, there was nothing political, nothing threatening towards the policy of Soviet Russia. But it was to be interpreted otherwise ...

Finno-Ugric Ethnicity as a Danger

At the beginning of the 1930s, history and ethnography were thoroughly reviewed by the Party, which decided that "bourgeois" tendencies had to be eradicated. Discourse about national issues had apparently not changed: local nationalism and "great-power chauvinism" were still in focus. But great-power was no longer Russian: in a programmatic article in the main ethnographic journal *Sovetskaya etnografiya* ['Soviet ethnography'] in 1931, N. M. Matorin (1931: 25–27) presented as "great-power chauvinism" Ukranian ethnographers protecting Ukrainian "kulaks" against Russian proletarians. And yet another category emerged, "national-chauvinism." Peoples that were "national-chauvinistic" were, for example, the Fennic peoples,[16] supported by

---
[15] Gerd also wanted to receive the same kind of scholarship, but his application was turned down, a few years after Lytkin had been granted his scholarship (Kuznetsov 1994:104).
[16] The Fennic peoples are communities speaking closely related languages in a continuum between the Courland coast (Livonians), Estonia, Finland and Karelia. In Russia, the

Finland, whose aim, allegedly, was to conquer Karelia and to create a "Great Finland" all the way to the Urals (Matorin 1931: 31). This was a very important theme that now appeared in public for the first time.

Illustration 10: Kuzebay Gerd (a.k.a. Kuz'ma Pavlovich Chaynikov, 1896–1937), Udmurt poet accused by the NKVD to be a leader of SOFIN in Udmurtia. Executed by the NKVD in November 1937 in Sandarmoh (Karelia). Courtesy of the Udmurt Institute of History, Language and Literature, Ural branch of the Russian Academy of Science.

While intellectuals—mainly Komi and Udmurt—tried to develop relations with the Western Finno-Ugrians for the sake of scholarly cooperation or developing knowledge of their own culture, other scholars attempted, in the 1920s, to develop Finno-Ugric studies within the USSR. They were aware that these studies did not exist in Russia, while research was quite advanced in Hungary, Finland and Estonia (LOIKFUN 1929a: 3). To this end, they created the Society of Researchers of Finno-Ugric Cultures (LOIKFUN)[17] in Leningrad in November 1925 and tried to coordinate the scholarly activities in the field.[18]

The most active scholars in Russia in Finno-Ugric studies, who were also involved in LOIKFUN, were Mordvinians like Mikhail Timofeevich Markelov (1899–1937),[19] and Komi, like Vasiliy Petrovich Nalimov (1873–

Fennic communities are mostly (with the exception of Karelians) smaller communities: Votes, Ingrians, Ingria Finns, and Vepsians.

[17] In Russian: *Leningradskoe Obshchestvo Issledovateley Kul'tury Finno-Ugorskikh Narodov*.
[18] Its leader was Vyacheslav Yegorov, a senior researcher whose course on the History of Fennic peoples had just been suppressed at Leningrad's University; he was not allowed to pursue his research after 1929 (see http://www.ethnology.ru/biobib/Result.php?fnc=459; accessed on 23 June 2014).
[19] For more details, see Churakov 2008.

1938). This is not surprising since both Mordvinians and Komi had been integrated into the Russian world long before the other Central Russia communities, which had long been encompassed into the Kazan Khanate, and thus kept at distance from Russian influence. In the 1920s, Udmurts[20] and Mari[21] started to develop scholarly research: they could not ignore Finno-Ugristics, as the discipline had collected huge amounts of precious materials. The creation of LOIKFUN allowed older and newer generations to conceive a development plan for Finno-Ugristics within Soviet Russia. LOIKFUN published at least one collection of articles in 1929, in which scholars from the different areas presented their works in different fields (for example, Kuzebay Gerd contributed the first article about contemporary Udmurt literature, cf. Toulouze 1996). LOIKFUN's plan to organise regular congresses (LOIKFUN 1929b: 1) that would coordinate Soviet Finno-Ugristics, associating several local and cultural organisations (Kuznetsov 1994: 300), would be realised later, in post-war Soviet Union. The first congress was to take place in Leningrad in 1931, and its preliminary outline contained nothing provocative. It emphasised the study of Soviet realities, as the theme proposed shows: "Report on and needs of socialist construction by Russia's Finno-Ugric peoples" (LOIKFUN 1929a: 2). No hint is made of any foreign scholar's possible participation. The project was accepted by the Udmurt Communist Party in 1929 (Kuznetsov 1994: 430–431). This was the last spark of hope for the proponents of Finno-Ugric studies in Russia.

In 1931 everything changed, as announced in Matorin's article in *Sovetskaya etnografiya*. LOIKFUN was severely criticised for its "bourgeois" tendencies and its board was renewed (Matorin 1931: 156). The society's orientations lost their independence and were harmonised with the overall goals of Soviet organisations. Attacks against Finland were multiplied. One goal was "to fight Finland's fascist territorial ambitions" (Kulikov 1997: 108). In the same issue of *Sovetskaya etnografiya*, the new chairman, M. Pal'vadre claimed that "the aim of Finnish ethnography is to create the scientific preconditions for [implementing] the idea of Great Finland" (Pal'vadre 1931: 41). These attacks against Finland were soon accompanied by attacks against "Great Estonia," presented as a parallel to "Great Finland" (Kulikov 1997: 109). The foreign dimension of Finno-Ugristics was explicitly formulated. At the same time, while political relations between the Soviet Union and Finland

---

[20] Grigoriy Vereshchagin (1851–1930) was the first Udmurt ethnographer and writer; but he was quite unique, and no other Udmurt acquired scientific reputation prior to 1917.

[21] Mari intellectuals before the Revolution dedicated their efforts to education; the first Mari to become a recognised scholar was Valerian Vasilev (see below).

were not the best, diplomatic relations stabilised a status quo: in 1932, a non-aggression pact was signed between the two countries. But what we are interested in here is not foreign policy or diplomacy, but the instrumentalisation of research. Actually, the Finnish situation[22] was interpreted according to the guiding principle of Soviet ethnography: the political dimension and instrumentalisation of science to state superior interests (Toulouze 2006: 35). The main scholarly organisations—SKS[23] and SUS[24]—were considered fascist organisations. Still, the most interesting point of view expressed in the two surrealistic articles mentioned above was that Soviet Finno-Ugristics was not strong enough to confront its Finnish and Estonian counterparts. Was this an appeal to security services to take in charge the problem researchers could not deal with? Was it a preparation for what was to follow? What was happening at the beginning of the 1930s was still not terror, but the beginning of the path leading to it.

The First Manifestations of National Repression

As the overall athmosphere was becoming tenser and tenser in the national regions, the authorities turned explicitly against the intellectuals of the

---

[22] Let us add some background information. Both Finland and Estonia were successor states and former parts of imperial Russia. Both states were anti-communist, and hence anti-Soviet, in their own political orientations, and communist parties were marginalised or excluded from social life. The Soviet Union could not attract much sympathy from these states, either as a proletarian state or as a coloniser. On the other hand, the language element was crucial in the national awareness that led to independence ambitions: both Finnish and Estonian identities were language-centred, and language was also at the core of Finno-Ugric research. In the new states, a portion of the public opinion wanted to develop particular links with the other analogous countries—newly independent states with strong patriotic feelings. In the three Finno-Ugric nations, motivated societies formed the so-called Finno-Ugric movement, which was rooted in society and not only in academic circles: *hõimuliikumine, heimotyö, rokonnépek mozgalma*. The focus of these civil society elements was not the Soviet Union's Finno-Ugric population. The societies were keen on developing relations among themselves, and as the Soviet Union was a closed country, they left it outside of their activities. But within this movement, especially in Finland, there were more political wings. Triggered by historical Karelia's position, and seeing in Karelia the actual roots of the Finns, some extreme groups, which were not the most influential ones in society, expressed ultra-nationalistic positions that may have provoked the Soviets' concerns.

[23] SKS = *Suomen Kirjallisuuden Seura*, the Finnish Literature Society, a scholarly organisation founded in 1831 on the initiative of Elias Lönnrot, Kalevala's author.

[24] SUS = *Suomalais-Ugrilainen Seura*, the Finno-Ugric society, founded in 1883 with the aim of promoting Finno-Ugric studies.

eponymous Finno-Ugric population. The first example ever of an operation against Finno-Ugric intelligentsia as such, with charges of nationalism and worse, took place in the Mari region.

I shall now focus on this first faked process, which is interesting for several reasons. It is the first example of something that in the following years would become a most common experience. Moreover, it seems to have been a rehearsal for a much wider operation two years later: all the mechanisms had already been identified and implemented.

At the end of January 1931, six Mari intellectuals were arrested.[25] They were not members of the Party, they all belonged to the older generation and were accused of nationalism. Moreover, they were charged with "having organised a counter-revolutionary group, helped by Finnish secret services" (*Tragediya* 1996: 26). These persons were among the most respected activists of Mari autonomy and Mari culture. The first to be arrested was the director of the regional museum, Timofey Yevse'yev, who only admitted that he had contacts with Finnish scholars (Kulikov 1997: 111). The elder of them, Valerian Vasilyev (called Üpö-Mariy, 'the Mari from Ufa'), a teacher in Kazan University, was arrested a few days later, and so were Leonid Mendiyarov (who worked at the Museum in Kozmodemyansk), A. Sayn (who was married to an Estonian) and a few others (*Tragediya* 1996: 111).

The arrested men were interrogated about their connections with Finland and asked to reveal their opinions about the situation in the Mari Oblast. They were interrogated for two weeks, both in Yoshkar Ola and in Nizhny Novgorod (Kulikov 1997: 111–113). Finally they were accused of planning, together with their group, "1. to separate the Mari Autonomous Oblast from the Soviet Union and 2. to gather intelligence for Finland" (*Tragediya* 1996: 113). There were also other charges.

In December 1931, the case file was examined in Moscow and the charges fizzled out. Moscow overruled the accusation that the Mari intellectuals were spies, and the accused were "only" exiled for three years for anti-Soviet activities (*Tragediya* 1996: 115). This ending, as well as the knowledge we have about future developments, is why we interpret this episode as a rehearsal for what follows.

This is the first example we have of clear criminalisation of being a national intellectual in a Finno-Ugric region. The accused Maris were all

---

[25] Actually at the same time, a smaller operation was led against a Hill Mari "nationalist" group. But we do not know whether this group had any links with Mari intelligentsia (*Tragediya* 1996: 27).

highly respected intellectuals, whose merits were directly connected with Mari nation-building. They were all involved in cultural "construction." Moreover, all their actions and declarations in favour of socialist construction show their loyalty towards the Soviet power and their sincere gratefulness cannot be doubted.

First Great Process against Finno-Ugric Intellectuals. The SOFIN

In the 1920s, the Udmurt leadership, as mentioned above, was reluctant to implement the pro-Udmurt policy promoted by Moscow—the Party was dominated by Izhevsk Factory Communists, a predominantly Russian proletarian organisation. The position of the Udmurt leadership had not changed, but Moscow had now chosen a more Russian-oriented policy. But there were tensions within the oblast. Can these tensions be explained by the new support local authorities received from the centre? Certainly, positions that were just hinted at in the previous decade, were now explicitly asserted. The Party leadership could express their dissatisfaction with intellectuals who felt involved in the Udmurt cause. Tensions accumulated around the number one poet, Kuzebay Gerd, who became the focus of harsher and harsher attacks and finally the victim of the first big process announcing wider and more systematic terror. The SOFIN affair is often also called the Gerd Affair (Kulikov 1997: 9).

Who was Kuzebay Gerd? Kuz'ma Pavlovich Chaynikov (1896–1937) was trained as a school teacher and participated enthusiastically in the revolutionary events. He was extremely active: he contributed to the establishment of Udmurt borders, wrote articles and poems in the press, had his plays performed in the countryside, lead an orphanage and was in charge of the Party's paper *Gudyri*. After this extraordinary period, he studied poetry in Moscow with Valeri Bryusov and came back in 1925 to fulfil several tasks in Udmurtia: director of the Udmurt Museum and leader of the writers' union. After some tension he went back to Moscow in order to prepare two doctoral dissertations (one in ethnography and one in folkloristics). He was called back to Udmurtia in 1931 and before he was arrested and tried, he was a university teacher. In those years, he published three collections of poems and several other works (textbooks, one short story, plays and collections of songs and folklore).

The Crescendo against Gerd

The first signs of serious disapproval of Gerd were apparent already in 1926 at a teachers' meeting where the Party's secretary accused Gerd, the chairman of the writers' union, of having bourgeois attitudes.[26] Certainly the poet's open, extrovert personality and his charm and charisma may have provoked personal jealousy and enmity. After this row, the Party dismissed him from his positions on the editing board of the literary journal *Kenesh* and as head of the writers' union and director of the Udmurt Museum (Yemelyanov 1988: 182–183). Later, he went to Moscow, where he spent some studious years in relative quiet and published in Kazan (not in Izhevsk) his second collection of poems, the reception of which was not very enthusiastic (Shklyaev 1988: 9; Yermakov 1988: 231).

But some of Gerd's fellow students denounced him in a letter to the Udmurt Communist Party and he was called back to Izhevsk without having completed his dissertations (Yermakov 1988: 14; Yermakov 1994: 36–37). I have not found any reason for this hostile attitude against a personality that was so appreciated by many. Two main hypotheses may be brought forth. The first is envy, in other words personal reasons. The second may seem paranoiac. But if Gerd had already been chosen as a culprit to be eliminated, the letter may have been inspired or even suggested by local authorities to students eager to get themselves into favour. But these are only conjectures.

Although he returned home, Gerd was increasingly targeted both in public speeches by Party officials and in the press, and accused of committing more and more political errors. Following a public letter in 1931 by Udmurt Bolshevik Nagovitsyn, which was quite critical of Gerd's political positions (Shumilov 1998: 217), Party Secretary Yelts'ov in a speech in 1932 expressed the official position:

> [T]he mouthpiece for national bourgeoisie in literature is a well-known poet, Gerd. Gerdism highly praises all our enemies, what remains of the kulak class, which we have eliminated, opposes all our initiatives and socialist construction [...]. In our press, this kulak fights against Russians, against Russian

---

[26] According to F. K. Yermakov, the Party secretary Baryshnikov said, when Gerd criticised the education authorities: "Gerd's behaviour is intolerable, he openly expresses contempt and disrespect towards the Education Office's civil servants [...]. Gerd has not changed his scornful attitude towards the Udmurts" (Yermakov 1988: 36). Gerd left the congress after this attack.

workers and he urges backward Udmurts not to learn Russian. (Kulikov 1995: 75–76)

This was a clear sign. Articles against Gerd, often signed by several persons, by colleague writers, became more and more frequent (Kuznetsov 1994: 150, Shklyaev 1990: 30).

Gerd's recent works were attacked. Gerd's wish not to provoke led him to more and more conventional works—his third[27] and last collection of poems, *Leget"es* ['Grades'] (1931) was not as original as his previous ones, either in form or content; while he praised the successes of the new life, his detractors found in his works negative metaphors against the Party's policies. For example in the poem "Storm in the village," an obsessive work with short verses, he was accused of slandering collectivisation (Shklyaev 1979: 79–80). But that is not all. All his poems were analysed from the point of view of the Party's policy and dogma, even those written before 1917: he was accused of idealising the past, praising the rich, exalting solitude and individualism, being melancholic and writing against the Russians (Shklyaev 1979; Shklyaev 1990).

Arrests

In 1932 the pressure was such that it was almost a relief to be summoned by the NKVD to Nizhny Novgorod (Kuznetsov 1994: 48). On 18 February, Gerd was asked to remain at his hotel and to write down everything about himself. He was being interrogated for the next two months (Kuvshinova 1998: 68–69). After 1994, these documents were found in KGB archives. As in other regions, a former Udmurt KGB official, Nikolay Spiridonovich Kuznetsov, published a book in 1994 informing the public about what had been forgotten and tabooed. The documents, which were undoubtedly written by Gerd, do not reveal under what pressure they were written. From what I know of their content, I do not doubt that, as far as the ones written during his confinement in Nizhny Novgorod are concerned, they certainly reflect Gerd's thinking. Gerd, who had been extremely wounded by the attacks against him, who did not understand what was happening, tried to sort things out for himself. His notes are extremely logical. He does not neglect self-criticism—but this was the praxis of the period—and at the same time he emphasises his willingness to act and to be useful (Kuznetsov 1994: 16, 309). In the first stage of the

---

[27] The first two are *Krez'chi* ['The citharist'] (Izhevsk 1922), and the second *Syas'kayas'kis' muz"em* ['The land in blossom'] (Kazan 1927).

procedure, he probably hoped that by providing an honest account of his thoughts, he would be able to convince the prosecutors of his good faith. Now we understand that this first stage was probably devised to obtain materials that could be turned against their author. Gerd was allowed to go back home, but as soon as on 13 May he was arrested together with some other Udmurt intellectuals. Gerd spent one year and seven months in an isolation cell in Nizhny Novgorod (Gerd 1988: 34; Kuznetsov 1994: 48). Later, other Finno-Ugric intellectuals were arrested as well.

Even though not all intellectuals were arrested, many were terrorised. The poetess and physician Akulina Vekshina (Ashalchi Oki) had stopped writing earlier, when she understood that it was no longer possible to be honest in one's writings. But in 1933 she was interrogated (Kuznetsov 1993: 61). She disappeared as a poet but was still able to go on working as a physician. But she was clearly traumatised, as she writes in 1956 to N. P. Kralina:[28]

> Who writes to a dead person? The Ashalchi Oki, whom you address, was buried long ago. A quarter of a century has passed since I wrote and I have forgotten everything. Anyhow, as far as I remember, I did not write anything after 1931. I have forgotten. I don't remember a single poem or story. As a result of my psychological trauma, I destroyed all the Udmurt literature that I had in my library. (Kralina 1990: 25)

The SOFIN

The process started in 1933 and finished in 1934. The files of this process comprise thousands of pages that have not been open to researchers, except for some scholars in Udmurtia, such as the former KGB official Kuznetsov. The examination of Gerd is long and extremely detailed. He was even brought to Lubyanka, where according to secondary information, he fell apart (Kuvshinova 1998: 70; Verner 1998: 227). There were several charges against the accused: ideological charges and reprehensible acts and intentions.

The ideological charges rested upon ambiguous elements, which, speciously put together, created the framework: a) nationalism, i.e., placing the interests of the Udmurts above the principle of class struggle; b) hostility to Russians or to Russian colonialism; c) anti-Sovietism, i.e., hostility towards

---

[28] Kralina had just discovered the existence of pre-war Udmurt literature and that one of the main names was still alive, working as an ophtalmologist in Alnashi, and she sent her a letter.

the power whose policy was not seen as favourable to the Udmurts; d) sympathy towards other countries, i.e., seeing Finland as a model.

The deeds the prosecution brought forth against the accused were all derived from these ideological premises: everything they did since the Revolution was interpreted as being inspired by these ideas. Thus Gerd was seen as an organiser, from the Association of Udmurt Culture Bölyak founded in Moscow in 1923–1924 (Kulikov 1991: 12) to the creation of the Udmurt Writers' Union. But all of these acts were not condemnable *per se*. Here the prosecutors were compelled to rely on imagination and invention: the creation of SOFIN as a counter-revolutionary organisation, whose aim was to work for the interests of Finland and Estonia in order to create a Finnish protectorate in Russia's Finno-Ugric regions. The SOFIN counter-revolutionary organisation was an invention. But it is well documented: we would call it a network. The NKVD reconstructed a Finno-Ugric network that existed in a non-formal way and replaced weak, occasional links with strong Party-like subordinate affiliation relations. All this was a paranoiac construction, but it was quite well structured: all groups that were interested in Finno-Ugrianness were related.

Within this construction, Gerd and his companions not only followed their own ideological beliefs, but had sold themselves to the enemy; they were also paid by Finland and Estonia to transmit intelligence about the Izhevsk weapon factory. It is clear that the most solid charges, the acts, were not consistent enough to be based on facts. Inventions were unavoidable.

The third component of the prosecution was about intention. As every act was illuminated by the ideological crimes, every act was potentially dangerous because of its possible consequences, i.e., the separation of the Finno-Ugric zones of the Soviet Union in order to have them join Finland. Words have no connection with reality. They have a meaning and a symbolism of their own.

The verdict of the process was extremely severe: at a time when the death penalty was rarely used, Gerd and his companion Yakovlev, whose sin was being a member of the Socialist Revolutionary Party[29] in the years following 1917, were actually condemned to death, while other "SOFIN members" were sentenced to less severe camp penalties. Gerd's life was allegedly spared by the interference of Gorky, who very much appreciated the Udmurt poet

---

[29] The Socialist Revolutionary Party, one of the Russian parties involved in the Revolution and later outlawed by the Bolsheviks.

(Kuznetsov 1994: 67; Gerd 1988: 35). The death penalties were finally commuted to 10 years in labour camps, and Gerd was in Solovkiy's camp when the Great Terror operations led to his execution along with thousands of other prisoners in Karelia at a place called Sandomokh (Loriya 1998: 152).

The other SOFIN accused received lighter penalties, such as exile or a few years in labour camps. The non-Udmurts were sentenced to shorter periods in camp: the Komis Lytkin and Nalimov were sentenced to two years and then released, while Markelov was exiled from Central Russia (Kulikov 1997: 238).

Conclusion

It is impossible to believe that the Soviet authorities at the beginning of the 1930s were afraid of Finland for territorial reasons. Hence this charge and the identity of the accused show that what was under process was indeed Finno-Ugrianness, which was seen as a menace to Stalinist power. How could this be? The only possible explanation is a wish to control all kinds of ethnicity more thoroughly than had been done before.

At the beginning of the 1920s, the central authorities had given a free hand to the ethnic intellectuals to work for them and to develop cultures innocuous for the Bolsheviks. In the 1930s the situation had changed. The Bolshevik power was well rooted. They could start to implement their project, in which ethnicity was not an issue. It was perhaps an important point for some of the old Bolshevik leadership (such as Lenin, who was himself from the Volga region), but not for those who had survived and for the majority of the Party, which was strongly Russian-minded. Great-Russian chauvinism was not only a political ideology: it was the default position of most Russians, who did not even question the righteousness of their supremacy over other, different and less "civilised" ethnic groups. Everything that was aimed at supporting a non-Russian nation became suspect. This analysis is not in contradiction with the importance of an ethnically structured country: it allowed the Bolsheviks to keep ethnicity but only under thorough control and to turn it towards their own goals. Too independent minds were dangerous for this project, because they would not be satisfied with just a national "form," they would demand a corresponding "content."

The SOFIN operation had deep consequences especially for the Udmurt population: one part of the national intelligentsia was silenced by physical elimination, another by fear; others were morally compromised and had lost their spiritual independence, although in the few more years they had to live before they were also caught in the Great Terror, some of them managed to produce works important for Udmurtness.[30] But in the towns, the fear provoked by the SOFIN process corresponded to the fear caused by kulak repressions in the countryside: after 1928–1929, life was a succession of unpredictable blows. Gerd's example showed that not even writing conventional communist-minded works would save one from punishment. For Volga peoples, terror was a part of life after the collectivisation. The succession of processes against Udmurts was fairly uninterrupted until the Great Terror. From the point of view of long-term political consequences, collectivisation terror and terror against intellectuals were certainly more relevant than the Great Terror: the latter was nothing new, fear had for a long time been dominating the country, and while during the Great Terror repression indeed touched groups that had not been victimised in the previous years, they, too, had lived under the empire of fear. Thus, the Great Terror did not bring anything totally new, except for its massive scale. So what are the conclusions we may draw from this experience?

- That the methods of the Great Terror had been thoroughly rehearsed;
- That the Great Terror was not an aberration, but a logical construct along the path Stalin had chosen since the collectivisation;
- That border and war problems are later phenomena. Ethnicity was dangerous as such. It had to be checked and subordinated to the state's interests;
- That the so-called Leninist nationality policy, which had structured the Soviet Union, while not being discussed as such, was a source of tension and one that was solved with the use of terror.

References

Churakov, V. S. (2008). Чураков, В. С. "Экспедиционный дневник М. Т. Маркелова – новый источник по этнографии удмуртов" ['M. T. Markelov's expedition diary. A new source for the ethnography of the Udmurt'], *Иднакар*, 1, pp. 94–111; http://udnii.ru/; access date 25 June 2014.

Dimanshteyn, S. M. (1937). Диманштейн, С. М. "Большевистский отпор национализму" ['The Bolshevik resistance to nationalism'], *Революция и национальности*, 4, pp. 1–13.

---

[30] Like, for example, writer Mikhail Konovalov, who could finish his novel *Gayan* (1936) before being arrested and eliminated.

Gerd, K. (1929). Герд, К. "Вотяцкая художественная литература" ['Belles-lettres of the Votyaks], in *Сборник ЛОИКФУН. Исследования и материалы по финноугроведению*, Leningrad, pp. 19–30.

Gerd, N. A. (1988). Герд, Н. А. "Воспоминания о моем муже. Удмуртском поэте" ['Remembrance of my husband. An Udmurt poet'], in *Современники о Кузебае Герде*, Izhevsk, pp. 22–42.

Haltsonen, S. (1964). "Muuan runoilijakohtalo" ['A poet's fate], *Valvoja*, Helsinki, p. 359.

Kralina, N. P. (1990). Кралина, Н. П. "К вопросу об изучении творчества К. Герда" ['On the question of studying K. Gerd's work'], in *Кузебай Герд и удмуртская культура*, Izhevsk, pp. 14–27.

Kreindler I. (1977). "A neglected source of Lenin's nationality policy," *Slavic Review*, 36:1–3, pp. 86–100.

Kulikov, K. I. (1991). Куликов, К. И. "Первое удмуртское научное общество 'Бöляк' (соседство) и археологические исследования в Удмуртии в периоде его деятельности" ['The first Udmurt intellectual society, "Bölyak" (neighbourhood) and archeological research in Udmurtia in the period of its activity'], in *Исследования по средневековой археологии лесной полосы Восточной Европы*, Izhevsk, pp. 4–13.

Kulikov, K. I. (1995). Куликов, К. И. "Политические взгляды Кузабая Герда" ['Kuzebay Gerd's political opinions'], *Финно-угроведение*, 2, pp. 72–91.

Kulikov, K. I. (1997). Куликов, К. И. *Дело СОФИН* ['The SOFIN affair'], Izhevsk.

Kulturnoe (1970). *Культурное строительство в Удмуртии. Сборник документов (1917–1940)* ['Cultural construction in Udmurtia. Collection of documents (1917–1940)']), Izhevsk.

Kuvshinova, R. A. (1998). Кувшинова, Р. А. "Как то было ..." ['How it happened ...'], in *Как молния в ночи ... Кузебай Герд. Жизнь. Творчество. Эпоха*, Izhevsk, pp. 68–71.

Kuznetsov, N. S. (1993). Кузнецов, Н. С. "Векшина Акулина Григорьевна – Ашальчи Оки" ['Akulina Grigor'evna Vekshina. Ashal'chi Oki'], in *Удмуртия. Массовые репрессии в 1930–1950 годов. Исследования, документы*, Moscow, pp. 58–62.

Kuznetsov, N. S. (1994). Кузнецов, Н. С. *Из мрака* ['From the darkness'], Izhevsk.

Lallukka, S. (1990). *The East Finnic Minorities in the Soviet Union. An Appraisal of the Erosive Trends*, Helsinki.

LOIKFUN (1929a). *Сборник Ленинградского Общества Исследователей культуры финно-угорских народностей. Исследование и материалы по финноугроведению* ['Articles of the Society of Researchers on the Finno-Ugric populations' culture. Research and materials on Finno-Ugric questions'], Leningrad.

LOIKFUN (1929b). *Бюллетен* ['Bulletin'], 2, Leningrad.

Loriya, E. (1998). Лория, Е. "Карельская Катынь" ['A Katyn in Karelia'], in *Как молния в ночи ... Кузебай Герд. Жизнь. Творчество. Эпоха*, Izhevsk, pp. 151–153.

Matorin, N. M. (1931). Маторин, Н. М. "Современный этап и задачи советской этнографии" ['Present stage and tasks of Soviet ethnography'], *Советская этнография*, 1-2, pp. 3–38.

Nikitina, G. A. (1998). Никитина, Г. А. *Удмуртская община в советский период* ['The Udmurt community in the Soviet period'], Izhevsk.

Pal'vadre, M. Yu. (1931). Пальвадре, М. Ю. "Буржуазная финская этнография и политика финского фашизма" ['The bourgeois Finnish ethnography and the policy of Finn fascism'], *Советская этнография*, 1-2, pp. 39–43.

Pavlov, N. P. (1991). Павлов, Н. П. *Трофим Борисов* ['Trofim Borisov'], Izhevsk.

Pesikina, E. I. (1956). Песикина, Е. И. *Народный комиссариат по делам национальностей и его деятельность в 1917-1918* ['The People's commissariat for nationalities and its activity in 1917–1918'], Moscow.

Shklyaev, A. G. (1979). Шкляев, А. Г. *На подступках к реализму. Удмуртская литература, литературное движение и критика в 1917-1934 гг.* ['Towards realism. Udmurt literature, literary movement and criticism in 1917-1934'], Izhevsk.

Shklyaev, A. G. (1982). Шкляев, А. Г. "Влияния романтизма А. М. Горького и финских поэтовна удмуртскую поэзию и период ее перехода к реализму" ['The influences of A. M. Gorky and of Finnish poetry on Udmurt poetry in the period of its evolution towards realism'], *Вопросы литературы народов СССР*, 8, Kyiv.

Shklyaev, A. G. (1988). Шкляев, А. Г. "Кузебай Герд и литературное движение 20х-годов" ['Kuzebay Gerd and the literary movement in the 1920s'], in *К изучению жизни и творчества Кузебая Герда*, Izhevsk, pp. 6–31.

Shklyaev, A. G. (1990). Шкляев, А. Г. "Герд и гердоведение" ['Gerd and research on Gerd'], in *Кузебай Герд и удмуртская культура*, Izhevsk, pp. 28–39.

Shumilov, E. (1998). Шумилов, Е. "Поэт и вождь" ['Poet and leader'], in *Как молния в ночи ... Кузебай Герд. Жизнь. Творчество. Эпоха*, Izhevsk, pp. 21–29.

Sidtikova, L. A. (1990). Сидтикова, Л. А. "Коренизация государственного аппарата в Удмуртии. Один из путей решения национального вопроса ['Indigenisation of the state apparatus in Udmurtia. One of the ways of solving the national question'], in *Народы Советского Союза. Удмурты*, Izhevsk, pp. 35–49.

Slezkine, Y. (1994). "The USSR as a communal apartment, or how a Socialist state promoted ethnic particularism," *Slavic review*, 53:2 Summer, pp. 414–452.

Toulouze, E. (1996). "Kuzebay Gerd et la littérature oudmourte" ['Kuzebay Gerd and Udmurt literature'], *Études finno-ougriennes*, 28, Paris, pp. 5–28.

Toulouze, E. (2006). "Le danger finno-ougrien en Russie (1928–1932). Les signes avant-coureurs des repressions staliniennes" ['Finno-Ugric danger in Russia (1928–1932). A harbinger of Stalinist repressions'], *Études finno-ougriennes*, 38, pp. 7–56.

Toulouze, E. (2010a). "Qui sont les Komis? Présentation générale" ['Who are the Komi? General presentation'], *Les Komis. Questions d'histoire et de culture*, eds. E. Toulouze & S. Cagnoli, Paris: ADEFO-L'Harmattan, pp. 13–35.

Toulouze, E. (2010b). "Les Komis Permiaks. Un peuple presque oublié," ['The Permyaks. A people almost forgotten'], in *Les Komis. Questions d'histoire et de culture*, eds. E. Toulouze & S. Cagnoli, Paris: ADEFO-L'Harmattan, pp. 47–83.

Tragediya (1996). Трагения народа. Книга памяти жертв политических репрессии Республики Марий Эл ['A people's tragedy. Memory book of the victims of the repressions in Mari El'], Yoshkar-Ola.

Turkin, A. (1995). Туркин, А. "К 100-летию со дня рождения В. И. Лыткина. Малоизвестные страны жизни I" ['For the 100th anniversary of V. I. Lytkin's birth. Little known pages of his life'], *Linguistica Uralica*, 31:3, pp. 207–213.

Turkin, A. (1997). Туркин, А. "V.I. Lytkinin päiväkirja" ['V.I. Lytkin's diary'], *V.I. Lytkin satavuosimuisto. Castrenianumin toimitteita* 52, Helsinki, pp. 27–34.

Verner, L. (1998). Вернер, Л. "Над пропастью во лжи" ['On the edge of lies'], in *Как молния в ночи ... Кузебай Герд. Жизнь. Творчество. Эпоха*, Izhevsk, pp. 225–228.

Yemelyanov, L. (1988). Емельянов, Л. "Обосновано ли столь строгое наказание ...?" ['Was so severe a punishment justified ...?'], in *Как молния в ночи ... Кузебай Герд. Жизнь. Творчество. Эпоха*, Izhevsk, pp. 182–185.

Yermakov, F. K. (1988). Ермаков, Ф. К. *Удмуртский поэт и писатель* ['An Udmurt poet and writer'], Izhevsk.

Yermakov, F. K. (1994). Ермаков, Ф. К. *Кузебай Герд (Кузьма Павлович герд-Чайников) Улмез но творчествоез* ['Kuzebay Gerd (Kuz'ma Pavlovich gerd-Chaynikov). His life and work'], Izhevsk.

PART 3
Religious Minorities under Soviet Repression

CHAPTER 7
The Ukrainian Evangelicals under Pressure from the NKVD, 1928–1939

Oksana Beznosova

A totalitarian rule in the USSR considered religious people unconditional enemies in the 1920s–1930s. Their suppression (i.e. literal restriction of citizens' rights to freedom of conscience) was the main task of the Soviet and the Communist Party authorities engaged in the affairs of the religious associations. Besides different kinds of actions of agitation and propaganda, various methods of persuasion, including violent coercion (political pressure), were applied by the political police (the VChK/OGPU/NKVD).[1] At the same time, the Soviet government pursued different policies in its relations with various religious bodies (churches and associations). Hierarchically organized churches—the Roman Catholic Church, the Evangelical Lutheran Church, the Ukrainian Greek Catholic Church (the so-called Uniates), and the Ukrainian Orthodox Church, which had the biggest influence on the society, were the most persecuted and the first to be oppressed. The so-called "cults" (Ru. *kul'ty*), which had a weaker vertical organizational structure, were regarded by the atheistic government as a unique ideological and social counterweight to the churches. Special attention was paid by the political police to the Baptists, the Evangelical Christians, the Pentecostals and the Adventists,[2] which were seen as the "most dangerous cults for the socialist society" among the non-hierarchical Christian confessions.

Subject and Field of Research

There were differences in both the occurrence of religious confessions and cultural traditions among the various areas of the USSR. In 1928, there were

---

[1] For more on the structure of the Soviet authorities which were supervising religious organizations, on the Soviet anti-religious propaganda, the League of the Militant Atheists (Ru. *Soyuz voynstvuyushchikh bezbozhnikov*) and the Anti-Religious Commission etc., see e.g. Nikolskaya 2009; Savin [ed.] 2004; Savin 2008; Kiridon 2008; Kurlyandsky 2011; Leont'eva 2012.

[2] Followers of Evangelical Protestantism (the Baptists, the Evangelical Christians, the Pentecostals, the Adventists, and the Mennonites) are, for the sake of brevity, designated as the "Evangelicals" in the following.

approximately 400,000 Baptists, 600,000 Evangelical Christians, 13,404 Adventists, 25,000 Pentecostals, and 200 Jewish Evangelists (Ru. *Obshchina yevreev-yevangelistov*) in the USSR[3] (Kravchenko & Sitarchuk 2005: 54–58). In addition, the Mennonites were quite similar to these groups as regards their organizational structure and confession. Some of the Mennonite denominations (*Mennonitskaya Al'yans-obshchina*) and the Mennonite Brethren Church (*Mennonitskaya bratskaya obshchina*) belonged to the Evangelical Protestant community, too. The main part of the Evangelicals of the USSR was located in the European part of the Union. More than one third of them lived in the Soviet Ukraine, the region that is selected as the topic of this study.

In the 1920s, there were still some differences between the administrative and civil laws of Ukraine and the all-Union ones, despite the fact that the Ukrainian SSR officially joined the USSR in 1922. Regulations concerning religious life had some special features in Ukraine, and there were both similarities and specific differences (including national ones) between the religious life of the Ukranian population compared to that of the Russian population. After the 1917 Revolution, the collapse of the Russian Empire and the declaration of an independent Ukrainian state, a number of Ukrainian Christian unions were created: an Evangelical Christian union, a union of Baptists associations,[4] an Adventist union and a Pentecostal one.[5] The Pentecostal movement started among the Baptists' Associations of the Odessa Oblast in the 1920s, and had a stronger development in Ukraine than in any other USSR region during the pre-war years. Mennonite religious life had some notable features too. All the Mennonites in the USSR were members of the public organization the Union of Citizens of Dutch Lineage (*Soyuz grazhdan gollandskogo proiskhozhdeniya*). Its organizational body, the Commission for Church Affairs (*Kommissiya po delam very*), was located in Molochansk in the Zaporizhia[6] Oblast of Ukraine. In 1928, the territory of the Soviet Ukraine was populated by approximately 300,000 Evangelicals (see Table 1).

---

[3] The number of Evangelicals at the beginning of the 1930s is debatable and the figures on which the majority of researchers are agreed are approximate. All data concern the number of adult (valid) members of religious associations only.

[4] The Ukrainian Union of the Baptists Associations consisted of the "Russian" (Ukrainian, Russian, Belorussian) Baptists, the German Baptists and the Jewish Evangelists.

[5] The All-Ukraine Union of Christians of the Evangelical Faith was organized in Odessa in 1926, while the all-USSR one was created in 1927.

[6] This city belonged to the Dnipropetrovsk Oblast in 1935–1939.

Table 1.[7]

Evangelical groups	USSR	Ukrainian SSR	Ukrainian Evangelicals' percentage of the USSR total
Baptists	400,000	65,000	16.25%
Evangelical Christians	600,000	95,000 (833 churches)	15.83%
Pentecostals	25,000	17,000 (105 churches)	68%
Adventists	13,404	5,703 (214 churches)	42.55%
Mennonites	85,000	65,000	76.47%
Jewish Evangelists		3 churches	100%

In this chapter, I focus on the Dnipropetrovsk and the Zaporizhia oblasts[8] for several reasons. First, this territory was one of the first regions where Evangelical Protestantism (Evangelism) arose in the Russian Empire (mid-nineteenth century), and strong traditions of both German and Russian-Ukrainian Protestantism existed in the region. Second, these two industrially developed oblasts were strongly involved in the processes of the "Stalin industrialization." Third, but not least important, the choice of region for this study is motivated by the available sources—a series of 27 books, *Reabilitovani istorieu*. This issue contains both biographical materials on the rehabilitated victims of political pressure in Ukraine (1920–1950) and additional documentary materials, as well as summarizing analytical articles on different periods of political persecutions and detailed statistics. These books present all 26 oblasts of Ukraine. Nevertheless, the biographical data of the rehabilitated differ a great deal in content among books on various oblasts. Therefore, the modern Dnipropetrovsk and the Zaporizhia oblasts were selected for this study, because there one finds the most exhaustive information (in *Reabilitovani istorieu. Dnipropetrovska oblast* 1–2, 2008;

---

[7] The figures are calculated from Kravchenko & Sitarchuk 2005: 54–58; *Istoriya yevangelskikh Khristian-baptistov v SSSR* 1989: 403; Yartsev 1930: 40; Nikolskaya 2009: 87; and Savin 2008: 5.
[8] Which in 1932–1938 were within the Dnipropetrovsk Oblast.

Reabilitovani istorieu. Zaporizka oblast 1, 2004; *Reabilitovani istorieu. Zaporizka oblast* 2–3, 2006; *Reabilitovani istorieu. Zaporizka oblast* 4, 2008; and *Reabilitovani istorieu. Zaporizka oblast* 5, 2010). Although these sources do not contain information on every servant or activist in the various denominations referred to as oppressed by witnesses or in the research literature (Mennonite ministers especially), there is plenty of information about people who are not yet included in martyrologiums. This gives us a chance to track down and analyze general tendencies in events of that time period.

The "cultists" were about 63,000, or approximately 2 per cent of the whole population of the Dnipropetrovsk and the Zaporizhia oblasts in 1928–1929. Half of them, nearly 33,000, were Mennonites, and nearly 4,000 were followers of "Orthodox cults" (Old Believers, Molokans, Tolstoyans, etc.). Another 40 per cent of the "cultists" were Evangelicals, most of whom (nearly 20,000 adult persons) belonged to the Evangelical Christians and the Baptists. There were also about 3,500 Pentecostals and nearly 1,000 Adventists.[9] Their growth in numbers was supported by active missionary activities both by non-Evangelical Christians and the followers of Baptism and the Evangelical Christianity (DADO P-7, op. 1, sprava 795, ark. 27; Franchuk 2002: 5; *Baptist Ukrainy* 1928: 38–41). Thus, the Evangelicals were a religious minority in the Dnipropetrovsk and the Zaporizhia oblasts in 1929–1930, but they were a very active and fast growing minority which was both ideologically and socially incompatible with the Bolshevik atheistic authority.

Underwater Rocks of the "Religious NEP"

Both research and, in particular, confessional literature (see e.g. Savinskiy 1999: 13, 118) have the following periodization of the history of the Evangelical confessions in the USSR in the pre-Second World War period:

- 1918–1928: "The Golden Decade," a period of relative religious freedom, the "Religious NEP" for the Evangelic confessions;
- 1929–1931: the first wave of trials and oppressions, related to the new act "On Religious Associations" and the closing of religious associations;
- 1935–1938: the period of massive repression;

---

[9] These figures are calculated from Kravchenko & Sitarchuk 2005: 54–58; and TsDAGOU 1, op. 20, sprava 1772, ark. 1. The author thanks Prof. R. Sitarchuk for providing additional data on the topic.

- 1939–1941: a decline in persecutions.

Undoubtedly, the "Golden Decade" was the most prosperous period for the Evangelicals during the Soviet period, but they did not enjoy full religious freedom. After the end of the Civil War and the establishment of Soviet authority in Ukraine in 1921–1923, the Bolsheviks declared themselves "militant atheists" and started a "crusade against religion." In the 1920s, the Soviet government mostly fought against the Orthodox, the Greek Catholics, the Roman Catholics and the Lutherans. However, the Bolsheviks did not exclude the followers of other religious groups (the "cultists") from their scope, but were trying to use them as a weapon against the larger churches (Boyko 2008: 741–742).

Suppression of the rights of religious minorities in the USSR started as early as in the process of preparations for the military reform in the mid-1920s. Most of the Evangelical followers were pacifists and this made them "inconvenient citizens" for the Soviet military state. Under the new military law of 1925, the right to alternative military service could be granted to members of pacifist confessions (the Adventists, the Mennonites, the Tolstoyans, the Baptists, the Doukhobors, the Molokans, the "Netovtsy"), who had this right also during the Russian Empire period. But this was a right that only pertained to the individual (Savin [ed.] 2004: 36). The Mennonites who were residing in Ukraine were obliged to prove their non-involvement in any self-defense squads during the Civil War (Beznosova & Beznosov 2011: 44–45). Besides, between 1925 and 1930, the authorities put pressure on pacifists in every possible way (by blackmailing, threats and bribery), forcing "voluntary" renouncements of the right to alternative military service (Nikolskaya 2009: 84–90; Savin [ed.] 2004: 30–38). Thus, when the All-Union and the All-Ukraine Union of Christians of the Evangelical Faith (the Pentecostals) approved a declaration of support for all the measures of the Soviet government (including military service) in October 1927, the movement against this decision among the Evangelical churches resonated through the USSR in the winter of 1928–1929. As a result, 17 people were arrested as *tryasuny* ['shiverers'] in Tomakovka (Dnipropetrovsk Oblast) and nearby villages in December 1928–February 1929. Two of them were imprisoned in labor camps for three years, while eight were released after a decision of 16 August 1929 by the Special Conference of the OGPU of the USSR. Nevertheless, all eight of the latter were exiled for three years with a "prohibition to live in certain places." One of the other arrested persons was exempt from punishment being a mental patient. Five were released in March

1929 having been found not to be *tryasuny*, but belonging to "another rationalistic cult" (*Reabilitovani istorieu. Dnipropetrovska oblast* 2, 2008). Considering the history of the Tomakovka settlement, one can assume that these released "rationalists" were Baptists or Adventists.[10]

The Evangelicals were considered by the Soviet authorities as "the most dangerous cultists" because of their missionary activity and civic stances. They created youth organizations (the Bapsomol, the Khristomol) and agrarian and other associations as alternatives to the Soviet ideology and practice. These public associations were in many cases more successful than their Bolshevik equivalents. The authorities were very disturbed by the economic, social and ideological achievements of the Evangelicals (Coleman 2005: 198–215). Therefore the political police (the OGPU)[11] and its Fifth Special Secret Department (the "Church Department") had been conducting secret preparations since 1923–1924 for a general and decisive attack on all the religious associations. The OGPU officers used a secret agency to destroy both churches and "cults" by instigating internal conflicts (DAKhO 1644, op. 1, sprava 1, ark. 5, 6, 12; Beznosova & Beznosov 2011: 43; Zubov [ed.] 2009: 873–880). Thus, tensions between the Baptists and the Evangelical Christians (Savin 2008: 12–13, 15–20; Savinskiy 1999: 97–98) and the struggle among the Evangelical Christians, the Baptists and the Adventists against the Voronaev's Pentecostals were used by the OGPU to reach its objectives (Franchuk 2002).

Increasing control of the political police over the activities of priests, ministers and religious associations started in 1925. A "New Statute of the Volost ['regional'] Administrations and the Selsovets ['settlement councils']"[12] was sent to the volost administrations on 25 January 1925. The statute's instruction was to "supervise the correct enforcement of the laws on separation of the churches from the state," and explained the duties of local administrations regarding the control of the activities of religious associations (Kulishova & Prigodina 2002). By order of this document, a re-registration of all religious associations at the local authorities was performed in February 1925. Extensive information on, *inter alia*, the administration

---

[10] At least one of them (S. M. Khrypko) was an Adventist (*Reabilitovani istorieu. Zaporizka oblast* 5, 2010: 484).
[11] The acronym OGPU (*Ob'edinennoe Gosudarstvennoe Politicheskoe Upravlenie* ['Joint State Political Directorate'] was interpreted by the people as *O, Gospodi, pomogi ubezhat'!* ['Oh, God, help me escape!'] (Wölk & Wölk 1981: 22; Shchuplov 2001).
[12] Ru. *Novoe polozhenie o volispolkomakh i sel'sovetakh*.

7 - UKRAINIAN EVANGELICALS UNDER PRESSURE, 1928-1939

(ministers, preachers and missionaries), active believers and property of the associations was gathered during the process.

On 14 August 1925 the administration of the OGPU of the Ukrainian SSR instructed their "field agents" to:

> Look for the political mood, anti-Soviet activities of the cult associations, their connections with foreign countries [...] and their religious centers, look for negative aspects of the indicated group's activity. That is, seek out anything that may compromise them in the eyes of their followers. (DAKhO 1644, op. 1, sprava 1, ark. 6)

At the same time, the "cultists" were considered by the OGPU as a less serious and dangerous threat than the "churches." Thus, at the end of 1927, the OGPU of the Ukrainian SSR was satisfied with having only one secret agent per region tasked with supervising the "cultists" and controlling local informants (Koshtoris vitrat na robotu DPU USSR [1928] 2011: 257-258). For example, in 1925, an analyst of the secret operative group of the Melitopol OGPU, Pavel Sudoplatov, worked with informants among the Mennonites, the Germans and the Bulgarians in the Melitopol Okrug of the Yekaterinoslav Government (DAKhO 1644, op. 1, sprava 1, ark. 5, 12). However, neither the Baptists nor the Evangelical Christians (who formed the major part of all the Evangelicals) were the main target of the OGPU operations among the *religiozniki* ['religious persons'], as H. Coleman (2005: 217) has pointed out. In "An explanatory note for the estimation of costs [for the OGPU of the Ukrainian SSR] to deal with the religious associations in the first half-year of 1928," the OGPU administration stated that "the work must be done among the All-Ukrainian Baptists' Union, the Evangelical Christians, the Christians of Evangelical Faith (*"tryasuny"*) and the Seventh-day Adventists" (Koshtoris vitrat na robotu DPU USSR [1928] 2011: 258). Thus the main blow was directed against the Evangelical pool as a whole.

The Beginning of Attacks

The beginning of the offensive strike on the rights of believers in Ukraine was the introduction of a new Administrative Code in 1927, in which the "cult ministers" (presbyters, deacons, pastors, preachers) were deprived of certain civil rights, including the right to vote for and be elected to public councils and authorities. The disfranchised, so-called *lishentsy*, had to pay additional taxes, had no right to be members of trade unions, could only be employed in low-paid jobs, etc. This was a hard blow to the ministers and their families, because some of them were forced to give up being "cult servants" (Reshetnikov & Sannikov 2000: 174). This legal provision relating to the disfranchised became official in the all-USSR jurisdiction in 1929, when the new law on the religious cults of 8 April 1929 and the NKVD instruction of 1 October 1929, "On the rights and obligations of religious associations" (which was based on the 1929 law) were passed (O pravakh i obyazannostyakh 1929).

Illustration 11: Members of the Union of the Baptists of the USSR, 1925. In the centre: Aleksey Markovich Bukreev (1884–1929), presbyter of Dnipropetrovsk Baptist Convention. Photo: Aleksey Sinichkin, Archive of the Union of Evangelical Christians-Baptists of Russia.

The persecution of religious representatives and activists started in mid-1928. Special attention was given by the political police to the initiators of the emigration movement among the Mennonites and persons who had contacts with foreigners (Beznosova & Beznosov 2011: 45–46). In this situation, travel abroad for whatever purposes, except governmental, was highly suspicious in the eyes of the authorities and provoked very negative reactions. Thus, in June 1928, when the Fourth Baptist World Congress was held in Toronto, it was openly proposed by the officials that the delegates of the Federative Baptist Union and the Union of Christians of the Evangelical Faith of the USSR should not be allowed to return to the Soviet Union. However, ten out of twelve members of the Soviet delegation did not accept this "good advice" (Ivanov & Sinichkin [eds.] 2007: 131). By the end of the year, A. M. Bukreev (1884–1929), one of the ten delegates, member of the Federative Baptist Union Council, vice-chairman and responsible secretary of the All-Ukrainian Baptist Union and presbyter of the Dnipropetrovsk Oblast Baptist Association, was accused of espionage and arrested. During the interrogation he was tortured and sent home in a bad physical and psychological condition.[13] He died in a sanatorium on 31 May 1929 (Bukreev 2011; Ivanov & Sinichkin [eds.] 2007: 131).[14] In the next few years, the remaining delegates were also arrested and imprisoned. The publishing of the All-Ukrainian Baptists' Union's journal *Baptist Ukrainy* ['The Baptist of Ukraine'] ceased in 1928.

Information on more than 240 Evangelicals who were repressed (arrested, imprisoned, exiled) on the territory of the Dnipropetrovsk and the Zaporizhia oblasts in 1928–1938 has been disclosed in the "The Rehabilitated by History" books, memoirs and research literature. Thus, the "peaks" of repressions against the Evangelicals in the oblasts took place in 1930, 1932–1933, 1935 and 1937–1938.

The 1928–1933 repressive measures were taking place during a process of massive collectivization and dekulakization. A contingent of "cultists" in Ukraine residing in villages resisted the plans of the authorities on ideological and organizational grounds. As a result, a lot of preachers and ordinary believers were arrested and exiled. For example, at the end of 1928, S. F. Rod'ko, the leader of "a religious cult of the Vodyanoe village," was arrested in the Vodyanoe village in the Kamyansko-Dniprovsk region of the Zaporizhia Oblast. He was accused of "preaching about the end of the world, the evidence of which was the existence of the current [Soviet] regime." He was sentenced by the OGPU of the Ukrainian SSR to be imprisoned in a labor camp for 3 years because of his alleged statement that "no one must bow to this Antichrist regime" (*Reabilitovani istorieu. Zaporizka oblast* 5, 2010: 435).

---

[13] Sending tortured suspects home to die in order to intimidate others was a characteristic feature of the 1928–1933 persecutions (Reshetnikov & Sannikov 2000: 174).

[14] The author thanks Pastor A. P. Nagirnyak for providing additional data on the biography of A. M. Bukreev.

Table 2: The table presents the number of repressed individuals and shows that the systematic persecution of "cultists" began in 1928 and reached climaxes in 1930, 1932–1933, 1935 and 1937–1938.

Oblast	1928	1929	1930	1931	1932	1933	1934	1935	1936	1937	1938	Total number of repressed Evangelicals
Dnipropetrovsk	14	7	20	5	4	4	1	15	2	37	46	158
Zaporizhia	1		8		9	15	1	8	4	26	11	83
Total	15	7	28	5	13	19	2	23	6	63	57	241

In 1927–1928, a struggle between two trends in Soviet authorities was won by the partisans of strict control of religious associations (Stalin, Kaganovich, and the administration of the OGPU/NKVD, among others). Thus, systematic attacks on religious groups started at the beginning of 1929. On 24 January 1929, the secret decree of the Politburo of the Communist Party's Central Committee "On the measures of intensification of anti-religious work" was approved. All religious associations were described in this document as "the only legally operating counter-revolutionary organizations which have an influence on the masses." A month later, the decree was sent out to the other Soviet republics. On 28 February 1929, the Politburo decided to amend the formulations in the Russian Soviet Federative Socialist Republic (RSFSR) Constitution regarding the religious and civil rights of Soviet citizens. As a result, all citizens of the RSFSR (and in practice all citizens of the USSR) lost their rights to spread religious propaganda (Pashchenko 1995: 233; Sovetov 2007). At the same time, a public mass propaganda campaign aimed at discrediting all "religionists" ("churchmen" and "cultists") was developed.[15]

A logical result of the preceding two years of increased control and limitations of religious associations and their leaders was the decree "On religious associations" which was developed by the Central Executive Committee (VTsIK) of the RSFSR on 8 April 1929 (O religioznych ob'edineniyach [1929] 1959).

---

[15] For more information on the press campaign and the Soviet anti-religious propaganda, see e.g. Savin [ed.] 2004: 46–64.

Although it was only intended for the RSFSR, in practice it became the law of the entire USSR during the whole Soviet period, even though it was subject to some amendments in 1932, 1962 and 1975. According to the decree, all cases involving "cultists" were to be handed over from the Secretariat of Cultist Affairs (*Sekretariat po delam kul'tov*) to the presidium of the Permanent Committee for Religious Matters at the Presidium of the VTsIK, which dealt with cases concerning all religious associations. This was a sign that the Soviet government was aiming at a uniform policy towards all religions.

According to the decree, only registered associations could operate in the USSR. Unregistered associations were declared illegal and their activities led to prosecution. In addition, the requirements for registering associations were tightened. Unlike stated in the previous act (of 1923), every religious body consisting of 20 (not 50) adult members ("actives") residing in one and the same settlement might be registered by the local authorities. However, this clause made it practically impossible for non-residents and youths to have a legal membership. On the other hand, large bodies of more than 20 persons (e.g. the Baptist and Evangelical Christian congregation in Dnipropetrovsk) were forced to reduce the official number of members, as it was specifically stated in the decree that "every religious association or group of believers may use one house of prayer only" (O religioznych ob'edineniyach [1929] 1959). The financial cost of registration and taxes for keeping a house of prayer had become so high that a considerable number of legal religious associations and houses of prayer had to close down in 1930–1931 (for example, the Chortitza Mennonites church) or turn into an illegal entity (*The Mennonite Encyclopaedia* 2, 1955: 235; Wölk & Wölk 1981: 19–20). In addition, any missionary and religious propaganda in public was forbidden, which led to a suspension in the production of church journals and religious literature. Charity and donations were also forbidden:

> Members of religious associations have a right to collect donations both in their house of prayer and outside of it, but only among the members of the association and only for the pupose of keeping up a house of prayer or property, hiring the servants of the cult and maintaining their executive organs. Non-voluntary payments for religious associations are punishable under the Criminal Code of the RSFSR. (O religioznych ob'edineniyach [1929] 1959)

Thus, the functions of religious associations were restricted to the organization of prayers:

Any activity beyond the gratification of religious needs was regarded as criminal (under paragraph 10 of Article 58 of the Criminal Code). Those accused of this crime could be imprisoned for 3 years or even executed for "using religious prejudices to weaken the state." (Courtois, Werth, Panne et al. 2006)

The inner life of religious associations was strongly restricted. Even those who managed to register faced arbitrary changes in the permission policy for prayer meetings. Associations were crossed off the register and their houses of prayer were closed immediately if the slightest indication of policy violation was found (Coleman 2005: 216–217).

Justification of such actions was given in a new decree from the VTsIK and the Sovnarkom (the Council of People's Commissars) of 11 February 1930, "On the struggle against counter-revolutionary elements in leading organs of religious associations." It instructed the authorities of allied republics to exclude "the Kulaks, the disfranchised and other persons who were antagonizing Soviet authority" and to refuse registration to religious associations that did not meet those terms (Sovetov 2007). Considering that all "servants of cults" of the Ukrainian SSR had been defined as disfranchised since 1927 (and since 1929 in USSR), this opened a wide field for administrative voluntarism and refusal of registration (Reshetnikov & Sannikov 2000: 176). Moreover, the authorities established a five-day working week: five days of work and one day off. Sunday was removed as a holiday for all people (Courtois, Werth, Panne, et al. 2006).

As a result of the decrees introduced in 1929–1930, most of the Evangelical associations had ceased to exist by 1931. If an association continued their meetings in private, the organizers of prayers were arrested. Thus, in 1929–1931, 40 persons in the Dnipropetrovsk and the Zaporizhia oblasts were arrested on charges of counter-revolutionary activities, anti-Soviet agitation and "involvement in a counter-revolutionary cult."[16] Eighteen of them were members of a religious commune, "The Kingdom of Light,"[17] which was forcefully liquidated in the process of mass collectivization. Among those arrested

---

[16] This figure is calculated based on *Reabilitovani istorieu. Dnipropetrovska oblast 1–2*, 2008; *Reabilitovani istorieu. Zaporizka oblast 1*, 2004; *Reabilitovani istorieu. Zaporizka oblast 2–3*, 2006; *Reabilitovani istorieu. Zaporizka oblast 4*, 2008, *Reabilitovani istorieu. Zaporizka oblast 5*, 2010.

[17] This religious commune may not have had a clear confessional identity. Some researchers consider its members as the "Tolstoyans" (Ru. *tolstovtsy*), "the Baptists-Subbotniks," the "Subbotniks," etc. All its repressed members are marked as "un-indicated confessions" in the column of the appendix table.

during these years were B. B. Dick, the preacher of the Morozovka village's Mennonite Church, and A. D. Brown, the deacon of the Shirokoe village's Mennonite Church in the Zaporizhia Oblast, both of whom had expressed dissatisfaction with the Soviet authority (*Reabilitovani istorieu. Zaporizka oblast* 3, 2006: 369; *Reabilitovani istorieu. Zaporizka oblast* 4, 2008: 69).

Active involvement by religious leaders in peasantry resistance to mass dekulakization, and the organization of hunger-fighting efforts by foreign co-religionists, led to another wave of repression. The general background to these events was the announcement of the years 1932–1936 as "The Godless Five Years." A new instruction, "On the order of organization, activity, accounts and liquidation of religious associations and registration of members and servants of cults of religious associations by state administration organs," was issued by the VTsIK and the Sovnarkom on 1 January 1932 (Instruktsiya sekretariata Presidiuma VUTsIK [1932] 1963). The instruction further tightened the registration terms and control over the lives of registered associations. All the "servants of religious cults" had the right to perform their duties only after registration with the corresponding executive committee (*ispolkom*) or local council (*sovet*). The freedom of action of ministers was limited to the place of residence of the members of their religious associations and the location of the prayer house. After that time, there was a mass closure of the houses of prayer and refusal of registration to communities, and the activities of many ministers became illegal (Reshetnikov & Sannikov 2000: 176). Among the (later rehabilitated) victims of persecutions in the Dnipropetrovsk Oblast due to religious activities in 1932–1933, 32 people were arrested. Only one of those arrested for missionary activities was a resident of a city, the others were village residents. In addition, seven "servants of cults" of Mennonite associations (of whom D. Raymer and J. Janz were shot in the Melitopol prison for having organized foreign aid to the starving people in 1933; see Wölk & Wölk 1981: 28–29), fifteen Baptists and Evangelical Christians, one Adventist, seven Pentecostals and two "members of counter-revolutionary cults" were repressed. Most of them were charged by the Special Council under the Collegium of the OGPU USSR or by the judicial troika of the GPU of the Ukrainian SSR to 3–5 years of imprisonment or to 3 years of exile in the North.[18]

---

[18] These figures are calculated from *Reabilitovani istorieu. Dnipropetrovska oblast* 1–2, 2008; *Reabilitovani istorieu. Zaporizka oblast* 1, 2004; *Reabilitovani istorieu. Zaporizka oblast* 2–3, 2006; *Reabilitovani istorieu. Zaporizka oblast* 4, 2008, *Reabilitovani istorieu. Zaporizka oblast* 5, 2010; Wölk & Wölk 1981: 19–20, 28–29; Fast 2001: 127–128.

This repressive action of 1929–1932, as T. G. Leont'eva has justly noted, did not only start the massive arrests of clerics and active laity, it also "played a fatal role during the next repressions: previous convictions becomes the 'recommendation' for including [previously convicted persons] into the shooting list in 1937–1938" (Leont'eva 2012: 224).

Mass Operations against the Evangelicals

A new wave of arrests, 1934–1936 (after the assassination of S. M. Kirov), led to the destruction of the central organs of the Federative Baptist Union, the Union of Christians of the Evangelical Faith and other associations, which were forced to close down. Recovery and re-registration of these associations took place under close supervision by the NKVD (Kravchenko & Sitarchuk 2005: 189; Nikolskaya 2009: 101–102; Savinskiy 1999: 122–123).

The arrest wave of 1934–1936 hit religious associations in both towns and villages on an oblast level. Eleven presbyters of the associations of the Baptists and the Evangelical Christians, the Adventists, the Pentecostals and the Mennonites were among those arrested.[19] Some of them (e.g. the activist of the Dnipropetrovsk Baptist association M. K. Avdeenko, the presbyter of the Pyatihatki Pentecostals' association G. G. Ponurko, and the preacher of the Molochna Mennonite Brethren Church G. I. Winter, see *Reabilitovani istorieu. Dnipropetrovska oblast* 2, 2008: 2, 747; Wölk & Wölk 1981: 28–29) were arrested for a second time. Ordinary active members of the congregations were arrested too. For example, more than five men of the church choir of the Dolgoe Mennonite Church were arrested in the Dolgoe (Conteniusfeld) village in the Chernigivka region of the Zaporizhia Oblast between December 1935 and the beginning of 1936 and were sentenced to 8–10 years of imprisonment in the Karaganda labor camps (Fast 2001: 127–128).

Meanwhile, the authorities prepared for the USSR census in 1936. Almost all houses of prayer and churches were closed and religious associations lost their registration. Following this, there were fewer than ten legal associations of the Baptists and the Evangelical Christians left in the Soviet Ukraine. Two of them (Baptist and Evangelical Christians) operated in Dnipropetrovsk (Reshetnikov & Sannikov2000: 177; Kravchenko & Sitarchuk 2005: 189; Nikolskaya 2009: 101–102). After all these measures, including an agitation

---
[19] This figure is calculated from *Reabilitovani istorieu. Dnipropetrovska oblast* 1–2, 2008; *Reabilitovani istorieu. Zaporizka oblast* 1, 2004; *Reabilitovani istorieu. Zaporizka oblast* 2–3, 2006; *Reabilitovani istorieu. Zaporizka oblast* 4, 2008, *Reabilitovani istorieu. Zaporizka oblast* 5, 2010.

campaign under the "Godless Five-Year Plan," the authorities seriously believed that the population would mainly identify themselves as atheists. However, they faced a very unpleasant surprise: only one third of the inhabitants of the USSR declared themselves as atheists in the 1936 census (Zhiromskaya 2000; Kravchenko & Sitarchuk 2005: 182). This fact was considered a failure on the anti-religious front. Development of specific measures for the elimination of religion, and for the predicted "breakthrough," was voted for by the February-March (1937) Plenum of the Central Committee of the Communist Party of Ukraine. Simultaneously, preparations for mass political repressions against religious persons started.

The attack on religious persons and associations began with a thorough gathering of information, conducted by the NKVD on the basis of Circular № 23 of 27 March 1937, "On the intensification of work for cultists and churchmen." The gathering of materials on the activities of religious associations was completed before the end of April. On 8 June 1937, a new directive of the NKVD demanded "initiation of strong measures for the liquidation of churchmen and cultists." This was the basis for mass arrests and for the planned "mass operations" (Kurlyandsky 2011: 490–491, 502–513). High taxation (40%) of the "cult leaders" as well as of persons having unearned income (Spravochnik rayonnogo prokurora 1942), was introduced by the Resolution of the Politburo of 14 July 1937 from 1 July 1937 (Kurlyandsky 2011: 510–511). This financial pressure often led to the complete ruin of religious ministers and to the forced abandonment of their official ministry. Therefore, a typical feature of questionnaires filled in by repressed religious leaders in the Dnipropetrovsk region in 1937–1939 (unlike in 1932–1935) was that they identified themselves not as "clerics," "presbyters," "elders," or "preachers," but as "factory workers," "farmers," "tailors," "photographers" or even as "unemployed."[20]

The "religionists" were oppressed by extrajudicial "troikas" in the kulak operation of the NKVD. I. A. Kurlyansky, who has studied the process of the elaboration of the provisions of Order 00447, notes that initially, the "religionists" were not included in the list of target groups of citizens subject to mandatory repression. They were added to the plan of repressions by Stalin personally after proposals from local party activists. In particular, the first Secretary of the Dnipropetrovsk Oblast Committee of the VKP(b), N. V.

---

[20] This is elucidated in *Reabilitovani istorieu. Dnipropetrovska oblast 1–2*, 2008; *Reabilitovani istorieu. Zaporizka oblast* 1, 2004; *Reabilitovani istorieu. Zaporizka oblast 2–3*, 2006; *Reabilitovani istorieu. Zaporizka oblast* 4, 2008, *Reabilitovani istorieu. Zaporizka oblast* 5, 2010; Oparin & Begas 2009: 36–38.

Margolin, was among those who demanded increased pressure on the counter-revolutionary organizations of "churchmen, cultists and other filth" in the Plenum of the Central Committee of the VKP(b), before the election of the Supreme Council in 1937 (Kurlyandsky 2011: 513–516). The result of these events was a circular of the NKVD of 5 October 1937, which included an order to "conduct a large-scale operation to destroy church and cultist counter-revolutionary persons as soon as possible" (Kravchenko & Sitarchuk 2005: 189). This resulted in a wave of arrests, especially of "churchmen" and "cultists," around the USSR. Some of those who were in labor camps after the first arrests in 1934–1936 were sentenced again to an extended period of imprisonment—for example, the presbyter of the Dnipropetrovsk Baptist association, N. I. Zubanov (*Reabilitovani istorieu. Donetska oblast* 4, 2007: 240; Slobodyanyuk 2003: 12–13)—or to execution—for example the leader of the Verhnyaya Chortitza village's Mennonite Church, A. P. Toews (*Reabilitovani istorieu. Zaporizka oblast* 4, 2008: 559).

186 "churchmen and cultists" were arrested according to the reports of the NKVD of the Ukrainian SSR. 178 of them were charged in the Dnipropetrovsk Oblast between July 1937 and January 1938. 74 "cultists" were arrested (14 executed) and 82 "churchmen" (36 executed) during the period between July and October 1937. Nevertheless, compared to other oblasts of the Ukrainian SSR in the second half of 1937,[21] these figures are the lowest indicators of the official zeal of the NKVD officers in the fight against "churchmen and cultists."

The names of 63 people repressed in 1937 (including 11 executed) were restored through materials of "The Rehabilitated by History" books, research literature and memoirs of witnesses.[22] From this information, it seems clear that the main strike was directed against leaders and activists of village-based and town-based religious associations: Baptists (Sinelnikovo, Berdyansk and Zaporizhia), Adventists (Melitopol), Mennonites (the Molochna Mennonite settlements and Melitopol) and Pentecostals (Pyatihatki and Krivoy Rog). Six of those had been charged as early as the beginning of the 1930s.

A notable feature of the verdicts of 1937 is the detailed information on the charged persons, in addition to standard phrases such as "anti-Soviet agitation" and "participation in a counter-revolutionary organization." However,

---

[21] This is elucidated in Bazhan 2010: 137.
[22] The figures are calculated from *Reabilitovani istorieu. Dnipropetrovska oblast* 1–2, 2008; *Reabilitovani istorieu. Zaporizka oblast* 1, 2004; *Reabilitovani istorieu. Zaporizka oblast* 2–3, 2006; *Reabilitovani istorieu. Zaporizka oblast* 4, 2008; *Reabilitovani istorieu. Zaporizka oblast* 5, 2010.

in 1938, sentences became more severe due to the acceleration of repression. Virtually all of the arrests ended with the arrested people being shot. Justifications such as "religious activity" practically disappeared from the wordings of court sentences. Thus, on 3 April 1938, the NKVD officers interrupted a meeting of the Baptist congregation of Dnipropetrovsk. Eighteen of the participating men were arrested on this and subsequent nights. On 29 April 1938, all of them were sentenced to death by a resolution of a troika of the NKVD for "participating in a counter-revolutionary organization." In May–June there was also a series of arrests in the Dnipropetrovsk association of the Evangelical Christians. 26 men were executed.[23] In the same months two members of the Novomoskovsk Adventist association were arrested and shot for belonging to the fabled "insurgent organization" (Oparin & Begas 2009: 44; *Reabilitovani istorieu. Dnipropetrovska oblast* 2, 2008: 93; *Reabilitovani istorieu. Dnipropetrovska oblast* 2, 2008: 589).

Among the citizens charged in 1938 who were later rehabilitated, only a small number were persecuted as "religionists." On 19 February 1938, J. J. Pris, the gardener of the kolkhoz named after Yezhov, was arrested as a "cultist who conducted counter-revolutionary agitation" in the Novoslobodka village of the Zaporizhia region. He was sentenced to execution by a Special Troika of the NKVD in the Dnipropetrovsk Oblast (*Reabilitovani istorieu. Zaporizka oblast* 4, 2008: 481). M. K. Streletz, a carpenter working in a factory in Zaporizhia, was arrested as a presbyter of a "Baptist group" that conducted anti-Soviet agitation during a worship service on 15 July 1938. He was sentenced to five years in a labor camp by a Special Meeting of the NKVD on 29 October 1939 (*Reabilitovani istorieu. Zaporizka oblast* 2, 2006: 625). Nine people (among them S. I. Salimonov, the second presbyter of the Zaporizhia Baptist association) were arrested together with Streletz and others. They were sentenced to ten years in labor camps.[24] Actual indicators of "religious activity" only appeared again in the cases of 1939, when the general terror decreased. However in 1940–1941 terror against "religionists" continued, but now it was mostly directed against the Adventists and the Pentecostals.

As a result of the "mass operations" of the NKVD, just before the beginning of the Second World War, it was mostly women and children who

---

[23] These figures are calculated from *Reabilitovani istorieu. Dnipropetrovska oblast* 2, 2008; Reshetnikov & Sannikov 2000: 177; Slobodyanyuk 2003: 14–15.

[24] These figures are calculated from *Reabilitovani istorieu. Zaporizka oblast* 2–3, 2006; *Reabilitovani istorieu. Zaporizka oblast* 4, 2008, *Reabilitovani istorieu. Zaporizka oblast* 5, 2010; Mokrenchuk 2010; *Evangelski Khristiani-baptisti Ukraini* 2012: 176.

remained official members of the Evangelical associations in the Dnipropetrovsk Oblast (Oparin & Begas 2009: 41; Reshetnikov & Sannikov 2000: 177).

Conclusion

The real scope of the repressions against Evangelicals, especially in 1937–1938 when terror struck a large number of ordinary members of the denominations, is still unknown. This is due to the fact that most believers were arrested on accusations not directly connected to their religious beliefs.

Summing up, on the basis of an analysis of personal data of more than 240 persons persecuted in the Dnipropetrovsk Oblast (modern-day Dnipropetrovsk and Zaporizhia oblasts) in 1927–1939, the following conclusions can be stated. The main blow to the "sectarians" took place in the 1930s and the main part of all repressed Evangelicals lived in the territory of the present-day Dnipropetrovsk Oblast. This region was an important center of Evangelism in the Ukrainian SSR where there were large legal (registered) Evangelical congregations before 1937. By 1941 all the legal Evangelical congregations had "voluntarily" ceased their activity due to repressions.

In denominational terms, the Pentecostals were the hardest hit. Although the number of repressed Pentecostals was three times lower than the number of repressed Baptists (45 versus 113), the total number of Pentecostal associations in Ukraine was only one sixth of the number of Baptist associations. Therefore, the relative losses of the Pentecostals in the process of repression were more significant. Unfortunately, little information is available on the Mennonites as religious persons, as the German population in general was repressed on national (i.e. ethnic) grounds in 1937–1938. The Mennonite preachers were persecuted the most, because of their involvement as the organizers of the foreign aid to starving people in 1932–1933.

The evolving totalitarian system demanded the completion of the processes of unification of the society, including unification in the ideological sphere. Therefore, all believers became victims of the repressive policies. Systematic aggressive propaganda campaigns consistently formed the image of the enemy—"vicious zealot cultists" in the eyes of the regime—which gave the actions of the authorities an ideologically grounded legal character. In the system of Soviet ideology, which denied any divine power, its own Marxist-Leninist-Stalinist theory actually had the character of a pseudo-religious doctrine. The Communist Party was like a totalitarian religion or "sect." In this way the political police (NKVD) performed the role of the "Holy Inquisition" in the liquidation of "heretics" of all kinds. In this situation with pressing political paranoia in the search for inner and outer enemies, mass terror against religious associations looked like a natural and unavoidable measure in the eyes of the authorities and society. This was the result of the relentless Civil War which started in 1917. The victims of the repressions and their butchers lived with its consequences for two decades.

Appendix
Repressions against the Evangelical of the Dnipropetrovsk and the Zaporizhia oblasts

Number of repressed individuals between 1928 and 1938														
Denomination	Evangelical Christians and Baptists		Pentecostals		Adventists		Mennonites		"Orthodox sectarians"		Unindicated confessions		Total	
Oblast	D	Z	D	Z	D	Z	D	Z	D	Z	D	Z	D	Z
1928	1		10								3	1	14	1
1929	1		2		1				2		1		7	
1930		5	2					3			18		20	8
1931	1		2		2								5	
1932	1	9	1								2		4	9
1933	3	2		6	1			7					4	15
1934	1							1					1	1
1935	9		5		1			8					15	8
1936							2	4					2	4
1937	15	11	17		1	3		6	1		3	6	37	26
1938	44	10			2			1					46	11
total	76	37	39	6	8	3	2	30	3		27	7	155	83
Total		113		45		11		32		3		34		238

D = Dnipropetrovsk Oblast
Z = Zaporizhia Oblast

References

Archives

DADO. Державний архів Дніпропетровської області ['State Archive of the Dnipropetrovsk Oblast'], Dnipropetrovsk, Ukraine.

DAKhO. Державний архів Херсонської області ['State Archive of the Cherson Oblast'], Kherson, Ukraine.

TsDAGOU. Центральний державний архів громадських об'єднань України ['Central State Archive of Public Organizations of Ukraine], Kyiv, Ukraine.

Literature

Baptist Ukrainy (1928). "Кто такой Воронаев" ['Who is Voronaev?'], *Баптист Украины*, 3, pp. 38–41

Bazhan, O. G. (2010). Бажан, О. Г. "«Шпигуни в сутанах». До питання про масштаби політичних репресій серед духовенства та віруючих в УССР у 1937–1938" ['"Spies in cloaks." Materials on a problem of political repressions against clergy and believers in the USSR in 1937-1938'], in *Сумський історико-архівний журнал*, 10–11, pp. 135–154; www.nbuv.gov.ua/portal/soc_gum/siaj/2010_10-11/10bogsdv.pdf; access date 1 March 2013.

Beznosova, O. & Beznosov, A. (2011). Безносова, О. и Безносов, А. "Религиозная жизнь меннонитов в середине 20-х гг. глазами советской политической полиции на примере поселения Фюрстенланд" ['The religious life of Mennonites in the mid-1920s through the eyes of the Soviet political police. The case of the Fuerstenland settlement'], in *History and Mission in Europe. Continuing the Conversation,* ed. M. Raber & P. F. Penner, Schwarzenfeld: Neufeld, pp. 33–47.

Boyko O. (2008). Бойко, О. В. "Репресії проти православного духовенства і віруючих на Дніпропетровщині у 1920–1930-ті роки" ['Repressions against the Orthodox clergy and believers in the Dnipropetrovsk region in 1920–1930s'], in *Реабілітовані історією. Дніпропетровська область* 1, pp. 743–763.

Bukreev (2011). "Алексей Маркович Букреев (1884–1929)" ['Aleksey Markovich Bukreev 1884-1929']; http://www.blagovestnik.org/bible/people/p0016.htm; access date 23 March 2016.

Coleman, H. (2005). *Russian Baptists and Spiritual Revolution, 1905–1929,* Bloomington: Indiana University Press.

Courtois, S., Werth, N., Panne J.-L. *et al.* (2006). Куртуа, С., Верт, Н., Панне, Ж.-Л. и др. "Государство против своего народа" ['The state against its people'], in *Черная книга коммунизма. Справочное издание в пяти частях*, 1:9; http://www.goldentime.ru/nbk_09.htm; access data 18 March 2016.

Evangelski Khristiani-baptisti Ukraini (2012). Євангельські християни-баптисти України. Історія і сучасність ['Evangelical Christians and Baptists of Ukraine. In history and in the present'], Kyiv: VSO EKhB.

Fast, V. (2001). Фаст, В. *Я с вами во все дни до скончания века. Жизнь верующих и общин евангельских христиан-баптистов и меннонитов Караганды и Карагандинской области (1931–1946 гг.)* ['I shall be with you in all days to the end of time. The life of the believers and the Evangelical Christians and Baptist churches in Karaganda and the Karaganda Oblast (1931–1946)'], Karaganda & Steinhagen: Samenkorn.

Franchuk, V. I. (2002). Франчук, В. И. *Просила Россия дождя у Господа* 2 ['As Russia has asked God for rain 2'], Moscow: N/A; http://www.iscelen.org/2515-istoriya-pyatidesyatnichestva-prosila-rossiya-dozhdya-u-gospoda.html; access data 2 March 2013.

Instruktsiya sekretariata Presidiuma VUTsIK [1932] (1963). "Инструкция секретариата Президиума ВУЦИК 'О порядке организации, деятельности, отчетности и ликвидации религиозных обществ и системы учета административными органами состава религиозных обществ и служителей культа (в развитие раздела Х Административного кодекса УССР – Правила о культах)'" ['Instruction of the Presidium of the VUTsIK Secretariat "On the order of organization, activity, accounts and liquidation of religious associations and registration of members and servants of cults of religious associations by state administration organs (added to chapter 10 of the Administrative Codex of the USSR—Regulations on religious cults")'], in *Хронологическое собрание законов, указов Президиума Верховного Совета, постановлении и распоряжения Правительства Украинской ССР*, 1, Kyiv: Gospolitizdat USSR (1963), pp. 346–498.

Istoriya yevangelskikh Khristian-baptistov v SSSR (1989). *История евангельских христиан-баптистов в СССР* ['A History of Evangelical Christians and Baptists in the USSR'], Moscow: VSECHB.

Ivanov, M. V. & Sinichkin, A. V. (eds.) (2007). Иванов, М. В. и Синичкин, А. В. (ред.). *История евангельских христиан баптистов в России* ['A history of Evangelical Christians and Baptists in Russia'], Moscow: RS EKhB.

Kiridon, A. (2008) Киридон, А. "Формування образу ворога як засіб антирелігійної пропаганди" ['Forming an image of an enemy as a tool of anti-religious propaganda'], in *Держава і церква в Україні за радянської доби. Збірник наукових статей за матеріалами II Всеукраїнської конференції (18–19 жовтня 2007 р.)*, Poltava: ACMI, pp. 52–62.

Koshtoris vitrat na robotu DPU USSR [1928] (2011). "Кошторис витрат на роботу ДПУ УССР серед релігійних угруповань на перше півріччя 1928 р. і пояснювальна записка до нього" ['A calculation of expenses on the DPU USSR activity among religious organizations during the first half of 1928 with an elucidative report'], in *Reabilitovani istorieu. Kyivska oblast*, 3, Kyiv: Osnova, pp. 257–258.

Kravchenko P. & Sitarchuk, R. (2005). Кравченко, П. и Сітарчук, Р. *Протестантські об'єднання в Україні у контексті соціальної політики більшовиків (20–30-і роки ХХ століття)* ['The Protestant Union in the context of the Bolshevik social politics during the 1920–1930s'], Poltava: ACMI.

Kulishova, S. V. & Prigodina, O. B. (2002). Кулишова, С. В. и Пригодина, О. Б. "Церковь и власть в Каргопольском уезде, 1918–1925 гг. По материалам архива милиции и местной печати' ['Church and rule in the Kargopole uezd during 1918–1925. On archive materials of the militia and local press']; http://www.booksite.ru/localtxt/svi/aty/nor/thr/uss/kih/zem/yel/28.htm; access date 12 March 2016.

Kurlyandsky, I. A. (2011). Курляндский, И. А. *Сталин, власть, религия (религиозный и церковный факторы во внутренней политике советского государства в 1922–1953 гг.)* ['Stalin, power and religion. Religious and church factors in internal politics of the Soviet state, 1922–1953'], Moscow: Kuchkogo Pole.

Leont'eva, T. (2012). Леонтьєва, Т. "Православне духовенство і більшовицький терор. Спроба регіонального дослідження" ['The Orthodox clergy and the Bolshevik terror. A topic in regional research'], *Ковчег*, 6, Lviv: Ukrainian Catholic University Press, pp. 220–234.

The Mennonite Encyclopaedia, 2 (1955). *The Mennonite Encyclopaedia. A Comprehensive Reference Work on the Anabaptist-Mennonite Movement*, Vol. 2, Scottdale: Mennonite Publishing House.

Mokrenchuk, Ye. (2010). Мокренчук, Е. "Жизнь и служение Якова Кузьмича Духонченко" ['The Life and Ministry of Jakov Kuzmich Dukhonchenko']; http://baptizm.info/index.php/skarbnichka/2010-01-10-20-41-46.html; access data 10 March 2016.

Nikolskaya, T. (2009). Никольская, Т. *Русский протестантизм и государственная власть в 1905–1991 годах* ['Russian Protestantism and state power in 1905–1991'], St. Petersburg: St. Petersburg European University Press.

O pravakh i obyazannostyakh (1929). "О правах и обязанностях религиозных объединений" ['On the rights and obligations of religious associations'], *Бюллютень НКВД*, 37, pp. 1–5

O religioznych ob'edineniyach [1929] (1959). "О религиозных объединениях" ['On the religious associations'], in *Хронологическое собрание законов, указов Президиума Верховного Совета и постановлений Правительства РСФСР*, 2: 1929–1939, Moscow: Gosyurizdat, pp. 29–45.

Oparin, A. A. & Begas, V. I. (2009) Опарин, А. А. и Бегас, В. И. *Белый камень. Очерки истории адвентизма на Екатеринославщине* ['A white stone. Essays on the history of Adventism in the Yekaterinoslav region'], Kharkov: Fakt.

Pashchenko, V. O. (1995). Пащенко, В. О. *Православя в Україні. Державно-церковні стосунки. 20–30-і рр. XX ст.* ['Orthodoxy in Ukraine. The relations between the state and the church. 1920s–1930s'], Poltava: "Poltava."

Reabilitovani istorieu. Dnipropetrovska oblast, 1–2 (2008). *Реабілітовані історією. Дніпропетровська область, у 2 кн.* ['The rehabilited by history. Dnipropetrovsk Oblast in 2 volumes'], eds. E. I. Borodin *et al.*, Dnipropetrovsk: Monolit.

Reabilitovani istorieu. Donetska oblast, 4 (2007). *Реабілітовані історією. Донецька область, у 9 кн.* ['The rehabilited by history. Donetsk Oblast in 9 volumes'], eds. O. L. Tretyak *et al.*, Donetsk: SPD Blednov.

Reabilitovani istorieu. Zaporizka oblast, 1 (2004). *Реабілітовані історією. Запорізька область, у 2 кн.* ['The rehabilited by history. Zaporizhia Oblast in 2 volumes], eds. P. P. Rebro *et al.*, Zaporizhia: Dniprovskiy metalurg.

Reabilitovani istorieu. Zaporizka oblast, 2–3 (2006) *Реабілітовані історією. Запорізька область, у 5 кн.* ['The rehabilited by history. Zaporizhia Oblast, in 5 volumes'], eds. P. P. Rebro *et al.*, Zaporizhia: Dniprovskiy metalurg.

Reabilitovani istorieu. Zaporizka oblast, 4 (2008). *Реабілітовані історією. Запорізька область, у 5 кн.* ['The rehabilited by history. Zaporizhia Oblast, in 5 volumes], eds. P. P. Rebro *et al.*, Zaporizhia: Dniprovskiy metalurg.

Reabilitovani istorieu. Zaporizka oblast, 5 (2010). *Реабілітовані історією. Запорізька область, у 5 кн.* ['The rehabilited by history. Zaporizhia Oblast, in 5 volumes], eds. P. P. Rebro *et al.*, Zaporizhia: Dniprovskiy metalurg.

Reshetnikov, J. E. & Sannikov, S. V. (2000). Решетников, Ю. Е. и Санников, С. В. *Обзор истории Евангельско-баптистского братства на Украине* ['Review of the history of Evangelical Christian and Baptist Brotherhood in Ukraine'], Odessa.

Savin, A. I. (ed.) (2004). Савин, А. И. (ред.). *Советское государство и евангельские церкви Сибири в 1920–1941 гг. Документы и материалы* ['The Soviet state and Evangelical churches in Siberia, 1920–1941. Documents and materials'], Novosibirsk: Posoch.

Savin, A. I. (2008). Савин, А. И. "'Разделяй и властвуй.' Религиозная политика советского государства и евангельские церкви в 1920-е годы" ['"Divide and rule." The religious policy of the Soviet state and Evangelical churches during the 1920s'], *Вестник Тверского государственного университета*, 15, pp. 3–23.

Savinskiy, S. (1999). Савинский, С. Н. *История евангельских христиан-баптистов Украины, России, Белоруссии (1917–1967 гг.)* ['A history of Evangelical Christians and Baptists in Ukraine, Russia and Belorus'], St. Petersburg: Bibliya dlya vsekh.

Shchuplov, A. (2001). Щуплов, А. "Короче, Склифосовский" ['Put it in a nutshell, Sklifosovskiy']; https://rg.ru/Anons/arc_2001/0831/hit.shtm; access date 28 February 2015.

Slobodyanyuk, M. A. (2003). Слободянюк, М. А. *Коротка історія Центральної церкви євангельських християн-баптистів м. Дніпропетровська* ['A short history of the Evangelical Christians and Baptists' central church in Dnipropetrovsk'], Kyiv: VSO EChB.

Sovetov, I. M. (2007). Советов, И. М. "Советское законодательство о религиозных культах в 20–30-х гг. XX в. Содержание и практика реализации, споры и дискуссии о реформировании его правовой базы" ['The Soviet legislation on religious cults in 1920–1930s. Content and practice, discussions on reforming of its regulatory framework']; www.rusoir.ru/president/works/217/; access data 11 March 2016.

Spravochnik rayonnogo prokurora (1942). *Справочник районного прокурора 1936-1942* ['Handbook of the regional prosecutor 1936-1942'], ed. V. M. Bochkov, Moscow: Yuridicheskoe izdatelstvo NKU SSSR; http://istmat.info/node/22562; access date 12 March 2013.

Wölk, H. & Wölk, G. (1981). *Die Mennoniten Brüdergemeinde in Rußland 1925-1980*, Fresno: The Historical Commission of the General Conference of Mennonite Brethren Churches of North America.

Yartsev, A. (1930). Ярцев, А. *Секта евангельских христиан* ['The Evangelical Christian sect'], Moscow: Bezbozhnik.

Zhiromskaya, V. B. (2000). Жиромская, В. Б. "Религиозность народа в 1937 году (По материалам Всесоюзной переписи населения)" ['Religiousness of the people of the USSR in 1937 (on materials of the All-Union census)']; http://krotov.info/history/20/1930/1937_zher.htm; access data 12 March 2016.

Zubov, A. B. (ed.) (2009). Зубов, А. В. (ред.). *История России. XX век. 1894-1939* ['A history of Russia. The twentieth century. 1894-1939'], Moscow: Astrel.

CHAPTER 8

The Cultural Bases in the North.
Sovietisation and Indigenous Resistance

Eva Toulouze, Laur Vallikivi & Art Leete

Fifteen culture houses, fifteen ethnographic centres, fifteen veterinary stations, fifteen medical care stations, fifteen boarding schools, fifteen production cooperatives, red tents, red boats, nomadic schools, model production workshops, agricultural stations, and radio-stations adorn as red circles the contemporary map of the Soviet arctic and subarctic zones. These are the fifteen complex culture bases, which at the beginning of the second Bolshevik five-year plan are in fact the forward bearing points of the Soviet power; they lead consequently and obstinately the Northern economy's socialist reconstruction on the basis of Leninist-Stalinist nationality policy in the faraway frontier of the great proletarian state, harsh but rich in natural strength. These are the future towns. They will grow and become real cultural and political centres.

Innokentii M. Suslov (1934: 28).

Sovietisation of the North was not an easy task.[1] The young Bolshevik power was aware of it, and of its inability to implement proper strategy and tactics because of its ignorance of the aborigines' world. Not only for the sake of the implementation of socialism, but also for the sake of the perspectives of economic exploitation of the North, they turned to the specialists for advice. This awareness probably emerged as early as 1921 or 1922,[2] when, at the People's Commissariat for the Affairs of the Nationalities (*Narkomnats*), the Polar Subcommittee was created. The instruments of Sovietisation in the North were the result of cooperation between two rather different worlds: the ethnographic expertise of renowned Russian scholars and Bolshevik administrators. While some of the researchers were internationally recognised, such as Vladimir Bogoraz-Tan,[3] they were not engaged in the Communist

---

[1] This research was supported by the Estonian Research Council (project PUT590 and PUT712) and the ERA.Net RUS Plus programme (project 189).
[2] The Soviet regime benefited from the initiative of the Commission for the Study of the Tribal Composition of the Population of Russia, formed in February 1917 with the aim of elaborating scientifically grounded colonial projects (see Hirsch 2005: 7–10, 57–61, 85–92).
[3] Vladimir Bogoraz-Tan (1865–1936) had been exiled to Eastern Siberia for revolutionary activities and became a specialist of the Chukchi. He spent some years in the United States

Party, even though they sympathised with the new leaders of Russia. As they had generally been hostile to tsarist autocracy, several of them had been exiled to the Far North. The bridge between them and the administrators were the Bolsheviks who had some knowledge of the North.[4] These groups produced policies that were clearly influenced by each other in different periods, while seemingly speaking with one voice.

This cooperation produced original forms of political and cultural action in the North. These were materialised through the peculiar governing board of the Northern areas, the so-called *Komitet Severa*, the Committee of the North,[5] which was founded in 1924 and whose composition reflected the new cooperation between scholars and politicians. The Committee of the North included representatives of the ministries and shaped the Soviet policy on the North.

The committee was conceived in order to satisfy both the needs of the Siberian natives and to integrate the North into the new political system. But it did not achieve its goal entirely, and triggered often quite resolute resistance in the native communities. The protest actions, often called uprisings (Ru. *vosstaniya*), led to relentless repression which deprived indigenous communities of their best men and vital resources for a long time. Numerous indigenous resistance actions, while they were not directly related to one another, took place between 1932 and 1950 in very different locations in Siberia. They were locally triggered by particular events in various ways, but they can be seen as one multifaceted phenomenon of reaction to homogenous Sovietisation policies.

The goal of this chapter is to focus on the culture bases, a peculiar instrument implemented by the Committee of the North, intended to be a kind of model Soviet villages for the indigenous peoples of the North. The construction of culture bases was decided in 1925 (Protokol 1925: 111). In this paper, we shall show what the aims of these culture bases were, how they were integrated into the whole Sovietisation process, how they functioned, and

—
(1901–1904), befriended Franz Boas, and started publishing there his famous three-part monograph *The Chukchee* (1904–1909) in English. When he returned to Russia, he became an active participant in policy-making towards the North, and well known for his proposal for creating native reservations and for his involvement in native higher education.

[4] For example, Avel' Enukidze (1877–1937) was exiled from 1914 to 1916 to the Yenisey government; Yemelyan Yaroslavskiy (Miney Guberl'man, 1878–1943) was born in Eastern Siberia and lived in Yakutsk from 1907 to 1917. Both men were so-called "old Bolsheviks."

[5] The full name was the Committee for the Assistance to the Peoples of the Northern Borderlands (*Komitet sodeystviya narodnostyam severnykh okrain*).

how the indigenous peoples of Siberia reacted to these initiatives. Our geographical focus will be Western Siberia.

To Civilise the Natives

Aims

This idea of bringing civilisation to the indigenous peoples of the North was shared by all the Soviet policy-makers, although the motivations were not always the same for everybody.

In the 1920s, the ethnographers became increasingly aware that there would be unavoidable changes in the natives' lives. From their evolutionist point of view, while largely accepting the need to preserve indigenous lifestyles, the ethnographers envisaged a future in which the natives had to take advantage of the achievements of the modern world from which they had been isolated. This would make the indigenous groups able to negotiate as equals with the state authorities. In short, there was a dream of converting natives into agents of their own fate. The one and only way imagined to be possible for making them modern was to educate them and help them become literate. The development of schools for indigenous peoples was one of the important measures suggested in the first political programmes, even before the constitution of the Committee of the North.

Also from the perspective of Bolshevik administrators, setting up schools throughout the Soviet North was an important goal to achieve. Their wish was to directly penetrate (not just with the help of scholars of dubious allegiance) remote communities through literate natives who would become mediators between the two worlds and of socialist reconstructions. Schools would allow the training of these mediators into firm believers of the Soviet construction project (Toulouze 2005: 140–148). Their understanding of school was highly practical and pursued immediate utilitarian aims:

> The boarding-school, taking children out of production activities, mobilises their attention on the reconstruction of Northern economy and gives them skills [...], both within school and by establishing links with the nearest cooperatives. (Suslov 1934: 34)

The politicians were clearly aware of the economic potential of the Northern areas and intended to exploit it in the state's interests.

In order to provide education for the natives, everything had to be built from scratch. As elsewhere, during the 1920s, schools were built and teachers were sent into the field. Very soon, the teachers discovered that education would only be of use if delivered in the pupils' mother tongue. So, languages and dialects were to be studied, orthographies and grammars to be established, literary languages adopted,[6] and textbooks written, both in Russian and vernaculars (Toulouze 1999). We shall here concentrate on the first point: the building of schools—often from scratch, and often by teachers sent by the Committee of the North, who were supposed to become the ultimate instruments of change.

Schools were of course only one of the means of penetrating into the tundra and the taiga, and a very slow one.[7] Hence the idea of establishing so-called culture bases, socialist outposts around schools (Campbell 2004: 41). They were expected to function as microcosms of the Soviet statehood aimed at hastening the pace and multiplying contacts with the local indigenous populations at every level.[8] Guidelines for the culture bases were provided by, amongst others, A. Lvov:

> These centres for providing all kinds of exemplary help to indigenous populations must thus also be the supporters of indigenous culture and prepare specialists among the indigenous people. These specialists will carry culture to their people and only with their help is it possible to serve all Northern territories as a whole, although culture bases themselves can serve only a small territory. (Lvov 1926: 31)

The culture bases were supposed to mediate what Soviet life in the tundra and in the taiga could look like. In practice, deprived of its ideological discourse, Soviet life was not very different from Russian life. For the "enlighteners" there was no practical difference between "culture" and "Russian culture," understood as an absolute category.[9] Therefore promotion of civilised life was paramount for promoting Russian life, and indigenous peoples recognised and understood this immediately.

---

[6] In a conference in 1932, 14 languages of the North were officially "given" a written form.
[7] Therefore already in 1925, a course was opened in the Workers University for training Northern aborigines. Vladimir Bogoraz-Tan was one of the most active teachers involved in this project.
[8] Schools were planned and built not only in the culture bases but also elsewhere.
[9] Forsyth, repeating Bogoraz-Tan's idea, speaks about "a kind of reforming missionarism without the Christian religion, but with an equally strong conviction of absolute enlightenment" (Forsyth 1992: 284).

The culture bases were to be founded in the remotest areas (Kantor 1933: 66; Shmyrev 1933: 69; Suslov 1934: 29). It hosted the personnel[10] of all the services and institutions needed for a fully functioning settlement,[11] which could reach 250 persons, as was the case for example in the Yamal culture base (Shmyrev 1933: 70). Besides the stationary institutions, every culture base had "nomadic appendices" that were sent out from the base to address the indigenous nomadic communities (Suslov 1934: 33). Particularly important were the Red tents or Red boats, used from 1929 by Party activists and medical doctors who had to convince the local population of the benefits of the Soviet statehood (Mazurenko 1979: 127). In 1934, there were fifteen culture bases in the Soviet Union (see Map).

When analysing the practice of culture bases and the discourse on them, we may define their function for the policy-makers as three-fold: to map, to show and to act.

To Map

Culture bases were supposed to be the meeting points out in the tundra and the taiga between the natives and the Soviets. Therefore, the latter would have the opportunity to discover and to study the local populations and their peculiarities, and to learn to communicate with them (Balzer 1999: 107; Forsyth 1992: 80; Suslov 1934: 28; Terletskiy 1935: 44). We may assume that the institutional members of staff, in other words the Party officials, wished to disentangle themselves from the authority of the specialists, by becoming themselves specialists. Culture bases had to be involved in research aimed at

---

[10] For example: instructors for the creation of local councils and the building of cooperatives, leaders of women's organisations, political instructors, physicians as well as medical and veterinary personnel, teachers, hunting specialists, ichthyologists, reindeer specialists, ethnographers, economists, etc. (Suslov 1934: 32). In 1935, there were more than 500 individuals working in the culture bases (not taking into account the builders) (V komitete 1935: 107).

[11] According to Terletskiy, who wrote not long before the decline of the bases in 1935, the institutions and buildings in a culture house were a "house of culture" (or a "house of the natives"), a hospital with a health centre, a boarding school, a kindergarten, a day nursery, a veterinary, zoological and agronomic stations, an ethnographic station with a laboratory allowing agrochemical and bacteriological scientific work, an electric generator, workshops, houses for the personnel, a sauna, warehouses. Moreover, there were the office of the cooperative and other economic institutions (Terletskiy 1935: 36). Zelenin adds some other details: bread reserves, a meteorological station and transportation (boats, motorboats, reindeer, dogs, and, in the last few years, all-terrain vehicles and even landing strips) (Zelenin 1938: 16).

Illustration 12: Map over culture bases in the Soviet Union, 1920s–1930s. Sources: Suslov 1934; Terletskiy 1935. Cartography: Johannes Vallikivi

acquiring a deeper knowledge of Northern peoples and Northern conditions (e.g., the health situation, natural resources, etc.). For instance, rich photo collections were created at the culture bases (Terletskiy 1935: 44). Moreover, culture bases had the duty to actively involve indigenous peoples in research. Even museums were to be created (Parkhomenko 1930: 125, 128; Suslov 1934: 35; Zelenin 1938: 16). Ethnographers were employed as specialists in all areas concerning the indigenous population, including issues of economy (for example such outstanding ethnographers as G. N. Prokof'pyev worked for two years at the Khoseda-Khard culture base, cf. Khomich 1999). For instance, when the class enemy concept became part of the Soviet policies in the late 1920s, they had to determine who was a kulak, deriving it from the number of reindeer owned and labourers used, all being relative to the local social and cultural circumstances.

To Show and to Act

Culture bases were supposed to cover most domains of local life and thus became small Soviet microcosms illustrating what life was supposed to be (Balzer 1999: 107). Even if they were not the only places where Soviet power was represented, they brought Sovietness to the depths of the local villages. The first way was through hosting. In the "house of the natives," guests from the tundra or taiga could find refreshments, newspapers, and spend the night. They could even file a complaint or repair a gun (Shmyrev 1933: 72–73).

Cultural and educational aspects

We have already mentioned the importance of the cultural and educational aspects. Schools were always to be the core of a culture base. They were financed by central funds[12] and provided with the "best teachers" (Lyarskaya 2003: 79). Debates about the forms of schools for natives had been going on since the middle of the 1920s. Although the policy-makers were well aware of the weaknesses of the boarding school system, they found no other working solution. As a result, boarding schools spread all over the North. The tuition was supposed to be in the native languages. In the 1920s, Soviet journals denounced many problems that occurred while setting up the school system. It was difficult to recruit children, to teach them, to feed them, to find teachers not only proficient in the native languages but also willing to work in arduous conditions, and also to communicate with reluctant parents. Thus school, while being an important issue, was also a critical one. Educational aspects were extended to adults as well. For instance, "courses for the liquidation of illiteracy," but also courses for accountants, herders, and nurses were introduced (Petrova & Kharyuchi 1999: 86–94).

From the non-locals' perspective, Russian habits, hygiene and way of life were generally considered civilised, while native customs were seen as backward: people were taught to wash, to go to sauna (Ru. *banya*), to reject conical tents, or at least adopt iron stoves (Khomich 1966: 308; Shmyrev 1933: 73). In this perspective, women were specifically targeted and introduced to the new rules of hygiene and prospects for "emancipation" (Khomich 1966: 298). One can see through these examples how sensitive all these issues could be, presenting without the shadow of a doubt Russian habits as being superior.

Political aspects

Culture bases were also tightly related to the political field. The local institutions of power like the native regional executive committees (*tuzrik*) were responsible for carrying out reforms in the area. Some of them had their offices in culture bases, making these settlements actual sites where the state enforced its laws. Moreover, they were places where the political power

---

[12] While this fact enhances the political and symbolic importance of schools and culture bases, it does not mean that the actual financing was satisfying. Lyarskaya (2003: 79) emphasises how in the Yamal culture base, opened in 1932, the boarding school there had no beds or chairs, and food was scarce.

expressed itself and advertised its goals, achievements, and programmes. These were sites for hosting natives and providing them with propaganda material: for example, culture bases used to print newspapers (e.g., the Yamal culture base published a newspaper, *Naryana Vy* ['The red tundra'], cf. Budarin 1968: 227; Shmyrev 1933: 72).

Economic aspects

In the 1930s, while "kulaks" and "shamans" were deprived of the political rights given to the rest of the indigenous population, natives were driven forcibly into kolkhozes and much of their possessions expropriated to the kolkhoz. The culture bases could have an important economic role as well. They were supposed to channel the work of the cooperatives, and some cooperatives had their office there. For instance, the Kazym culture base was criticised for poor results in its efforts to establish cooperatives (Kantor 1933: 67). In some places, the culture base even established cooperatives, for example in Sakhalin (Grant 1993: 232); in others, especially at the end of the 1930s, the culture base was responsible for collectivisation and sedentarisation, for example the one in Yamal, according to its director M. M. Brodnev. He recollects that he had to carry out electrification of the base as well (Lipatova 2008: 70–71). The bases were also supposed to teach northerners horticulture (Kantor 1933: 71), which was a challenge in the harsh climatic conditions. Culture bases functioned as commercial hubs where natives could exchange furs, fish or berries for bread, sugar and other imported goods. Many stores were situated in the culture bases. Private commercial activities had been disrupted first by the Civil War and then by anti-merchant policies, which had resulted in trade becoming almost exclusively a state concern. Like later collectivisation and the sedentarisation of nomads, this way of concentrating commercial activities was part of the wider Soviet project of economic rationalisation.

Medical and veterinary aspects

Another important service offered by the culture bases was medical and veterinary as well as birth care. Veterinary care was at first mainly oriented towards controlling meat production, especially during the slaughter of reindeer, but also towards spreading "knowledge" about a scientific approach to reindeer husbandry and research on reindeer diseases (Suslov 1934: 35; Terletskiy 1935: 43). Veterinary staff was supposed to visit reindeer herds in the tundra (Leete 2004a: 56).

Illustration 13: Photo from Tura culture base, Krasnoyarsk krai, 1920s. Public domain.

Medical care can be seen from two complementary points of view. Firstly, there was certainly the aim to provide the natives with services that they did not have in the tundra and taiga, thus saving both human and animal lives. Soviet authors mention proudly the achievements in this field: in 1934, 13 hospitals were functioning in the culture bases (Skachko 1934: 18). But from another point of view, the culture bases had an ideological—and hence political—aspect as well: they were in direct competition with what the Soviets called "superstitions" and the role of the "shamans" in the communities (Khomich 1966: 312; see further Leete 2004b).

Results and consequences

How did all this actually function? One difficulty we always meet when working with Soviet sources is the abundance of programmatic literature and the scarcity of reliable assessment materials. Reports must be read with previous knowledge of the local conditions in order to understand the possible realities behind the printed text. Undoubtedly, the ambitions were high. Still, we know that culture bases lacked means of various kinds. They lacked material means, as money was scarcely distributed from the central authorities; for example, they often did not have means of transportation, and they also ran short of food and heating (Terletskiy 1935: 46). Being isolated, they did not receive support from the local administrators. Often Party and government leaders in the regions did not understand why money and energy had to be spent on a handful of "savages" who were not interested in socialism and could not understand it properly anyway. Moreover, the culture bases did not have enough human resources. As Lunacharskiy (1927: 18–19) observed, there were some fairly enthusiastic specialists associated to the culture bases. But it is important to emphasise that the so-called "missionaries of the new culture and of Soviet statehood," as Bogoraz-Tan (1925: 48; cf. also Leete & Vallikivi 2011) put it, were very few compared to the needs defined by the Committee of the North. Even Soviet authors emphasise the lack of appropriate personnel (Kantor 1933: 41, 66). Although textbooks in languages of Northern natives were being published in Leningrad, we do not know how many of them were actually used or how many teachers were able to use vernacular languages in their work. This problem was not only encountered in Siberia but also elsewhere in the Soviet Union, where the demand for trained staff largely exceeded the supply.

The results presented by Soviet journalists on, for example, medical care are, as a rule, bombastic: in the Kazym culture base, in two years, 5,833 individuals were supposed to have gone for check-ups (Kantor 1933: 68). This number is confusing and seems exaggerated, especially when one considers the actual population of the region. At the beginning of the 1930s, the population of the Kazym tundra was 1,630 (81 per cent of them Khanty, 13 per cent Nenets and 6 per cent Komi).[13] Still, one explanation for the very high statistics is that more than 60 per cent of the people attending medical care institutions were Russians who could attend more than once (Terletskiy 1935: 41). The attendance of the local population declined noticeably between the first and the second year. Curiosity may well have been a determining reason for the first visits, while rising tensions explain quite well the regression. On the other hand, children in boarding schools made up a considerable portion of the native attendance.

Soviet authors, while emphasising the difficulty of working with the indigenous population and convincing them of the usefulness of the Soviet project (Suslov 1934: 31), wrote at length about the issues of class struggle, especially about sabotage acts by kulaks, shamans and even by interpreters, who reportedly misinformed and frightened the poorer natives (Suslov 1934:

---

[13] Source: Museum of History and Local Heritage of Berezovo District, Khanty-Mansi Autonomous Region.

31–33). Undoubtedly, the state's impact was considerably limited by the resistance. The culture bases were not as effective as the authorities had hoped. Moreover, since the beginning of the 1930s, the development of kolkhozes and kolkhoz centres-to-be had competed with the culture bases.

A hearth of socialism. The Kazym culture base

The implementation of Soviet policy was the most important goal. All of the above-mentioned activities were supposed to be a contribution towards achieving the programme's goals. But the vision of the policy-makers, and of some of the theoreticians they relied upon, was much wider and had a long-term and global scope.

The culture bases were at the centre of a nucleus-based strategy: they were the hearth from which, through a domino effect, socialism was to win round the taiga and the tundra. We shall illustrate this theory with an account of what was expected in the case of the Kazym culture base.

The project of opening a base in the region emerged right after the extended plenum of the Committee of the North and an expedition was organised in 1926 under the leadership of V. M. Novitskiy, an ethnographer and member of the Committee of the North of the Tobolsk area (Leete 2004a: 57).

Novitskiy's leading ideas are particularly interesting, because they illustrate one strand of missionary thinking in the Committee of the North. The first point in his strategy was to identify areas almost entirely inhabited by natives, surrounded by native regions and characterised by a traditional way of life. This he calls "the main hearth of the indigenous culture," the place where a culture base, a "cultural awakener," had to be established, in order to develop friendly relations with the natives and thus influence them as well as the surrounding communities. Through a chain mechanism of "self-influence," by getting into Soviet control the "strongest" natives, the other, weaker links would follow the example of the strongest ones. When the work was done, the culture base would be moved elsewhere. The Kazym region was specifically chosen. By empowering the strongest Kazym Khanty, the aim was to "better the indigenous race." The chosen method for colonising the North was what Novitskiy called the "Iceland method," i.e., to increase the local work force, not by importing labourers, but through a reduction in mortality (Novitskiy 1928a; Novitskiy 1928b: 77–79).

Novitskiy's plans were a failure, as they did not measure up to reality. While he did not doubt that the stronger natives would accept and welcome Soviet power, the cultural workers confronted with the "fierceness" and "stubbornness" of the Kazym Khanty saw the same features as proof of savageness (Kantor 1933: 66; cf. also Leete 2004a: 64–65). To impose an alien presence in a context where resistance was supposed to be the strongest was a risk; in Kazym, this triggered the natives' resistance, as we shall see below.

Resistance to Sovietisation. Changes in Policies and an Example of Protest

Undoubtedly, the resistance was connected with the actual changes that the culture bases were intended to implement. But these changes, which originated from global processes, were mediated to the indigenous peoples, among other forms, through the culture bases.

We shall briefly dwell on the global processes that provoked the resistance, and then concentrate on native views on the culture bases, in order to explain the mechanism of protest.

From Lenient to Harsh Methods

The Soviet goal to integrate all the Union's populations into one rational state project never actually changed. However, different approaches to implementing this goal were used in different periods.

While for the overall Soviet Union the chronology is punctuated by the New Economic Policy (NEP) and collectivisation with enhanced class struggle afterwards, there are some peculiarities that deserve to be pointed out in the North, even though the general pattern is the same as elsewhere.

Within the Committee of the North, the ethnographers' ideas had dominated in the first period from 1924 to 1928. They had argued that class struggle was unknown to the native peoples untouched by "the capitalist phase of development." The indigenous peoples as such were the proletarians of the North and they were expected to pass directly from primitiveness to communism (Slezkine 1994: 146–147). With this general orientation, the Committee of the North was able to implement some measures intended to satisfy the native communities. Moreover, the attitude of the scholars who were sent to the area was often friendly and sensitive.

This situation gradually changed at the end of the 1920s, because of a change in the internal balance of power within the Committee: "the Party line"—which emphasised that class struggle was everywhere, including in the North, and therefore required fighting against the "people's enemies"—became dominant in the Committee at the 6th Plenum in 1929. Many of the promoters of the "lenient" approach (e.g. Bogoraz-Tan) tried to adapt and soften the consequences for the natives, without directly confronting the Party's voice.

This change of approach was immediately reflected in concrete policies. So-called kulaks and shamans were deprived of their civil rights and forbidden to vote for and be elected to local councils (Karshakova 1996: 39; Slezkine 1994: 199–201). An extensive interpretation[14] of these notions deprived a considerable number of citizens of the right to vote (for example 569 individuals in the Yamal-Nenets national okrug; more than 1,000 in Khanty-Mansi national okrug, cf. Onishchuk 1986: 135). Herds of livestock were confiscated and tax pressure increased. Moreover, the Russians showed increasing presence and power in these remote areas.

How was this reflected in the culture base and how was all this perceived by the natives?

The Example of the Kazym War

We shall illustrate this issue with the example of the so-called Kazym war. Firstly, we shall briefly present the complex events of this protest wave, in order to provide a more concrete understanding of rebellion forms adopted by the natives. More details are to be found in the synthetic work by Art Leete dedicated to this event (Leete 2002; Leete 2004a; Leete 2007) and his overall comments about native resistance in Siberia (Leete 2007).

This summary is based on various different sources: Party archive documents, written memoirs of contemporaries, oral history, scholarly work both in Russia and abroad and literary works by Khanty authors (Leete 2004a: 17–25).

Various events led to the Kazym Khanty leaders confronting Soviet power through its representatives. The uprising of the Khanty and Forest Nenets began in the autumn of 1931, after the representatives of the local soviet (council) had taken 48 native children to the boarding school at the Kazym culture base. On 28 December the same year, the Khanty raided the culture base and took 43 of their children back.

After a relatively peaceful period of about two years, while discontent with the elimination of the most respected indigenous leader from the Soviet elections (in 1932) was growing, four Khanty "shamans" were arrested in

---

[14] E.g. a Khanty possessing 200 or 300 reindeer was considered a "kulak" (Kantor 1935: 10).

March 1933. Rumours had also circulated about further arrests. This stirred a violent conflict between the authorities and the native peoples.[15]

At the same time, the fishing co-operative of Kazym was sent to fish in Lake Num-To. The local people informed the fishermen that the lake was sacred and that fishing was not allowed there.[16] Because of the tensions between the local people and the communist staff of the culture base, several Russian "propaganda teams" (*agitbrigady*) were sent to the area. However, they did not encounter any of the protesters, who had withdrawn to less accessible areas. The participants of the fourth *agitbrigada* were made up of local Party leaders, whose involvement demonstrates the authorities' growing concern. These were Pyotr Astrakhantsev, the head of both the propaganda team and the executive committee of the Beryozovo district, female communist activist Polina Shnaider, Pyotr Smirnov, the head of the culture base, Zakhar Posokhov, a representative of the security service and also some local "activists," including Prokopi Spiridonov, a Khanty and head of the Kazym soviet.

On 26 November 1933, the *agitbrigada* reached Num-To. Polina Shnaider, in spite of being informed about the local peoples' beliefs, went to the island in the middle of Num-To. The island, on which there was a sacred site, was taboo for women. This action of sacrilege deeply disturbed the locals' feelings.

Then Astrakhantsev's group moved to the forest tundra, and on 3 December they met a group of Khanty and Forest Nenets. On 4 December, the members of the brigade were taken prisoners. The Khanty and Forest Nenets presented their demands in written form: release of arrested shamans, a ban on fishing in the waters of Num-To, restoration of voting rights to shamans and kulaks, abolishment of taxes on richer natives, termination of reindeer confiscations and forced labour for the culture base, free fish and fur

---

[15] There is also another piece of information on possible factors triggering the Kazym resistance. Soviet scholar M. Budarin (1968) wrote that the native leaders brought photographs of Kliment Voroshilov (a Soviet politician), in which he wore a white navy uniform, and then showed them to the Khanty with the accompanying message that a white leader would soon come from the upper courses of the Ob and Irtysh rivers, with twenty steamers full of soldiers and armaments, and that the Soviet domination of this area would not then last long (Kopylev & Retunskiy 1965).

[16] Lake Num-To is not far from the upper course of several tributaries of the Ob River (e.g. the Tromyugan, Pim, Lyamin and Kazym rivers), and is a sacred site for local people. In winter, the Khanty and Nenets of the neighbouring regions used to go there and carry out sacrifices.

trade and closing of all trading posts in the tundra. In addition, they demanded that children not be sent to the boarding school, that natives should not have to appear in court outside the indigenous areas and that all Russians, i.e. the culture base staff, must leave Kazym.

In this extraordinary situation, with the Party's envoys held prisoners, the Khanty and Nenets held a shamanic ritual: the ritual leaders stated that gods ordered the offering of the captured Russians. The members of Astrakhantsev's group were tied up and taken to a hill in reindeer sleds. They were strangled with a long rope tied around their necks, imitating the way reindeer were killed for sacrifice. After that the Khanty and Nenets sacrificed seven reindeer and held a traditional ceremony.

When news of the event emerged some weeks later, retaliation started. Troops were sent to the Num-To area, and on 18 February 1934, there was a 30-minute skirmish between security service troops and natives in a Khanty camp owned by Grigoriy Sengepov. Two Russians and Sengepov with his wife were killed during the fight. Other local people were arrested. It is said that only Engukh, a Forest Nenets, was able to escape.

Sometime before 21 February, another larger group of locals involved in the fighting were arrested, including the leaders of the uprising, Ivan Yernykhov and Yefim Vandymov (in Khanty named Yänkow-iki, 'White Head'), the shamans who had carried out the ritual killing of the members of Astrakhantsev's brigade. Spiridonov, the head of the Kazym soviet, was also arrested. He was accused of having collaborated with the local fighters throughout this period.

The eventual outcome of the events is confused and sources are hazy and contradictory. According to different official sources, 60 or 88 local people were arrested after the conflict, 9 or 34 of whom were later released. Two persons died before the trial (either from heart problems or suicide). The others were condemned to prison sentences of various lengths. 11 had previously been condemned to death, but they appealed and the death penalty was commuted into 20 years of detention. According to archive material, the rest soon died in prison. However, the official data may not be reliable. Researcher G. Bardin has for example reported (without indicating his sources) that several hundred people were arrested (Bardin 1994: 6). The present-day fieldwork materials—conversations with Khanty or Nenets people, oral history recollections among descendants of the convicted—also suggest that the number of killed or otherwise repressed people was considerably higher than 50 (Leete 2002: 127–130). To avoid retaliation and repression, some natives left for the upper reaches of the neighbouring rivers

(Nadym, Pur, Taz, Yugan, Lyamin, Pim, Tromyugan, and even Agan) and for the Yamal Peninsula. Security service troops pursued participants of the uprisings in the forest tundra until 1935 (Kopylev & Retunskiy 1965).

In 1993, the relatives of the killed natives made an application for the rehabilitation of those who participated in the uprising as protectors of their traditional rights and basic patterns of Siberian native life. However, this was turned down by the authorities.[17] We may add that the impact of these events on the communities was enormous. Tatiana Moldanova, a contemporary Khanty writer elaborates in her story how women who were not directly involved in the operations became direct victims of the repressions as they were deprived of their men, the providers for the family, and were left alone without hunting devices. Many of them starved with their children. The survivors kept silent about the events for several decades.

The Culture Bases Seen by the Natives

While in the first part of this chapter, we described the culture base from the point of view of its programmatic goals and its activities, and in the second part the mode of the resistance in one indigenous community, we shall now attempt to analyse the indigenous point of view and delve into the natives' critical relations with the cultural base.[18]

Of course, we lack direct information from the participants of the events in the 1930s, for the natives were not the history writers of these experiences. Still, we have indirect sources such as press accounts, archival documents, memoirs of Soviet activists and oral history, and through them we know quite clearly what they wished to achieve. Resistance was triggered by measures and events that were part of the cultural base initiatives. While keeping silent about the indigenous reactions, the press of the time reflects them in two ways, both typical to Soviet discourse—firstly, by emphasising class struggle and sabotage by kulaks and shamans (for example, Al'kor 1934: 29) and

---

[17] Out of a total of 60, 49 participants in the uprising were found guilty and sentenced to imprisonment of different durations (including 10 persons who had initially been sentenced to death) in a session of the Ob-Irtysh Oblast court held in Khanty-Mansiysk on 25 July 1934. On 29 December 1993, the Tyumen Oblast Prosecution Office retried the Kazym War case, and decided not to restore the rights of the 49 participants of the war.

[18] It is important to mention that no generalisation should be drawn from this example. All cases of resistance were shaped by local conditions and traditions.

secondly by observing "errors"[19] in the activity of the cultural base (Suslov 1934: 36). However, we argue that, while some attitudes of Soviet activists may have exacerbated the conflict, the causes lay deeper in Soviet state policy. They were to be found in the project as a whole and in the wider ambitions of Soviet construction, which were completely unacceptable from the indigenous perspective. Not only resolute resistance actions, such as not sending their children to school or taking them out of school, but also acts of avoidance such as not attending school or not using the services offered by the cultural bases proved that the spontaneous chain reaction impact predicted by Novitskiy, was far from becoming true. Let us examine this in more detail.

Cultural Misunderstandings

Cultural confrontation is not a new phenomenon in the North and is not to be found just in the activities of culture bases. The main cause was the Russians' racial prejudice towards the indigenous peoples, often manifested in attitudes ranging from disrespect to hostility or even violence (for example in the case of Khanty herders who wanted to create their own kolkhoz instead of working in a Russian-Komi cooperative and who were simply murdered by the cooperative leadership; see Skachko 1931: 105–107). Being a pivotal place of contact, the culture base was also a privileged place for communication and often enough for miscommunication.

The Kazym culture base was opened in a remote area with few contacts with Russians, and hence the natives had hardly any knowledge of Russian. The mere name of the institution was ominous for them. Thus, for the Khanty, culture base in Russian, *kul'tbaza*, reminded them of the Khanty concept *kul'*, which denotes an evil spirit (Balzer 1999: 107).[20] The culture bases must have appeared as dangerous places, especially because of the boarding schools, where children were exposed to alien influences without the protection of their parents. The Russians, however, who were ignorant of the local culture and language, were not aware of the unhappy choice of name.

---

[19] For example, Suslov enumerates the "errors" committed by the Kazym culture base: "substitution of the local committee of the base; raw administration instead of political work." While it is not explicitly stated, clearly Suslov presents these "errors" as causes of the Kazym rebellion.
[20] There are various Khanty deities with similar names, in which *kul'* is one element: *Kul'-iki* or *Kul'-lunkh* is associated with diseases and the underworld, also identified with the Christian devil; *Kul'-Ortyr* is an underworld god-spirit (Balzer 1999: 85, 87).

Other misunderstandings with the same origin—ignorance on both sides—concerned the children's diet. As noodles were not part of the natives' diet, parents thought that their children were being fed worms (Leete 2004a: 120). Conflicts and miscommunication took place on all levels, including what the Soviets defined as "everyday issues," such as refusals to go to the sauna, wear underwear or undress before going to bed, and girls residing on higher floors of a building than boys, which was seen by the natives as ritually polluting.[21]

The Natives and School

As mentioned above, school was a critical issue in the natives' view. As experienced by the Russian Orthodox missionaries, who had also attempted to set up schools for natives, native families were reluctant to "give" their children to the boarding school (Irinarkh 1904; Irinarkh 1905). This did not change under the Soviet regime. Having a child in the boarding school meant being deprived of labour, being separated for long months from the children and exposing them to unknown teaching practices, actions and forces, and consequently natives were reluctant to send their children to school.

Various different administrative measures were used against parents who did not want to send their children to school: sequestration, court summons, penalty taxes and forcible abduction. Parents were frightened, and some yielded. This brutal approach, as shown by archival materials, was instigated by the director of the Kazym culture base, Filipp Yakovlevich Babkin and decisions were taken by the local council. While some "results" may have been formally achieved, dissatisfaction was the main consequence of these constraints: Khanty leaders started discussing among themselves ways to oppose the Russians (Leete 2004a: 119–121).

The parents also feared more specific dangers, especially after epidemics started to spread very quickly in the community. In the Kazym school there was an epidemic of chickenpox and a quarantine was declared during which children were isolated from their parents (Yernykhova 2003: 50–51). In general, children were weakened by a life very different from the one they were accustomed to live and were probably more sensitive to infections, as they were not resistant to the germs brought by the Russians. Mortality and

---

[21] In the Khanty and Nenets traditions, it was not acceptable for a female to be situated higher than a male or above a male. A female walking over a male was thus considered particularly shameful.

disease were actually a traditional plague in Russian schools for several centuries (Efirov 1934: 54). Justified or unjustified rumours of casualties were certainly one of the reasons why schools were shunned.

Moreover, parents were right in their fears of acculturation. True enough, in Soviet discourse and in the enlighteners' understanding, education was not supposed to Russify the children (it was supposed to be delivered in vernacular languages) but to give them instruments to get accustomed to the wider world. But in spite of the absence of this explicit goal in the discourse, parents were well aware that their children were taught how to live in a different world that was going to swallow them in the end (Golovnev & Osherenko 1999: 79). A good example of this reality is to be found in Soviet accounts of achievements: braid cuttings are considered as positive achievements that the leaders of the bases were proud of (Terletskiy 1935: 42).

It is thus understandable that protest against school was one of the most common points raised in the uprisings. The Kazym events started with the parents invading the school building and taking their children back to the tundra.

The Natives and Economic Exploitation

Building culture bases was not the easiest of tasks: they were situated in remote locations and often building materials had to be brought to the area (for difficulties in connection with building, see Bazanov & Kazanskiy 1939: 68–70). Some bases compelled natives to work, often without being paid, as in Kazym where Khantys were forced to participate in the building of the school. Other forms of economic exploitation, illegal by definition, were the use of the natives' reindeer, which were just taken without any compensation, or the illegal appropriation of furs brought by Khantys in order to be traded (Yernykhova 2003: 99–100). Clearly, this was not part of the official Soviet project and can be seen as part of the denounced "defects and errors."

The Natives and the Soviets

The indigenous communities had lived for centuries under Russian rule. While until the Soviet period, the authorities had not interfered much in the natives' lives, they had still had a presence and had institutions that shaped their interaction. The natives did not contest the existence of these institutions. But when the wealthier communities and the most respected people, such as the "shamans," were indicted and forbidden to take part in political life, the local communities protested and took action against the Soviets' decision. Thus, on 8 January 1932 in Kazym, when the council wanted to exclude two men as kulaks, the Khanty population elected a board favourable to indigenous interests which did not allow the exclusion of the so-called kulaks (Leete 2004a: 128–129).

The principle of class struggle, so central to Marxism-Leninism, was alien to the natives' not yet ideologised worldview. The exclusion of people who were considered leaders (which was the very reason why they were eliminated) was one of the causes for dissatisfaction. In some cases, the protest went further: we have examples where the communities demanded the return of their priest and the restoration of an Orthodox church, which was seen as a source of efficient rituals. They were reluctant to accept the kind of changes Soviet power wanted to impose on them.

The Natives and the Staff of the Culture Base

Clearly the behaviour of the people that the Khanty and the Nenets happened to get in touch with determined, at least partially, the indigenous reaction to the culture bases. We have already mentioned the role of Babkin in the campaign for bringing children to school, and the predatory acts of taking furs or reindeer, as well as compelling people to work for free. Some other attitudes during the conflict worsened the relations: when fishing in the lake triggered protests and intervention from the natives, the authorities responded by sending to Num-To various representatives who, as a rule, did not meet with the indigenous representatives. But their attitudes were undoubtedly provocative enough to worsen the conflict. The first delegation was mainly composed of people connected with the base: its subsequent director A. D. Shershnev and the Party secretary and head of the cooperative. While waiting for the natives to appear, they made grenades and prepared a rope for restraining the Nenets in case they were "kulaks." These preparations were made openly, and the Nenets, undoubtedly, were informed of them, as stated in an official report (*Sud'by narodov Ob'-Irtyshskogo Severa* 1994: 12). There were other Russian provocations during these events, but they came from people unconnected with the culture base, for example the Party member Polina Shnaider.

Conclusion

In the case of the Kazym events, the natives' reactions were triggered by two distinct but yet connected provocations. One involved actions and behaviour that were not in agreement with the Soviet project and were not justified by it. The above-mentioned actions must have been all too familiar to the local indigenous population accustomed to the Russians' insolence and arrogance. They were due to the same sense of superiority that pervaded the "white" persons' attitudes towards the natives: this is discernible even in the official writings (Tolkachev [ed.] 1999: 13). But even without these provocations, the core of the project was destined to spark off reactions.

The bases were developed on the basis of an ideology that ceased to be relevant in the mid-1930s. They were not intended to implement a policy of constraint, but to trigger spontaneous development, and thus their importance decreased. They did not disappear as locations, but they lost their central role in the process of sovietisation. Resistance due to the principles along which the bases had been established deprived them of any sense of purpose. They were the brain-children of the Committee of the North and with the decline of the committee's influence, the bases lost their impact and with its liquidation in 1935, the management of Northern policies was devolved to an economic organ in charge of the Northern Sea Route (*Glavsevmorput'*). This shows clearly that the Northern areas were seen as economic resources rather than human habitats. With this new vision of the North, in which the human element was insignificant, a deep silence settled on the North.

As a Khanty scholar emphasises: "the culture bases in the northern territories attract attention as a specific social experiment of the Soviet state" (Yernykhova 2010: 102). We would take this further and see culture bases as imaginary sites, the kernel of a utopian world, and from this point of view their failure may be seen as the embodiment of Soviet failure.

References

Al'kor, Ya. (1934). Алькор (Кошкин), Я. "Задачи культурного строительства на Крайнем Севере" ['Tasks of cultural construction in the Far North'], *Советский Север*, 2, pp. 22–35.

Balzer, M. M. (1999). *The Tenacity of Ethnicity. A Siberian Saga in Global Perspective*, Princeton: Princeton University Press.

Bardin, G. (1994). Бардин, Г. "Народ югорский, право на жизнь" ['The Yugra people, right to live'], *Новости Югры*, 30 March.

Bazanov, A. G. & Kazanskiy N. G. (1939). Базанов, А. Г. и Казанский, Н. Г. *Школа на Крайнем Севере* ['School in the Far North'], Leningrad: Gosudarstvennoe Uchebno-pedagogicheskoe Izdatel'stvo Narkomprosa RSFSR.

Bogoraz-Tan, V. G. (1925). Богораз-Тан, В. Г. "Подготовительные меры к организации малых народностей" ['Preliminary measures to organise the small peoples'], *Северная Азия*, 3, pp. 40–50.

Budarin, M. (1968). Бударин, М. *Были о сибирских чекистах* ['Stories of the Siberian chekists'], Omsk: Zapadno-Sibirskoe knizhnoe izdatel'stvo, Omskoe otdelenie.

Campbell, C. A. R. (2004). "Cultural *stroitel'stvo* and the Tura culture base," in *Этносы Сибири. Прошлее. Настоящее. Будущее*, ред. Н. П. Макаров, Krasnoyarsk: Krasnoyarskiy kraevoy kraevedcheskiy muzey, pp. 41–47.

Efirov, A. F. (1934). Эфиров, А. Ф. "Руссификаторские новокрещенские школы" ['The Russifying schools for newly converted'], *Просвещение национальностей*, 4, pp. 51–58.

Forsyth, J. (1992). *A History of the Peoples of Siberia. Russia's North-Asian Colony, 1581–1990*, Cambridge: Cambridge University Press.

Golovnev, A. & Osherenko, G. (1999). *Siberian Survival. The Nenets and their Story*, Ithaca: Cornell University Press.

Grant, B. (1993). "Siberia hot and cold. Reconstructing the image of Siberian indigenous peoples," in *Between Heaven and Hell. The Myth of Siberia in Russian Culture*, eds. G. Diment & Y. Slezkine, New York: St. Martin's Press, pp. 227–254.

Hirsch, F. (2005). *Empire of Nations. Ethnographic Knowledge and the Making of the Soviet Union*, Ithaca: Cornell University Press.

Irinarkh (1904). Иринарх (иеромонах), "К вопросу об организации школьного дела среди кочевников крайнего Севера" ['About the organisation of school education among the nomads of the Far North'], *Православный благовестник*, 15, pp. 297–307.

Irinarkh (1905). Иринарх (иеромонах), "К вопросу о необходимости школьного обучения девочек обдорких инородцев" ['About the need of school education for the girls of the Obdorsk nomads'], *Православный благовестник*, 19, pp. 137–140.

Kantor, E. D. (1933). Кантор, Е. Д. "Казымская культбаза" ['The Kazym culture base'], *Советский Север*, 6, pp. 66–68.

Kantor, E. D. (1935). Кантор, Е. Д. "Перевыборы Советов в северных нацокругах и районах" ['Re-elections of the soviets in the northern national regions and districts'], *Советский Север*, 1, pp. 9–16.

Karshakova, N. V. (1996). Каршакова, Н. В. "К вопросу о политических, экономических и культурных преобразований на Обь-Иртышском Севере в 1920–1930 годах" ['About the issue of political, economic and cultural reforms in the Ob-Irtysh North during the 1920s and 1930s'], Tyumen, pp. 32–46.

Khomich, L. V. (1966). Хомич, Л. В. *Ненцы. Историко-этнографические очерки* ['The Nenets. Historic and ethnographic essays'], Moscow: Nauka.

Khomich, L. V. (1999). Хомич, Л. В. "Георгий Николаевич Прокофьев – исследователь языков и этнографии самодийских народов (к столетию со дня рождения)" ['Georgiy Nikolaevich Prokof'yev, a researcher of languages and ethnography of the Samoyed peoples (for the centenary of his birth)'], *Курьер Петровской Кунсткамеры*, 8–9, St. Petersburg, pp. 274–277; online version: www.kunstkamera.ru/siberia; access date 30 January 2013.

Kopylev, D. I. & Retunskiy, V. F. (1965). Копылев, Д. И. и Ретунский, В. Ф. *Очерки истории партийной организации Тюменской области* ['Essays on the history of the Tyumen Oblast Party organisation'], Sverdlovsk: Sredne-Ural'skoe knizhnoe izdatel'stvo.

Leete, A. (2002). *Kazõmi sõda. Šamanistliku kultuuri allakäik Lääne-Siberis* ['The Kazym War. The decline of shamanic culture in Western Siberia'], Tartu: Tartu University Press.

Leete, A. (2004a). Леэте, А. *Казымская война. Восстание хантов и лесных ненцев против советской власти* ['The Kazym War. Revolt of the Khanty and the Forest Nenets against Soviet power'], Tartu: Tartu University Press.

Leete, A. (2004b). "Invasion of materialism into the Soviet North. Sedentarisation, development of professional medicine and hygiene in the 1920–40s," in *Everyday Life and Cultural Patterns. International Festschrift for Elle Vunder* (Studies in Folk Culture 3), eds. A. Leete & E. Kõresaar, Tartu: Tartu University Press, pp. 69–86.

Leete, A. (2007). *La guerre du Kazym. Les peuples de Sibérie occidentale contre le pouvoir soviétique 1933-1934* ['The Kazym War. The peoples of Western Siberia against Soviet power 1933–1934'], Paris: ADÉFO-L'Harmattan.

Leete, A. & Vallikivi, L. (2011). "Adapting Christianity on the Siberian edge during the early Soviet period," *Folklore. Electronic Journal of Folklore*, 49, pp. 131–146; https://www.folklore.ee/folklore/vol49/leetevallikivi.pdf; access date 30 January 2013.

Lipatova, L. F. (2008). Липатова, Л. Ф. *"Сава луца, хороший человек Броднев"* ['"Sava Lutsa, a good man, Brodnev"'], Tyumen: Siti-press.

Lunacharskiy, A. V. (1927). Луначарский, А. В. "Задачи Наркомпроса на Крайнем Севере" ['The tasks of the People's Commissariat for Education in the Far North'], *Северная Азия*, 3, pp. 18–22.

Lvov, A. K. (1926). Львов, А. К. "Культурные базы на Севере" ['The culture bases in the North'], *Северная Азия*, 3, pp. 28–37.

Lyarskaya, E. V. (2003). Лярская, Е. В. "Северные интернаты и трансформация традиционной культуры (на примере ненцев Ямала)" ['The northern boarding schools and the transformation of traditional culture (on the example of the Yamal Nenets'], diss., European University at St. Petersburg.

Mazurenko, G. A. (1979). Мазуренко, Г. А. "Деятельность партийных организаций по формированию социалистического быта народностей Севера" ['The activity of Party organisations in constructing socialist way of life among the peoples of the North'], *Социалистический образ жизни*, pp. 126–128.

Novitskiy, V. M. (1928a). Новицкий, В. М. "Казымский тузрайон как основной очаг туземной культуры на Тобольском севере" ['The Kazym indigenous district as the main hearth of indigenous culture in the Tobolsk North'], *Уральское краеведение*, 2, pp. 117–124.

Novitskiy, V. M. (1928b). Новицкий, В. М. "Туземцы Тобольского Севера и очередные вопросы по устроению их жизни" ['The indigenes of the Tobolsk North and present issues about the organisation of their life'], *Северная Азия*, 5–6, pp. 68–73.

Onishchuk, N. T. (1986). Онищук, Н. Т. *Создание советской национальной государственности народностей Севера* ['Creating Soviet national statehood for the Northern peoples'], Tomsk: Izdatel'stvo Tomskogo universiteta.

Parkhomenko, S. G. (1930). Пархоменко, С. Г. "Краеведческая работа в культбазах" ['Studying local history in culture bases'], *Советский Север*, 1, pp. 125–129.

Petrova, V. P. & Kharyuchi, G. P. (1999). Петрова, В. П. и Харючи, Г. П. *Ненцы в истории Ямало-Ненецкого автономного округа* ['The Nenets in the history of the Yamalo-Nenets autonomous okrug'], Tomsk: Izdatel'stvo Tomskogo universiteta.

Protokol (1925). "Протокол расширенного пленума Комитета Севера совместно с делегатами XII Съезда советов РСФСР" ['The protocol of the extended meeting of the Committee of the North with the delegates of the 12th Congress of the Soviets of the RSFSR'], *Северная Азия*, 3, приложение 3, p. 111.

Shmyrev, V. (1933). Шмырев, Б. "Ямальская культбаза" ['The Yamal culture base'], *Советский Север*, 6, pp. 69–74.

Skachko, A. (1931). Скачко, А. "Земля Югорская и Обдорская в лето 1930 г. (Историческая справка)" ['The land of Yugor and Obdorsk during the summer of 1930. (Historical information)'], *Советский Север*, 2, pp. 58–113.

Skachko, A. (1934). Скачко, А. "Десять лет работы Комитета Севера" ['Ten years of work of the Committee of the North'], *Советский Север*, 2, pp. 9–21.

Slezkine, Y. (1994). *Arctic mirrors. Russia and the Small Peoples of the North*, Ithaca: Cornell University Press.

Sud'by narodov Ob'-Irtyshskogo Severa (1994). Судьбы народов Обь-Иртышского Севера. Из истории национально-государственного строительство 1822–1941 гг. Сборник документов ['The fate of the peoples of the Ob-Irtysh North. From the history of state-national construction 1822–1941. A collection of documents'], ред. Д. И. Копылов, Tyumen: Gosudarstvennyy Archiv Tyumenskoy Oblasti.

Suslov, I. M. (1934). Суслов, И. М. "Пятнадцать северных культбаз" ['The fifteen Northern culture bases'], *Советский Север*, 1, pp. 28–37.

Terletskiy, P. (1935). Терлецкий, П. "Культбазы Комитета Севера" ['The culture bases of the Committee of the North'], *Советский Север*, 1, pp. 36–48.

Tolkachev, V. F. (ed.) (1999). Толкачев, В. Ф. (ред.). *Ненецкий край. Сквозь вьюги лет. Очерки. Статьи. Документы* ['The Nenets region. Through the blizzard of years. Essays. Articles. Documents'], Arkhangelsk: Pomorskiy gosudarstvennyy universitet imeni M. V. Lomonosova.

Toulouze, E. (1999). "The development of a written culture by the indigenous peoples of Western Siberia," *Pro Ethnologia*, 7, pp. 53–85.

Toulouze, E. (2005). "The intellectuals from Russia's peoples of the North. From obedience to resistance," in *The Northern Peoples and States. Changing Relationships* (Studies in Folk Culture 5), Tartu: Tartu University Press, pp. 140–164.

V komitete (1935). "В комитете Севера" ['In the Committee of the North'], *Советский Север*, 1, pp. 106–110.

Yernykhova, O. D. (2003). Ерныхова, О. Д. *Казымский мятеж (Об истории Казымского восстания 1933–1934)* ['The Kazym revolt (From the history of the Kazym uprising 1933–1934)'], Novosibirsk: Sibirskiy khronograf.

Yernykhova, O. D. (2010). Ерныхова, О. Д. "Казымская культурная база как социальный эксперимент советского государства" ['The Kazym culture base as a social experiment of the socialist state'], *Вестник Тюменского Государственного Унтверситета*, 1, pp. 101–108.

Zelenin, D.K. (1938). Зеленин, Д. К. "Народы крайнего Севера после Великой Октябрьской социалистической революции" ['The Peoples of the Far North after the Great Socialist October Revolution'], in *Советская этнография. Сборник статей*, pp. 12–52.

CHAPTER 9
Repression of Shamans and Shamanism in Khabarovsk Krai. 1920s to the early 1950s

Tatiana Bulgakova & Olle Sundström

> Shamanism is and will be an obstacle to socialist construction. The struggle against shamanism cannot and must not be conducted in isolation from the general construction. The struggle against shamanism is a part of the socialist construction itself.
>
> Innokentii M. Suslov (1931: 128)

In the 10th congress of the Soviet Communist Party in 1921, it was decided that the indigenous peoples of the North should be assisted, by the Party, to take the leap from a "primitive," "pre-class" society to a socialist one. The economic, political, and cultural level of the indigenous societies was to be raised through the implementation of Soviet administration, law, and economics as well as through the development of schools, newspapers, and other cultural institutions. Not least, the spreading of modern medicine and information about the importance of hygiene was seen as imperative for improving living conditions in the Soviet North (Eidlitz Kuoljok 1985: 34–35; Slezkine 1994: 143–144). The aim of Soviet policies concerning the indigenous peoples of the North was to combat poverty and backwardness and what the communists saw as unjust social and economic relations in the traditional indigenous societies. The old society was to be replaced by a new and better one. As M. M. Balzer (2011: 45) puts it, in this revolutionary atmosphere shamans "as quintessential symbols of tradition and conservatism, became a focus of repression." Together with the liquidation of economic exploitation, poverty, analphabetism, ignorance, poor hygiene, disease, patriarchalism, and the abuse of women and children, shamanism should also be ousted. But how was this struggle against shamanism enacted in practice? How, and in what sense, did it turn into repression of so-called shamans and shamanism?[1]

---

[1] The concepts "shaman" and "shamanism" are in this context Russian or Soviet concepts. "Shaman" and "shamanism" were (and still are, to a large extent) used to designate certain, in many respects different—but also, of course, in other ways similar—ritual functionaries. The world-views they acted within among the indigenous peoples of the

The official methods of combatting shamans and shamanism included propaganda, enlightenment, and modernisation in the form of anti-religious and pro-materialist agitation, schools, and the sending out of medical doctors and midwives to the northern fringes of the Union.[2] In addition, legal restrictions with the aim of marginalising the influence of purported shamans and some of their activities were established in the 1920s. There are, however, also examples of, and above all many narratives about, arrests and even executions of shamans in the 1930s. This has led some scholars to conclude that shamans, just like, for example, Russian Orthodox priests, were violently purged in the socialist reconstruction of the indigenous societies. For instance, P. Vitebsky claims that the Soviet communists

> started to "civilize" the native peoples by building them permanent wooden villages and providing basic schooling and medical facilities, introducing State bureaucracy and teaching them Communist values. At the same time they imprisoned or killed their spiritual support, the shamans. (Vitebsky 2005: 35)[3]

On Nanai shamans, S. V. Bereznitskiy writes:

Eurasian North also varied. It is important to be reminded about this particularly when speaking about the ritual functionaries among the indigenous peoples touched upon in this chapter because the very term *shaman* is borrowed into the Western academic vocabulary from the Manchu-Tungus languages, to which most indigenous languages in Khabarovsk krai belong. Thus, a Nanai *saman* was considered a "shaman" in the Soviet discourse under study (just as a *tadebya* among the Nenets was labelled a "shaman" in this discourse). The "shaman" in the Soviet mind should not, however, be confused with the *saman* in the traditional Nanai. The conceptions of a "shaman" among advocates of the Soviet ideology were very different from the conceptions of a *saman* among proponents of a traditional Nanai world-view. For a more exhaustive discussion on the concepts of "shaman" and "shamanism" in the Soviet and Russian context, see Sundström 2012; and Leete 2015.

[2] The most well-organized project for implementing socialism and further modernisation among the peoples of the Soviet North was the culture bases, run by *Komitet Severa*. On the culture bases and *Komitet Severa*, see Chapter 8 by Tolouze, Vallikivi & Leete in this volume.

[3] In a popular science book, Vitebsky (1995: 136–137) claims that shamans "were often sentenced to exile and sometimes dropped out of helicopters and challenged to fly." He also retells a story of a KGB officer in a remote Siberian area, who had the habit of visiting known shamans while pretending to be sick. The officer lured the shamans to a secluded place and shot them, taking their drums back home as trophies. These stories have the character of legends, and the author does not give any references as to their origins.

Nanai shamans, like other shamans of the indigenous peoples of the Lower Amur, were called the enemies of the people, and many of them were executed during the repressions in the 1930s. An entire era of Nanai spiritual life and Nanai world-view was liquidated together with them. (Bereznitskiy 2003: 215, *our translation*)

The Sakha scholar P. N. Il'yakhov-Khamsa (1995: 22) also contends that "mass arrests" of shamans took place and that Evenk shamans were arrested and shot without inquiry or trial, accused of being "deceivers of the people." He exemplifies the purge of shamans with Konstantin I. Chirkov, who was disfranchised (Ru. *lishenets*) and arrested in February 1932, charged with being a kulak. Chirkov was accused of many things: of having traded with and helped the White Guard during the Civil War; of pursuing systematic anti-Soviet agitation against collectivisation and the fur companies; of using his position as shaman to influence the ignorant people; of spreading counter-revolutionary rumours about the imminent downfall of Soviet rule; and of persuading youngsters not to join the Komsomol. His livestock and hunting rifle were confiscated in the arrest. A troika from the security service sentenced him, according to the notorious paragraph 58-10 in the penal code, to six months of incarceration in the penitentiary of Yakutsk (Il'yakhov-Khamsa 1995: 22–23). Chirkov was released after four months because of the time he had served in prison before the trial (Vasil'eva 2000: 61).

Even if there are claims in previous research that shamans were subjected to "mass arrests" and executed after summary trials, and even if several concrete examples of both arrests and executions can be presented, there is still a lack of substantial evidence to estimate the scale of the repression of shamans. Therefore, it is still difficult to assess the character of the Soviet struggle against shamanism.

In this chapter, we will investigate how this rather complex struggle was carried out in the Soviet North in the 1920s up until the 1950s, with special focus on the Nanai and Ulchi[4] shamans in what is today Khabarovsk krai in the Soviet Far East. We shall try to shed light on the situation using, together with previous research, the data that Tatiana Bulgakova has collected during her field work among the Nanai from the late 1980s to the present,[5] as well as

---

[4] The Nanai and the Ulchi (or Ulch) are two of the main indigenous peoples inhabiting the Lower Amur region. Together with the Udege, Negidal, Orok, and Orochi, they belong to the southern branch of the Manchu-Tungus language group. The Nanai today constitute some 12,000 individuals and the Ulchi just over 3,000. They are closely related linguistically and culturally—traditionally subsisting on hunting and fishing.

[5] For a complete list of Bulgakova's informants, see Bulgakova 2013: 239.

the material that Olle Sundström[6] has obtained from the State archives in Khabarovsk and Nikolaevsk-on-Amur (2010–2012).

The 1920s. The Beginning of Sovietisation

As related above, Evenk shaman Konstantin Chirkov was accused of lining his own pockets by collaborating with the Whites during the Civil War. Even if putative shamans in the 1930s, in sweeping statements by the communists, were held to be reactionary elements that resisted socialist reconstructions, it is difficult to say whether this was the actual case with shamans or indigenous spiritual leaders in general. There are several examples of so-called shamans who in the 1920s both assisted the Red Army during the Civil War and who took leading positions in the new Soviet local administration. The Soviet North was vast, and conditions most likely varied between the different parts of the area. There is, for instance, evidence that the persecution of shamans was quite severe in Yakutia already during the Civil War. N. D. Vasil'eva (2000: 27–28) concludes that in the first years of the 1920s shamanic ritual objects were forcefully confiscated and destroyed, and shamans were "subjected to political discrimination and morally discredited." Some shamans were also brought to public court trials. But there is no evidence of such severe punishments, such as executions, that Orthodox priests were subjected to at the time (see Pospielovsky 1988: 1–18; Corley [ed.] 1996: 14).

In the initial period of its formation, the Soviet regime strove to engage the indigenous peoples themselves in the construction of socialism and in the political struggle against the old society. Before the repression of shamans and shamanism began, not only some representatives of the indigenous population, but also some shamans were actively involved in the governing bodies. Those who had had leading positions among the indigenous groups before the Revolution were often elected as leaders in the newly invented native clan councils (Ru. *rodovye sovety*), which were supposed to rule and judge partly according to local indigenous custom. For example, V. G. Bogoraz-Tan (1932: 142–143) described three shamans who became the leaders of the native council in the Chukchi village of Uelen. In some Yakut villages, shamans actively assisted the Red Army in establishing Soviet power and in suppressing counter-revolutionary actions (Vasil'eva 2000: 29). The

---

[6] Sundström's research in Khabarovsk krai was made possible by a grant from the Swedish Research Council (*Vetenskapsrådet*) for the project "Repression of 'shamans' in the Soviet North from the late 1920s through the 1950s: an archival study," as well as a travel grant from the Swedish Institute (*Svenska institutet*).

Yakut shaman Spiridon G. Gerasimov was elected in the 1920s as a member of the local council and the local Revolutionary Committee and as assessor of the village law court. In 1925–1930 he was recruited as a guide for a Red Army squad that was sent from Irkutsk to eliminate the remnants of bandit leaders in the Anabar and Bulun districts. Afterwards, Spiridon was granted honorary awards by the Red Army for his military prowess (Bravina & Illarionov 2008: 16).

There is also reason to believe that Party members at times turned to shamans for help. At all events, the Yakut provincial committee of the Bolshevik Party, in its plenary meeting on 27 May 1924, found it necessary to prohibit members of the Party and the Komsomol from consulting shamans for their needs (Il'yakhov-Khamsa 1995: 11).

The support of the new system consisted not only of material assistance and participation in military activities, but also by means of rituals. For example, among the Nanai the establishment of Soviet power in the beginning of the 1920s coincided with the time when a certain spirit, *Kheri mapa*, obtained great popularity. Nanai shamans are reported to have believed that the Revolution was undertaken according to the will of *Kheri mapa* and that the Red Army was triumphing over the Whites because of the supplication that Nanai partisans, on the Red side, directed towards the spirit (Koz'minskiy 1927: 49).

Perhaps these shamans, in collaborating with the communists, put their hopes in the revolutionaries and saw their chance to turn against the former Russian tsarist regime, with its Orthodox Church, that in its own way had combatted shamanism and traditionalism among Siberian natives. If so, these hopes were initially fulfilled, at least partially. The Soviet League of the Militant Atheists (Ru. *Soyuz voinstvuyushchikh bezbozhnikov*)—a voluntary organization with close ties to the Communist Party founded in 1925 with the purpose of propagating atheism and combatting religion (Peris 1998: 44–45)—concluded in 1929 that shamanism, and the indigenous, non-Christian, religions in general, had gained strength after the Revolution and the Civil War (Kosokov 1930: 4). The same was reported by *Komitet Severa* (Suslov 1931: 129).

L. P. Potapov (1991: 163) even presents a statistical survey conducted in 26 villages in the Altai-Sayan region in 1924 that, at least in this particular area, confirms the strengthening or renaissance of shamanism. The survey showed, among other things, that 45 out of the 71 confirmed shamans had started practicing their art less than 5 years earlier, and only 11 of them had been practicing shamans for more than 10 years. Only 14 of them were 50 years or older, while 30 of them were under the age of 35. Even if Potapov could not say how reliable the results of the survey were, he confirmed the tendencies from his own experiences during his fieldwork in the region from 1926 to 1932 that shamanism became more popular during the years after the Revolution, not least among young people.

One important reason for the upsurge of shamanism after the Revolution was probably that the antireligious measures in the beginning were directed towards the liquidation of mainly Russian Orthodox Christianity. Persecutions in northern areas in the beginning of the 1920s therefore first and foremost fell upon Orthodox missionaries and priests, as well as on those members of the indigenous peoples who were Christians. Because most northern indigenous peoples were officially and nominally Christians by the time of the Revolution (Balzer 2011: 39), the first anti-church measures had consequences also for them. In fact, regarding the Nanai in Khabarovsk krai, only 675 persons (13.5% of the entire Nanai population) considered themselves "heathens" according to the 1897 census (Patkanov 1906: 17). Y. V. Argutsyaeva confirmed that by 1916 the Christianisation of the Nanai was almost complete and that there were already several Nanai catechists and priests (Argutsyaeva 2009). Many of Bulgakova's Nanai informants remembered that their grandparents went to church services, studied in parish schools, and used to have orthodox icons—items that, during the time of Soviet persecution, they had to hide away in the attic. Witnesses to the eradication of the church buildings recalled that the icons were removed, chopped into pieces, and burned and that the church bells were taken away to Khabarovsk, the main city along the Amur River.

The chapels had been one of the few Russian infrastructures on the northern frontier as the regime reached out to the perimeter of the empire to spread literacy, education, Russian culture, and Christianity. When the priests and other servants of the church were forced to withdraw, the new regime took over this infrastructure during the second half of the 1920s. Former church buildings were oftentimes transformed into Soviet schools or "clubs," where meetings, concerts, and theatre plays dedicated to the new ideology and system were held. So-called Red tents or yurts (Ru. *Krasnye Chumy/Yurty*)—mobile units of the culture bases (see Chapter 8 in this volume)—turned former chapels into their headquarters. This was, for example, the case with the chapels in the Nanai villages of Nizhnye Khalby and Kondon (Putintseva 2010: 17, 56, 268). In Troytskiy, another Nanai village, the former chapel, turned into a school, was still standing until it burned down in the 1950s—an event that some Nanais interpreted as a sign that (the

Christian) God took it away (informants Olga Yegorovna and Kseniya Ivanovna).

Because the Orthodox Church, with the help of state authorities, earlier had persecuted shamans and shamanism (banning rituals and drums, destroying sacred places, and incarcerating shamans), the Bolshevik attack on the church made it possible for the indigenous religions to be practiced more openly and to gain ground in the 1920s (Potapov 1991: 91–92, 219–220). Andrei Znamenski concludes:

> At first, communists and their sympathizers rarely crusaded against shamanism, preferring mainstream Christianity as a target for their attacks. In such a climate, practicing shamanists felt relaxed. Moreover, many earlier indigenous converts to Orthodox Christianity found it possible to return to their polytheistic spirituality. (Znamenski 2007: 328)

That the early anti-religious campaigns targeted mainly the Orthodox Church also meant that the measures that were elaborated to combat religion were designed after the structure of that church (and other institutionalized religions such as Judaism, Islam, and Buddhism). T. M. Mikhaylov (1979: 148) suggests that these measures did not apply in the case of shamanism because it had no organizations to infiltrate or dissolve, no temples to close or eradicate, no literature to censor or ban, and no set calendar of services to interfere with. C. Humphrey (1983: 416–417), who like Mikhaylov writes about the Buryat, adds that shamanism's lack of hierarchical structure, dogmatism, and strict ethical demands on its practitioners made it less of a competitor to the new communist regime, and thus initially less important to combat. As suggested by Balzer (2011: 39), yet another reason for the return to shamanic practices in the beginning of the Soviet era could have been that the turmoil and confusion—as well as famine—caused by the Revolution and the Civil War led to an increased demand on shamans:

> Individual and community catharsis occurred in troubled times through séances, intense emotional dramas, usually involving trance (of the shaman and sometimes others) with poetic chants, drumming, dancing, and group participation. (Balzer 2011: 40)

Balzer's remark is important because it suggests that the shamanism of the 1920s was perhaps not so much a "renaissance"—in the sense of an upsurge of lingering ancient ideas and ritual practices—as it was a response to a particular historical and social situation.

The 1930s. Cultural Revolution and Collectivization

The hopes that the various indigenous communities in the North could administrate and rule themselves both according to their own manners and customs as well as according to the Soviet system came to a close by the end of the 1920s, partly, it seems, because shamans and shamanism in some cases had gotten the upper hand among the natives. From the Soviet point of view, the problem with shamanism was both social and ideological—that it helped sustain the old social structures and that it was "superstitious." I. M. Suslov, an ethnographer specializing in shamanism among the Evenks and vice-chairman of the *Komitet Severa*—and thus one of the leading ideologues regarding the policy on the peoples of the North around 1930—argued that the recent resurgence of shamanism was a consequence of the will of the "indigenous kulaks" and "clan aristocracies" to safeguard their own authority and economic power, which they felt were threatened after the Revolution. Therefore they supported the shamans, whom they saw as the guardians of tradition (Suslov 1931: 129–130).

There are also concrete examples of so-called shamans taking control over the governing of an area in opposition to the new Soviet rule. In the Karaga district of Kamchatka, a certain Savva, allegedly a shaman and leader of an indigenous Itelmen organization with several shamans, managed to stay in unofficial control of the people during the entire 1920s, despite the fact that Soviet administrative rule was established in the area already in 1923. He repudiated Soviet schools, Russian food and clothes, and the new bathhouses, claiming that they were detrimental to the people. However, in 1930–1931 Savva was ousted by the new executive committee in the Karaga district when the Koryak National Okrug was formed (Stebnitskiy 2000: 159).

Among communists, it was agreed that shamanism was "superstitious" and anti-scientific, and thus did not belong in a future socialist or communist society. To what degree it was also "religious" or a "religion" was a slightly different matter. In his address at the plenary meeting of the Yakut provincial committee of the Bolshevik Party in May 1924, a certain I. Vinokurov contended that "the basis of the origin of shamanism is found in primitive animism, i.e. the attribution of spirits to the forces of nature" and that "in its subsequent development shamanism encountered Christianity and did not develop into a religious system." Therefore, according to Vinokurov, shamanism in general is a "cult" that has degenerated and taken the forms of "quackery" or "sorcery" (Ru. *znakharstvo*). In accordance with the directives of the central Soviet policy on the authorities' "relation to religious and other cults," the presidium of the Central Executive Committee of the Yakut ASSR decided in November 1924:

1. to consider shamanism a particularly harmful phenomenon that hampers the cultural-national awakening as well as the political development of the peoples in the Yakut ASSR;

2. that the struggle against shamanism should be carried out by means of enlightenment, agitation and propaganda;

3. that certain shamanic activities should fall within the penal code and that shamans should be prosecuted for those activities; and

4. to suggest to the NKVD of the Yakut ASSR and the health authorities that they initiate a plan for prohibiting medicaments and medical treatments that are not approved by medical science (see Il'yakhov-Khamsa 1995: 10–12).

The decisions of the committee were, in essence, a campaign against quackery, even if they also contained important aspects of what was conceptualized by the communists as raising the "cultural," "national" (in the sense "ethnic"), and "political" level of awareness among the natives. But it was not a campaign against shamanism as a "religion."

Around the turn of the 1930s, the rhetoric against shamans and shamanism changed towards categorizing them together with other religious functionaries and religions. In the original constitution of 1918, "monks and spiritual servants of churches and religious cults" (Ru. *monakhi i dukhovnye sluzhiteli tserkvey i religioznykh kul'tov*) had been disfranchised and prohibited from being elected to decision-making bodies (Ru. *sovety*).[7] Because shamans were not generally viewed as the equivalents of monks and priests—and because shamanism was not generally considered a *religious* cult—they were generally not denied these civic rights in the early 1920s and could, apparently, be elected to local councils. However, in November 1926, prior to the re-elections to local councils in the Soviet North, an instruction from the Central Committee was issued. In that instruction, the "servants of religious cults" were expressly specified as "monks, novices, deacons, psalmers, mullahs, rabbis, lamas, shamans, pastors [...] and all those who fulfil similar

---

[7] Konstitutsiya (Osnovnoy Zakon) Rossiyskoy Sotsialisticheskoy Federativnoy Sovetskoy Respubliki (prinyata 5 Vserossiyskim S'ezdom Sovetov v zasedanii ot 10 iyulya 1918 g.; http://constitution.garant.ru/history/ussr-rsfsr/1918/chapter/13/#block_4600; accessed on 14 September 2016.

functions." Shamans were thus, together with their family members, denied the right to vote or be elected (Pospielovsky 1987: 137). The disfranchised were also locked out from participation in kolkhozes and cooperatives, were not allocated hunting or fishing grounds, nor land for farming, and their belongings were expropriated. Their children were not allowed to enter boarding schools or higher education (Il'yakhov-Khamsa 1995: 19).

With the launching of the Cultural Revolution by the Stalin regime in the spring of 1928, the class struggle was intensified and all "exploiters" were to be liquidated. In the crucial 6th plenary meeting of the *Komitet Severa* in March 1929, the committee was severely criticized by high-ranking Party officials for not having used a class perspective in their work among the indigenous peoples of the North. The gist of the critique was that the committee had not been able to identify "exploiters" because it regarded northern indigenous communities as "primitive communists" lacking social classes. This had impeded socialist reconstruction in the North. In his concluding speech at the meeting, the chairman of the *Komitet Severa*, Petr Smidovich, admitted that the committee had not implemented serious class struggle. But he reassured that now, when the Soviet governmental and administrative bodies were in place, the work with improving the position of women and disfranchising kulaks and shamans—the latter now being seen as the equivalent of priests—among the natives would be strengthened (Slezkine 1994: 191–192, 226–227).

As a response to the demands from the Party, ethnographers engaged in the League of the Militant Atheists and the *Komitet Severa* started emphasizing that shamanism should be treated as religion. In a pamphlet issued by the League's publishing house *Bezbozhnik* ['the Atheist'] in 1930, I. Kosokov argued against those who denied that shamanism was a religion:

> In our days, to deny shamanism the character of religion, means denying the necessity of a resolute struggle against shamanism, which serves as a major obstacle to the construction of socialism among the most backward peoples of the Soviet Union, and which serves as a direct instrument for the kulaks in their exploitation of the working masses among the indigenous peoples of Siberia. (Kosokov 1930: 6, *our translation*)

Illustration 14 (next page): 'Elect workers to the indigenous council. Don't let the shaman and the kulak in.' Soviet propaganda poster by Georgiy Khoroshevskiy, 1931.

Bogoraz-Tan, a prominent member of the *Komitet Severa*, also emphasized the importance of including the struggle against shamanism in the general fight against religion:

> For the native class-elite and for their ideological spokesmen now comes the time of liquidation. [---] Now neither the shaman nor the priest has a place in the socialist society, and they will both perish entirely. [---] Provided that the struggle against the shaman can and should be linked to the struggle against the kulaks, the struggle against the shamanic religion, i.e. against shamanic animism, must be tightly linked to the struggle against Orthodoxy.
>
> [---]
>
> Icons must constantly be placed on par with indigenous idols, priestly rituals with shamanic rituals, and Christ himself, his death and resurrection placed on par with [...] the mysteries of the bear cult, which in the same way includes the death and resurrection of the powerful animal—god. (Bogoraz-Tan 1932: 157, *our translation*)

As seen above, the concept of "shaman" was tied to the most intimidating catchword of the time, *kulak*, sometimes conflated in the accusation *kulak-shaman*. Even if shamans were not themselves rich and wealthy, they were perceived as the ideological supporters of the kulaks and thus in essence "exploiters." In a telling formulation in a document from the Yamal-Nenets Party Committee, the category "kulak" is defined as "big reindeer-owners, former heirs of the fishing industry, princes, elders and shamans" (*Sud'by narodov Ob'-Irtyshskogo Severa* 1994: 242).

Even if the idea of shamanism as "religion" or "religious" was not new—it had existed before the Revolution as well[8]—the new emphasis on shamanism as the indigenous religion of the northern peoples, instead of as mere "superstition" and "quackery," meant two important changes in the Soviet attitude towards it. First it made the so-called struggle against shamanism a part of the general struggle against religion. Second it meant that shamanism was seen as a whole system of ideas and practices that people lived within and according to. Thus, it could not be overcome by merely confiscating drums and prohibiting rituals and certain healing practices.

---

[8] Opinions on the question of whether shamanism was a religion or not diverged also among nineteenth-century ethnographers and Orthodox missionaries; for examples, see Znamenski 2003: 43–130.

In a 1931 publication addressed to Party workers, anti-religious activists, indigenous students, and others who were involved in the reconstruction of the indigenous cultures and societies in the North, I. M. Suslov criticized the measures that had, up until then, been taken towards shamans. He described trying to coerce shamans to cease their activities by forcing them to hand over their drums and other ritual regalia as absurd, shallow, and counter-productive because these measures had only forced the shamans underground and caused opposition among the natives towards the reconstructions. Suslov also quoted a resolution of the 12th Party congress (in 1923) where such methods were condemned:

> Deliberately brutal methods, [and] insults to objects of belief and cult, instead of a serious analysis and explanation, does not hasten the liberation of the working masses from religious prejudices, but obstructs it.

To yield to "spontaneity" could easily lead to "exaggerations" (Ru. *peregiby*), Suslov argued. Instead, what he was proposing was intensified education, enlightenment, and the creation of indigenous cadres of atheist propagandists who could agitate for the materialist world-view. Particular emphasis should be laid on the engagement of indigenous women and youngsters—the women because they were the most oppressed among the indigenous peoples and the young because they were the future and also the easiest to (re-)educate (Suslov 1931: 128 ff.). At the institutes for higher learning, founded in the 1920s to foster an intelligentsia of the indigenous peoples of the North—the Institute for the Peoples of the North in Leningrad, and the institutes of technology for indigenous peoples in Irkutsk, Khabarovsk, and Tomsk—cells of the League of Militant Atheists should be created. All education at these institutes should be imbued with an anti-religious, and particularly anti-shamanic, content, as Suslov suggested: "Not one single student should be allowed to finish these institutions of learning without having received the necessary atheistic tempering" (Suslov 1931: 138, 147–148).

Bogoraz-Tan, in an article in *Komitet Severa*'s journal *Sovetskiy Sever* ['The Soviet North'], thought it important to distinguish between the "religious ideology" and the "religious organization." Among the peoples of the North, the religious ideology was animism, and the religious organization was shamanism. He found that the measures Suslov suggested were proper for the fight against shamanism because religious organizations are always counter-revolutionary and an impediment to development and progress. But in order to combat animism, a total reconstruction of the communities in the North would be necessary—the local social structures must be demolished and the traditional means of production must be replaced by new ones. What Bogoraz-Tan was suggesting was in essence the industrialisation of the North as a means to come to terms with the indigenous religion (Bogoraz-Tan 1932: 144, 148).

The Fight against Shamanism in Khabarovsk Krai

Kosokov's, Suslov's, and Bogoraz-Tan's articles were published in the organs of the most important actors concerning the policy toward shamanism of the time, *Komitet Severa* and the League of the Militant Atheists. Together with a few other similar texts, they constitute the closest we get to an official blueprint for the Soviet struggle against shamanism. In these articles, the analysis was made, the conclusions were drawn, and the guidelines were set (for a further discussion on these articles, see Sundström 2007: 146–164). But how was this plan carried out in practice in the Khabarovsk krai? What happened on the ground in indigenous villages and settlements?

It is not very easy to paint a coherent picture of what happened, but a few general traits can be discerned. T. V. Mel'nikova (2006: 73, 76) has suggested four phases in the repression of shamanism during the Soviet era in what is present-day Khabarovsk krai:

1. In the first phase, from the middle of the 1920s to the beginning of the 1930s, shamans were disfranchised together with, for example, Orthodox priests. This meant that they were not allowed to vote or to be elected to local councils, should not be members of the newly founded kolkhozes, and were sometimes exiled from the region where they lived.

2. During the second phase, taking place in the middle of the 1930s, shamanic equipment and ritual attributes were forcibly confiscated and destroyed, and many members of kolkhozes were expelled after being accused of practicing shamanism.

3. The third phase, at the end of the 1930s, was a time characterised by arrests. However, Mel'nikova notes that, so far, no mass arrests of shamans during this period have been confirmed in research.

4. The last phase stretches from the end of the Second World War until the downfall of the Soviet Union. Mel'nikova argues that, on paper, the ban on shamanic activities remained unchanged between 1945 and the 1980s, but that the observance of the ban gradually decreased. In the 1960s, there were still occasional instances of administrative measures taken against

shamans, but from the 1970s onwards the struggle against shamanism was reduced to mere formal atheist propaganda.

This approximate periodisation can, at least partly, be confirmed by our sources.

Disfranchisement of Shamans

Already in 1926 there is evidence of people being disfranchised on the grounds that they were shamans. But the process of disfranchisement seems to have been conducted at a varying pace in different villages during the following years up until 1934.

Judging from the documents in which shamans are listed with names and ages, the average age of a shaman being denied her or his civic rights in Khabarovsk krai was between 48 and 49 years (the youngest being 32 years old and the oldest 72).[9] In Mel'nikova's (2006: 73) account of disfranchised shamans in the Ulchsky-Negidalsky district in 1932, approximately the same age distribution is shown. One conclusion to be drawn from this information is that disfranchised shamans belonged to the middle aged and fairly old segment of the population, rather than the younger generation born after the turn of the century. It is interesting to note that among the named shamans there are as many women as men. This is not in accordance with previous suggestions in research that it was mainly male shamans that were subjected to repressive measures in the Soviet North (Balzer 1999: 94). For this reason, perhaps there are other explanations to the observed "feminisation" of Siberian shamanism in the twentieth century, as Znamenski (2007: 344) has indicated. Znamenski has identified the same process of feminisation of similar ritual practices in both Japan and Korea in connection with modernisation during the same time period. Moreover, whether male or female shamans among a certain ethnic group were targeted was, most likely, also dependent on whether the high profile ritual functionaries (the "shamans") were male or female among that particular group. Among the Tungus-speaking peoples in Khabarovsk krai, both men and women could be shamans, whereas among, for example, the Samoyedic-speaking peoples on the far northern tundras, so-called shamans were almost exclusively men.

One of the shamans recorded in the archives was the 69-year-old Podi (or Podya) Tumali, who, together with his wife Mariya, was disfranchised in 1926

---

[9] GAKhK, f. 1213, op. 1, d. 106, l. 84; GAKhK, f. 1213, op. 1, d. 106, l. 144; GAKhK, f. 1817, op.1, d. 39, l. 29; GAKhK, f. r3372, op. 1, no. 1, l. 4, 103; MANAR, f. 303, op. 1, d. 53, l. 12.

by the local council in the village of Mongol in the Ulchsky district. Even though the couple were denied their civic rights, they apparently continued to take part in the work at the kolkhoz, and from 1933 there are reports of them both working diligently (fishing) for the kolkhoz and not agitating against or opposing the socialist reconstruction.[10] These reports imply that Podi Tumali had support among at least some members of the kolkhoz. However, it seems that the younger generation among the indigenous peoples sided with the Soviet order and turned against the shamans and the traditionalists. In some cases, children of shamans tried to persuade their parents, verbally or with forcible means, to abandon shamanism because they were ashamed. For example, Podi Tumali's son, Pavel, told Mel'nikova in 1992 how he had taken his father's shamanic belt—a part of an Amur shaman's equipment almost as essential as the drum—and thrown it in the river with the words: "Don't disgrace us!" (Mel'nikova 2006: 74–76).

There are other examples that disfranchised shamans had the support of many of their fellow natives. In documents from the regional committee of the Communist Party in the Lower Amur region, as well as from the executive committee in the Ulschsky district in 1935 and 1936, it is stated that 38 shamans were disfranchised in the entire district. But almost all of these 38 were still members of kolkhozes. In 1934, one village council even petitioned that their shamans should be rehabilitated on the grounds that they were "good people," did not perform any "hostile work" against the kolkhoz, and were *udarniki* ('shockworkers,' i.e. exemplary and unusually productive workers). Without waiting for the decision of the district executive committee, the village council had arbitrarily torn up the list of the disfranchised and rehabilitated them. The regional Party committee was very concerned about this because they found that the shamans and kulaks that were still members of kolkhozes used their influence to sabotage the reconstructtion work. Therefore, they claimed, production quotas of fish and fur (the main products of these kolkhozes) were not fulfilled, and the emancipation of women was impeded. In general though, the committee noted that the average health conditions among the indigenous peoples had improved considerably since 1929, when the first medical centres (Ru. *medpunkty*) were established in the district—the number of healthy Ulchi[11] had, according to their

---

[10] GAKhK, f. r3372, op. 1, no. 1, l. 122, 123, 124, 126.
[11] According to the regional Party committee, there were 1,786 Ulchi living in the Ulchsky district in 1936.

information, risen from 53 per cent in 1932 to 75 per cent in 1935. The conclusion was that this was because the monopoly of shamans and "quacks" on health care had been broken and that the natives now instead mostly turned to medical doctors. But the committee still complained that the active fight against shamans was too weak. The judicial authorities in the district did not fulfil their duties in combatting "vestiges of the past" and the influence of shamans, and no Ulchi shaman had ever been brought to court. One Party delegate contended that the attorney's office did not even know about shamans, and therefore was incapable of bringing them to justice.[12]

The diaries of Aleksandra P. Putintseva give on-the-spot accounts of the struggle against shamanism in the Nanai villages of the Nizhne-Tambovsk district between 1929 and 1932 (see Putintseva 2010; Sundström 2011). Putintseva, a Russian woman in her late twenties, was the head of a Red yurt with the mission to bring healthcare and enlightenment to the indigenous peoples in the area. In concrete terms, the work consisted of carrying out vaccination programs and teaching basic personal hygiene, reading, writing, arithmetic, etc. But it also consisted of teaching the new Soviet ideology, ethics, and law—particularly regarding the rights of women and children in what seems to have been a strongly patriarchal and gerontocratic Nanai society. In Putintseva's lectures, wall magazines, theatre plays, and individual conversations with the villagers, she agitated against what she saw as the patriarchalism and superstitions of the traditional Nanai way of life. The topics of the study groups that she, together with the Red yurt's *politprosvetchik* ['political educator'], conducted are telling examples of the essence of the yurt's work: "On the rearing of children (why one should not give [corporal] punishment to children)," "The rights of women according to Soviet law," "On women's diseases," "First aid to infants," "Tending toddlers," "Masturbation among children and how to come to terms with it," "Eczema," "Medical self-treatment," "On clean air and the role of sunlight," and "Organizing a kolkhoz."

As the chair of the election committee for the elections to one of the village councils, Putintseva sorted out the kulaks and shamans that were to be prohibited from voting and from being elected. For example, out of 15 disfranchised for the elections in the village Kondon, with some 300 inhabitants, 3 were defined as shamans (Putintseva 2010: 109). But still the "clan elite" supported the disfranchised shamans, she reported. During a meeting, one member of the village council, Luka Samar (noted as the "brother of a

---

[12] GAKhK, f. 1213, op. 1, no. 120, l. 76–172.

shaman" by Putintseva), expressed that he did not think that shamans could be blamed for anything. It was the people who sought their help, and if no one would consult them, they would not shamanise at all. In that sense, they were just like the Russian doctors (Putintseva 2010: 49, 268). Others complained about the doctor, or the "Russian Devil" as they called him, saying that he was no better than a shaman—neither of them could help the newborn babies who died (during one winter seven infants died in one of the villages) (Putintseva 2010: 95–96).

Some of the disfranchised shamans petitioned in writing to be given back their civic rights if they gave up shamanism, and they handed over their drums and other shamanic equipment to the village council.[13] If they kept away from shamanism for three years, they would be rehabilitated. This was, for example, the case with the shamans Bali Digor and Bargina Kile. However, another shaman asked Putintseva to tear up his submitted petition because he had been sick ever since he had quit shamanising and therefore needed to pick up his ritual practice again (Putintseva 2010: 101–103, 112, 175, 210). This shaman's request can be explained by the notion among the Nanai that a shaman could not turn away from her or his helping spirits by choice. If not attended to properly by the shaman, the spirits would take revenge, which could lead to sickness and eventually the death of the shaman. According to Bulgakova's informants, this was the fate of several Nanai shamans during the Soviet anti-shamanic campaign (see further Bulgakova 2013: 213).

Makar, yet another Nanai shaman, had stopped shamanising in the village where the Red yurt was present, but he had apparently continued practicing his art in another village. One man confronted Putintseva and asked her why she did not arrest Makar when she knew that he was still an active shaman (Putintseva 2010: 42, 48). This example shows that at least some Nanai expected that Putintseva and the Red yurt could arrest shamans in 1930. But this was obviously not something Putintseva saw as a possibility. In the local law courts that she arranged—mostly for didactic purposes to teach the natives the new judicial system under Soviet rule—no one was prosecuted for shamanic activities. Only one shaman, Aleksandr M. Digor, was put on trial. However, he was not charged for practicing shamanism, but for exchanging his grown up daughters for a second wife. For this offence he was sentenced to 8 months of forced labour (Putintseva 2010: 194).

---

[13] In other instances, the equipment could be handed over to the executive committee of the district, see Mel'nikova 2006: 73.

In one of her final reports on the doings of the Red yurt, Putintseva noted that the shamans and "class enemies" constantly tried to obstruct the yurt's work by "stirring enmity among nationalities," depicting all the Soviet enlightenment measures and reforms as Russification, and continually trying to protect the Nanai traditions. She concluded, however, that if the influence of the shamans among the Nanai was evident when the yurt arrived, the shamans' authority was drastically diminishing. After some successful cures by the medical doctor, the Nanai had started believing in Russian medicine, and the Nanai themselves were beginning to write anti-shamanic slogans on the wall magazines (Putintseva 2010: 269). Soviet ethnographers of the 1930s reported the same decline of the Nanai religion and that the natives were turning away from their shamans. These scholars attributed this decline to Soviet modernisation and the atheist enlightenment (or propaganda, if you will). Thus, one V. Lidin enthusiastically reported that in the home of a Nanai hunter, where he had expected to see the hunter's sevens (three dimensional images of guardian spirits in wood or skin), instead a radio hung. In newspaper style, D. K. Zelenin wrote that "shamans and quacks have forever been banished; their place has been taken by Soviet teachers, doctors and paramedics, who have come from the midst of the indigenous working population" (Zelenin 1938: 38, 46).

Confiscation and Destruction of Shamanic Equipment

Besides notes on disfranchised shamans handing over their drums and other equipment in order to be rehabilitated, there are only occasional reports in the archives on the confiscation and destruction of ritual objects connected to shamanism in the 1930s in Khabarovsk krai, and only a few of these objects ended up in museum collections (cf. Mel'nikova 2006: 74). However, in the oral history of the Nanai and Ulchi, collected from the 1980s and onwards, there are plenty of memories of these events. The campaigns directed towards the material manifestations of shamanism seem to have affected most villages in the area. Bulgakova's informants remember well how the Komsomol organized raids, going from house to house in the villages collecting shamanic equipment—drums, belts (with bells), *seven*s, shamans' robes, *mio*s (a *mio* is a particular kind of cloth with names of deities written on it), etc. According to informant Konstantin M. Bel'dy (b. 1930), the Komsomol gathered once in the Ulchi village of Ukhta on the order of the regional Party committee of the Ulchsky district. The crowd searched through every attic for *seven*s, and they even collected *seven*s from the tombs of deceased shamans. Then they continued to the next villages of Nizhnyy Gavan and

Illustration 15 (this spread): Images of *seven*s, kept at the museum in the village Troytskiy,

Khabarovsk krai. Photos: Tatiana Bulgakova.

Bogorodskoe. Afterwards, the expropriated *seven*s were publicly burned in a large bonfire (much the same way icons had been burned in the campaigns against Christianity). Another informant recalled a similar event taking place in the village of Dzhuen where not only *seven*s, but also shamanic drums and belts, were expropriated, leaving only the small metal images of *seven*s that hung around people's necks. In the Nanai village of Naykhin, *toro*s (wooden poles with carved images of spirits) were set on fire, and in Dokiada a *saola* was destroyed by anti-shamanic zealots. A *saola* is a clay vessel in which the helping spirits of a deceased shaman are believed to be contained. To this particular *saola*, Nanai from all over the region used to come and sacrifice pigs. The informant Aleksandr S. Khodzher (1914–2000) asserted that it was the executive committee of the Nanaysky district that had instigated the eradication of the object (see further Bulgakova 2013: 195–197; cf. Mel'nikova 2006: 76).

Illustration 16: A *saola* of the Zaksor clan, supposed to contain the helping spirits of a female shaman, who died in the 1950s. In front of the *saola* are offerings of vodka and candy. Daerga village, Khabarovsk krai, 1994. Photo: Tatiana Bulgakova.

In Dzhari, another Nanai village, a similar *saola* was destroyed. However, the spirits residing in this *saola* did not go away because of that, according to the village shamans. Therefore a new *saola* was made for the spirits, but was kept secret from the anti-shamanic activists. Judging from the interviews Bulgakova made with Nanai informants—preserving either their own recollections of the 1930s or stories from their parents' generation—it was common practice to secretly restore or exchange expropriated or destroyed religious objects, as well as to hide away the religious items that were left. In that way shamanism continued to be practiced, in private or concealed from those who combatted religion—just as the 12th Party congress in 1923 and Suslov in 1931 had warned. People hid *seven*s, *mio*s, and robes in their homes (sometimes even burying them in the garden), and they exchanged the banned drums for ordinary pot lids (cf. Smoljak [1991] 1998: 227; for similar practices among other Siberian peoples, see Balzer 1995: 26). "If you happened to have a drum," informant Ivan T. Bel'dy (1916–2001) said, "you would be arrested." Therefore, "people practiced shamanism at night, clanging the pot lids" (Bulgakova 2013: 196–197).

Arrests of Shamans

Ivan T. Bel'dy testified that practicing shamanism could result in being arrested. As we have seen above, this was seen as a possibility already during the first half of the 1930s, both among members of indigenous peoples and among Party officials. However, these assertions were made together with complaints that no one was actually arrested or brought to trial.

In December 1936, article 135 on disfranchisement of certain citizens was changed in the new Soviet constitution on the suggestion of Stalin himself. The new article read that every Soviet citizen that had reached the age of 18 had the right to vote and be elected "irrespective of racial or national belonging, sex, creed, social background, economic situation and former activities."[14] The only ones exempt from voting rights were convicted criminals and the mentally ill. This meant that all "servants of religious cults," including shamans, were rehabilitated (see Vasil'eva 2000: 49–50). The change in the constitution seems to have led to growing activity by shamans in some places. From Dadi, in the Nanaysky district, it was, for example, reported in 1937 that two years earlier there was only one active shaman in the village. Since the new constitution, the authorities now counted nine active shamans, and

---

[14] See http://constitution.garant.ru/history/ussr-rsfsr/1936/red_1936/3958676/chapter/11/; access date 9 November 2016.

neither the village council nor the kolkhoz management conducted any anti-shamanic work.[15]

The alleviation of administrative and legal measures against shamans coincided with the beginning of the Great Terror. According to some of Mel'nikova's informants, threats to arrest shamans increased in 1937 and 1938, and shamans' ritual equipment was expropriated not only by Komsomol crowds, but by the police (Mel'nikova 2006: 74). One of Bulgakova's informants, the shaman Lingdze I. Bel'dy (1912–1999), stated that shamans were arrested *en masse* and that many of them disappeared: "Shamans were arrested, taken away, and quite a few of them were reported missing." Ivan T. Bel'dy claimed that there was a decree sent out to local authorities that a certain number of shamans should be arrested: "They assaulted shamans; they used to call it a troika. They purged shamans. Arrested them! Shot them! [---] Many shamans were imprisoned." His own grandfather, a known shaman, was among those taken into custody. However, the grandfather was released almost at once because the prison in Khabarovsk was overcrowded with incarcerated people (being tortured). The grandfather himself had also indicated that personnel from Moscow were present, and if they had not been there he would have been detained (see further Bulgakova 2013: 198–202).

The plan for arresting a certain number of shamans led to arbitrariness, according to Ivan Bel'dy. A troika could note down anyone as a "shaman," and this gave free scope for private vendettas.

> In 1937 there was a troika working in each village. They did whatever they wanted. They could take down that a person was a shaman and a vermin, and that was it. After them came people from the NKVD, took [the accused] away and that was it. Shot them! (Ivan T. Bel'dy)

In fact, Ivan Bel'dy suspected that local authorities hesitated to arrest actual shamans, and instead picked out other persons to fulfil the stipulated quotas. The reason for this hesitance could have been a fear among local officials of some sort of revenge from shamans, their spirits, or their families. Ivan Bel'dy explained the arrest and killing of the only shaman he could name that was caught during these years—the elderly Sangila from the village Dzhari[16]— with the fact that Sangila had no sons and daughters who could avenge him

---

[15] GAKhK, f. R-353, op. 1, d. 386, l. 39, 40.
[16] "They came and took him [Sangila], and they did not even put him in prison. They shot him somewhere" (Ivan T. Bel'dy).

(Bulgakova 2013: 198-202). It should be mentioned that we have not found any evidence in other sources on Sangila's arrest and disappearance.

All in all, Bulgakova received information from her informants about four Nanai shamans being arrested. The only one of these four that there are any details on is Bogdan Londonovich Onenko from the village of Naykhin. At the age of 65, he was arrested on 12 September 1937, sentenced by a decision of a troika of the NKVD to capital punishment, and shot on 22 November the same year. In the published files on his case, it is not mentioned that he was a shaman—his occupation is recorded as "fisherman" (*Khotelos' by vsekh poimenno nazvat'* 2 1999: 176). But he was sentenced in accordance with the paragraph 58-10, which criminalized counter-revolutionary activity and agitation, among other things by "exploiting religious and national prejudices among the masses." From her informants Bulgakova, has been able to obtain details on the events leading to Bogdan Onenko's arrest. What happened was that several of the shaman's patients, who had been cured, had not delivered the sacrificial animals (roosters or pigs) that the *seven*s demanded in return for the cure. The reason why his clients did not live up to their obligations—which was very well known to them—was allegedly that they had been influenced by the new Soviet propaganda that told them that shamanism and sacrifices were all superstition. After this, Onenko fell badly ill, something that he explained as the revenge of the *seven*s who had not received their rightful share. According to the shamanic world-view within which Onenko was acting, he had two choices, either releasing his clients' "souls" (*panian*) from the safe abode where he, as a result of the preceding healing rituals, kept them—and thus jeopardizing their lives—or collecting the sacrificial animals himself. For presumably altruistic reasons he chose the second option and went to his former patients' homes and took their pigs to sacrifice to the *seven*s. For this, he was accused of stealing according to Soviet law (see further, Bulgakova 2013: 183-192). Yet another aspect of Bogdan Onenko's story is that he is supposed to have been arrested by the Nanai policeman Anton P. Bel'dy, who was a member of another, competing, shamanic family (Anton Bel'dy's mother Dekhe Kile was a famous shaman and later his brother Nikolay and his two sisters Maria and Toyo also became shamans).

It is difficult to say for what reason Bogdan Onenko was arrested and shot. Was it because he practiced shamanism, an activity not tolerated by the Soviet authorities? Or was his crime the quite civil offence of stealing from his fellow citizens? Or could it be that he was framed by members of another shamanic family, which saw their chance to eliminate a competitor in the turmoil of the Great Terror? Perhaps it was all these circumstances taken together that led to his death. In any event, Onenko was posthumously rehabilitated by the attorney's office of Khabarovsk krai on 18 July 1989. Thus, eventually, the authorities considered his sentence to be unjust.

Despite the above-mentioned instances of arrested shamans, some of Bulgakova's informants denied altogether that shamans were arrested. Sofia S. Bel'dy from Naykhin—the very same village where Bogdan Onenko lived—did not know of any stories about arrests of shamans: "There were no repressions. Did they imprison anyone? No!" Nikolay Ch. Bel'dy of the village Bolan, admitted that there was a lot of anti-shamanic propaganda and that shamanic objects were expropriated. But shamans were always active, albeit in secret, and "nobody was arrested." The Nanai author Konstantin M. Bel'dy, who recalled well the expropriation campaigns of religious objects, contended that "not too many people suffered during the repression." There are even a couple of examples of Nanai shamans—for instance the above-mentioned Dekhe Kile—who received official permissions on paper to continue practicing shamanism because they had helped cure someone in an authoritative position. Thus, there are very different, and somewhat contradictory, recollections of the events of these days among the Nanai (Bulgakova 2013: 198, 202–203).

Accusations of being a shaman or having shamanic descent also appeared among Nanai in decision-making bodies within the Communist Party. One example of this is the rather complicated struggle between the Party officials Bogdan Khodzher and Pavel Kile in 1935–1937. At the time, Khodzher was the chairman of the executive committee of the Bolshevik Party in the Nanaysky district. Based on the documents from the Communist Party, Mel'nikova (2004) has described how Khodzher and Kile were both charging each other with conducting anti-Soviet work. One important ingredient in these mutual allegations was the opponent's connection with shamanism, something that possibly can be explained by the fact that Khodzher and Kile belonged to two rivalling clans and two rivalling lineages of shamans. The affair ended in the arrest and execution of Khodzher on 26 August 1937. At the same time, he was dismissed as the chairman of the executive committee and excluded from the Party. The accusations towards him were many, but among them he was supposed to have conducted "clan-enmity" between the two clans and intimidated the Nanai population in his capacity as the representative of a prominent shaman lineage—and as chairman of the executive committee nobody dared to criticize him. He was also said to have concealed and protected shamans, stating that there were only 6 active shamans in the district, while others in the committee knew of 130 (or 71 according to another Party member). After Khodzher's arrest, the affair also led to a reckoning within the Bolshevik Party in the Nanaysky district where other Party members' connections with Khodzher and shamanism—or what in the protocols was called the *Khodzhershchina*[17]—were to be exposed.[18]

In July 1938, Pavel Kile was also arrested for counter-revolutionary activities and sentenced to five years in a labour camp (Mel'nikova 2004: 133). Kile had earlier claimed that Khodzher only fought against those shamans who were hostile to him, and at the same time secretly supported other shamans who were loyal to him. In his written defence to that complaint, Khodzher pointed out that since 1932 the Party had started rehabilitating the shamans who had not practiced exploitation in recent years and who diligently worked and did not resist the socialist construction. A lot of the shamans worked for the kolkhozes and were *udarniki*, and there were only a few bad shamans left (Mel'nikova 2004: 111). Some of Bulgakova's informants still remembered Bogdan Khodzher as a "great shaman" and a keeper of the family's *saola*, even though he had to practice shamanism in secret because of his position in the Party's executive committee.

It is worth noting that, from what we know, the struggle against shamanism in Khabarovsk krai was to a large extent carried out on the ground by the indigenous peoples themselves. It was indigenous members of the Komsomol who performed the raids against peoples' homes, took the religious objects, and burned them. Several of Bulgakova's informants testified that it was considered an "expression of patriotism" and heroism at the time to combat their own traditional religious culture. It was the young generation, educated in the Soviet system in which they had received "atheistic tempering" and become animated by the new ideology, that was at the forefront of combatting shamanism. Thus, a divide between the generations erupted. This development was all in accordance with the blueprint for the struggle against shamanism outlined by *Komitet Severa*, The League of the Militant Atheists, and the Bolshevik Party.

---

[17] *Khodzhershchina* can approximately be translated the 'Khodzherist inclination' and can be compared to another concept, the *Yezhovshchina*, which in the 1950s became the popular name of the most intense purges during the Great Terror. This concept was construed after the name of the head of the NKVD between 1936 and 1938, Nikolay P. Yezhov. Eventually Yezhov himself became a victim of the purges and was executed on 4 February 1940.

[18] GAKhK P-399, op. 1, d. 368, l. 202–203; GAKhK P-399, op. 1, d. 369, l. 50–52.

A Lingering Ban on Shamanism

As has been mentioned, people in authoritative positions complained in the beginning of the 1930s that the efforts to liquidate shamanism in Khabarovsk krai were too feeble, or even non-existent, and that shamanism continued to be practiced among the indigenous peoples in the region. At a meeting with the district committee of the Bolshevik Party of the Nanaysky district in June 1937, the same complaints were made. The executive committee reported that no anti-religious work had been carried out during the preceding years. It was claimed that "hostile elements" were increasingly utilizing religion in order to strengthen their influence on the "backward" portion of the population, and because there was no branch of the League of the Militant Atheists in the district there was no actual resistance against "the hostile actions of Baptists, shamans, etc." Therefore the executive committee urged all Party organizations to give priority to anti-religious work, to commission new agitators to conduct conversations and lectures on anti-religious issues, and to reinforce anti-religious propaganda through mass media and atheistic literature. Above all, the "correct interpretation" of paragraph 124 in the Soviet constitution—which guaranteed the citizens' freedom of conscience and "the freedom to exercise religious cults as well as the freedom to [spread] anti-religious propaganda"[19]—should be disseminated because it had been misinterpreted by the masses. No religious gatherings and rituals that contradicted Soviet law were from now on to be allowed. The meeting ended with the decision that the executive committee should consider a plan for anti-religious actions by the Komsomol.[20]

Material on the struggle against shamanism in Khabarovsk krai during the Great Terror and the Second World War is scarce. Therefore, we cannot say anything for certain about what happened to shamans and shamanism during these years. But it is likely that the fight against shamanism was not a prioritized concern either in this region or in other parts of the Soviet North during these chaotic years—despite the above-mentioned ambitions of the Bolsheviks on the eve of the Great Terror. Vasil'eva, who has studied the repression of shamans in the Yakut ASSR, finds the same calls for a strengthening of anti-religious and anti-shamanic work in 1937. But in reality the fight against shamanism in Yakutia slacked off in the last years of the 1930s, according to Vasil'eva, for mainly two reasons. First, shamanism had

---

[19] See http://constitution.garant.ru/history/ussr-rsfsr/1936/red_1936/3958676/chapter/10/#block_1010; access date 14 November 2016.
[20] GAKhK op. 1, d. 368, l. 150.

in fact diminished and was at the time practiced mostly by the elderly and in hiding. Second, during the Great Terror the "enemy of the people" was not first and foremost identified as an "exploiter" but rather as a "spy," a category in which "shamans with their 'otherworldly relations' could not fit in" (Vasil'eva 2000: 50–51).

It is also well known that the harsh attitude of the Stalin regime towards religion and religiosity in general was mitigated during the war. The government sought the support of first and foremost the Orthodox Church in creating national unity in the defence of the country. In 1941, the League of the Militant Atheists was dissolved and Stalin ordered a halt to the anti-religious campaigns. This led to a certain religious revival in the country; churches were reopened and religion was increasingly manifested in public. To some extent, this also seems to have been the case with the indigenous religions of the peoples in some parts of the North (Corley [ed.] 1996: 130–131; cf. Balzer 1993: 236).

One thing the regime did during the war was to found two new councils to handle the affairs of religious associations, one for the affairs of the Russian Orthodox Church (in 1943) and one for the affairs of other "religious cults" (in 1944). The basic duties of these councils were to register religious associations and buildings for worship, collect information on the organizations, and surveil and control their doings, as well as to see to it that the relations between the religious associations and Soviet authorities were correct. The constitution guaranteed freedom of conscience and religious worship, while the ruling Communist Party had on its (by then long-term) agenda to liquidate religion. As M. B. Serdyuk (2011: 100) points out, this made the work of the councils rather ambiguous. On the one hand they should protect the religious associations' constitutional rights; on the other they should take measures to prevent the growth of the same associations.

Among the assignments of the Council for the Affairs of Religious Cults in Khabarovsk krai was to gather information on and control shamanism. Judging from the reports and letters of the head of the council (between 1948 and 1952), B. M. Grebennikov, this was not an easy task because the area of inspection was so vast and shamanism existed only in the countryside. What is more, shamanism seemed so disorganized and incomprehensible to the administrators in Khabarovsk—it was not even possible to predict when and where shamanic rituals would be performed.[21]

---

[21] The following account is based on the documents from the Council of the Affairs of Religious Cults in Khabarovsk krai found in GAKhK, f. 1359, op. 3, no. 3–6.

In his reports, already from the beginning of his term of office in 1948, Grebennikov voiced the same complaints that were common among Soviet administrators in the 1930s—that nothing, or at least too little, was done to combat shamanism, and shamans were acting quite openly. He even claimed that shamans had become more active, both in the Amur area and in Kamchatka and Chukotka, which were also part of Grebennikov's jurisdiction. Local authorities obviously knew about all of these shamans, but still allowed them to perform their rituals.

In order to get a full picture of the situation in the region, Grebennikov had consulted a certain comrade Khodzher,[22] himself a Nanai and instructor of the organizing department of the executive committee in Khabarovsk krai. Khodzher, who knew the people and the language, was sent out to the villages in the Nanaysky and Komsomolsky districts in 1948 to survey the activities of shamans. Later he would report that there were shamans in several of the villages and because no one prohibited shamanism the population remained tolerant of them. He reported that most of the time the Nanai laughed at the shamans and did not believe in their "sorcery" (Ru. *koldovstvo*), but the elderly continued to consult them when they needed a cure for some illness. During his round trip, Khodzher talked to the shamans and tried to convince them to cease their trade by informing them that shamanism was now prohibited. Many of them agreed to this and promised to destroy their drums, belts, costumes, and masks. All of the local authorities had also been instructed to prohibit shamanism and to take legal proceedings against those shamans who continued their practice. There were, of course, cases when shamans declined to give up their craft. Grebennikov reported that when the administrators of the Komsomolsky district had requested seven shamans to quit, threatening them with a special fine, four of them had willingly paid the imposed 500 roubles.[23]

A year later Grebennikov himself visited the Nanai settlement Gvasyugi, where there was a shaman by the name of Kimonno. The chairman of the village council had declared that Kimonno was a capable hunter and fisherman who worked well for the kolkhoz. But the shaman now and again performed rituals if someone asked him to. Grebennikov and the chairman sent for Kimonno and persuaded him to give up shamanism. The latter promised

---

[22] Not to be confused with the above mentioned Bogdan L. Khodzher.
[23] The law that was used in this case was probably paragraph 123 in the penal code, which prohibited "deceitful acts with the purpose of rousing superstition among the masses for one's own benefit." The penalty for breaking this law was one year in labour camp or a fine of 500 roubles.

to do that, saying that it was better to go to the medical doctor if one was ill. Then he fetched his drum, drumstick, bells, costume, and different fineries, and "ceremonially destroyed everything" in front of Grebennikov's and the chairman's eyes. However, this was only one shaman out of many, and Grebennikov suspected that the chairman of the village council protected and concealed several other shamans in the area.

In a letter to the secretary of the regional committee of the Bolshevik Party in Khabarovsk krai in May 1949, Grebennikov complained about the lack of measures taken against shamans (as well as Baptists and members of other sects), and he noted that because "shamanism is not recognized as a religion at all, at present no one struggles against this evil, nor takes any steps to stop [the shamans'] activities." But paradoxically, in some places indulgence was shown towards shamans with reference to paragraph 124 in the constitution and the "freedom to practice religious cults." What people did not understand, according to Grebennikov, was that the constitutional freedom of religion only pertained to registered religious associations, and not to shamanism, because shamanism could not be registered. In another letter he gave a vivid example of this indulgence with the story of Pavel Gekker, a Nanai hunter who had visited Grebennikov a few weeks earlier. In April 1949 a shaman (by the name of Onenko), dressed up in full regalia, had come to Gekker's village Koyminskiy, in the Ulchsky district, to conduct a ritual in broad daylight. After the ritual, which had attracted a large crowd of both old and young, the shaman demanded that the people sacrifice meat, fish, vodka, clothes, and money to the "spirit of fishing and hunting." A police officer who was present had arrested Onenko and brought him to the main police station in the district centre Bogorodskoe. But the chief of police had scolded the police officer and immediately released the shaman claiming that "religion is allowed according to the constitution."

Grebennikov gave further examples of what he regarded as the overindulgent attitude among officials towards shamans. In one village in the Ulchsky district, the shaman Angina Enako was openly shamanising. But instead of arresting and prosecuting her for deceiving the people and spreading superstition, the local officers of the secret service (MGB at the time) had merely confiscated her drum. Then they had suggested to the chairmen of the village council and the local kolkhoz that they should see to it that she was given medical and material aid. Thus, Grebennikov concluded that, in effect, they suggested that a shaman was to be given maintenance by the kolkhoz.

There were other instances when members of the Party and the Komsomol took active part in shamanic rituals and sacrificial ceremonies.

Grebennikov related a ritual performed in Dzhari that gathered around 30 participants, among them several Party members, including the head of the kolkhoz. During the ritual a pig and 18 chickens were slaughtered, all at the expense of the kolkhoz, and because of the heavy drinking many workers could not attend work for several days afterwards.

To come to terms with shamanism, Grebennikov suggested to his superior in Moscow, the head of the central Council for the Affairs of Religious Cults Ivan V. Polyanskiy, that a letter be sent out to all executive committees of the region in districts where shamans were to be found. In this letter, the executive committees were recommended to disrupt the activities of shamans and to commission the police and the village councils to take the "most severe measures" (Ru. *samye zhestokie mery*) against shamans, for example expropriating and destroying shamanic objects and prosecuting particularly hostile shamans for deceiving the people and for fooling superstitious individuals.

Even though Polyanskiy agreed that the practicing of shamanism was illegal *per se* (because shamanism could not be registered as a religious association), he recommended that Grebennikov not send out the letter to local authorities. Instead, he suggested that administrative and legal measures should be taken against shamans only when they were caught in the very act of violating Soviet law. Polyanskiy did not give any explicit explanation as to why he considered the letter to be inappropriate, so we can only speculate. But perhaps he did not want to instigate a "witch hunt" or the kind of "terror" that had characterised the end of the 1930s. Since Polyanskiy himself had been an official of the secret service from 1921 until he took office in the Council for the Affairs of Religious Cults in 1947, he was likely to have known all too well the possible consequences of such campaigns.

Conclusion

That shamanism was repressed by the Communist Party and the authorities in Khabarovsk krai is quite obvious. It was the official policy of the Party and the state that shamanism should be liquidated by means of anti-shamanic propaganda (slandering what the authorities saw as the superstition that was the foundation of shamanism), education (instilling a materialist, scientific, and Marxist world-outlook among the indigenous peoples), modern medicine (making ineffective shamanic healing practices obsolete), and legislation (disfranchising and thus marginalising shamans, as well as prohibiting certain ritual practices deemed as quackery and fraud). Local authorities and local communist activists—often of indigenous descent—at times also carried through campaigns in which they confiscated shamanic ritual objects by force. Even if this last method was not officially sanctioned by the legislation or the leading ideologues behind the Soviet struggle against shamanism, there is nothing to suggest that the authorities took action against or punished such measures, although they were sometimes condemned as "exaggerations." Rather, the instances of outright mocking and more or less violent outbursts against shamans appear to be logical consequences of the stigmatisation of shamans that the official anti-shamanic propaganda and legislation brought about.

In the beginning of the Great Terror, the legislation aimed at marginalising shamans was somewhat eased, and together with other categories of disfranchised citizens shamans were given back their civic rights in 1936. There are also some reports that anti-shamanic (and generally anti-religious) work was slackening by the end of the 1930s. But the information on the fate of shamans during the Great Terror is somewhat contradictory. On the one hand, authorities complained—as they indeed had done already in the beginning of the decade, and would be doing a decade later—that nothing or too little was done to fight shamanism and that shamans escaped punishment. On the other, there are testimonies in the oral history of the indigenous peoples that shamans were arrested *en masse* and summarily killed. All testimonies from informants do not agree, however. Some claim that several shamans were arrested, but immediately released. Others contend that non-shamans were pointed out as shamans and then arrested, or that the communists often threatened to arrest shamans and participants of shamanic rituals, but that they did not fulfil their threats. There are even those who deny altogether that shamans were arrested, let alone shot.

It has not been possible, as of yet, to find support in the archival records for the claim that shamans in general were arrested (or executed), and there is no evidence of any special operation against shamans nor of any general plan to fill arrest quotas with shamans. This may, of course, be due to a lack of sources. We have not been able to obtain permission to look into this matter in the archives of the NKVD (FSB). Upon Sundström's request, the answer has been that no such information or documents are available in the archive of the security service. Nor has it been possible to find such information in the state archives of the area.[24] From what we have seen of the documentation of indigenous persons arrested or executed during the years of the

---

[24] This according to letters sent to Sundström from the archive of the Federal Security

Great Terror, "shaman" is not among the accusation points. The confirmed shaman Bogdan L. Onenko, shot in 1937, was not listed as a "shaman" in the records; he was recorded as a "fisherman." That Ivan T. Bel'dy (and perhaps others) interpreted the many arrests, combined with accusations of the practice of shamanism, as an official plan might be due to the fact that "shaman" was one of the main stigmas of the time. Thus it could have functioned, on the local level, in the same way as the accusation "enemy of the people." As such, the accusation "shaman" could have been used to discredit and betray competitors and personal enemies—and perhaps to help fulfil the lethal quotas of the terror (cf. Leete 2015: 101–102). This seems to have been the case even among Nanai representatives in the highest ranks of the Communist Party, as evidenced by the purges of Bogdan Khodzher and Pavel Kile. There are even some indications that superiors from Moscow released shamans when locals had arrested them, just as the head of the Council for the Affairs of Religious Cults in Moscow in 1950 did not recommend a campaign to take general legal actions towards shamans as was suggested by his local subordinate in Khabarovsk krai.

Balzer concludes, regarding the Soviet repression of shamans in the entire Soviet North, that:

> The full scope of this repression is unlikely to be known, even with open archives, for some shamans were charged with other offences when their true "crime" was the practice of shamanism. (Balzer 2011: 44)

If it is the case that many shamans were arrested and executed without inquiry or trial, state archives would, for obvious reasons, not get us far. The somewhat contradictory versions of the arrests of shamans, in the oral history of the local population, should also make us wary of drawing too far-reaching conclusions. A lack of substantial historical evidence could lead to myth-making that fits the circumstances of the present rather than reflecting actual past events. It is far from certain that shamans were particularly targeted or represented among the victims of the terror in Khabarovsk krai, even if there are some examples of arrests. From the available evidence, the execution of shamans does not seem to have been a conspicuous method in the struggle against shamanism in this region. It is clear that shamanism was practiced through the entire period studied in this chapter, and indeed it continued to

---

Service of the Russian Federation (FSB) and the State Archive of the Amur Oblast of 14 May 2010 and 8 June 2010, respectively, as well as Sundström's searches in archives (GAKhK and MANAR).

be practiced by some individuals in Khabarovsk krai through the whole Soviet period, even if the number of both shamans and their clients gradually diminished. The same ambivalence regarding how to combat shamans with legal and administrative means was voiced by officials in both the beginning and the end of the 1930s, as well as around 1950.

References

Archives

GAKhK. Государственный Архив Хабаровская Края ['State archive of Khabarovsk krai], Khabarovsk, Russia.

MANAR. Муниципальный Архив Николаевского-на-Амуре Района ['Municipal archive of the Nikolayevsk-on-Amur district'], Nikolayevsk-on-Amur, Russia.

Literature

Argutsyaeva, Yu. V. (2009). Аргуцяева Ю.В. "Миссионерская деятельность Русской Православной Церкви среди коренных народов Дальнего Востока" ['Missionary work of the Russian Orthodox Church among the indigenous peoples of the Far East'], *Религиоведение*, 4, pp. 32–41.

Balzer, M. M. (1993). "Dilemmas of the spirit. Religion and atheism in the Yakut-Sakha Republic," in *Religious Policy in the Soviet Union*, ed. S. P. Ramet, Cambridge: Cambridge University Press, pp. 231–251.

Balzer, M. M. (1995). Балзер, М. М. "От бубнов к сковородам. Парадоксальным изменениям шаманизма в истории саха (якутов)" ['From drums to frying pans. Paradoxical changes of shamanism in the history of the Sakha (Yakut)'], in *Шаманизм и ранные религиозные представления. К 90-летию доктора исторический наук, профессора Л. П. Потапова. Этнологические исследования по шаманству и иным ранным верованиям и практикам 1*, ред. Д. А. Функ, Moscow: Institute of Anthropology and Ethnography, pp. 25–35.

Balzer, M. M. (1999). "Shamans as healers, rebels and philosophers. Exploring cultural repression and resilience in Siberia," in *Материалы международного конгресса Шаманизм и иные традиционные верования и практики*, ред. В. И. Харитонова и Д. А. Функ, Moscow: Institute of Anthropology and Ethnography, pp. 59–69.

Balzer, M. M. (2011). *Shamans, Spirituality, and Cultural Revitalization. Explorations in Siberia and Beyond*, New York: Palgrave Macmillan.

Bereznitskiy, S. V. (2003). Березницкий, С. В. "Современная обрядовая практика" ['Modern-day ritual practice'], in *История и культура нанайцев. Историко-этнографические очерки*, ред. В. А. Тураев, St. Petersburg: Nauka, pp. 212–218.

Bogoraz-Tan, Vladimir G. (1932). Богораз-Тан, В. Г. "Религия как тормоз соцстроительство среди малых народностей Севера" ['Religion as an obstacle in the socialist construction among the small peoples of the North'] *Советский Север*, 1–2, pp. 142–157.

Bravina, R. I. & Illarionov, V. V. (2008). Бравина, Р. И. и Илларионов, В. В. "О шаманских текстах А. А. Попова" ['On the shamanic texts by A. A. Popov'], in Попов, А. А., *Камлания шаманов бывшего Вилюйского округа. Тексты*, 2-е издание, отв. ред. Ч. М. Таксами, Novosibirsk: Nauka, pp. 13–24.

Bulgakova, T. D. (2013). *Nanai Shamanic Culture in Indigenous Discourse*, Fürstenberg: Kulturstiftung Sibirien.

Corley, F. (ed.) (1996). *Religion in the Soviet Union. An Archival Reader*, London: Macmillan Press LTD.

Eidlitz Kuoljok, K. (1985). *The Revolution in the North. Soviet Ethnography and Nationality Policy*, Uppsala: Almqvist & Wiksell International.

Humphrey, C. (1983). *Karl Marx Collective. Economy, Society and Religion in a Siberian Collective Farm*, Cambridge: Cambridge University Press.

Il'yakhov-Khamsa, P. N. (1995). Ильяхов-Хамса, П. Н. *Борьба с шаманизмом в Якутии (1920–1930 гг.)* ['The struggle against shamanism in Yakutia (1920–1930)'], Yakutsk: Respublikanskiy Dom Narodnogo Tvorchestvo.

Khotelos' by vsekh poimenno nazvat' 2 (1999). *Хотелось бы всех поименно назвать. Книга мартиролог* 2 ['One would have wanted to name them all. A martyrolog 2'], Khabarovsk.

Kosokov, I. (1930). Косоков, И. *К вопросу о шаманстве в северном Азии* ['On the question of shamanism in northern Asia'], Moscow: Izd. "Bezbozhnik."

Koz'minskiy, I. (1927). Козьминский, И. "Возникновение нового культа у гольдов" ['The origin of a new cult among the Golds'], in *Сборник этнографических материалов* 2, ред. В. Г. Богораз-Тан, Leningrad: Leningrad State University, pp. 43–52.

Leete, A. (2015). "Reconsidering the role of shamans in Siberia during the early Soviet era," *Shaman*, 23:1–2, pp. 89–108.

Mel'nikova, T. V. (2004). Мельникова, Т. В. "Проявление родовой вражды у нанайцев в условиях социалистических преобразований в 1930-е годы" ['Manifestation of clan-enmity among the Nanai under the conditions of socialist reformation in the 1930s'], *Записки Гродековского музея*, 9, Khabarovsk: Khabarovsk kraevedcheskiy muzey, pp. 89–133.

Mel'nikova, T. V. (2006). Мельникова, Т. В. "Шаманы под запретом власти" ['Shamans banned by the power'], *Словесница искусств*, 17, pp. 73–76.

Mikhaylov, T. M. (1979). "Влияние ламаизма и христианство на шаманизм бурят" ['The influence of Lamaism and Christianity on Buryat shamanism'], in *Христианство н ламаизм у коренного населения Сибири (вторая половина XIX начало XX в.)*, ред. И. С. Вдовин, Leningrad: Nauka, pp. 127–149.

Patkanov, S. (1906). Патканов, С. *Опыт географии и статистики тунгусских племен Сибири* 1 ['Geographical and statistical data on the Tungus tribes of Siberia 2'], St. Petersburg.
Peris, D. (1998). *Storming the Heavens. The Soviet League of the Militant Godless*, Ithaca & London: Cornell University Press.
Pospielovsky, D. V. (1987). *A History of Marxist-Leninist Atheism and Soviet Antireligious Policies. Volume 1 of A History of Soviet Atheism in Theory and Practice, and the Believer*, New York: St. Martin's Press.
Pospielovsky, D. V. (1988). *A History of Marxist-Leninist Atheism and Soviet Antireligious Policies. Volume 2 of A History of Soviet Atheism in Theory and Practice, and the Believer*, New York: St. Martin's Press.
Potapov, L. P. (1991). Потапов, Л. П. *Алтайский шаманизм* ['Altay shamanism'], Leningrad: Nauka.
Putintseva, A. P. (2010). Путинцева, А. П. *Дневники красной юрты* ['Diaries of a red yurt'], Khabarovsk: Khabarovsk kraevedcheskiy muzey.
Serdyuk, M. V. (2011). Сердюк, М. Б. "Институт уполномоченных Совета по делам Русской православной церкви и Совета по делам религиозных культов на Дальнем Востоке, 1944–1954 гг." ['The heads of the Council for the Affairs of the Orthodox Church and the Council for the Affairs of Religious Cults in the Far East, 1944–1954'], *Азиатско-Тихоокеанский Регион. Научный и общественно-политический журнал*, 24:2, pp. 94–101.
Slezkine, Y. (1994). *Arctic Mirrors. Russia and the Small Peoples of the North*, Ithaca: Cornell University Press.
Smoljak, A. [1991] (1998). *Der Schamane. Persönlichkeit, Funktionen, Weltanschauung*, Berlin: Reinhold Schletzer Verlag.
Stebnitskiy, S. N. (2000). Стебницкий, С. Н. *Очерки этнографии коряков* ['Studies in the ethnography of the Koryaks'], St. Petersburg: Nauka.
Sud'by narodov Ob'-Irtyshskogo Severa (1994). *Судьбы народов Обь-Иртышского Севера. Из истории национально-государственного строительство 1822–1941 гг. Сборник документов* ['The fate of the peoples of the Ob-Irtysh North. From the history of state-national construction 1822–1941. A collection of documents'], ред. Д. И. Копылов, Tyumen: Gosudarstvennyy Archiv Tyumenskoy Oblasti.
Sundström, O. (2007). *Kampen mot "schamanismen." Sovjetisk religionspolitik gentemot inhemska religioner i Sibirien och norra Ryssland* ['The struggle against "shamanism." Soviet religious policy towards the indigenous religions of Siberia and Northern Russia'] (Studies on Inter-Religious Relations 40), Uppsala: Swedish Science Press.
Sundström, O. (2011). "Struggling for a new way of life. A. P. Putintseva, the Red Yurt, and the Nanai (Review of Aleksandra Petrovna Putintseva, *Dnevniki Krasnoi Yurty*, Khabarovsk 2010)," *Sibirica. Interdisciplinary Journal of Siberian Studies*, 10:1, Spring 2011, pp. 78–93.
Sundström, O. (2012). "Is the shaman indeed risen in post-Soviet Siberia?" in *Post-Secular Religious Practices. Based on Papers Read at the Symposium on Post-*

Secular Practices Held at Åbo/Turku on 15-17 June, Finland, 2011, ed. T. Ahlbäck, Turku: The Donner Institute for Research in Religious and Cultural History, pp. 350–387.

Suslov, I. M. (1931). Суслов, И. М. *Шаманство и борьба с ним* ['Shamanism and the struggle against it'], Moscow: Izd. Komiteta Severa.

Vasil'eva, N. D. (2000). Васильева, Н. Д. *Якутское шаманство 1920-1930-е гг.* ['Yakut shamanism in the 1920s and 1930s'], Yakutsk: Akademiya nauk Respubliki Sacha (Yakutia).

Vitebsky, P. (1995). *Shamanism*, Norman: University of Oklahoma Press.

Vitebsky, P. (2005). *Reindeer People. Living with Animals and Spirits in Siberia*, London: HarperCollins.

Zelenin, D. K. (1938). Зеленин, Д. К. "Народы крайнего Севера после Великой Октябрьской социалистической революции" ['The peoples of the far North after the Great October socialist revolution'], *Советская этнография*, 6, pp. 15–52.

Znamenski, A. (2003). *Shamanism in Siberia. Russian Records of Indigenous Spirituality*, Dordrecht: Kluwer Academic Publishers.

Znamenski, A. (2007). *The Beauty of the Primitive. Shamanism and the Western Imagination*, New York: Oxford University Press.

CHAPTER 10

Where Have the Amur Region's Shamans Gone?

Yana Ivashchenko

Nothing that brings about unexpected change in our lives is ever truly accidental: it is rather what hides inside us and is only waiting for an external cause or pretext to spring into action.

Alexander S. Grin

"Paganism," "superstition," "savage habits," "primitive religion," "opium for the people," "traditional beliefs," "ethnic symbolism," "culture memory"—this is by no means a complete list of designations used by researchers and journalists in the nineteenth and early twenty-first centuries in descriptions of Far Eastern shamanism, being the manifestation of an external view of this aboriginal tradition. First, this string of denominations naturally falls into two large categories: one contains definitions assuming a negative and the other a positive evaluation of the phenomenon. A seeming prevalence of negative connotations cannot be viewed simply as the result of random sampling. This negative attitude was the way shamanism had been viewed and evaluated by the so-called "civilized" nations until the end of the twentieth century. Second, the above-listed words, in their succession, reflect the historiography of the study of shamanism over the last three centuries: they were first inspired by imperialistic and evolutionist characterizations of shamanism common during the eighteenth and nineteenth centuries, then by the ideological enthusiasm of the twentieth century and, finally, by the elements of the thesaurus of ethnology and ethnic studies of the late twentieth and early twenty-first century when local tradition and ethnic culture were proclaimed to be one of the key values in need of protection from modern civilization. All these scientific paradigms and attitudes have largely influenced the destiny of shamanism in the Amur River basin—a destiny about which we know much less than enough today.

Goals of the Study

However, I will not delve in the discussion into issues such as scientific ethics and the history of the study of shamanism and its early development. Instead,

I am going to draw extensively upon field study materials collected in the lower reaches of the Amur River in 2000–2012 and concentrate on the Soviet times—the period when shamanism in the Amur River regions practically came to naught—and the post-Soviet era when the traditions formerly practised by the indigenous peoples of Russia, including primeval rituals, have become re-actualized. My goal in this paper is to find out what happened to the shamans of the Amur region in the twentieth century and why these things happened to them. I will do so by trying to answer a range of questions, which, in my view, still remain matters of argument:

- Were shamans really purged and punished by ostracization, deportation, arrests, etc., which other scholars of ethnography and ethnology have claimed on more than one occasion?
- When and why did such a persistent phenomenon as shamanism cease to be practised in the region of the lower reaches of the Amur River?
- Why and in what form was shamanism revived in this region in the late twentieth century?
- Can we be justified in calling the modern, purportedly ancient ceremonies, "true shamanism"?

We should not delude ourselves by the seeming simplicity of answers such as: shamanism became extinct due to the fact that it was strictly prohibited by the Soviet government (this is the version given by most indigenous informants, when asked specifically about this). Revival of the tradition may be accounted for by the context of the so-called cultural-national renaissance, when it became a socially important thing again (or, as the bearers of the tradition put it, "these have been and are *our* traditions, and we *must* support them").

Source Data

During my primary processing of field materials, as is often the case, I had the intention both to draw a historical picture of shamanism in the region by providing definitive answers to the above questions, and to describe the very mechanism of social cultural processes that led to the extinction and later revival of this social group, the shamans, which had been and is again so significant for the indigenous peoples of Russia's North. This is the reason why data offered by the bearers of the tradition, including the children, grandchildren and townsmen of a famous Nanai shaman, Semen P. Saigor (1890–1975), are compared with other known facts and materials from earlier expeditions.

The Vanishing of the Shamans

Talking to informants/residents of the villages of Nizhnye Khalby, Belgo and Verkhnyy Ekon of the Komsomolsk district, in the villages of Malyshevo, Naykhin and Dzhari of the Nanaysky district of the Khabarovsk region,[1] and using the resulting data for a study of the life of the legendary shaman from the Verkhnaya Ekon village to whom many a resident of other locations in the Lower Amur region would come for healing and ritual help, have demonstrated that shamanic medical practices were still alive in this region in post-Second World War times and up to the 1970s. These practices, which could not ensure a better living for its practitioners and only brought them extra troubles with the authorities, which, on the other hand, neither Christianization of the nineteenth century nor Sovietization of later times could exterminate, faded away quite unexpectedly in the 1970s (I suggest that this was exactly the point at which the thread of this tradition was cut, since neither ethnographic sources nor our informants can name any "true" shamans of the 1980s). There are also grounds to believe that the perishing of shamanist traditions in the lower reaches of the Amur River was not the result of the implementation of harsh anti-shamanic approaches: our informants from the above-mentioned villages could not recall any cases of arrest, exile, deportation or any other type or form of persecution directed against shamans and other participants in rituals. Nevertheless, the majority of the informants

---

[1] Ms Lidiya N. Adzhar, born 1938, resident of the village of Nizhnye Khalby of the Komsomolsk district (July 2010); Mr Aleksandr V. Popov, born 1944, resident of the village of Belgo of the Komsomolsk district (September 2009); Ms Aleksandra D. Digor, born 1927, resident of the village of Verkhnaya Ekon of the Komsomolsk district (March 2000); Ms Zinaida S. Digor, born 1953, resident of the village of Verkhnaya Ekon of the Komsomolsk district (July 2012); Ms Valentina S. Olchka, born 1940, resident of the village of Malyshevo of the Nanaysky district of the Khabarovsk region (July 2012); Mr Mikhail Z. Bel'dy born 1930, resident of the village of Naykhin of the Nanaysky district (April 2004); Mr Maksim P. Bel'dy, born 1962, resident of the village of Naykhin of the Nanaysky district (April 2004); Ms Sofia S. Bel'dy, born 1934, resident of the village of Naykhin of the Nanaysky district (April 2004); Ms Tatyana F. Bel'dy, born 1938, resident of the village of Dzhari of the Nanaysky district (April 2004); Ms Svetlana A. Onenko, born 1961, resident of the village of Dzhari of the Nanaysky district (April 2004).

pointed out that while a ban on indigenous religious practices did exist, people successfully circumvented it by hiding ritual paraphernalia in cold cellars and placing them under heaps of stored potatoes,[2] or by relocating the shamanic ritual site to a forest or a river's shore.[3]

According to other sources, in both pre- and post-Second World War times in the lower reaches of the Amur River, shamans would conduct their rituals at people's homes in the evening or at night;[4] which is when the sound of their drums could be easily discerned by local authorities in the calm and quietness of the countryside. Children would have a chance to observe these rites. Later, as adult informants, they have been able to tell me about what they were witnessing and how they hid under their beds, trembling with fear. The above facts also seem to demonstrate that indigenous populations were not in awe of, or enthusiastic about, the "new Soviet order," which could have been the key reason for abandoning their centuries-old tradition. So, I have convincing enough grounds to reject the widespread version of the decline of shamanism in the Amur region being the result of purges of shamans, and I shall therefore try to find more plausible explanations.

Interview with Valentina S. Olchka, Daughter of the Prominent Amur River Region Shaman Semen P. Saigor

Ms Valentina S. Olchka, the younger daughter of the shaman Semen P. Saigor, told us about her childhood. Among other things, I learned a number of small details allowing us to form a different view of the problem. Valentina told our interviewer that once during a ritual performed by her father, a female schoolteacher entered the house. She hesitated at the door and then left the room without attracting attention. Judging by the date of birth of the informant (1940) and the time of the beginning of her father's shamanic practices (according to her, he started offering ritual services to people in the 1940s and 1950s), this story took place after the Second World War, i.e. at a time when all cultural differences and "superstitions" were considered to be "by and large subdued" (Tugolukov 1971: 205). In reply to my question concerning how Valentina's "non-proletarian" descent bore upon her relations

---
[2] Information on this method of storing a shaman's ritual paraphernalia was kindly provided by Valentina S. Olchka (July 2012).
[3] This information was kindly provided by Zinaida A. Digor.
[4] This information was kindly provided by Mr Mikhail S. Bel'dy born 1930, resident of the village of Dzhari of the Nanaysky district (April 2004), Aleksandra D. Digor and Zinaida S. Digor.

with her schoolmates and the school administration, she could recall only a few cases of being teased and nicknamed as a "shaman's daughter." On the whole, according to the informant, there was no victimization or persecution. Back then, being a child, she was not able to realize certain educational subtleties of the historical context, for instance, that the policy of latent, although still obviously existing, isolationism directed against her—and others like her—as a "shaman's daughter" could have been inspired and initiated not by her classmates but by an authoritative adult, their teacher.

It seems possible that it was due to this sort of invectives and insults that Valentina decided to reject her father's intention to hand down his "gift" to her, as the tradition required (Semen Saigor's father and grandfather were also shamans). She also told me that till this day she cannot forgive one of her sisters-in-law for making condescending remarks about her being a "shaman's daughter." Valentina, who confessed to me that she had an inner feeling of possessing the necessary shamanistic "talents," explained her rejection of the "gift" as follows: "I simply do not need this yoke upon my neck!" What did the laconic Nanai woman mean by the word "yoke"? Despite the well-known fact that in many history as well as fiction books from Soviet times, including Nanai folk texts of this period, shamans are described as "relentless blood-suckers and exploiters of the people." Ethnographic data collected at the turn of the twentieth century give evidence that many such shamans had a rather unenviable lot. Shamans, unlike other types of religious specialists in traditional societies, had not formed themselves as a distinct social group or as bearers of a "profession." In short, shamans did not make a living out of their practices as shamans. Instead, they represented the poorest section of the society they served with their rituals. Along with that, they had to do ordinary work to earn their living and provide themselves with everything they needed (Shirokogorov 2001: 177–178). In addition to the above, all future "ministers" of the shamanic religion who had been "called" to their service by "spirits," suffered for long years from various mental disorders and occasionally demonstrated coma-like states. Children, grandchildren and fellow villagers of Semen P. Saigor have more than once highlighted that before he started his shamanic practices he had for nearly 10 years had some form of mental illness.[5]

---

[5] Ms Yevgeniya V. Samar, born 1984, resident of the village of Verkhnaya Ekon (May 2012), Ms Yelena A. Kapustina, born 1976, resident of the village of Verkhnaya Ekon of the Komsomolsk district (May 2012) (granddaughters of the shaman Semen P. Saigor), and Valentina S. Olchka.

In my view, however, it was not simply the burden of a shaman's work and life difficulties that demotivated Valentina from becoming a shaman herself, but rather her unwillingness to be looked upon as an outsider, the "white raven"[6] among "red eaglets,"[7] an attitude nurtured by her school teacher—diplomatic, patient but pertinacious in her striving to educate children in the spirit of the "new" Soviet times. Although being fundamentally atheists, the bearers of the "new life, light and culture" who were bringing this into the life of indigenous peoples of the Amur River region still tried to be cautious in tackling religious issues, including traditional rituals during which the participants made wild screams in order to repel evil spirits. The above-mentioned schoolteacher was hesitant about engaging in open combat against the established shaman and the followers who respected and admired his "powers" and supported the tradition that was still alive at that time. Instead she set her feet on a 25-year long bypass route, which proved the right one in the end. It may be no accident that the 1970s—the period of a "decline" in shamanic practices in the Amur River region—was the time when some fundamental reforms were introduced into the education system, including the total abandonment of the use of indigenous languages in education and practically expelling these languages from the communicative context of native communities (Bobyshev & Akhmetova 2008: 90). This was possible due to the fact that in native villages the majority of active adults were already people who had received secular education in boarding schools established by the new Soviet government.

One of the female informants (Valentina S. Olchka), nevertheless maintained that participants in shamanic rituals would be threatened with arrest, but she could not recall any particular case of such threats having been carried out. It seems to be the case that while banning shamanic rituals and warning the local population from participating in them, authorities did not actually intend to follow up on such threats.

---

[6] A "white raven" is metaphorically an outsider, *rara avis*.
[7] "Red eaglets"—a Soviet ideologeme of the early twentieth century which meant the younger generation raised and educated in the spirit and letter of the new socialist ideology; it was also extensively used in fiction symbolizing the revolutionary heroism, brave youthfulness and the Bolshevik pioneer youth movement.

Illustration 17: 'Attack shamans—a band of charlatans!' Page from *Antireligioznaya azbuka* ['Anti-religious ABC'], Leningrad-Moskva: Utilbyuro Izogiza, 1933.

Causes for and Mechanisms of Change in the Shamanic Culture

This rather ambiguous situation in which Valentina Olchka found herself and which was characteristic of the whole Soviet period, may to some extent be illustrated by a dialogue between two communist activists from a book by N. E. Shudrik:

> – Gosh, what sort of strange people are they? You drag them, by your teeth and claws, to the clean air and bright light, but they are balking like a roped caribou!

> – You shouldn't rope-and-drag. Call them, use your heart to make them trust you, let them go themselves, freely and voluntarily; this is the right way. If you drag someone anywhere, he'll always be balking, no doubt about it. (Slezkine 2008: 372)

The same spirit of philanthropical reform permeates the story told by a Nanai writer, G. G. Khodzher, in his novel *Gaychi* (1978) describing the process of Sovietization in the Nanaysky district (the birthplace of many of our informants) in 1924 (Khodzher 1978: 269). It must be pointed out here that this novel, a text of fiction, seems to provide a rather true-to-fact depiction of the events and, most particularly, the everyday life of people in those times, as far as I can judge based on my knowledge of the culture of the region. On the other hand, as is often the case with Soviet literature, the reader has to first disengage him-/herself from the inevitable ideological clichés, such as the idea of the "salvatory" advent of Soviet rule to the region, or the operatic glorification of a Nanai who disobeyed "the shaman and the monger" and then joined a Soviet collective farm. The depiction of the reality of the Nanaysky district in the 1920s, though transformed by the socialist realism discourse, still reflects much of the mentality of that epoch. As I view it, similarities between the reality and literary fiction here are possible only if the initiators and executors of the Soviet reformist project among the indigenous peoples of Russia's North were inspired by and acting in line with the same fundamentally optimistic values and goals as the socialist realism literature tried to implant in the nation's mentality.

The described events were only an external factor bearing upon the process under scrutiny. But can we be justified in definitively reducing all possible causes for the change to an outside interference? Every culture must have its own internal mechanism of sanctioning change and implementing it. My contemplation here of the factors that can bear upon the process of change in the spiritual culture has paradoxically enough led to ritual practices which, at the first glance, must work to the contrary, i.e. to keep the tradition unchanged. So, without dismissing the role of the protagonists of the reform project in these processes, I have to admit that factors leading to change in the traditional shamanic culture must be looked for in shamanism itself. It occurred more than once that the "keeper of the tradition"—the shaman—was the one who actually sanctioned the transformation. Adaptation of cultural borrowings by way of subjecting them to the "shamanist censorship" has been observed in other indigenous Northern cultures, for instance among the Nenets (Golovnev 1992: 159).

We have at our disposal ethnographic and literary materials which will allow us to track the action of this mechanism in the culture of the peoples of the lower reaches of the Amur River at the dawn of social reform. Let us now look more closely at these issues in the context of the cross-culture communication theory. Broadly, the mechanism of socio-cultural dynamics, including the transitional phase of innovation (when innovation is still being viewed as something "alien," but already interesting for the recipient culture, and therefore step by step introduced in daily use while at the same time assuming all new forms and connotations characteristic of the recipient culture), was personified in the mythological and ritual culture of the indigenous hunting and fishing societies of the Far East. For them, the spirit named *Dona* was the personification of all that was new and alien and that should be "tamed" or "domesticated." Its significance, its rules of incarnation and "domestication" of new elements in the culture of hunters and fishermen living in boreal coniferous forests was outlined in the works by S. V. Shirokogorov (2001: 135). In these cultures, *Dona* belonged to the class of "alien" spirits that came when other peoples came to their territory. These non-material creatures, after having "spent" some time among the local population as *Dona*, could later become "domesticated" and even accepted as a clan's spirit-helpers, should the shaman find their "taming" practicable and his own powers sufficient to subdue them.

In the context of the study of the semiosphere of the southern part of the Far East, it seems rather significant that the word *dono* is also applied here to the upper flap of the smoke hole in a house's front wall (*Sravnitel'nyj slovar' tunguso-man'chzhurskikh yazykov* 1975: 215), which in folk texts, fairy tales and rituals practised in the region plays the role of a mediator object between people's "own" space and the other world, just as it was a mediator between the home and the exterior world. For all spirits, including the "ethnically ambiguous" ones, a shaman would make a wooden "capsule" or "shell" enabling him to control the spirit's activity. Such a "shell" into which an alien spirit would be installed was the material incarnation of the idea of *Dona*.

In the context of the active change of life in which the indigenous peoples of the Amur River region had found themselves in the second half of the nineteenth century and later on, their own cultural thesaurus was not sufficient for interpreting formerly unfamiliar problems and phenomena, often linked to epidemics, reforms of education, economy, social structures, etc.; therefore shamans relying on the oral tradition had to improvise and draw upon ideas which "were in the wind of change." Adding new spirits to the ones already "affiliated" with a tribe or clan had to improve the shaman's "powers" in decisions on vital problems of the changing society; from this follows that a minister of shamanic religion was interested in the enlargement of his pantheon. From this follows that "domesticating" an "alien" spirit, providing explanations of new phenomena by engaging the symbolic means of "the Big Other," a shaman, who still retained his status and authority in the community, would legitimize adoption of other innovations and any change in general. This was the reason why aboriginal peoples of the Amur River and Sakhalin regions living close to Russian migrants in the early twentieth century followed another logic, such as: "The Russian god is more powerful than the Gilyaks', and therefore, Russian shamans are more powerful than Gilyaks' shamans" (Shternberg 1933: 76).

The Change of the Role of a Shaman in the Society of the Amur River Aboriginals in pre- and post-Soviet Times

The indigenous word *shaman* was applied by the natives to priests, and later also to medical doctors and paramedics, i.e. the specialists who appropriated to themselves one of the essential roles of a minister of the indigenous religions—healing people's bodies and souls. The conflict between the shaman and the medic (i.e. between the old and the new order of life) and the final symbolic replacement of the former by the latter have been depicted in the already mentioned novel *Gaychi* by Khodzher. An old shaman who had proved forceless in fighting the "black death" (the term applied to the small pox disease in the novel) gives up his place and authority to a young couple of medical doctors able to eradicate the deadly illness in the Nanaysky district. Here the figure of a shaman is represented as doubting his own powers and ability to combat the epidemic. There is only one scene in the novel, although a rather exemplary one, which depicts the inertia of obedience to the shaman: only after the shaman himself, fearing imminent death, agreed to be inoculated against the disease was his example followed by his fellow Nanai villagers, who had formerly doubted the "power" of this medication. The Nanai are depicted in the novel as torn between the two Truths, and the shaman, unwittingly, influences their decision.

It seems obvious that the novel's author—an established indigenous writer of the Soviet times who had to work in a situation of harsh censorship and therefore strictly followed the canons of socialist realism—strove to show a well-known mythologeme of a combat between Light and Darkness, rather than a mere superstition. This idea was very popular in the time of socialist reforms in post-revolutionary Russia. From the moment of the inevitable victory of everything that was "Light," free of "superstition" and future-bound, shamans were thrown away in the realm of "Darkness" and became a symbol of regression and cultural past. On the other hand, these ideas, largely shared by many aboriginal peoples of Siberia and the Far East, did not spring up all of a sudden at the beginning of the Soviet period, as is widely believed, but were the result of much earlier processes of change in material production, social relations, cognition and spiritual culture driven by the contacts with neighbouring pastoralist and agriculturalist tribes. Due to these changes, the indigenous peoples in Siberia and the Far East underwent a gradual separation of ritual from everyday life. Thus, the Tungus tribes—genetically related to the Amur Region peoples—had become reindeer herders but retained their shamanic religions and believed they needed to somehow segregate the shaman from the rest of the village because, according to them, his "spirits" interfered negatively with the normal life of the village and even caused the death of livestock (Shirokogorov 2001: 178–179). Relocating shamans to the outskirts of an inhabited locality or to the opposite coast of a water basin was known to indigenous people of the southern part of the Far East region,[8] who actively traded with neighbouring agricultural tribes and consequently hoped for both the favour of spirits controlled by their shamans and for successful trade when furs would be exchanged for starch-containing food. Apparently, such isolation in the Amur River region was characteristic of the shamans considered most powerful and skilled, the *kasa*-shamans, while the majority of other shamans in this area continued to reside within the settlements.

---

[8] This information was kindly provided to us by residents of the villages of Naykhin and Dzhari of the Nanaysky district of the Khabarovsk region (2003-2004): Mr Mikhail S. Bel'dy, Mr Maksim P. Bel'dy, Ms Sofia S. Bel'dy, Ms Tatiana F. Bel'dy, and Ms Svetlana S. Onenko.

The significance of shamans was gradually reduced as a result of the appearance of many indigenous specialists in healing, whose work was assumed to possess more rational knowledge of flora and fauna (Shirokogorov 2001: 172). According to V. V. Podmaskin (2008: 71–72), the spread of such medical practitioners among the indigenous peoples of Siberia and the Far East was due to Buddhist influences coming from neighbouring Turkic and Mongol-speaking pastoralist tribes and from the population of cross-border areas of China. Along with other forms of livelihood activity and migrants coming to the Amur River area, institutionalized forms of rational knowledge also penetrated the region. It is known that some Nanai people would send their children to schools in Manchuria (MAE RAN, Lipskaya, f. 5, op. 4, d. 5), or to Russian educational institutions set up by ecclesiastical missions. Later, the latter were replaced by a system of boarding schools.

Thus, the processes of desacralization of knowledge, whose results became so evident by the mid-twentieth century in the form of the shamans losing their former authority, were in part prepared by the advent of more efficient and less costly ways of livelihood activity, by contacts with other cultures that had introduced these new methods, and by the spread of this new rational knowledge that allowed the local population to benefit regularly and efficiently from all this. The shaman's key roles and functions—such as healing, preservation and transmission of knowledge about the traditional worldview—were taken over by specialists of secular vocational activities such as modern healthcare, education and political education. There was only one role of a shaman that could not be taken over by secular institutions— the "sending off" of the soul of a dead to the other world. On the other hand, the sheer existence of a human "soul" had been totally abandoned by the official culture of the Soviet Union many years ago. Folk narratives of the Amur River region that were collected by folklorists in the second half of the twentieth century demonstrate that shamans—as the "non-labouring" elements of the society—were already looked upon as antagonists and even cannibals. Shamanism along with anthropophagic practices was interpreted in these folk-tales as the manifestation of cultural backwardness and "decline back to nature."

Illustration 18: 'Anti-religious skittles.' Children's board game with figures of a "Mongolian shaman," a "German minister," a "Russian priest," the "Jewish god," a "Tungus hunting god," a Nanai "idol," and the "Christian god." From the Soviet children's magazine *Murzilka* (1932).

Conclusion

All the above arguments give us grounds to maintain that shamanism became extinct by the 1970s, not primarily because it was banned, but due to the fact that against the background of all the changes and innovations it was becoming a socially unpopular and non-prestigious phenomenon among the bearers of the tradition themselves. On the other hand we cannot disagree with the opinion that such attitudes were intentionally incorporated into the mentality of Northern indigenous peoples. Shamanism was again spoken of positively and revived in the 1980s–1990s, when the status of a shaman began to bring some social, psychological and even material benefits. This period brought up the idea of reviving the culture and traditions of indigenous peoples of the North on the basis of ethnographic materials collected in the nineteenth and early twentieth centuries and during later expeditions specifically aimed at "saving what remained of the tradition." For Siberia and Russia's Far East, this work can be viewed as the second wave of the so-called "Siberia boom."[9] However, unlike the first wave, dating back to the turn of the twentieth century, this activity involved the most advanced intellectuals and professionals of indigenous origin. Interest in shamanism in Russia was also provoked, in my view, by another factor: the increased curiosity in various mystical ideas and occult practices, which is not a rare thing during transitional periods and times of crises in the life of a society.

This cultural-national renaissance seemed to be, on the one hand, a hope for relief for ethnophores (the bearers of a specific ethnic tradition) facing, like millions of other Russian citizens, the harsh problem of survival; on the other, it could be viewed as the "opium for the people" distracting them from serious economic and political problems of the post-Perestroika life in the country. In order to legitimize these phenomena and their roles in the social and political realm of today, the mythologeme of "going back to the origins" or "revival" has been, and still is, largely used. However, such "bridging back" to the "true source," to the "cosmos," the "forefathers" etc., is being actualized now not in the context of the archaic—or primitive—indigenous syncretism of cultural forms, but on the basis and by the agency of the following elements:

- systematic knowledge of the principles of ethnic culture and its mechanisms, to the accumulation, systematization and enlargement of which individual researchers and research communities have been putting their constant efforts;
- improvement of the legislative framework needed for the development of local communities subsisting from traditional means of exploiting natural resources;

---

[9] This is an expression in the Russian ethnographic discourse that denotes periods of active research of the indigenous populations of Siberia and the Far East.

- development of social and commercial projects involving traditional mythologemes, symbols, material and spiritual values of indigenous ethnic cultures.

It was, thus, in this social and cultural context that shamanism was revived in the Amur River region. In connection with the above, it seems only appropriate to find the answer to my last question: How should we view and interpret this purportedly "traditional" reality that has been reconstructed on the basis of research materials and is being performed by aboriginal theatre groups? What is today's shamanism, the one where a shaman rehearses his or her "show" before putting it on, or where the Shaman mountain—only forty years ago the source of powers for the last of the traditional Nanai shamans—has now become merely a popular tourist attraction? Today's residents of indigenous settlements and villages may "become" shamans if they are awaiting some important guests from afar. Traditional links and relations are being substituted by scientific and social concepts, the true reality by simulacra, vital necessity by economic expediency, and the religious rite itself by a theatrical show. Should we therefore talk about rational and artistic forms of this phenomenon rather than the archaic tradition?

Still, shamanism remains the cultural constant that has defined the culture of the indigenous peoples of the Amur River region for centuries. No wonder therefore that the figure of a shaman, along with such symbols as the sun and waters whose signifiers are linguistic or ornamental elements, are consciously or subconsciously chosen as the emblem for innovative economic or social cultural projects aimed at attaining regional branding purposes. Therefore we are justified to conclude that shamanism, which until the mid-twentieth century had performed all key cultural functions of the indigenous peoples of the lower reaches of the Amur River, is now becoming a symbol of this local cultural tradition, i.e., it exists today in a form that seems to be most adequate to the modern social cultural realm and is most efficient for the task of preserving this tradition in the memory of humankind.

References

Archives

MAE RAN. МАЭ РАН. Музей Антропологии и Этнографии Российской Академии Наук (Кунсткамера), Липская, Н. А. Нанай (гольды), Ф. 5. Оп. 4. Д. 5 ['Peter the Great Museum of Anthropology and Ethnography, Russian

Academy of Sciences (Kunstkamera). Lipsakaya, N. A., The Nanai (Golds), f. 5, op. 4, d. 5'], St. Petersburg, Russia.

Literature

Bobyshev, S. V. & Akhmetova, A. V. (2008). Бобышев, С. В. и Ахметова, А. В. *Коренные малочисленные народы Дальнего Востока на завершающем этапе социалистической модернизации (50-х–середина 80-х гг. XX века)* ['Indigenous minorities of the Far East at the final stage of socialistic modernization of the 1950s–1980s'], Khabarovsk: Izdatelstvo DVGUPS.

Golovnev, A. V. (1992). Головнев, А. В. "Модель в культурологии" ['Models in Cultural Studies'], in *Модель в культурологии Сибири и Севера. Сборник научных трудов* ['Models in cultural studies of Siberia and the North. A collection of scientific papers'], Yekaterinburg, pp. 142–169.

Khodzher, G. G. (1978). Ходжер, Г. Г. *Гайчи. Роман* ['Gaichi. A Novel'], Moscow: Sovremennik.

Podmaskin, V. V. (2008). Подмаскин, В. В. *Введение в этнографию Дальнего Востока России. Народная медицина и культура питания* ['Introduction to the ethnography of Russia's Far East. Folk medicine and diet'], Vladivostok.

Shirokogorov, S. M. (2001). Широкогоров, С. М. "Опыт исследования основ шаманства" ['A study on the basics of shamanism'], in Широкогоров, С. М., *Этнографические исследования. Кн. первая. Избранное. Сост. и примеч. А. М. Кузнецова и А. М. Решетова* ['Ethnographic works. Book 1. Selected writings. Ed. and comm. by A. M. Kuznetsov & A. M. Reshetov'], Vladivostok, pp. 116–186.

Shternberg, L. Ya. (1933). Штернберг, Л. Я. *Гиляки, орочи, гольды, негидальцы, айны. Статьи и материалы, под ред. и с предисл. Я. П. Алькор (Кошкина)* ['The Gilyaks, Orochis, Goldis, Negidals and Ainu. Papers and materials'], Khabarovsk: DalGIZ.

Slezkine, Yu. (2008). Слезкин, Ю. *Арктические зеркала. Россия и малые народы Севера*; автор. пер. с англ. О. Леонтьевой ['Arctic mirrors. Russia and indigenous minorities of the North'], Moscow: Novoe Literaturnoe Obozrenie.

Sravnitel'nyj slovar' tunguso-man'chzhurskikh yazykov (1975). *Сравнительный словарь тунгусо-маньчжурских языков. Материалы к этимологическому словарю*, отв. ред. В. И. Цинциус. Т. 1 ['A comparative dictionary of the Tungus and Manchur languages. Materials for an etymological dictionary. Vol. 1'], Leningrad: Nauka, Leningradskoe Otdelenie.

Tugolukov, V. A. (1971). Туголуков, В. А. "Преодоление старого в быту и сознании эвенков" ['Overcoming the past in the everyday life of the Evenkis'], in *Осуществление ленинской национальной политики у народов Крайнего Севера*, ред. И. С. Гурвич, ['Implementing Lenin's nationality policy among the indigenous peoples of the Far North'], Moscow, pp. 200–212.p

Contributors

Oksana Beznosova, PhD in history, is a project manager at the International Union of German Culture in Moscow, Russia. Previously she worked as a senior researcher at the Center of German Studies at Dnipropetrovsk National University, Ukraine. Her list of publications includes "Regionale Besonderheiten in den antideutschen Kampagnen im Russischen Reich. Gouvernement Ekaterinoslav" in *Besetzt, interniert, deportiert. Der Erste Weltkrieg und die deutsche, jüdische, polnische und ukrainische Zivilbevölkerung im östlichen Europa* (Essen 2013) and "Die Missionstätigkeit deutscher Evangelisten in der Ukraine im 19. Jahrhundert" in *Forschungen zur Geschichte und Kultur der Russlanddeutschen* (1996:6).

Tatiana Bulgakova is a professor of cultural studies at the Department of Ethnic and Cultural Studies, Herzen State Pedagogical University, St. Petersburg, Russia. Some of her recent publications include the monographs *Nanai Shamanic Culture in Indigenous Discourse* (Fürstenberg 2013) and *Kamlaniya nanayskikh shamanov* ['Shamanic performances of Nanai shamans'] (Fürstenberg 2016), and the articles "Contest in Nanai shamanic tales" in *Journal of Ethnology and Folkloristics* (2015:9/1), "Le choix entre traditions et modernisation. L'éducation comme moyen de transformer les cultures autochtones en Sibérie," in *Quelle éducation pour les peuples autochtones?* (Paris 2017) and "Nevostrebovannoe issledovanie tunguskogo shamanstva" ['Unclaimed research on Tungus shamanism'] in *Etnograficheskoe obozrenie* (2017:5).

Victor Dönninghaus is a professor of history at the Department of History, Freiburg University, and the deputy director of *Nordost-Institut* in Lüneburg, Germany. His research focuses on Soviet nationality politics, the German minority in Russia and the Soviet Union, Stalinism, and Leonid Brezhnev and his rule. His recent publications include *Minderheiten in Bedrängnis. Die sowjetische Politik gegenüber Deutschen, Polen und anderen Diaspora-Nationalitäten 1917–1938* (München 2009), *Revolution, Reform und Krieg. Die Deutschen an der Wolga im ausgehenden Zarenreich* (Essen 2002), *Die Deutschen in der Moskauer Gesellschaft. Symbiose und Konflikte 1494–1941*

(München 2002), and "Don't be seen repealing the decree on the Jews—just don't enforce it. L. I. Brezhnev, Détente, and Jewish emigration from the USSR" in *Russian Studies in History* (2014, 52:4, co-authored with Andrey Savin).

Yana Ivaschenko is doctor of Cultural Studies and professor at the Department of History and Political Science, Novosibirsk State Technical University, Russia. Her research focuses on the indigenous peoples and dynamics of the culture of the Far East region. The list of her publications includes the monograph *Kul'tura zhizneobespecheniya tungus-manzhurov. Sistemno-strategicheskiy analiz* ['Life-sustenance culture of the Manchu-Tungus peoples. A systematic-strategic analysis'] (St. Petersburg 2011) and the article "The figure of cannibal in the traditional Nanai culture" in *European Journal of Science and Theology* (2015).

Marc Junge is a senior researcher at the Faculty of History, Ruhr-University of Bochum, Germany. His main fields of research are Stalinism, Soviet rehabilitation policy 1938–1991, and the Russian revolutionary movement of the nineteenth century. His most recent publications include *Stalin's Mass Repression and the Cold War Paradigm* (New York 2016); *Revolyutsionery na pensii. Vsesoyuznoe obshchestvo politkatorzhan i ssyl'noposelentsev 1921–1935* ['Revolutionaries on a pension. All-Union society of political prisoners and exiles. 1921–1935'] (Moscow 2015), and *Bol'shestskiy poryadok v Gruzii. Bolshoy terror v malen'koy kavkazskoy respublike* ['Bolshevik order in Georgia. The Great Terror in a small Caucasian republic'] (Moscow 2015, co-authored with Bernd Bonwetsch).

Andrej Kotljarchuk is a senior researcher at the School of Historical and Contemporary Studies, Södertörn University, Sweden. His research focuses on minorities, propaganda, mass violence, and the role of expert communities. His most recent publications include the monograph *In the Forge of Stalin. Swedish Colonists of Ukraine in Totalitarian Experiments of the Twentieth Century* (Stockholm 2014), the book chapters "Nordic fishermen in the Soviet Union. Ethnic purges and the cleansing of cultural landscapes" in *The Barents and the Baltic Sea Region. Contacts, Influences and Social Change* (Rovaniemi 2017); "The Nordic threat. Soviet ethnic cleansing on the Kola Peninsula" in *The Sea of Identities. A Century of Baltic and East European Experiences with Nationality, Class, and Gender* (Stockholm 2014) and "Ethnic cleansings and 'Russification'" in *Encyclopedia of the Barents Region*

(Oslo 2016), and the articles "Kola Sami in the Stalinist terror. A quantitative analysis" in *Journal of Northern Studies* (2012:6:2) and "Norwegians in the Stalinist terror. New perspectives for research" in *Fortid* (2015:2).

Hiroaki Kuromiya is a professor of history at the Department of History, Indiana University, USA. He specializes in the history of modern Russia, modern Ukraine, and more broadly modern Eurasia. His most recent publications include the books *Conscience on Trial. The Fate of Fourteen Pacifists in Stalin's Ukraine, 1952–1953* (Toronto 2012), *Między Warszawą a Tokio. Polsko-Japońska współpraca wywiadowcza 1904–1945* ['Between Warsaw and Tokyo. Polish-Japanese intelligence cooperation 1904–1944'] (Warsaw 2009, co-authored with Andrzej Pepłoński), and *The Voices of the Dead. Stalin's Great Terror in the 1930s* (New Haven 2007).

Art Leete is a professor of ethnology at the Institute of Cultural Research and Arts, University of Tartu, Estonia. His research focuses on indigenous peoples' reactions to the early Soviet reforms. His list of publications includes the monographs *La guerre du Kazym. Les peuples de Sibérie occidentale contre le pouvoir soviétique, 1933–1934* (Paris 2007), *Muutused ja meeleheide. Põhjarahvad ja nõukogude võim 1920.–40 aastatel* ['Changes and desperation. The northern peoples and Soviet power during the 1920s–40s'] (Tartu 2007) and *Guileless Indigenes and Hidden Passion. Descriptions of Ob-Ugrians and Samoyeds through the Centuries* (Helsinki 2014) as well as the articles "Reconsidering the role of shamans in Siberia during the early Soviet era" in *Shaman* (2015:23) and "Imitating enemies or friends. Comparative notes on Christianity in the indigenous Russian Arctic during the early Soviet period" in *Asian Ethnology* (2011:70:1, co-authored with Laur Vallikivi).

Daniel Müller is the director of the postgraduate centre at the University of Siegen, Germany. His main fields of research are Soviet nationality policies in Transcaucasia, media-minority relations in Germany, and the history of journalism. His publications include the monograph *Sowjetische Nationalitätenpolitik in Transkaukasien 1920–1953* (Berlin 2008), the edited collection *Gruziya v puti. Teni stalinizma* ['Georgia on its way. Shadows of Stalinism'](Moscow 2017, with M. Junge and B. Bonwetsch), and contributions in Junge, M. & Bonveč, B. (eds.), *Bol'shevistskiy poryadok v Gruzii. Tom 1. Bol'shoy terror v malen'koy kavkazskoy respublike* ['The Bolshevik order in Georgia. Vol. 1. The Great Terror in a small Caucasian republic'] (Moscow 2015).

Andrey Savin is a senior researcher at the Institute of History of the Siberian Branch of the Russian Academy of Sciences in Novosibirsk, Russia. His main fields of research are ethnic and religious minorities in the Soviet Union, Stalinism, repressions, inter-war Soviet-German relations, Soviet heroism, and Leonid Brezhnev and his rule. His list of publications includes *Ethno-Confession in the Soviet State. Mennonites in Siberia, 1920–1989. Annotated List of Archival Documents* (Fresno 2008), *Die Sibiriendeutschen im Sowjetstaat. 1919–1938* (Essen 2001, co-authored with Detlef Brandes), "Don't be seen repealing the decree on the Jews—just don't enforce it. L. I. Brezhnev, Détente, and Jewish emigration from the USSR" in *Russian Studies in History* (2014, 52:4, co-authored with Victor Dönninghaus).

Olle Sundström is associate professor of the History of Religions at Umeå University, Sweden. In his doctoral thesis *"Vildrenen är själv detsamma som en gud"* ['The wild reindeer is itself the same as a god'] (Umeå 2008), he analyses how Soviet ethnographers conceptualised and theorised "supernatural beings" in the world-views of the Samoyed peoples. He has also published studies on Soviet policies towards "shamanism" among the indigenous peoples of the North, as well as on the revival of shamanism in post-Soviet Siberia, e.g. in the book *Kampen mot "schamanismen." Sovjetisk religionspolitik gentemot inhemska religioner i Sibirien och norra Ryssland* ['The struggle against "shamanism." Soviet religious policy towards the indigenous religions of Siberia and Northern Russia'] (Uppsala 2007) and in the article "Is the shaman indeed risen in post-Soviet Siberia?" in *Post-Secular Religious Practices* (Turku 2012). His most recent project concerns the historical relations between the Sami and the Church of Sweden (2016 and 2017). Sundström is editorial secretary of the multi-disciplinary *Journal of Northern Studies*.

Eva Toulouze is an anthropologist and professor of Finno-Ugric studies at INALCO (Paris) and researcher at the Department of Ethnology, University of Tartu, Estonia. Her research focuses on Russia's Finno-Ugric communities, especially the Udmurt and Forest Nenets cultures. Written culture and its history, evangelisation, and the present religious situation and oral cultures are among the most developed issues. She has edited several collections of articles on Finno-Ugric peoples; among the most recent are *Les Maris, un people finno-ougrien de Russie centrale* (Paris 2013), *Les Komis, questions d'histoire et de culture* (Paris 2010), and *Deux écrivains autochtones de Sibérie, Eremeï Aïpine et Iouri Vella* (Paris 2010). She has published more than 130 academic articles in Finno-Ugric studies in French, English, Estonian, Italian, and Russian.

Laur Vallikivi is a senior researcher at the University of Tartu, Estonia. His research focus is on the anthropology of Siberian indigenous peoples in the context of past and present cultural contacts. His publications include a monograph on the impact of Russian evangelical missionaries among Nenets reindeer herders, *Arktika nomaadid kristluse ja šamanismi vahel* ['Arctic nomads between shamanism and Christianity. The conversion of Yamb-to Nenets to Baptism'] (Tartu 2005), the book chapter "Christianisation of words and selves. Nenets reindeer herders joining the state through conversion" (2009), and the article "On the edge of space and time. Evangelical missionaries in the tundra of Arctic Russia" in *Journal of Ethnology and Folkloristics* (2014:2).

Södertörn Academic Studies

1. Helmut Müssener & Frank-Michael Kirsch (eds.), *Nachbarn im Ostseeraum unter sich. Vorurteile, Klischees und Stereotypen in Texten*, 2000.
2. Jan Ekecrantz & Kerstin Olofsson (eds.), *Russian Reports: Studies in Post-Communist Transformation of Media and Journalism*, 2000.
3. Kekke Stadin (ed.), *Society, Towns and Masculinity: Aspects on Early Modern Society in the Baltic Area*, 2000.
4. Bernd Henningsen et al. (eds.), *Die Inszenierte Stadt. Zur Praxis und Theorie kultureller Konstruktionen*, 2001.
5. Michal Bron (ed.), *Jews and Christians in Dialogue*, ii: *Identity, Tolerance, Understanding*, 2001
6. Frank-Michael Kirsch et al. (eds.), *Nachbarn im Ostseeraum übwer einander. Wandel der Bilder, Vorurteile und Stereotypen?*, 2001.
7. Birgitta Almgren, *Illusion und Wirklichkeit. Individuelle und kollektive Denkmusterin nationalsozialistischer Kulturpolitik und Germanistik in Schweden 1928–1945*, 2001.
8. Denny Vågerö (ed.), *The Unknown Sorokin: His Life in Russia and the Essay on Suicide*, 2002.
9. Kerstin W. Shands (ed.), *Collusion and Resistance: Women Writing in English*, 2002.
10. Elfar Loftsson & Yonhyok Choe (eds.), *Political Representation and Participation in Transitional Democracies: Estonia, Latvia and Lithuania*, 2003.
11. Birgitta Almgren (eds.), *Bilder des Nordens in der Germanistik 1929–1945: Wissenschaftliche Integrität oder politische Anpassung?*, 2002.
12. Christine Frisch, *Von Powerfrauen und Superweibern: Frauenpopulärliteratur der 90er Jahre in Deutschland und Schweden*, 2003.
13. Hans Ruin & Nicholas Smith (eds.), *Hermeneutik och tradition. Gadamer och den grekiska filosofin*, 2003.
14. Mikael Lönnborg et al. (eds.), *Money and Finance in Transition: Research in Contemporary and Historical Finance*, 2003.
15. Kerstin Shands et al. (eds.), *Notions of America: Swedish Perspectives*, 2004.

16. Karl-Olov Arnstberg & Thomas Borén (eds.), *Everyday Economy in Russia, Poland and Latvia*, 2003.
17. Johan Rönnby (ed.), *By the Water. Archeological Perspectives on Human Strategies around the Baltic Sea*, 2003.
18. Baiba Metuzale-Kangere (ed.), *The Ethnic Dimension in Politics and Culture in the Baltic Countries 1920–1945*, 2004.
19. Ulla Birgegård & Irina Sandomirskaja (eds.), *In Search of an Order: Mutual Representations in Sweden and Russia during the Early Age of Reason*, 2004.
20. Ebba Witt-Brattström (ed.), *The New Woman and the Aesthetic Opening: Unlocking Gender in Twentieth-Century Texts*, 2004.
21. Michael Karlsson, *Transnational Relations in the Baltic Sea Region*, 2004.
22. Ali Hajighasemi, *The Transformation of the Swedish Welfare System: Fact or Fiction? Globalisation, Institutions and Welfare State Change in a Social Democratic Regime*, 2004.
23. Erik A. Borg (ed.), *Globalization, Nations and Markets: Challenging Issues in Current Research on Globalization*, 2005.
24. Stina Bengtsson & Lars Lundgren, *The Don Quixote of Youth Culture: Media Use and Cultural Preferences Among Students in Estonia and Sweden*, 2005.
25. Hans Ruin, *Kommentar till Heideggers Varat och tiden*, 2005.
26. Ludmila Ferm, *Variativnoe bespredložnoe glagol´noe upravlenie v russkom jazyke XVIII veka* [Variation in non-prepositional verbal government in eighteenth-century Russian], 2005.
27. Christine Frisch, *Modernes Aschenputtel und Anti-James-Bond: Gender-Konzepte in deutschsprachigen Rezeptionstexten zu Liza Marklund und Henning Mankell*, 2005.
28. Ursula Naeve-Bucher, *Die Neue Frau tanzt: Die Rolle der tanzenden Frau in deutschen und schwedischen literarischen Texten aus der ersten Hälfte des 20. Jahrhunderts*, 2005.
29. Göran Bolin et al. (eds.), *The Challenge of the Baltic Sea Region: Culture, Ecosystems, Democracy*, 2005.
30. Marcia Sá Cavalcante Schuback & Hans Ruin (eds.), *The Past's Presence: Essays on the Historicity of Philosophical Thought*, 2006.
31. María Borgström & Katrin Goldstein-Kyaga (ed.), *Gränsöverskridande identiteter i globaliseringens tid: Ungdomar, migration och kampen för fred*, 2006.

32. Janusz Korek (ed.), *From Sovietology to Postcoloniality: Poland and Ukraine from a Postcolonial Perspective*, 2007.
33. Jonna Bornemark (ed.), *Det främmande i det egna: filosofiska essäer om bildning och person*, 2007.
34. Sofia Johansson, *Reading Tabloids: Tabloid Newspapers and Their Readers*, 2007.
35. Patrik Åker, *Symboliska platser i kunskapssamhället: Internet, högre lärosäten och den gynnade geografin*, 2008.
36. Kerstin W. Shands (ed.), *Neither East Nor West: Postcolonial Essays on Literature, Culture and Religion*, 2008.
37. Rebecka Lettevall & My Klockar Linder (eds.), *The Idea of Kosmopolis: History, philosophy and politics of world citizenship*, 2008.
38. Karl Gratzer & Dieter Stiefel (eds.), *History of Insolvency and Bankruptcy from an International Perspective*, 2008.
39. Katrin Goldstein-Kyaga & María Borgström, *Den tredje identiteten: Ungdomar och deras familjer i det mångkulturella, globala rummet*, 2009.
40. Christine Farhan, *Frühling für Mütter in der Literatur?: Mutterschaftskonzepte in deutschsprachiger und schwedischer Gegenwartsliteratur*, 2009.
41. Marcia Sá Cavalcante Schuback (ed.), *Att tänka smärtan*, 2009.
42. Heiko Droste (ed.), *Connecting the Baltic Area: The Swedish Postal System in the Seventeenth Century*, 2011.
43. Aleksandr Nemtsov, *A Contemporary History of Alcohol in Russia*, 2011.
44. Cecilia von Feilitzen & Peter Petrov (eds.), *Use and Views of Media in Russia and Sweden: A Comparative Study of Media in St. Petersburg and Stockholm*, 2011.
45. Sven Lilja (ed.), *Fiske, jordbruk och klimat i Östersjöregionen under förmodern tid*, 2012.
46. Leif Dahlberg & Hans Ruin (eds.), *Fenomenologi, teknik och medialitet*, 2012.
47. Samuel Edquist, *I Ruriks fotspår: Om forntida svenska österledsfärder i modern historieskrivning*, 2012.
48. Jonna Bornemark (ed.), *Phenomenology of Eros*, 2012.
49. Jonna Bornemark & Hans Ruin (eds.), *Ambiguity of the Sacred: Phenomenology, Politics, Aesthetics*, 2012.
50. Håkan Nilsson, *Placing Art in the Public Realm*, 2012.

51. Per Bolin, *Between National and Academic Agendas: Ethnic Policies and 'National Disciplines' at Latvia's University, 1919–1940*, 2012.
52. Lars Kleberg & Aleksei Semenenko (eds.), *Aksenov and the Environs/Aksenov iokrestnosti*, 2012.
53. Sven-Olov Wallenstein & Brian Manning Delaney (eds.), *Translating Hegel: The Phenomenology of Spirit and Modern Philosophy*, 2012.
54. Sven-Olov Wallenstein and Jakob Nilsson (eds.), *Foucault, Biopolitics, and Governmentality*, 2013.
55. Jan Patočka, *Inledning till fenomenologisk filosofi*, 2013.
56. Jonathan Adams & Johan Rönnby (eds.), *Interpreting Shipwrecks: Maritime Archaeological Approaches*, 2013.
57. Charlotte Bydler, *Mondiality/Regionality: Perspectives on Art, Aesthetics and Globalization*, 2014.
58. Andrej Kotljarchuk, *In the Forge of Stalin: Swedish Colonists of Ukraine in Totalitarian Experiments of the Twentieth Century*, 2014.
59. Samuel Edquist & Janne Holmén, *Islands of Identity: History-writing and identity formation in five island regions in the Baltic Sea*, 2014.
60. Norbert Götz (ed.), *The Sea of Identities: A Century of Baltic and East European Experiences with Nationality, Class, and Gender*, 2015.
61. Klaus Misgeld, Karl Molin & Pawel Jaworski, *Solidaritet och diplomati: Svenskt fackligt och diplomatiskt stöd till Polens demokratisering under 1980-talet*, 2015.
62. Jonna Bornemark & Sven-Olov Wallenstein (eds.), *Madness, Religion, and the Limits of Reason*, 2015.
63. Mirja Arnshav & Anna McWilliams, *Stalins ubåtar: en arkeologisk undersökning av vraken efter S7 och SC-305*, 2015.
64. Carl-Gustaf Scott, *Swedish Social Democracy and the Vietnam War*, 2017.
65. Jonna Bornemark & Nicolas Smith (eds.), *Phenomenology of Pregnancy*, 2016.
66. Ulrika Dahl, Marianne Liljeström & Ulla Manns, *The Geopolitics of Nordic and Russian Gender Research 1975–2005*, 2016.
67. Annika Öhrner (ed.), *Art in Transfer in the Era of Pop*, 2017.
68. Jan Öhrming, *Allt görs liksom baklänges: verksamheten vid Nya Karolinska Solna*, 2017.
69. Piotr Wawrzeniuk, *Med osäker utgång*, (forthcoming)

70. Niklas Eriksson, *Riksäpplet: Arkeologiska perspektiv på ett bortglömt regalskepp*, 2017.
71. Christine Bladh, *Hennes snilles styrka - Kvinnliga grosshandlare i Stockholm och Åbo 1750–1820*, (forthcoming).
72. Andrej Kotljarchuk & Olle Sundström (eds.), *Ethnic and Religious Minorities in Stalin's Soviet Union: New Dimensions of Research*, 2017.

Northern Studies

The *Journal of Northern Studies* is a peer-reviewed academic publication issued twice a year. It is published by Umeå University and Sweden's northernmost Royal Academy, the Royal Skyttean Society. There are two monograph series connected to the journal: Northern Studies Monographs (publication languages English, French and German) and Nordliga studier ['Northern Studies'] (publication languages Danish, Norwegian and Swedish).

The editor-in-chief of the *Journal of Northern Studies* is:

Professor Lars-Erik Edlund
Dept of Language Studies
Umeå University
SE-901 87 Umeå
lars-erik.edlund@umu.se
www.jns.org.umu.se

Northern Studies Monographs (ISSN 2000-0405)

1. Heidi Hansson & Catherine Norberg (eds.), *Cold Matters: Cultural Perceptions of Snow, Ice and Cold*. Umeå 2009.
   ISBN 978-91-88466-70-9

2. Giuseppe Nencioni, *The Italians in the Arctic Explorations: A Critique of the Reinterpretation of Nationalism*. Umeå 2010.
   ISBN 978-91-88466-76-1

3. Ann-Catrine Edlund, Lars-Erik Edlund & Susanne Haugen (eds.), *Vernacular Literacies: Past, Present and Future*. Umeå 2014.
   ISBN 978-91-88466-86-0

4. Ann-Catrine Edlund, T.G. Ashplant & Anna Kuismin (eds.), *Reading and Writing from Below: Exploring the Margins of Modernity*. Umeå 2016.
   ISBN 978-91-88466-88-4

5. Andrej Kotljarchuk & Olle Sundström (eds.), *Ethnic and Religious Minorities in Stalin's Soviet Union: New Dimensions of Research*. Stockholm & Umeå 2017.
   ISBN 978-91-7601-777-7

Nordliga studier (ISSN 2000-0391)

1. Olle Sundström, *"Vildrenen är själv detsamma som en gud": "gudar" och "andar" i sovjetiska etnografers beskrivningar av samojediska världsåskådningar.* Umeå 2008.
   ISBN 978-91-88466-74-7

2. Gunnar Gjengset, *Matti Aikio: verk og virke.* Umeå 2011.
   ISBN 978-91-88466-77-8

3. Ann-Catrine Edlund (eds.), *Att läsa och att skriva: två vågor av vardagligt skriftbruk i Norden 1800–2000.* Umeå 2012.
   ISBN 978-91-88466-81-5

4. Ann-Catrine Edlund & Susanne Haugen (eds.), *Människor som skriver: perspektiv på vardagligt skriftbruk och identitet.* Umeå 2013.
   ISBN 978-91-88466-85-3

www.ingramcontent.com/pod-product-compliance
Lightning Source LLC
Chambersburg PA
CBHW061249230426
43663CB00022B/2959